Google™ Apps Deciphered

Google™ Apps Deciphered

Compute in the Cloud to Streamline Your Desktop

Scott Granneman

PRENTICE
HALL

An Imprint of Pearson Education

Upper Saddle River, NJ ■ Boston ■ Indianapolis ■ San Francisco

New York ■ Toronto ■ Montreal ■ London ■ Munich ■ Paris ■ Madrid

Cape Town ■ Sydney ■ Tokyo ■ Singapore ■ Mexico City

Many of the designations used by manufacturers and sellers to distinguish their products are claimed as trademarks. Where those designations appear in this book, and the publisher was aware of a trademark claim, the designations have been printed with initial capital letters or in all capitals.

The author and publisher have taken care in the preparation of this book, but make no expressed or implied warranty of any kind and assume no responsibility for errors or omissions. No liability is assumed for incidental or consequential damages in connection with or arising out of the use of the information or programs contained herein.

The publisher offers excellent discounts on this book when ordered in quantity for bulk purchases or special sales, which may include electronic versions and/or custom covers and content particular to your business, training goals, marketing focus, and branding interests. For more information, please contact:

U.S. Corporate and Government Sales
(800) 382-3419
corpsales@pearsontechgroup.com

For sales outside the United States please contact:

International Sales
international@pearson.com

Visit us on the Web: www.informit.com/ph

Library of Congress Cataloging-in-Publication Data is on file

ISBN-13: 978-0-137-00470-6
ISBN-10: 0-137-00470-2
Text printed in the United States on recycled paper at Courier in Stoughton, Massachusetts.
First printing December 2008

Editor-in-Chief
Mark Taub

Executive Editor
Debra Williams Cauley

Development Editor
Songlin Qiu

Managing Editor
Kristy Hart

Project Editor
Andy Beaster

Copy Editor
Barbara Hacha

Indexer
Heather McNeill

Proofreader
Language Logistics, LLC

Technical Reviewer
Corey Burger

Cover Designer
Alan Clements

Composition
Bronkella Publishing, LLC

To Robin—I can't thank you enough.

Contents at a Glance

Contents

Foreword

Whether Microsoft likes it or not, thousands of people are moving from office applications on their own computers to free, collaborative applications in the cloud. In the arena of Internet-based cloud applications, no company has made a bigger splash of late than Google and the offering featured in this book: Google Apps.

With Google Apps, you can create websites, email accounts, and calendars for your business or organization under the umbrella of your own customized domain name. You can write documents, build spreadsheets, and use instant messaging—all done collaboratively with other users. And you can do all this with no investment in infrastructure on the backend and simple Internet-connected web browsers on the frontend.

Google Apps give you the opportunity to replace the headache of maintaining the basic office applications your business or organization needs with the freedom to focus on your own business. Everything is stored on Google servers and run with web-based applications. In fact, you'll find that you don't even need separate office applications.

Now, if you find it a bit scary to leave the comfort of your cranky old Word, Excel, and Outlook applications, you may appreciate some reassurance and guidance before jumping into Google Apps. You may wonder how to choose the exact Google Apps service that will work for you. You may have questions about the security and control you'll have of the content you create. To address those and other concerns with getting into Google Apps, I leave you in the capable hands of Scott Granneman.

With the focus of our series on software freedom, we were thrilled when Scott proposed this book on Google Apps. Linux and other free software makes Google Apps possible. As someone using the service, you may not know that you are running free software. The results of software freedom will shine through to you in many ways, such as:

- Freedom to access your email, calendars, documents, and spreadsheets from any web browser (whether from Windows, Mac, Linux or even your mobile phone).
- Freedom to collaborate live with co-workers and friends.
- Freedom from maintaining your own server infrastructure.
- Freedom from constant software upgrades (as Google Apps developers express their freedom to modify and rapidly develop and improve the software behind the scenes).
- And did I mention freedom from paying for software (at least beginning with basic service)?

If you don't have technical expertise to set up your own servers, don't worry. Google Apps takes care of most of that. For the rest, Scott walks you through the more technical aspects. For example, you'll learn how to set up DNS records for your own domain and how to transition your current email accounts, documents, and address books into Google Apps. If your IT staff is afraid of losing control of your critical communications and data, Scott describes how they can maintain control and oversight of your organization's Google Apps accounts.

After you have finished with Scott's descriptions, you could end up with your own website under the domain name of your choice and hosted in Google Apps. You could have email accounts for all your people set up under that domain name. And you could have a full range of collaborative documentation and communications tools configured for everyone to access (within or outside of your organization as you choose).

So I leave you to Scott Granneman and Google Apps. I trust that you will find his writing both useful and entertaining, as I have. Good luck!

—*Christopher Negus, Series Editor*

Preface

I've been using Google Apps since it came out, back when it was known as Google Apps for Your Domain (or GAFYD by many). I was impressed from the beginning with Google Apps's products and even more impressed by Google's goals: to create an online suite of software and services that anyone could use from anywhere in the world, with everything stored online in the cloud.

Over the past several years Google has expanded Google Apps in many directions. New Apps have appeared, and new features have shown up on an almost-weekly basis. In fact, the constant improvements have made this book hard to write—every time I would finish a chapter, I'd have to revise it again after Google changed something or in some cases added new programs.

NOTE

To keep up with these changes, visit my blog dedicated to this book and Google Apps. Titled "1 and 100 Zeroes," you'll find it at www.1and100zeroes.com.

This book isn't for the absolute beginner to Google Apps—I don't spend endless chapters explaining how to use Gmail, Google Calendar, or Google Docs in mind-numbing detail ("Click this button to do foo. Press here to do bar. Drag this to do foobar."). Instead, I assume throughout this book that you have the basics down and you're looking for something more. You want tips and tricks for using Google Apps that will make you more productive. You want the skinny on cool features that may not be obvious. You want details about programs that you can't find in any other book.

xxviii | Preface

If that's what you want, you're holding the right book in your hands.

Much of what I write about in this book is based on my personal experience using Google Apps, but the book wouldn't have been possible without the thoughts, experiences, and writings of lots of other folks who contribute daily to some excellent blogs. If you want to keep up with Google Apps, let me suggest the following resources.

First are the official Google blogs, which are often full of good stuff:

- The official update feed from the Google Apps team
  http://googleappsupdates.blogspot.com
- Official Google Blog
  http://googleblog.blogspot.com
- Official Gmail Blog
  http://gmailblog.blogspot.com
- Official Google Docs Blog
  http://googledocs.blogspot.com
- Google Code Blog
  http://google-code-updates.blogspot.com
- Google Sites Blog
  http://googlesitesblog.blogspot.com
- Google Talkabout
  http://googletalk.blogspot.com
- Official Google Data APIs Blog
  http://googledataapis.blogspot.com
- Official Google Mobile Blog
  http://googlemobile.blogspot.com

As great as Google's own blogs are, there's more great stuff out there written by non-Googlers. The following blogs contain information about Google Apps that I read, use, and learn from every day (they're in alphabetical order, not preference):

- Digital Inspiration
  www.labnol.org
- Download Squad
  www.downloadsquad.com
- Google Blogoscoped
  http://blogoscoped.com

- Google Operating System
  http://googlesystem.blogspot.com
- Googling Google
  http://blogs.zdnet.com/Google/
- Lifehacker
  http://lifehacker.com
- Mac OS X Hints
  www.macosxhints.com
- TechCrunch
  www.techcrunch.com
- TidBITS
  http://db.tidbits.com

Finally, there's my own contribution to the furtherance of Googly knowledge, which I also use as a place to keep you, my readers, up-to-date with changes to Google Apps:

- 1 and 100 Zeroes: A Google Apps Blog
  www.1and100zeroes.com

If you don't know how to read all those blogs, sign up to use the fantastic and free Google Reader with your Google account at http://reader.google.com. It's great software, and I honestly couldn't do all my jobs—teaching, writing, and running a web dev business—without it.

Finally, if you want to drop me a line, feel free to do so. I can't provide tech support for every problem you might have (that's why I included "Further Reading" at the end of most chapters), but I'd love to hear from you if you find problems in the book, if something is confusing, or if you just want to let me know what you think. Email me at scott@granneman.com and share your thoughts.

Thanks for reading my latest book, and I hope you find it enjoyable, entertaining, and really, really useful!

Acknowledgments

I wrote this book in many locations over the span of several months, including Web-Sanity's office, Denise Lieberman's house, Carrie Jaeger's house, my Mom's house in Marshall, on a plane flying back and forth to Cleveland, in the St. Louis airport, in a car between St. Louis and Marshall, at CWE-LUG meetings (www.cwelug.org), at several coffee shops, at Jans Carton's house, at Washington University in St. Louis, and last, but certainly not least, at the home Robin Woltman and I share.

My executive editor Debra Williams Cauley was awesome as always, and she believed in this book. Thank you, Debra—it's always a pleasure working with you!

Songlin Qiu, Corey Burger, and Andrew Beaster were my other editors, and they all helped improve the book in hundreds of ways. Thank you all so much for your hard work—I truly appreciate it.

Yusef Jeffries-El, Jeffrey Joslin, and David Wasserman from the WWWAC list answered several questions I posed in a timely and informative manner, proving once again why the WWWAC list is so great (www.wwwac.org).

My best friend and business partner (ay yi yi…what a combination) Jans Carton answered several Google Apps queries I had and always knew his stuff. Thanks!

Denise Lieberman read over several chapters and suggested some very clever edits. She also fed me more than once, and it was always yummy!

Jerry Bryan has looked over virtually everything I've written in the last six years, and he did so again on this book. He was a tremendous help, and I can't thank him enough.

Robin Woltman read every line of this book and found little boo-boos and errors everywhere and also forced me to think about what I was trying to say. She also provided moral support and knew how to entertain me with Laurel & Hardy movies when I needed a break. Robin, you're the greatest!

Gabe Gibert and Fiona Carton, two very dear six-year-old friends, kept me entertained and laughing—and therefore distracted!—while I was writing this book, but it was a great way to take my mind off of the book and onto more important matters, like soccer and aliens and dogs. I wouldn't have it any other way.

Around the time this book appears, another production will have made his appearance—Finn Scott Granneman Jaeger—and so I wanted to give him a shout-out now. Welcome to the world, Finn!

And finally, my lil' shih-tzu Libby always knew when to demand ear scratches and belly rubs, even when I was engrossed in a chapter, and I was always glad to give them to her.

About the Author

Scott Granneman is an author, educator, and consultant. Scott has written three books (*Don't Click on the Blue E!: Switching to Firefox*, *Hacking Knoppix*, and the seminal *Linux Phrasebook*), co-authored one (*Podcasting with Audacity: Creating a Podcast With Free Audio Software*), and contributed to two (*Ubuntu Hacks* and *Microsoft Vista for IT Security Professionals*). In addition, he is a monthly columnist for *SecurityFocus*, with op/ed pieces that focus on general security topics, and for *Linux Magazine*, in a column focusing on new and interesting Linux software. He formerly blogged professionally on *The Open Source Weblog* and *Download Squad*.

As an educator, Scott has taught thousands of people of all ages—from pre-teens to senior citizens—on a wide variety of topics, including literature and technology. He has worked to educate people at all levels of technical skill about open source technologies, such as Linux and Firefox, and open standards. He is currently an Adjunct Professor at Washington University in St. Louis, where he teaches a variety of courses about technology, the Internet, and security.

As a Principal of WebSanity, he works with businesses and non-profits to take full advantage of the Internet's communications, sales, and service opportunities. He researches new technologies and manages the firm's UNIX-based server environment, thereby putting what he writes and teaches into practical use, and works closely with other partners on the underlying WebSanity Content Management System (CMS).

Computing in the Cloud

Microsoft Office is the undisputed 800-pound gorilla in the office suite jungle, with millions of users and billions of dollars in sales. However, as we saw in King Kong, even the mightiest gorilla can be hurt by enough buzzing planes. If one of those planes is actually a mighty jet named Google, then good ol' Kong may be facing more trouble than he's anticipated.

Over the last few years, Google has been polishing Google Apps, its online suite of software that includes most of the features found in mainstream office suites and then some:

- Word processing, spreadsheets, and presentations
- Email and contacts, including message security and recovery
- Calendar
- Wikis and websites
- Instant messaging
- Video sharing

Google is seeing phenomenal success with Google Apps. Over 3000 businesses a day are signing up at a rate of over one million per year. In total, over 500,000 businesses use Google Apps, with more than ten million active users. Of those, hundreds of thousands pay for the Premier Edition of Google Apps, which costs $50 per year. In the realm of education, thousands of universities, with more than one million active students and staff on six continents, are using Google Apps.

Some of those clients in business include the following:

- Brasil Telecom
- The District of Columbia (38,000 employees)
- Genentech
- Indoff (500 employees)
- Intel
- L'Oreal R&D
- Procter & Gamble Global Business Services
- Prudential Real Estate Affiliates (450 employees)
- Telegraph Media Group (1400 employees)
- Valeo (32,000 employees)

As for clients in education, there are many impressive wins in that list as well:

- Arizona State University (65,000 students)
- George Washington University
- Hofstra University
- Indiana University
- Kent State University
- Northwestern University (14,000 students)
- University of Delhi
- University of North Carolina—Greensboro
- University of Southern California
- University of Virginia

Just to give one example, Arizona State University has 65,000 students, which is obviously a huge number, but it took only two weeks to deploy Google Apps. As a result of the switch, ASU is now saving $500,000 a year, which is nothing to sneeze at.

This might all seem like a drop in the bucket compared with Microsoft's reach and profits, and in strictly numerical terms, it is. However, remember that Google makes its money primarily through ad sales, and it therefore has an overwhelming interest in moving as much of our lives as possible online. The more we move online, the more opportunities Google has to place ads in front of our eyeballs.

In addition, every person who starts using Google Apps is potentially one less customer for Microsoft, which hurts Google's biggest competitor in the long run. Microsoft has finally woken up to the fact that software and services are inexorably moving to the Net, and it has responded with its own attempts in this area, called Microsoft Online Services.

> ## NOTE
>
> Microsoft also markets a service called Office Live (www.officelive.com), but don't be fooled. That's just rebranded Hotmail, document storage (you still have to have Word, Excel, and PowerPoint installed on your PC), and el cheapo website hosting.

Microsoft's involvement, however, remains tied to its "software plus services" model, in which online tools still require the use of software running on a PC to work. This protects Microsoft's cash cows, Windows and Office, first and foremost, while allowing the company to trumpet its participation in moving online as well.

If you look more closely at Microsoft's offering, you see that it still requires software that runs on your computer beyond just a web browser. Sure, the cheapest offering —$3 per user per month—provides email through a web browser, but that's just Outlook Web Access pointed to an Exchange server. To use other tools such as SharePoint server access for document sharing and collaboration, expensive licenses for Microsoft Office are still mandatory.

Prices go up from there so that the full package, with hosted Exchange and SharePoint and other tools, starts at $15 per user per month, which comes to $180 per year per person. And of course it works only with Microsoft software, which means Windows and Office. You can use a Mac to read email, but you have to use Entourage, Microsoft's Outlook-like program that's part of the company's Office suite, for Macs. Linux users? Don't be silly!

It's not just Microsoft, however. Yahoo is sniffing around the hosted services concept with the formation of a new Cloud Computing & Data Infrastructure Group. And Amazon has been doing this for years with its Amazon Web Services (http://aws.amazon.com), which includes Elastic Compute Cloud, Simple DB, Simple Storage Service, and Simple Queue Service.

Something is changing in business, on the Internet, and in technology. The term that is increasingly used to apply to this change is *cloud computing*.

THE RISE OF CLOUD COMPUTING

As a term of technical slang, the "cloud" refers to the Internet, so cloud computing refers to Internet-centric software and services that are outsourced to someone else and offered on pay-as-you-go terms. In the case of Google Apps, organizations don't have to install software on their computers (and it doesn't matter if those computers are running Windows, Mac OS X, or Linux), and they don't have to install and maintain expensive servers and the associated software they require to run. Instead, they simply access Google's services in a web browser.

Everything is on Google's infrastructure—the software, the data, the backups, everything—and is therefore accessible in the cloud from anywhere. It doesn't matter if you're getting to Google Apps from your computer at work or at home, or from your iPhone or BlackBerry, or from your office or somewhere in Timbuktu because everything you need is always available in Google's cloud.

It's not a new idea *per se*—decades ago, Sun co-founder John Gage proclaimed that "the network is the computer"—but it's finally been able to reach a period of reality and even hypergrowth thanks to the spread of reliable high-speed Internet access coupled with the virtually limitless supplies of computer storage and processing power. As it gets cheaper and cheaper for companies such as Google and Amazon to build out massive server farms and then connect those mind-bogglingly powerful resources to users across the world via the Internet, new and exciting technologies become possible. Case study number one: Google Apps, the subject of this book.

Of course, there are problems that companies building services in the cloud and users of those services will face.

To start with, there's reliability. Yes, even the mighty Google has stumbled. In July 2008, for example, Google Docs was unavailable to many users for an hour or so. Virtually all companies have suffered downtimes, however, ranging from eBay to Amazon to Royal Bank of Canada to AT&T. This is simply a fact of life. Downtimes will happen. Humans can attempt to plan for every eventuality, but mistakes, errors, and even natural events beyond our control intrude and cause problems. It's an interesting psychological fact, though, that we humans exhibit something called the illusion of control. For instance, we are far more likely to die in a car than on a plane, but people are often psychologically more comfortable driving in their cars than riding on planes due to the fact that drivers feel in control of the situation, while passengers may not.

For this reason, many people feel safer running their own servers instead of outsourcing to Google because they want that feeling of control over their machines and their data. However, Google now offers a service level agreement (SLA) for the Premier Edition of Google Apps that guarantees 99.9% uptime for Gmail (that means about 9 hours of downtime a year). SLAs for other services are coming soon as well.

In addition, take a look at this 99.9% uptime guarantee. Before you refuse to even consider using Google Apps, think honestly about your own organization's infrastructure. I know you work hard, and you do the absolute best you can, but can you honestly say that your servers are down less than 9 hours a year? If so, then maybe you should continue doing things the way you've been doing them. But if not, maybe you should think a bit more about cloud computing the Google way.

In fact, more than just a lack of downtime, I would argue that customers actually want honest communication about problems and what cloud computing providers are doing about them. If a service I use is down, that's annoying, but if I can see that the service providers know about the issue and follow along as they fix it, I'm fine. I'm in the loop, and that reduces my stress and annoyance. Google has been okay at communication so far, but it is working on improving it, which is always a good thing.

And finally, there is security. Again, many organizations have their own internal security matters they need to attend to long before they begin to worry about Google Apps' security. And besides, Google does take security seriously. For an overview, read The Official Google Blog's "How Google keeps your information secure" (http://googleblog.blogspot.com/2008/03/how-google-keeps-your-information.html) for the company's four-prong strategy: philosophy, technology, process, and people. But on top of that, realize that Google eats its own dog food—it uses Google Apps itself. If there's a security vulnerability, no one feels it more acutely than Google. When your business is run on what you're selling, you can bet that you'll make darn sure that everything is as safe as it could possibly be.

In the end, cloud computing, especially as it is embodied by Google Apps, brings enormous benefits to users, administrators, and organizations that simply cannot be ignored.

- **Access from anywhere**—I have several computers at home, one at work, one at Washington University in St. Louis where I teach, and I use computers that aren't mine at various locations all the time. On top of those, I carry my iPhone with me everywhere I go. With Google Apps, I'm always connected to my email, my calendar, and my data. If I'm online, I can access and use Google Apps. And even if I'm not online, I can still use most everything I need with Google Apps as well.

- **Platform- and browser-agnostic**—I use a Mac mostly, but I also use Linux and sometimes Windows. When it comes to web browsers, I'm running Firefox and Safari constantly, but I'll also open Google Chrome and Opera, and even every once in a while if a really have to, and I'm forced, Internet

Explorer. Google Apps doesn't really care what operating system I'm running, and it does a heck of a job working with my menagerie of web browsers. That's the way it should be, and I appreciate it.

- **Costs less**—I don't need to buy special servers, operating systems, and software to access and use Google Apps. All I have to have is a free web browser on an Internet-enabled device, and I can work with Google Apps. Further, Google Apps has only two price points: free, which provides the services most users and organizations need, and $50 per user per year for the Premier Edition of Google Apps that is more suited to businesses with specialized needs. Even at $50 per user per year, that's a negligible expense for an incredible set of services.

- **Constant improvements**—Google rolls out new features for Google Apps at least every month, thereby constantly making its software better. Those new features arrive as part of Google Apps without the need for additional software installs. And they're free. Something that gets better all the time without inconveniencing me or costing me extra money? Sounds great!

- **Someone else worries about the plumbing**—I don't have millions of dollars and thousands of smart folks at my immediate disposal, but Google does. The company has smart and experienced programmers, admins, and engineers, as well as money, and an amazing infrastructure of computers and networks—and by using Google Apps, I can use all of that for my own benefit. I don't have to concern myself with the hard stuff that Google takes care of; instead, I can focus on using Google Apps to make my life and work more productive.

- **Backup and reliability**—As part of that massive infrastructure, Google provides backup for my data. Of course, it's always a good idea to back up things yourself, and I cover doing just that in Appendix A, but know that you don't need to worry about day to day losses. And Google's network has been remarkably reliable, with next to no downtime, so you know you can count on it.

- **Security**—It's a fact of life that companies have to worry about security. Google Apps takes care of much of that, for instance, by scanning automatically for viruses and spam. Even better, its tools for detecting those nasties are excellent and highly effective. You can access most Google Apps services via an encrypted connection, which stymies snoops, and there are other security tools available for those that need them.

- **Collaboration and sharing**—No one is an island, and that's never been more true than in today's interconnected world. We don't work today as much as we collaborate and share, and Google Apps makes this interesting. The first time you find yourself editing a file in Google Docs with another person on a different computer, and you realize that both of you are able to edit the same file at the same time, you'll gasp. The second time you edit a file with someone else, you'll start to wonder why all software doesn't work that way. It's that easy and that natural, and Google Apps makes it simple.

- **Search instead of find**—Google is the king of search, and it's no surprise that its super-powerful search tools are embedded throughout Google Apps. Forget filing your email messages; instead, search for them. Don't worry about pawing through subfolder after subfolder looking for that document you need; just search for it. Can't find the details you need for that upcoming appointment? Search your Google Calendar and find past meetings that tell you what you need to know.

- **Work with your existing programs**—As great as Google Apps is, the company still realizes that many people are wed to one or more desktop tools that they feel they can't live without (actually, I'd argue that most of the time, they just don't yet realize that they can in fact live without them). Outlook often falls into this category, but it's not just Outlook. Maybe you're a huge fan of Apple's iCal, or Thunderbird, or OpenOffice.org. In most cases, you can still use your favorite desktop tools with Google Apps. I will show you how in several chapters throughout this book.

Cloud computing is very much a popular buzzword right now, but Google Apps shows that there is a large and growing business behind that buzzword. It's an exciting time to be in business and technology, as several forces that have been improving for years—networks, computers, and mobility, to name but a few—have converged to create something that offers a new computing paradigm that can benefit virtually everyone who uses a computer for their work and life. As you'll see in this book, Google Apps provides those benefits, in spades.

FURTHER READING

There's always more to learn, so here are some resources that you might find handy if you want to learn more about Google Apps and cloud computing:

- Google's clients
  - John Cox's "Google, Microsoft woo higher ed with freebies" from eWeek (August 4, 2008).
  - "Businesses share their stories": www.google.com/apps/intl/en/business/customers.html

- "Google Apps to Meet iPhone at Texas University": www.eweek.com/c/a/Messaging-and-Collaboration/Google-Apps-to-Meet-iPhone-at-Texas-University/

- "Google Apps Premier Edition Takes Aim at the Enterprise": www.eweek.com/c/a/Enterprise-Applications/Google-Apps-Premier-Edition-Takes-Aim-at-the-Enterprise/

- "Customers Compile Wish List for Google Apps": www.eweek.com/c/a/Messaging-and-Collaboration/Customers-Compile-Wish-List-for-Google-Apps/

- "One year mark for Google Apps Education Edition": http://googleblog.blogspot.com/2007/10/one-year-mark-for-google-apps-education.html

- "Back to school with more than 1 million users worldwide": http://googleblog.blogspot.com/2008/07/back-to-school-with-more-than-1-million.html

- "Google Apps tops 1 million businesses": http://news.cnet.com/8301-13953_3-10029861-80.html

- "No One's Paying For Google Apps, But That's Okay (GOOG)": www.alleyinsider.com/2008/7/no-one-paying-for-google-apps

- "Customers": www.google.com/a/help/intl/en-GB/admins/customers.html

- Microsoft's Cloud Computer Offerings

  - "Microsoft Launches Hosted Exchange Deals": www.techcrunch.com/2008/07/08/microsoft-launch-hosted-exchange-deals/

  - "Microsoft Unveils Pricing and Partner Model for Web-Based Messaging and Collaboration Services": www.microsoft.com/presspass/press/2008/jul08/07-08BOSGWPCAPR.mspx

  - Microsoft Online Services: www.microsoft.com/online/

- Cloud Computing

  - "Twenty Experts Define Cloud Computing": http://cloudcomputing.sys-con.com/read/612375_p.htm

  - "Cloud Computing: So You Don't Have to Stand Still": www.nytimes.com/2008/05/25/technology/25proto.html

  - Nicholas Carr's The Big Switch: www.nicholasgcarr.com/bigswitch/ (especially see www.nicholasgcarr.com/bigswitch/readings.shtml)

  - "Can you trust your business to Google's cloud?": http://news.cnet.com/8301-17939_109-9989019-2.html

- "Google Docs goes down, user data does not": http://news.cnet.com/8301-17939_109-9985608-2.html
- Google Apps
  - Interactive Video Guide: http://services.google.com/apps/resources/overviews/welcome/topicWelcome/index.html
  - Product Overview and Tour Videos
  - Google Apps Quick Tour: www.youtube.com/watch?v=kJT3pagjd8s
  - Rajen Sheth demos Google Apps: www.youtube.com/watch?v=wY2bpr1TAA4
  - Google Apps Overview Screencast: https://services.google.com/apps/site/overview/index.html
  - Official Google Apps Discussion Group: http://groups.google.com/group/apps-discuss
  - The official update feed from the Google Apps team (blog): http://googleappsupdates.blogspot.com
  - Webinars: www.google.com/a/help/intl/en/admins/seminars.html
- News and Announcements
  - News: www.google.com/a/help/intl/en/admins/news.html
  - New features for users and admins: www.google.com/a/help/intl/en/admins/new.html
  - Google Apps Frequently Reported Issues: www.google.com/support/a/bin/request.py?contact_type=known_issues
  - Support Options: www.google.com/support/a/bin/static.py?page=contacting_support.html

Part I

Getting Started with Google Apps

CHAPTER 1

Choosing an Edition of Google Apps

You've decided Google Apps is right for you—congratulations! But you can't just start using Google Apps in the same way that you can't just start using Microsoft Office. If you tell me that you want to use Office, my first question is, "What version of Office is appropriate for you?" (For many people, the answer is "None.") Microsoft has decided, for various reasons—some good, some silly, mostly incomprehensible—to create and market different versions of Office with different features and for different audiences. Likewise, before you register and start using Google Apps, you have to choose between what Google calls its "editions" of Apps.

Currently, Google has five editions available:

1. Standard
2. Premier
3. Team
4. Education and Nonprofits
5. Partner

Google provides a table to show the differences between its editions, but it really covers only three of the five. So I've created one that covers all five editions and calls out key differences and similarities (see Table 1.1).

TABLE 1.1   The Five Editions of Google Apps

	STANDARD	PREMIER	TEAM	EDUCATION (AND NONPROFITS)	PARTNER (FREE) / PARTNER (PAID)
Price	Free	$50/account/year	Free	Free	Free / $0.15/account/month
Gmail	✓	✓		✓	✓
99.9% uptime guarantee for email		✓	N/A		✓
Storage amount per account	6.75GB	25GB	N/A	6.75GB	6.75GB
Ads next to mail	Standard	Optional	N/A	Optional for students, full-time staff, and volunteers	Standard / No
Email routing controls for dual delivery		✓	N/A	✓	
Google Calendar	✓	✓	✓	✓	✓
Conference room scheduling		✓		✓	
Google Docs	✓	✓	✓	✓	✓
Google Talk	✓	✓	✓	✓	✓
Google Sites	✓	✓	✓	✓	
Start Page	✓	✓	✓	✓	✓
Web Pages	✓	✓		✓	
Message Security and Recovery		✓			
App Engine	✓	✓		✓	✓
Integration APIs		✓		✓	✓
24/7 phone support		✓		✓	
					✓

STANDARD

In terms of the programs offered, or even in the amount of email storage, the Standard Edition of Google Apps doesn't offer more than users with normal, non-Apps Google accounts would see. Instead, Google Apps offers administrators a way to control exactly what services the users will have available and even what they can do with those services. For instance, the administrator of a Google Apps domain could decide not to make Google Talk available to her users because her organization has standardized on a different client. Or an administrator might allow employees access to Google Docs but disallow document sharing with folks outside of the company's domain to keep the necessary information confidential.

For many organizations, the Standard Edition of Google Apps will be perfect. It provides great services, the price is right (free!), and it's no big deal that text ads appear next to email when it's checked using the Web or that full-time phone support isn't included.

PREMIER

Other organizations, however, will need the extra features provided by the Premier Edition of Google Apps. They have heavy email users who need a lot more storage space or require an uptime guarantee and someone to call on the phone when things aren't working smoothly. Perhaps their email admins salivate at the powerful email management and recovery tools provided by Google's purchase of Postini, or maybe they don't like to see ads while they're reading their email. No matter the specific reason, for only $50 per user account per year, Google has those businesses covered.

TEAM

The Team Edition is the newest member of the group of five, but it fills an interesting, though perhaps slightly controversial, niche in Google's Apps portfolio. The basic idea behind the Team Edition is that you have a group of workers in an organization who want to use collaborative tools, but their IT department—or the lack of one—makes this difficult or even impossible. If these users enter their work email addresses, which will all end in the same domain name—say colostomo.com—at Google Apps, they can use several Google tools to work together as a group. Email isn't included, which makes sense because the IT staff isn't involved and therefore can't make the necessary changes to DNS to use Gmail, but most of the other major software offerings are there, such as calendaring, IM and VoIP, and documents.

The controversy concerning the Team Edition is around the lack of IT involvement. Some pundits have seen the Team Edition as an end run around IT staff, with their often very legitimate worries about security, training, and unified tools. Google counters with two arguments. First, Google correctly points out that employees frequently use software and services that aren't blessed by IT. At least when employees are using the Google Apps Team Edition, IT can be reassured by knowing that Google, a large, Internet-centric company, is working behind the scenes to guarantee security, usability, and unification of tools.

Second, if an IT department finds out that its clients are using the Team Edition of Google Apps, it can easily control what is going on if it wants to. IT needs to sign on to the Team Edition that employees have created. After it has done that, it can prove that it controls the domain name in question by either creating a CNAME record in the company's DNS records, by uploading a Google-generated HTML file to the company's website, or by altering the domain's MX records for email (for more information, see "Signing Up for the Team Edition" in Chapter 2 or www.google.com/support/a/bin/answer.py?hl=en&answer=86647). At that point, the Team Edition switches over to either the Standard or Premier Edition, fully under the control of IT.

EDUCATION (AND NONPROFITS)

If you're an accredited not-for-profit K-12 school, college, or university, or a registered 501(3) nonprofit, you're going to love the Education Edition of Google Apps (it's called the Education Edition, but it's also available to nonprofits). It's basically the same as the Premier Edition, with a few small differences. Foremost is that it's free, which is perfect for that target audience. It doesn't come with the 99.9% uptime guarantee, and email storage is the same as the Standard Edition (still a whopping 7GB and counting, though), and Postini's policy management and recovery service isn't available. But that's about it. Virtually everything else is the same as the Premier Edition, which demonstrates a smart effort on Google's part to attract and keep as many users as possible with an attractive, powerful solution.

One thing about this version is a bit confusing, however—if you're a nonprofit, you still need to use the Education Edition signup form. At this time, there isn't a specific form for nonprofits. Also, international nonprofits are still out in the cold, but they're free to use the Standard Edition if they'd like.

PARTNER

For years, many ISPs and hosting providers have offered webmail to their subscribers. Unfortunately, the vast majority of those webmail implementations have presented underpowered, unusable interfaces to users, with especially poor anti-spam and anti-malware protections. The Partner Edition of Google Apps seeks to solve that problem for both ISPs and their subscribers. An ISP or portal can sign up for the Partner Edition, customize and integrate Google Apps to match their needs and branding, and then turn around and offer Gmail, Google Calendar, Google Docs, and Google Talk to users. Best of all for the ISPs and hosting providers of the world, they don't have to host anything themselves, so it allows them to focus on their core business.

Unlike the other editions, however, Google offers two versions of the Partner Edition, based on whether the ISP wants to pay for the service. The free version removes 24/7 phone support, custom Gmail headers, and uptime guarantees as options; in addition, it shows ads to users in Gmail. If a hosting provider requires extended support and customization, the decision comes down to whether it wants to display ads to users when they're using Gmail. If ads are okay, the Partner Edition costs $0.15 per month per user account; if ads are not kosher, it costs $0.18 per month per user to remove them.

Because the minimum number of mailboxes is 20,000, an ISP is looking at either a starting expense of $3,000 per month with ads or $3,600 per month without ads. If a hosting provider or ISP has the minimum number of subscribers that the Partner Edition requires, $3,000 or so a month can be a small price to pay for the advantages that Google will bring it.

> **NOTE**
>
> If you think your organization qualifies for the Partner Edition, head over to www.google.com/a/help/intl/en/admins/partner_getting_started.html to find out more.

CONCLUSION

Like Microsoft Office, Google offers its Apps in several versions with different price points and feature levels. Unlike Office, however, Google Apps' versions range from inexpensive to free, and there aren't a great many differences among offerings. All provide an extensive list of features to users, and all are updated constantly. The choice comes down to you and your organization's status and needs and how much hand-holding you need from Google. It's easy to get started with Google Apps, however, and anyone can begin using it for free with at least the Team Edition, making it a nearly painless way to jump into cloud computing.

FURTHER READING

There's always more to learn, so here are some resources that you might find handy if you want to learn more about the various editions of Google Apps:

- Video case studies: www.youtube.com/view_play_list?p=CAC2420E3E3EF1DC
- Comparing Editions
  - Table comparing Standard, Premier, and Education Editions: www.google.com/a/help/intl/en/admins/editions_spe.html
  - Comparison of Standard and Premier Editions: www.google.com/a/help/intl/en/admins/editions.html
  - Choose the Edition That Fits Your Needs video: http://services.google.com/apps/resources/overviews/welcome/topicWelcome/page15.html
- Standard Edition
  - Overview: www.google.com/a/help/intl/en/org/
- Premier Edition
  - Purchases and Renewals: www.google.com/support/a/bin/answer.py?answer=56904
  - Phone Support: www.google.com/support/a/bin/answer.py?answer=65260&topic=9193
  - Video testimonials from businesses: www.youtube.com/view_play_list?p=5D03DA3C38B5AA78
- Education and Non-profit Edition
  - Overview for Education: www.google.com/a/help/intl/en/edu/
  - Overview for Non-profits: www.google.com/a/help/intl/en/npo/
  - Administrator's Circle – For Education Edition discussion group: http://groups.google.com/group/apps-edu-circle/topics
  - Video testimonials from universities: http://www.youtube.com/view_play_list?p=F75FFEC752E33053
  - Video testimonials from non-profits: http://www.youtube.com/view_play_list?p=DC86D9E5EE317326

- Phone Support: www.google.com/support/a/bin/ answer.py?answer=65260&topic=9193
- Team Edition
  - Overview of Team Edition: www.google.com/apps/business/
  - Overview of Team Edition for students: www.google.com/apps/edu/
  - How is my Google Apps Team Edition account different from a Google Account?: http://www.google.com/support/a/bin/ answer.py?answer=86646&hl=en
  - The User Dashboard And Google Apps Team Edition: http://google.com/ support/a/bin/static.py?page=faq.html
  - Video Overview: www.google.com/apps/video/team_edition_video.html
- Partner Edition
  - Overview: www.google.com/a/help/intl/en/partners/
  - Feature Comparison (free and pay): www.google.com/a/help/intl/en/ admins/editions_partner.html
  - FAQ: www.google.com/a/help/intl/en/admins/partner_faq.html
- For developers: Google Apps APIs by Edition: http://code.google.com/apis/apps/start.html
- Support options: www.google.com/a/help/intl/en/admins/support.html
- List of clients and success stories: www.google.com/a/help/intl/en/ admins/customers.html

CHAPTER 2

Setting Up Google Apps

Now that you understand the various editions of Google Apps that we looked at in Chapter 1, it's time to pick one and walk through the process of setting it up. This can be a detailed process, but it's not incredibly difficult, as long as you're patient and careful.

SIGNING UP FOR THE VARIOUS GOOGLE APPS EDITIONS

As you saw in the first chapter, Google offers five editions of Google Apps. I'm not going to cover setting up the Partners Edition because much of what I cover in this chapter applies to that edition and because those who use it are in a small, select group. If you have more than 20,000 users about to move to Google Apps, Google is going to give your organization special, customized attention that will fully address the specifics not covered in this book.

I'm going to spend a lot of time on the Standard Edition because it's the most popular, and it makes a great base for understanding the other three editions. Let's go!

Signing Up for the Standard Edition

A few months ago I woke up from a dream with the perfect domain name lingering in my mind: heavymetalmassage.com. I don't have any plans to become a masseuse, much less to give massages to the dulcet strains of Black Sabbath and Metallica, but I thought it was a fun domain name nonetheless, and buying a domain name is pretty cheap nowadays, so I snagged it. Let's suppose my dreams of writing computer books come to naught, however, and after months at massage school and securing the rights to play "Iron Man" and "Ride the Lightning" during sessions with clients, I finally decide to open my new business: Heavy Metal Massage.

Of course, I'm going to use Google Apps to manage my email, calendar, docs, and so on. In addition to the proprietor—me—I've also convinced my buddy Jans to help with all things Web, my Mom to oversee bookings, and my friend Jerry to take care of the money stuff. That's four users right there: Scott, Jans, Betty Sue (AKA Mom), and Jerry. I'm planning to use the Standard Edition of Google Apps, so four users are as free to me as forty would be.

Why the Standard Edition? Based on what I wrote in Chapter 1, I don't need 25GB for each email account, and I don't need the 99.9% uptime guarantee because Gmail is up every time I've tried to use it. Ads in email don't bother me, and at this time I don't need conference room scheduling, as it's just me giving massages, and I have only one room. I'm pretty paranoid when it comes to backups, so I don't need the message recovery services provided by Postini. Finally, because I'm writing a book on Google Apps, hopefully I won't need the 24/7 phone support.

As Heavy Metal Massage grows as a business and I hire employees, I very well might find that I need to upgrade to the Premier Edition and start paying $50 per account per year. One of the nicest features of Google Apps is that it's very easy to upgrade my account at any time, so I can do it when I need to, not when the software forces me.

To begin the process of setting up Heavy Metal Massage to work with Google Apps, I first need to sign up at Google. I head over to www.google.com/a/ (an easy-to-remember domain!) and click the blue button labeled Compare Editions and Sign Up. Under the Standard Edition is a big blue button that reads Sign Up, so I click it.

At this point, I have to enter the domain name that's going to be used with Google Apps. Google gives me two choices on two separate tabs:

```
I want to use an existing domain name
I want to buy a domain name
```

In the case of Heavy Metal Massage, I already own the domain name, heavymetalmassage.com, so I'm going to use the first tab. But what if I didn't already own the domain name? I could either go register it with my domain registrar of choice and then come back to Google and choose the first tab (since by that point the domain name would already exist somewhere else), or I could choose to use Google as my domain registrar and register the domain with it. Later in this chapter I'll register a domain name through Google so you can see how that process works, but for now let's continue with a domain name that's already been registered.

If you want to use a domain that already exists, you have to identify how much control you have over the domain name. Google determines this by asking you to check one of the following:

```
Administrator: I own or control this domain
End-User: I am a member of this domain
```

If you select End User, you're asked to enter your email address. If you instead select Administrator, you're asked to enter your domain name. Google does this to funnel people on this form to the correct version of Google Apps. If you're an end user, you don't have control over your domain name, so you can't register and set up the Standard (or Premier, Education, or Partner) Edition of Google Apps for everyone in your organization. In that case, you will be funneled to the Team Edition, which we'll look at later in this section.

> ## NOTE
>
> If you put in an email address for a domain that's already associated with Google Apps, you'll see an informational message from Google: "This domain has already been registered with Google Apps. Please contact your domain administrator for instructions on using Google Apps with this domain."

I indicate that I'm the Administrator, enter **heavymetalmassage.com**, and press the Get Started button. On the next screen, I'm asked to fill in some details about the number of users I'll need, the new Google Apps administrator account, and the organization itself.

First is the number of expected users. This isn't a hard and fast number that you're held to; it's just giving Google an idea of how many people are using Google Apps. I need four accounts today. Eventually I may need up to ten if my massage business really takes off. But I don't need to go ahead now and enter 100 just to make sure I have enough.

For the Account Administrator, I'm asked to fill in first name, last name, email address, phone, country or region, and job title. These aren't that difficult, but there are a few things you need to think about when you run through this process. I'm creating what will become an administrator account, and I might conceivably sell the company some day or grow it to the size where we have an entire IT department, which means that having an administrator account tied to my name (Scott Granneman) and my email address (scott@heavymetalmassage.com) wouldn't be a good idea. Besides, I can always add additional accounts later and assign them administrative functions—scott@heavymetalmassage.com, for instance.

For these reasons, I'm going to put the first name in as **Heavy Metal Massage** and the last name as **Admin**. For email, I shouldn't put in something@heavymetal-massage.com, even if I already get email at that address, considering that I'm about to associate that domain name with Google Apps' email. Instead, I'll enter some other email address that is valid and that I can access, such as my gmail.com address. Also notice that all these fields are required, with the exception of Job Title, so I'm not going to fill that one in.

> ## NOTE
>
> Why didn't I put in **Scott** and **Granneman** for the first and last names? You'll find out why in just a few paragraphs! The short answer: the name I put in here cannot later be changed, so I'll go ahead and create a "name" for my administrator account.

Next I need to check a box stating that I realize that I'm going to have to alter DNS records for my domain and that I understand that if I can't, using Google Apps is going to be a bit difficult. Check it.

Now for some nonrequired stuff about my organization, including its name, its type of business, and its size. In addition, I'm asked if it currently provides email, and if so, what I'm using. This is purely to help Google understand who's using Apps and why, so don't feel obligated to enter anything in here unless you want to.

I press Continue to go on to the final screen. Now I'm asked to create an administrator account—one that is tied to the Google Apps Account Administrator I created earlier. The person's name is already onscreen and unchangeable (Heavy Metal Massage Admin), based on the Administrator I created earlier, so that's easy enough.

I do need to create a username—one that's going to serve as an email address at heavymetalmassage.com as well. In this case I'm going to go along with the Heavy Metal Massage Admin persona I'm creating and use admin@heavymetalmassage.com.

Next is the password for admin@heavymetalmassage.com. Enter a good password—one that's a mix of capital letters, small letters, numbers, and symbols, that's not in the dictionary or related to your life, and that's hard to guess, and reenter it to make sure they match.

Now it's time for two check boxes asking if I want emailed tips and news and if I'm willing to provide feedback to Google if it contacts me. I check yes to both, but feel free to put in whatever you're comfortable with.

TIP

Don't know some of the rules for creating a good password? Check out an article I wrote for SecurityFocus titled "Pass the Chocolate," available at www.securityfocus.com/columnists/245.

Below that are the Terms and Conditions for using Google Apps. Scroll through it if you'd like and then press the button labeled I Accept. Continue with Set Up. You're now ready to rock and roll, so skip ahead to the section later in this chapter titled "Configuring DNS." If you'd instead like to learn how to set up other editions of Google Apps, keep reading.

Signing Up for the Team Edition

You can sign up for the Team Edition in a couple of ways. You can point your browser to www.google.com/a/, select Compare Editions and Sign Up, press Sign Up under the Standard Edition, and then, on the tab labeled I Want to Use an Existing Domain Name, select End User: I Am a Member of This Domain. Put your email address in the text field, press Get Started, and you're on the Team Edition sign-up page.

WARNING

Be sure your email address has the same domain name as the other members of your team! If you work at Widget Co. and your team members are all fellow Widget Co. employees, use me@widgetco.com here, not your gmail.com, yahoo.com, or att.com email address—and make sure everyone else does the same.

The other way to sign up for Team Edition is to go to www.google.com/apps/business/, the Team Edition info page. Enter your email address into the text box on the right, press Get Started, and you're on the Team Edition sign-up page, shown in Figure 2.1.

After you're there, things are pretty straightforward: enter a password, verify that you're a human being and not a spambot, type in your contact info, read the Terms and Conditions, and press the button that reads I Accept. Continue to Google Apps. You're ready to start using the Team Edition of Google Apps, which does not require any changes to DNS.

FIGURE 2.1 It's easy to create an account for Google Team Edition.

Upgrading from the Team to the Standard or Premier Edition

If you're the IT administrator at an organization and you encourage or allow your users to employ Google Apps Team Edition—or you discover that they are doing it without your say-so— you can always take control of things by upgrading to the Standard or Premier Edition, or even deleting Google Apps entirely.

NOTE

You could block access to Google Apps via your firewall or some other network security tool, but that could spark resentment and anger from your users. Better to talk things over with them and explain your position and reasoning first before you do anything drastic. Maybe you already have tools available that your users can implement, or maybe you just can't allow stuff outside your network for regulatory reasons. Maybe Google Apps would be perfect, but you need a level of control over its use. No matter the reason, talk with your users first and *then* act (unless the use of Google Apps means that the company is violating some regulation that could land people in very hot legal water—then act first and explain later!).

If you want to start managing Google Apps, you'll first need to create an account with your company's Team Edition, as detailed previously. The domain name of your email address must match the domain name used by everyone else. Log in to the Control Panel for the Team Edition and then look for the text near the bottom of the page that reads If You Are the IT Administrator, You Can Access Administrative Features for Your Organization. Next to that, follow the Learn How link.

On the next page, you'll be asked to enter an email address that is unconnected with the domain in question, so it's time to dust off your gmail.com or att.com address. You'll need to agree with Terms and Conditions by pressing the button labeled I Accept. Continue to Activate.

At this point, you'll have received instructions explaining how to verify that you control the domain. You can either create a CNAME record for the domain in DNS or upload a specified HTML file to the domain's website. Do one and then click Verify to tell Google to check it out and thereby prove that you are, in fact, the master of your domain. You are now free to sign up for the Standard or Premier edition of Google Apps, and it is all under the control of IT admins.

> **NOTE**
>
> I go over the two methods, CNAME and HTML file, in much greater depth later in this chapter.

Signing Up for the Premier Edition

Ready to spend some money for the features you really need? Head over to www.google.com/a/ in your web browser, select Compare Editions and Sign Up, and press Sign Up under the Premier Edition. Again, you're asked if you're an Administrator or an End User. If you're an end user and you enter your email address, you'll be shunted over to the sign-up form for the Team Edition (that's the third way you can get to that form!). But because you're an administrator, choose that, enter your domain name, and press the Get Started button.

The second screen is exactly like the one used by the Standard Edition. You're asked for the standard information about the number of users, account admin info, and details about the organization.

The third screen is the big difference: you're asked to pay up! Google multiplies the number of accounts you specified on the second screen by $50 and gives you the grand total you owe. You can change the number on this screen, however, and you can always add more users later.

By default, you're asked to use a credit card through Google Checkout, Google's PayPal-like online payment service. If your company doesn't want to use Google's system, there's a link to a form on which you can request a different payment method.

If you're not 100% sure that you want to use the Premier Edition, you can try it out free for 30 days. Your credit card is authorized, but it's not actually charged until 30 days have passed, and you can cancel anytime. It's a nice way to try out Google Apps Premier Edition without a big monetary commitment.

NOTE

Google says this is just a limited time option, but they've been doing it for quite a while, and it makes good sense for them to reassure companies who might be hesitant about moving over to Google Apps, so I don't think this option is going to go away soon.

If you're ready, click the I Accept. Proceed to the Google Checkout button and fill out the information on the following screen. After you've paid Google, you'll end up on the final screen, on which you create an administrator account, just as in the Standard Edition. Go through that process, and you're at the Google Apps Control Panel, ready to set up DNS.

Upgrading from the Standard to the Premier Edition

Remember that you can always sign up for the Standard Edition first and upgrade to the Premier Edition later. After you have everything set up and running the way you'd like, log in as a user with administrative privileges, go to your Control Panel, select the Domain Settings tab, and then choose Account Information. (From the Dashboard, you can also click the Manage Account Information link for a shortcut.) There you'll see the Upgrade to Google Apps Premier Edition link, shown in Figure 2.2.

Google Google Apps for heavymetalmassage.com - Standard Edition admin@heavymetalmassage.com Inbox Help Sign out

(Search accounts) (Search Help Center)

Dashboard | User accounts | Domain settings | Advanced tools | Service settings▾

Domain settings

General | **Account information** | Domain names | Appearance

Account type | Google Apps Standard Edition

Upgrade to Google Apps Premier Edition
For added email storage (25 GB per user), phone support and more advanced tools, upgrade to Google Apps Premier Edition. Learn more

FIGURE 2.2 You can upgrade to the Premier Edition if you need its extra features.

You'll get a chance to review how many accounts you're going to need, and then it's off to Google Checkout to pay the bill. You're now using the Premier Edition!

Signing Up for the Education (and Nonprofit) Edition

If you're an accredited educational institution or a licensed 501(3) nonprofit, aim your browser at www.google.com/a/, press the blue Compare Editions and Sign Up button, and then under Education Edition press the blue Sign Up button. Again, you're asked if you're an Administrator or an End User. If you're an end user and you enter your email address, you'll be taken to the sign-up form for the Team Edition (the fourth way you can get to that form). Because you're an administrator, choose that, enter your domain name, and press the Get Started button.

The next step in setting up the Education Edition is very similar to the Standard Edition. You're asked the number of users, the name and contact info of the administrator, and details about the organization—with one difference. Other editions don't require the name of the organization and its type, but the Education Edition does. You must enter the name of your school or nonprofit and indicate whether it is an educational institution or a nonprofit organization. Press Continue and you'll go to the third and final screen. Create an administrator account, enter the necessary data, and click through to reach the Google Apps Control Panel. Now it's time to set up DNS.

NOTE

What's to stop some wiseacre from setting up Google Apps for his local high school or a nonprofit he wants to harass? First, Google checks things out and promises on the second setup screen that it will "contact you via email about the status of your Education Edition upgrade." Second, our budding hooligan would have to control the DNS for the organization, which effectively puts the kibosh on any shenanigans.

ENABLING ADDITIONAL SERVICES

By default, a new Google Apps account comes with most services already enabled: Start Page, Email, Chat, Calendar, Docs, and Sites. You can remove those services at any time by going to your Control Panel, choosing Service Settings, and then the name of the service you want to remove. Scroll down to the Disable Service section and click the link to turn the service off. It's no longer on, nor available to users, nor on the Dashboard.

You can reenable a disabled service at any time or enable a new service by going to your Dashboard and clicking Add More Services. The next page that loads, shown in Figure 2.3, lists any services that you can add.

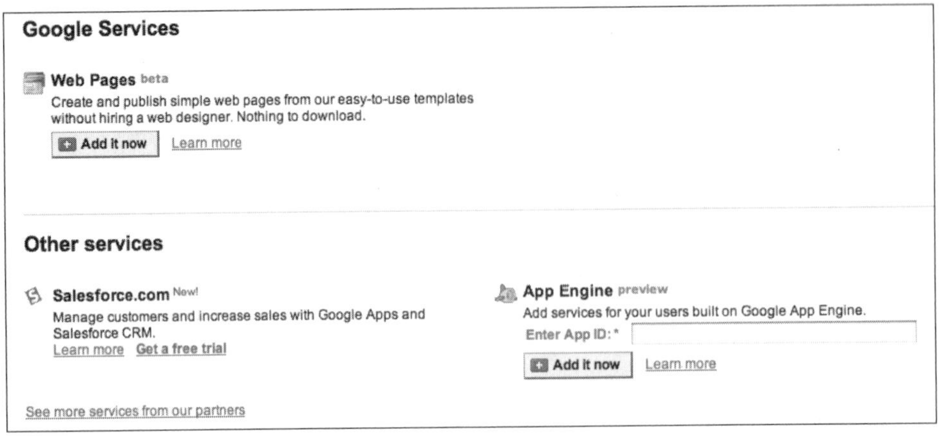

Google Services

Web Pages beta
Create and publish simple web pages from our easy-to-use templates without hiring a web designer. Nothing to download.
[+] **Add it now** | Learn more

Other services

Salesforce.com New!
Manage customers and increase sales with Google Apps and Salesforce CRM.
Learn more   Get a free trial

App Engine preview
Add services for your users built on Google App Engine.
Enter App ID: *
[+] **Add it now** | Learn more

See more services from our partners

FIGURE 2.3   The Standard Edition has three services that are not turned on by default.

Currently, four possible services are not turned on by default, but you can enable them on the Other Services page: Salesforce.com, Web Pages, App Engine, and Message Security and Recovery. As you saw in Chapter 1, the list of services available depends on the edition of Google Apps you're using. Table 2.1 shows the various editions and what's available.

I'm not going to cover Salesforce.com in this book because it's not a service provided by Google. Instead, it's a third-party web-based program (albeit a very good one) provided by another company partnering with Google. But I will walk through the other three services in this book and in this chapter.

TABLE 2.1   The Additional Services Available to You Depend on the Edition of Google Apps You Are Using

	STANDARD	PREMIER	TEAM	EDUCATION & NONPROFITS	PARTNER
Salesforce.com	✓	✓			
Web Pages	✓	✓		✓	
App Engine	✓	✓		✓	✓
Message Security and Recovery		✓			

Enabling Web Pages

Go to your Dashboard, click Add More Services, and press the Add It Now button under Web Pages. The page will reload, and you should see that the Web Pages option is no longer present. Go back to the Dashboard, and there it is: Web Pages, now an available service.

You still need to set up DNS so that this service, like the others, will work. For that information, look in "Configuring DNS" later in this chapter.

Enabling App Engine

Although many users and organizations will not use App Engine, it's important that those who are interested in it know how to enable it. Go to your Dashboard, click Add More Services, and...you can't just add App Engine. First you have to acquire an App ID.

To get an App ID, you need to jump through several hoops, the biggest of which includes actually creating something that runs under App Engine. For that reason, we'll look at Google App Engine in Chapter 21, "Things to Know About Using Google Video."

Enabling Message Security and Recovery

One of the services available only to those using the Premier Edition is Message Security and Recovery, which came about through Google's purchase of Postini. Before you can enable the Postini services available for Google Apps, you first have to activate email, which I detailed previously in this chapter, and mail must be working through Google.

To start the process, go to your Dashboard and click Add More Services. On the following page, press the Add It Now button next to Policy Management and Message Recovery, which places that new tool on your Dashboard. It's labeled as Inactive, however, so you now need to click Activate Postini.

You're taken to a registration form that asks you for basic company information (virtually all required), your admin contact info (also required; use the same admin account that you set up for Google Apps), and your acceptance of terms and conditions (accept them or else!). Submit it, and you should receive an email confirming your registration, shortly followed by one with an activation key (an incredibly long string of numbers, letters, and some symbols), instructions, and a link to the Email Protection Service Setup and Activation web page.

Follow that link, paste in the activation key, click the Log In button, and then you're asked for some vital data required by Postini. First is the domain name associated with your Google Apps Premier account. Type it in carefully, or better yet, paste it in. Next is an email address that is in your domain, that has already been given administrator privileges, and that will have the responsibility of administering Postini services for that domain. Enter a good password twice, choose a time zone, and press Set Up Account.

On the final setup page, you're told that you're going to receive yet another email with instructions for changing your MX records (yep—again!) to work with Postini. You can go ahead and log in and start adding users to the service, but realize that Postini won't protect them until the MX records have been switched over.

Instructions for setting up those MX records, as well as more DNS-related information having to do with Postini, can be found in the next section, "Configuring DNS."

CONFIGURING DNS

Okay, so I've done the initial setup of the Standard Edition of Google Apps for my business, Heavy Metal Massage. I'm at the Control Panel's Dashboard, pictured in Figure 2.4. But nothing is ready to work yet. For starters, Google isn't positive I own the domain name heavymetalmassage.com, and none of my services have been activated. I could go ahead and activate them, but that wouldn't make much sense because I haven't verified the domain. So let's start by doing that, and then we'll configure DNS as necessary.

FIGURE 2.4 Services are active, but none of them are available at my organization's domain.

Verifying Domain Ownership

Right on my Dashboard I see a Verify Domain Ownership link. I click it, and Google gives me two ways to prove that I own and administer heavymetalmassage.com: Upload an HTML File or Change Your CNAME Record.

NOTE

Don't know what DNS is? The quick definition, provided by Wikipedia, is

The Domain Name System (DNS) associates various information with domain names; most importantly, it serves as the "phone book" for the Internet by translating human-readable computer hostnames, e.g. www.example.com, into IP addresses, e.g. 208.77.188.166, which networking equipment needs to deliver information. It also stores other information such as the list of mail servers that accept email for a given domain.

You can read more (a lot more) at http://en.wikipedia.org/wiki/Domain_Name_System.

Uploading an HTML File

If I choose to upload the HTML file, Google tells me to create a file named google-hostedservice.html and put some specified text into it, something along the lines of google9c85d7ea61b55571 (it's always the word "google" followed by a string of letters and numbers). If you've never created an HTML file before, it should look something like this:

```
<html>
<head></head>
<body>
google9c85d7ea61b55571
</body>
</html>
```

I save the file and upload googlehostedservice.html to the root of heavymetalmassage.com.

After that's done, I make sure I can see the file by clicking the supplied link, and if I'm successful, I press the Verify button.

Changing Your CNAME Record

If you know how to edit your DNS records, this can be easier than creating an HTML file. When I choose this option, Google gives me a string to enter as a CNAME—it's the same string that it gave me if I'd chosen to upload an HTML file: google9c85d7ea61b55571. I use Go Daddy to manage heavymetalmassage.com, so I log in to the website, click My Account, choose Manage Domains, select heavymetalmassage.com, and then click the tiny link that says Total DNS Control and MX Records, resulting in the screen shown in Figure 2.5.

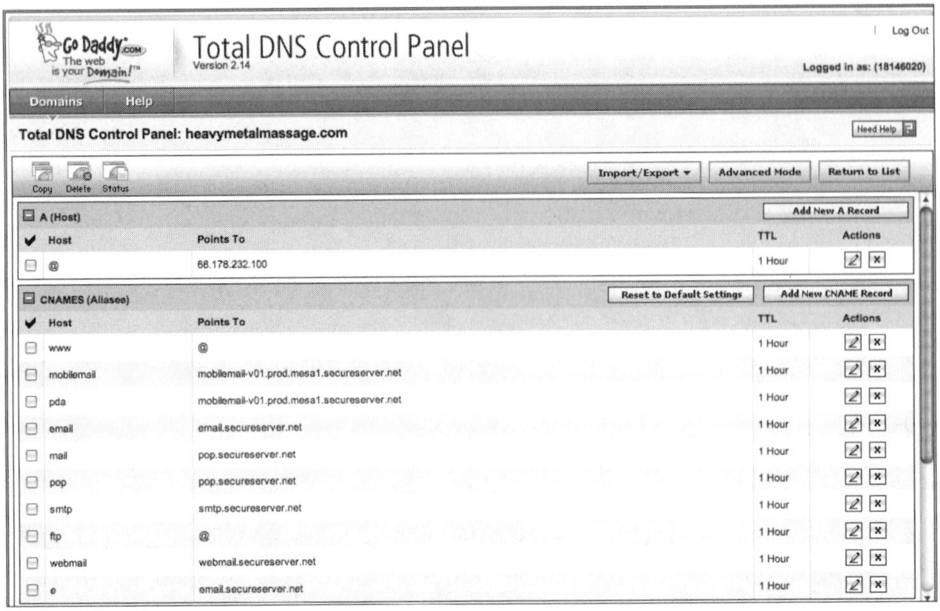

FIGURE 2.5 Go Daddy gives its users a good level of control over their domains' DNS records.

NOTE

I vastly prefer DynDNS (www.dyndns.com) and its interface for managing DNS. But I know a lot of readers use Go Daddy, and I registered heavymetalmassage.com at that registrar, so I thought it would be instructive to demonstrate this process using that website. You can find specific instructions for configuring CNAME records at many popular registrars and DNS services on www.google.com/support/a/bin/answer.py?answer= 47283. Some of the more well-known providers on that page include

- GoDaddy.com
- 1and1
- EveryDNS.net
- Yahoo! SmallBusiness
- eNom
- Network Solutions
- Dreamhost
- register.com

I now click Add New CNAME Record, which displays the fields shown in Figure 2.6. For Enter an Alias Name, I enter the string given to me by Google: `google9c85d7ea61b55571`. For Points to Host Name, I enter `google.com`, as ordered by Google. I can set the TTL (Time To Live) to whatever I'd like; the default is 1 Hour, but I usually set it to 1/2 Hour due to old habits.

CNAME (Alias)

To create a new CNAME record for your domain, please complete the Alias Name, Points To Host Name, and TTL fields below; then click "Continue."

Note: The Points To Host Name should be defined as your domain name (i.e., "www.domainnamegoeshere.com") or "@" (Entering "@" will automatically insert your domain name as the host name for the CNAME Record). The Alias field should be the subdomain of your top-level domain the CNAME record points to your domain.

Enter an Alias Name:
Points To Host Name:
TTL: 1 Hour

OK   Cancel

FIGURE 2.6   Add a new CNAME using Go Daddy's user interface.

It takes Go Daddy a bit of time to get everything completely finalized on its side. After it says the CNAME is in place, I can test that it's working by clicking the link to http://google9c85d7ea61b55571.heavymetalmassage.com. If I end up at Google's home page, things are copacetic; if not, I need to wait a bit longer for everything to propagate. If after 24 hours things still aren't working right, I should check my CNAME entry and make sure I did it correctly.

If my CNAME is working, it's time to go ahead and press the Verify button. I'm immediately taken back to my Control Panel's Dashboard, where a small message shown in Figure 2.7 informs me "We are checking domain ownership. This may take 48 hours to complete."

Fortunately, I've never seen it take that long. Reload the Dashboard in five minutes or so, and that message should be gone. If it is, I'm golden—Google has verified my domain ownership, and it's now certain that I own and administer heavymetalmassage.com. Time to (finally) configure DNS.

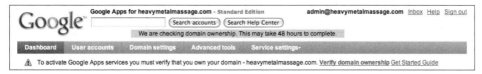

FIGURE 2.7   Google says it may take 48 hours, but it never has for me.

> **NOTE**
>
> You can delete the CNAME you created for google9c85d7ea61b55571 (or whatever string Google assigned to you) after you're sure that Google has verified your domain.

Creating Custom URLs

By default, my Google Start Page is set to go at http://partnerpage.google.com/heavymetalmassage.com, my Calendar at http://www.google.com/calendar/a/heavymetalmassage.com, and my Docs at http://docs.google.com/a/heavymetalmassage.com. The first problem: those addresses aren't exactly easy to remember. The second: not only are they hard to remember, they're all organized differently, so the Calendar has the word "calendar" in the path, followed by /a/, whereas Docs has "docs" in the domain name, followed by /a/ as the first part of the path. So they're virtually impossible to keep straight and remember!

Fortunately, Google allows you to create custom URLs that are much easier to remember. Personally, I'd much rather tell my coworkers to go to docs.heavymetalmassage.com or mail.heavymetalmassage.com. In fact, you should plan out what domains you want for each of the Google Apps you plan to use. Table 2.2 shows what I decided to do with mine (and several of these are suggested by Google in the interface you'll examine in just a few paragraphs):

TABLE 2.2 Suggested Fully Qualified Domain Names for Google Apps

GOOGLE APPS SERVICE	FULLY QUALIFIED DOMAIN NAME
Start Page	my.heavymetalmassage.com
Email	mail.heavymetalmassage.com
Calendar	calendar.heavymetalmassage.com
Docs	docs.heavymetalmassage.com
Sites	wiki.heavymetalmassage.com

To set up custom URLs, I go to the Dashboard and decide what services I want to set up at this time. I could set up two now, one tomorrow, two a week later, and so on, but that doesn't seem very efficient. By default, as you saw in Figure 2.4, Google has enabled Start Page, Chat, Docs, Email, Calendar, and Sites. Of these, Chat doesn't have any DNS work to do, so I can ignore it for now.

TIP

Here are some other ideas for your domain names that you might want to consider:

- start.domain.com for Start Pages because, after all, it *is* a "start" page (in fact, this is Google's default, as you'll soon see)

- email.domain.com for Email

- cal.domain.com for Calendar because "cal" is shorter to type than "calendar"

- office.domain.com for Docs because word processing, spreadsheets, and presentations are the components that make up office suite software

- sites.domain.com for Sites because it's a collection of websites (another one of Google's defaults)

- pages.domain.com for Web Pages, especially if you have an official website already set up and running at www.domain.com

Feel free to use your imagination; just be as simple and intuitive as possible.

The process for setting up a custom URL for one service or all services starts the same: under the Service Settings menu on the Control Panel, choose a service. If I wanted to change only one service, I'd select that one. I want to change all of them, so I select any of them. Start Page is at the top, so that's the one I'll pick. On the Start Page Settings page is a section in the middle labeled Web Address, which you can see in Figure 2.8 (and which you'd see no matter which service you'd picked, with the exception of Google Talk, which has no URL associated with it). Google tells me the current address for the Start Page, which is http://partnerpage.google.com/heavymetalmassage.com (yuck!) and provides a Change URL link.

When I click that link, I'm taken to a web page that allows me to change the URL of the Start Page, shown in Figure 2.9. If that's all I wanted to do, I could go ahead and fill out the form here, submit it, and that would be that. But I'm more efficient than that, so I'm going to click the link at the top, Change URLs for All Domain Services.

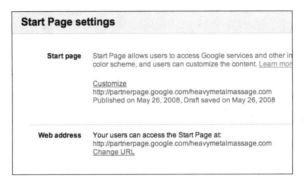

Start Page settings

Start page   Start Page allows users to access Google services and other in
color scheme, and users can customize the content. Learn mor

Customize
http://partnerpage.google.com/heavymetalmassage.com
Published on May 26, 2008, Draft saved on May 26, 2008

Web address   Your users can access the Start Page at:
http://partnerpage.google.com/heavymetalmassage.com
Change URL

FIGURE 2.8 It's time to change that awfully unfriendly URL!

Change URL for Start page
Select a simple, easy-to-remember address that redirects to the login page for Start page. Change URLs for all domain services

⦿ http://partnerpage.google.com/heavymetalmassage.com (default)

◯ http:// start .heavymetalmassage.com/ (custom)
To enable your custom URLs, you must create CNAME records with your domain host.

(Save changes) (Cancel)

FIGURE 2.9 I could change just this one link, but there are so many left to change.

I'm now taken to a page, shown in Figure 2.10, which will allow me to do just that: change the URLs of all the services I'm using with Google Apps in one fell swoop.

For each service, I need to select the option button next to the custom address and then enter my new subdomain into the textbox. You don't have to accept what Google has by default in those text fields—those are just suggestions. For instance, Google suggests start.heavymetalmassage.com for the Start Page, which is logical enough, but I like having people go to my.heavymetalmassage.com because it's more personal, so I'm going to enter that instead. After making the changes I listed in Table 2.2, I press Continue.

On the following page, Google has figured out who I use to manage my DNS registration (not too difficult but still slick and very helpful on Google's part) and tells me to go there and create CNAME records matching the subdomains I chose. Each of them is to point to the same address: ghs.google.com. Then I am to come back to this page and press the I've Completed These Steps button at the bottom.

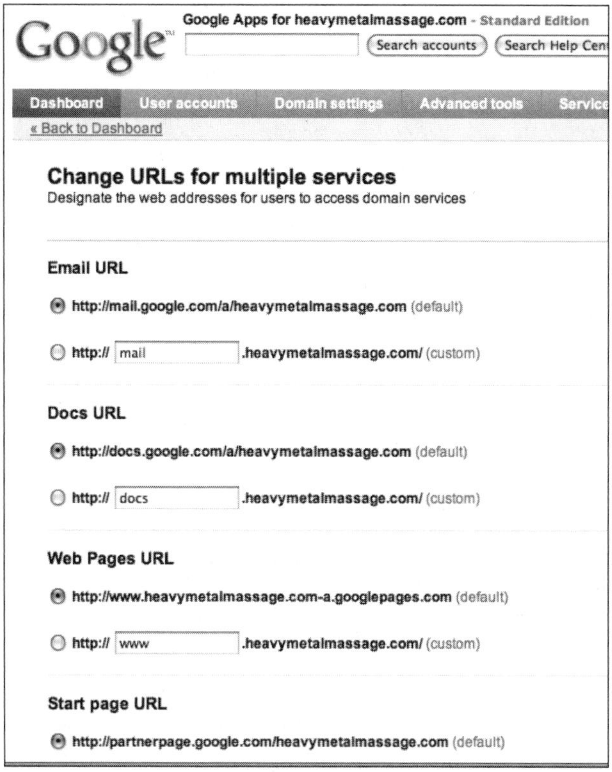

FIGURE 2.10   Now I can change all the URLs of all my services at one time, which is much more efficient.

Because I'm using a web browser with tabs, I open up www.godaddy.com in another tab and follow Google's instructions. When I get to Go Daddy's DNS Control Panel, I remember that Go Daddy created several CNAME records for me automatically when I registered heavymetalmassage.com with it (your registrar may or may not do this), which you can see back in Figure 2.5.

I need to delete the CNAME records for mobilemail, pda, email, pop, smtp, ftp, webmail, and e, since I do not and will not use them. Then I need to change the CNAMEs for www and mail. Finally, I need to add CNAMEs for my, calendar, docs, and wiki. Your tasks at your registrar will undoubtedly differ; just follow the general principle that you need to set up your CNAME records so they match what Google asked you to do.

After I'm done, my DNS Control Panel at Go Daddy looks very Google-centric, as shown in Figure 2.11.

☐ CNAMES (Aliases)			Reset to Default Settings	Add New CNAME Record
✔ Host	Points To		TTL	Delete
☐ mail	ghs.google.com		1/2 Hour ↕	☐
☐ my	ghs.google.com		1/2 Hour ↕	☐
☐ calendar	ghs.google.com		1/2 Hour ↕	☐
☐ docs	ghs.google.com		1/2 Hour ↕	☐
☐ wiki	ghs.google.com		1/2 Hour ↕	☐
☐ www	ghs.google.com		1/2 Hour ↕	☐

FIGURE 2.11   All my CNAME records are now correct for Google Apps.

It takes Go Daddy only a few moments to make the necessary changes, and then I go back to Google, to the page I left open, where I click the I've Completed These Steps button. My Dashboard opens back up, and like magic all the URLs now point to the CNAMEs I created.

TIP

If you close your browser or otherwise find that the page isn't open, no biggie—go back to your Google Apps Control Panel, repeat the steps we took to set up custom URLs, and you're ready to go again.

There is one exception: Email doesn't confirm that it's accessible via http://mail.heavymetalmassage.com. According to my Dashboard, I still need to Activate Email. That will involve, as we're about to find out, editing MX records in DNS.

WARNING

Although you are free to delete the CNAME you created earlier in this chapter to verify your domain, do not delete the CNAME records you created for your custom URLs. If you do, your custom URLs won't work any longer, and you'll have to deal with confused and possibly panicked phone calls from your end users, which would be terrifically unpleasant.

Setting Up MX Records for Email

After setting up CNAME records so I have custom URLs for my Google Apps services, it might seem like I'd be all done and could now jump into using Google Apps. However, one look at my Dashboard shows me that email still isn't working because it needs to be activated.

To begin that process, I click Activate Email and find myself on a page titled Set Up Email Delivery, which is really all about setting up MX, or Mail Exchange, records in DNS. Basically, you need to change your MX records wherever you manage your DNS so that they point to Google's servers.

NOTE

For an overview of MX records, see Wikipedia's article at http://en.wikipedia.org/wiki/MX_record.

Google detects who manages your DNS and automatically tries to tell you what to do for that service. In my case, Google knows I'm using Go Daddy, so it displays the appropriate information. However, if Google makes a mistake, or if you want to see what to do for a different registrar, the Showing Instructions For drop-down menu allows you to pick from a long list of more than 35 services, or you can see generic instructions by selecting Any Hosting Company.

For those who already know what they're doing DNS-wise, the quick and dirty instructions are to remove any existing MX records and add the following MX servers and priorities:

```
ASPMX.L.GOOGLE.COM.            10
ALT1.ASPMX.L.GOOGLE.COM.       20
ALT2.ASPMX.L.GOOGLE.COM.       20
ASPMX2.GOOGLEMAIL.COM.         30
ASPMX3.GOOGLEMAIL.COM.         30
ASPMX4.GOOGLEMAIL.COM.         30
ASPMX5.GOOGLEMAIL.COM.         30
```

NOTE

In case Google ever changes these MX records (although it's highly unlikely), you can see the list yourself at www.google.com/support/a/bin/answer.py?hl=en&answer=33352.

As for me, I go to Go Daddy and again head to the DNS Control Panel, where I see what you see in Figure 2.12—the MX records created by default.

I delete both of the existing MX records and add my first MX record. Priority is 10, Host Name is @ (which is something Go Daddy and perhaps a few other services use; it's a shortcut for my domain name, heavymetalmassage.com), Goes To Address is ASPMX.L.GOOGLE.COM. (note the dot at the end—it has to be there), and the TTL is 1/2 Hour. You can see these settings in Figure 2.13.

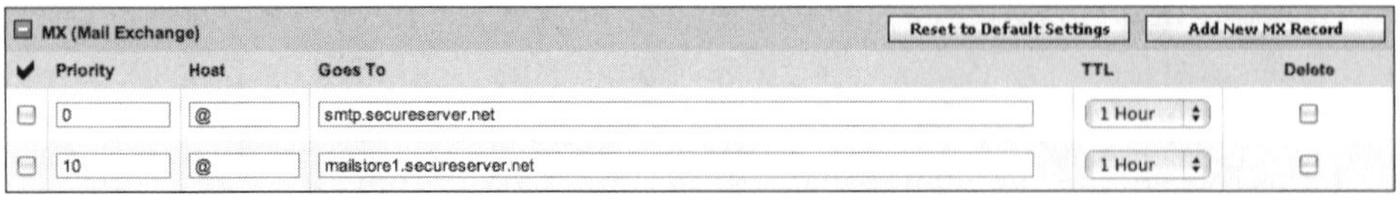

FIGURE 2.12 The default MX records Go Daddy created, which need to be deleted.

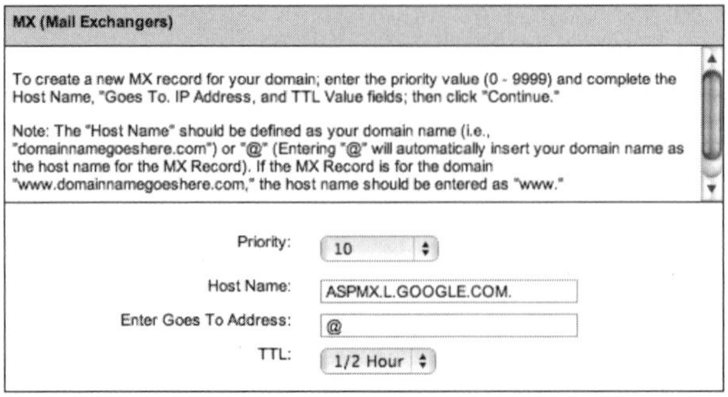

FIGURE 2.13 A sample MX record for Google Apps made at Go Daddy.

The instructions given by Google for Go Daddy ask me to create only five MX records, which might seem like a contradiction with the list of seven MX records you saw just a few paragraphs earlier, but it's not; five should be more than enough, and the end result of either list is in practice pretty much the same thing. After I've finished, my list of MX records at Go Daddy looks like Figure 2.14.

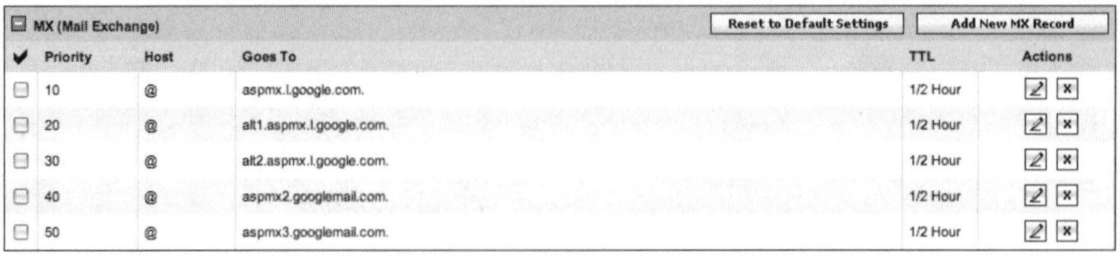

FIGURE 2.14 The final list of MX records at Go Daddy, all filled in and ready to go.

Back at Google, I can click the I Have Completed These Steps button, which takes me back to my Control Panel's Dashboard. As you can tell from Figure 2.15, Google tells me that it is checking the MX record additions I made. This shouldn't take too long; in my experience, it can be almost instantaneous depending on the company managing your DNS.

> **M Email** beta - Updating...
> We are checking MX records for your domain. This may take 48 hours to complete.
> View instructions again

FIGURE 2.15   Google is checking my MX record changes, which shouldn't take too long.

Now that my custom URLs and MX records are working correctly, my Dashboard shows, as in Figure 2.16, that it's time to jump to the "Creating Users" section later in this chapter.

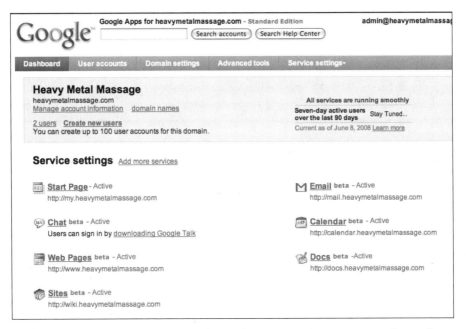

FIGURE 2.16   My Dashboard shows that my services are up to date. It's time to create some users.

Setting Up SRV Records for Google Talk Federation

You're going to learn more about Google Talk, Google's chat client, in Chapter 18, "Things to Know About Using Google Talk," but you should know now that it's possible for Google Talk to interoperate with other Instant Messaging networks. Underlying Google Talk is Jabber, an open, extensible IM protocol. One of the huge benefits of using Jabber is that Google Talk can connect to other messaging systems built around Jabber through a process known as *federation*.

> **NOTE**
>
> For more on Jabber, see Wikipedia's article at http://en.wikipedia.org/wiki/Jabber.

That means that if your Google Apps users want to IM—or even use Google Talk like a telephone—with people who aren't using Google Talk, it's possible, as long as you make a few DNS changes first.

> **NOTE**
>
> Keep in mind that your Google Apps users will be able to chat with each other just fine without any DNS changes. They'll also be able to chat with any other Google Apps users on any other domain, as well as any non-Google Apps Gmail users, again without any DNS changes. You will need to make these DNS changes only if you want them to be able to chat with people who aren't using Google Apps or Gmail.

You need to add the following SRV records into your DNS records. Change mydomain.com to your Google Apps domain; in my case, I would enter heavymetal-massage.com. Do not change google.com and leave all the underscores in place, or things won't work at all.

```
_xmpp-server._tcp.mydomain.com. IN SRV 5 0 5269 xmpp-
server.l.google.com.
_xmpp-server._tcp.mydomain.com. IN SRV 20 0 5269 xmpp-
server1.l.google.com.
_xmpp-server._tcp.mydomain.com. IN SRV 20 0 5269 xmpp-
server2.l.google.com.
_xmpp-server._tcp.mydomain.com. IN SRV 20 0 5269 xmpp-
server3.l.google.com.
_xmpp-server._tcp.mydomain.com. IN SRV 20 0 5269 xmpp-
server4.l.google.com.
_jabber._tcp.mydomain.com. IN SRV 5 0 5269 xmpp-server.l.google.com.
_jabber._tcp.mydomain.com. IN SRV 20 0 5269 xmpp-server1.l.google.com.
_jabber._tcp.mydomain.com. IN SRV 20 0 5269 xmpp-server2.l.google.com.
_jabber._tcp.mydomain.com. IN SRV 20 0 5269 xmpp-server3.l.google.com.
_jabber._tcp.mydomain.com. IN SRV 20 0 5269 xmpp-server4.l.google.com.
```

At Go Daddy, go to the DNS Control Panel and click the Add New SRV Record button, which shows you an interface like that in Figure 2.17.

NOTE

In case Google ever changes the DNS requirements for these SRV records, you can find its original instructions at www.google.com/support/a/bin/answer.py?answer=60227&hl=en and www.google.com/support/a/bin/answer.py?hl=en&answer=34143.

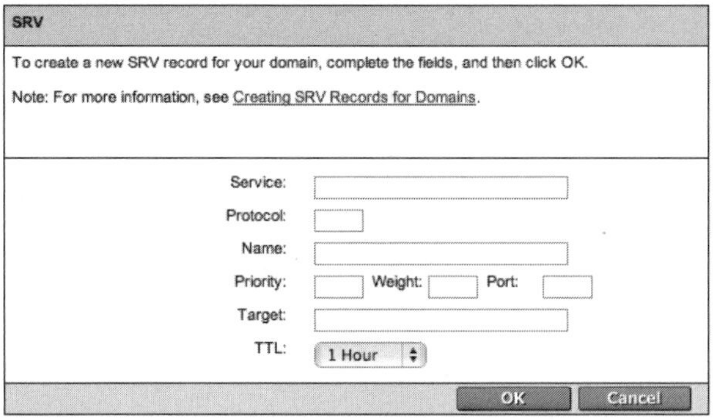

FIGURE 2.17 Even though SRV records can be complicated, Go Daddy makes it fairly easy to add them.

Based on what Google tells me to add, I'd put the following data in the fields provided by Go Daddy if I were adding the first SRV record for heavymetal-massage.com:

- Service: _xmpp-server
- Protocol: _tcp
- Name: @ (Go Daddy wants me to use @ instead of heavymetalmassage.com)
- Priority: 5
- Weight: 0
- Port: 5269
- Target: xmpp-server.l.google.com.
- TTL: Accept the default provided by Go Daddy, which is 1 hour

Note the underscores in what I entered since they are required.

If I were using DynDNS instead, I would see an interface similar to Figure 2.18:

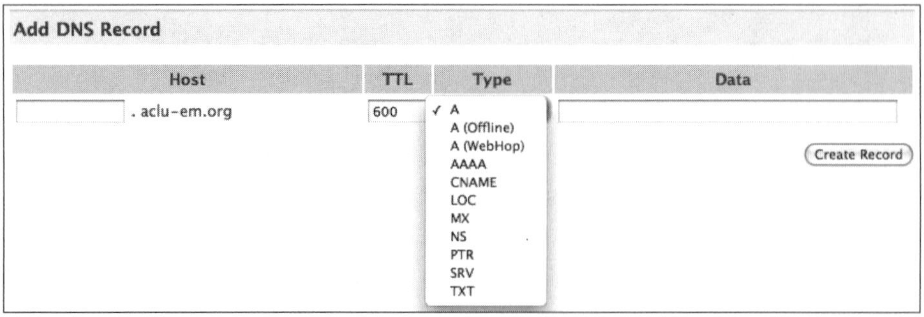

FIGURE 2.18 DynDNS doesn't hold your hand as much as Go Daddy, but I still like it better.

Based on what Google tells me to add, I'd put the following data in the fields provided by DynDNS if I were adding the first SRV record for heavymetal-massage.com:

- Host: _xmpp-server._tcp
- TTL: Accept the default provided by DynDNS, which is 600
- Type: SRV
- Data: 5 0 5269 xmpp-server.l.google.com.

Your DNS provider may very well have an interface different from both Go Daddy and DynDNS. Because of the relative complexity of SRV records when compared to other DNS records, you'll have to read your DNS provider's help files to make sure you enter the right data for your SRV records.

After you get the SRV records set up correctly, you ensure that your users can federate Google Talk with other supported networks.

> **TIP**
>
> Want to learn more about SRV records? Check out Wikipedia's article on the subject, available at http://en.wikipedia.org/wiki/SRV_record.

Setting Up MX Records for Policy Management and Message Recovery

The email you'll receive has the info you'll need for your MX records. Basically, you're changing things so that incoming emails flow through Postini before heading on to Google App's mail servers and out through Google App's SMTP servers and then to Postini's servers before hitting the wider Internet. (Yes, both mail servers are in fact owned by Google, but it's easier to treat them here as though they're separate.)

Postini's desired MX records almost always follow this pattern:

```
[yourdomain].com.s[system #]a1.psmtp.com. 10
[yourdomain].com.s[system #]a2.psmtp.com. 20
[yourdomain].com.s[system #]b1.psmtp.com. 30
[yourdomain].com.s[system #]b2.psmtp.com. 40
```

You would replace [yourdomain] with your domain name and [system #] with your assigned Postini system number, which is always either 7 or 200. With that pattern in mind, therefore, the MX records for heavymetalmassage.com would look like this:

```
heavymetalmassage.com.s7a1.psmtp.com. 10
heavymetalmassage.com.s7a2.psmtp.com. 20
heavymetalmassage.com.s7b1.psmtp.com. 30
heavymetalmassage.com.s7b2.psmtp.com. 40
```

Remember that you've already set up MX records for Google Apps email earlier, which looked like this:

```
ASPMX.L.GOOGLE.COM. 10
ALT1.ASPMX.L.GOOGLE.COM. 20
ALT2.ASPMX.L.GOOGLE.COM. 30
ASPMX2.GOOGLEMAIL.COM. 40
ASPMX3.GOOGLEMAIL.COM. 50
```

NOTE

One group is all lowercase, and one is all uppercase. It really doesn't matter one whit what the cases are, as long as they end with a dot, a space, and a ranking number.

When you're adding the new Postini-based MX records, you need to make their numbers lower—or closer to zero—so that they have higher priorities than the older MX records. That way, mail will be delivered to Postini first. After you're sure that email is going where it should—through Postini to Google Apps and from there to users—you can remove the original, older, lower-priority MX records.

You need to make one other mandatory setting for things to work correctly with Postini: You need to add Postini's SMTP servers to your Google Apps config. In your activation email, you were provided with an SMTP address, something along the lines of outbounds7.ga.obsmtp.com. But don't put that SMTP address into your favorite email client! Instead, go to your Google Apps Control Panel, then to Service Settings, then Email. In the text box for Outbound Gateway, enter the SMTP address provided by Postini; then scroll down and press Save Changes.

> **NOTE**
>
> Google has provided instructions for most major registrars, including Go Daddy, Network Solutions, 1&1, Dreamhost, Yahoo!, and my fave, Dyn-DNS. You can find the guide at www.postini.com/webdocs/activate_pg/ wwhelp/wwhimpl/common/html/wwhelp.htm?context=activate_pg&file= mx_switch.html#960868.

You're basically finished setting up Postini—not configuring everything, just setting it up—unless you're using SPF records in DNS to help with spam. For that, keep reading.

Fighting Spam with SPF Records

SPF, short for Sender Policy Framework, is designed to prevent spammers from forging the From line that identifies the sender of an email. Ever had a friend ask why you sent them spam when you know for sure that you didn't send it? In that case, a spammer lied in the From line to say it was from you. It's shockingly easy to fake the From, so SPF (along with several other complementary—and sometimes competitive—technologies) was developed.

To set the SPF record for your domain, you need to log in to wherever you manage your DNS and create a TXT record that looks like this:

```
v=spf1 include:aspmx.googlemail.com ~all
```

For Go Daddy, you'll need to log in, get to your DNS Control Panel, and scroll down to the TXT section. There's a helpful button labeled Add New SPF Record, but after that, it's a bit confusing.

On the first screen of the resulting wizard, choose An ISP or Other Mail Provider and press OK. On step 2, select the Outsourced tab and then, in the box in which you are supposed to Enter Outsourced Domains, paste in aspmx.google-mail.com. Press OK, and Go Daddy shows you the SPF record it's going to insert:

```
v=spf1 include:aspmx.googlemail.com ~all
```

> ⚠️ **WARNING**
>
> Do not check the box on screen 2 next to Exclude All Hosts Not Specified Here (-all). Note that if you do, you will be inserting a "minus all" (-all), not the required "tilde all" (~all), which will probably result in completely hosing your ability to send email using Google.

At some registrars, the record you create will need to look a bit different. Dyn-DNS, for instance, which handles my main domain granneman.com, requires the TXT record to include quotation marks, like this:

```
"v=spf1 include:aspmx.googlemail.com ~all"
```

Wait a while for the DNS changes to get propagated and then test what you've put into place.

You have a couple of options for testing. The people behind the SPF Project provide one service: Just send an email to spf-test@openspf.org, and you'll get back what looks like a bounce notification, with a Subject of Delivery Status Notification (Failure). Read the email, though, and you will hopefully see a line like this:

```
SPF Tests: Mail-From Result="pass"
```

Port25 provides another email-based service. Send an email to check-auth@verifier.port25.com, and you'll receive in reply a detailed message containing the information you can see in Figure 2.19, and even more.

```
==========================================
Summary of Results
==========================================
SPF check:           pass
DomainKeys check:    neutral
DKIM check:          neutral
Sender-ID check:     pass
SpamAssassin check:  ham


==========================================
Details:
==========================================

HELO hostname:   wx-out-0506.google.com
Source IP:       66.249.82.227
mail-from:       scott@granneman.com

------------------------------------------
SPF check details:
------------------------------------------
Result:          pass
ID(s) verified:  smtp.mail=scott@granneman.com
DNS record(s):
    granneman.com. 600 IN TXT "v=spf1 include:aspmx.googlemail.com ~all"
    aspmx.googlemail.com. 7200 IN TXT "v=spf1 redirect=_spf.google.com"
    _spf.google.com. 121 IN TXT "v=spf1 ip4:216.239.32.0/19 ip4:64.233.160.
ip4:209.85.128.0/17 ip4:66.102.0.0/20 ip4:74.125.0.0/16 ?all"
```

FIGURE 2.19   Port25 tells me whether SPF is set up correctly for my domain.

Easily the nicest web-based service is at http://senderid.espcoalition.org, from the Email Service Provider Coalition. Scroll to the bottom of the page, and you'll notice that a unique email address has been generated, along the lines of fBk6J@senderid.espcoalition.org. Send an email to that address and then press the View Sample button. When the following page loads, you'll find an attractive, complete report covering not only SPF, but also other DNS-based antispam and anti-spoofing technologies. You can see parts of that report in Figure 2.20.

Make sure you test your SPF record before you start to rely on it. Be patient, though—although some registrars seem to update and propagate DNS changes almost instantaneously, others can take hours, even up to the standard boilerplate time period of 48 hours.

```
MAIL FROM: scott@granneman.com

PRA: scott@granneman.com

SPF-Record-Classic: v=spf1 include:aspmx.googlemail.com ~all

SPF-Record-MFROM Scope: v=spf1 include:aspmx.googlemail.com ~all

SPF-Record-PRA Scope: v=spf1 include:aspmx.googlemail.com ~all

SPF-Method Result: pass(granneman.com: domain of
        granneman.com designates 66.249.82.237 as permitted sender)

SenderID-MFROM-Method Result: pass(granneman.com: domain of
        granneman.com designates 66.249.82.237 as permitted sender)

SenderID-PRA-Method Result: pass(granneman.com: domain of
        granneman.com designates 66.249.82.237 as permitted sender)

DomainKey-Status: bad format: No DomainKey signature found
```

FIGURE 2.20   The ESPC provides a very useful report for those testing SPF.

USING A DOMAIN PURCHASED THROUGH GOOGLE

Not everyone who wants to use Google Apps already has a domain name registered and ready to configure. In fact, many people interested in Google Apps probably don't have any idea how to register a domain name, much less how to fiddle with DNS. Recognizing that this problem exists, in December 2006 Google announced that it had partnered with two of the larger domain name registrars, Go Daddy and eNom, to make it drop-dead simple to register domains that would work seamlessly with Google Apps. The pitch? You buy the domain name (ending in .com, .org, .net, .biz, or .info) through Google for $10 per year (which is pretty cheap), and everything is automatically configured for you so it works immediately with Google Apps.

You actually get a nice range of domain-related services along with the deal. Your registration information is made private automatically, at no charge, which a lot of people will like because it protects that data from spammers (Personally, I think this is a bad idea because it's important that Netizens be able to contact domain owners for a variety of very legitimate reasons, but I'm not running the service.) Another service made available at no charge is domain locking, which prevents unauthorized domain transfers.

Contrary to what some might expect, you have complete control over your DNS. If you want to configure things to work with non-Google services, you are more than free to do so. Things are simplified for you, but you don't lose functionality or control, which is vitally important—and fair.

Buying a Domain Through Google

Since I was a little kid, I've enjoyed playing games with words and names, and one of my favorites is the backwards game: take a person's name, turn it around backwards, and then try to say it (yes, I know this is weird—maybe that's why I'm a writer).

I'm Ttocs Namennarg. My brother is Sug. My friends include Snaj Notrac, Sumaes Rekced, Nibor Namtlow, and Ebag Trebig (and I can pronounce all of those flawlessly). So when it's time for me to buy a domain name for fun to test Google's ability to provide the domain-name-less with a domain, I decided to go for it and register namennarg.com. After all, I already own granneman.com, so why not get the same domain, just backwards? And it's only $10 per year!

Again, I head to www.google.com/a/, click Compare Editions and Sign Up, and choose Sign Up under Standard Edition. This time, however, I select I Want to Buy a Domain Name, where I am first asked to search for the domain name I'd like. I enter **namennarg**, opt for .com as my top-level domain, and press the Check Availability button. The next page, displayed in Figure 2.21, tells me that the name is available (what a surprise!) and its cost, along with the services I'll receive with the domain name registration.

If you look carefully at the bottom of Figure 2.21, you'll notice that Google lets me know that this registration will be "powered by eNom." Hmmm. I'm not sure that's what I want. I already have accounts at DynDNS and Go Daddy, and the last thing I need is yet another account with a domain registrar. I click Learn More next to eNom, and I'm taken to a page on which Google allows me to select either eNom or Go Daddy as my registrar. I pick Go Daddy, press Continue, and I'm back at Step 1: Choose a Domain Name, but now my purchase will be "powered by GoDaddy.com," which is what I want. I press Continue to Registration to do just that.

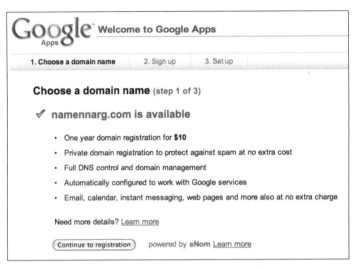

FIGURE 2.21 Hey, who would've guessed? Namen-narg.com is available!

On the page for step 2, I'm asked if I want to Keep My Registration Information Unlisted. Many people will want to do this to possibly frustrate spammers, but I really do think it goes against the spirit of the Internet, and I'm also going to be using Gmail, which has the best spam filters in the world, so I'll uncheck it.

Next I'm asked for personal information—the same personal data you could expect from any domain registrar—which is no problem to enter. I have two check boxes to deal with. One, which must be ticked to continue, says I've read the Go Daddy Terms of Service, and the other automatically renews my registration every year and is completely optional. On the bottom of the page is a button that, when pressed, takes me to Google Checkout so I can pay for the domain.

> **NOTE**
>
> Yep, you need a Google Checkout account to buy a domain. But don't worry—if you don't have one already, you'll be prompted to create one on the next page.

I already have a Google Checkout account, so I sign in and pay Google. On that page, shown in Figure 2.22, I have a few interesting choices to make.

Google Checkout

rsgranne@gmail.com | Help | Sign out

Change Language [English (US)   ‡]

Order Details - Google Apps, 1600 Amphitheatre Parkway, Mountain View, CA 94043 US

Qty	Item	Price
1	**Domain Registration namennarg.com** - 1 year registration for namennarg.com, powered by GoDaddy.com	$10.00
	Tax (MO) :	$0.00
	Total: $10.00	

☐ Keep my email address confidential.
Google will forward all email from Google Apps to rsgranne@gmail.com. Learn more

Pay with: **VISA xxx-3589**Change

☑ I want to receive promotional email from Google Apps.

(Place your order now -- $10.00)

Billing Information & Privacy
Your credit card will be charged by Google. "GOOGLE * GoDaddy " will appear by the charge on your credit card statement. Learn more

Return Policy for Google Apps
All sales are final. If you have any questions or concerns, please contact our support at www.google.com/support/a/.

FIGURE 2.22   Buying a new domain with Google Checkout isn't hard to do.

It's standard operating procedure for Google Checkout to offer to hide your email address from sellers. If I check the appropriate box, Google will forward all emails sent from the seller to the email address I used, which was my gmail.com address to which my Google Checkout account is tied. But the seller here was itself Google Apps, so I just don't see the point!

Under that is a check box, already ticked, that says I want to receive junk…er, "promotional email" from the seller. Don't need it. Unchecked.

I press the button to place my order, and I am the proud owner of a new domain name: namennarg.com. The next page, shown in Figure 2.23, thanks me and provides a link so that I can "retrieve [my] purchase."

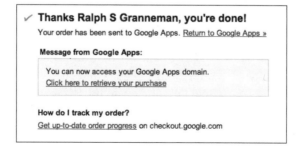

✓ **Thanks Ralph S Granneman, you're done!**
Your order has been sent to Google Apps. Return to Google Apps »

Message from Google Apps:

You can now access your Google Apps domain.
Click here to retrieve your purchase

How do I track my order?
Get up-to-date order progress on checkout.google.com

FIGURE 2.23   Time to claim what's now
mine: namennarg.com!

At the same time, two emails arrive in my Inbox, one a receipt and the other containing information about activating my Google Apps account. I save both.

I click the link found on the thank you web page, and I'm invited to create my first administrator account for the namennarg.com Google Apps account. The username is "ttocs," of course, and the password is "kltpzyxM" (Or is it? How mischievous of me not to say!). Do I want to receive tips? Nope, don't need 'em. Do I want to give feedback? Sure. I press Continue, and the Dashboard for namennarg.com loads, which you can see in Figure 2.24.

FIGURE 2.24   The Dashboard for my domain bought through Google, namennarg.com.

You'll notice that the custom domains for the Start Page, Email, Calendar, and Docs are all set automatically for me, which is very cool. As I said earlier in the "Creating Custom URLs" section, I'd prefer my.namennarg.com to start.namennarg.com, but that's no biggie. I can always change it. But a bigger problem is that the URLs for Web Pages and Sites are not very customized at all: http://www.namennarg.com-a.googlepages.com and http://sites.google.com/a/namennarg.com? Who wants that? I thought that's why I was buying the URL from Google and one of its partners—to remove my need to fiddle with changing URLs. Now I find out that I have to in fact fix things. Sigh.

This is a pretty easy fix, however. At my Google Apps Control Panel, go to Service Settings and then Web Pages. In the Web Address section, I click Change URL, and on the Change URL for Web Pages, I select the second option button, which automatically inserts "sites" into the custom URL text field. Then I press the Continue button, and I repeat the same process for Sites. In just a few moments, all my custom URLs are in place. It wasn't too bad, but I sure hope Google fixes this little issue. It's not a huge thing, but it is annoying.

> **NOTE**
>
> I could have changed both URLs at the same time, but I was only changing two, so it wouldn't have saved me that many clicks. That's why I did them separately.

Accessing Advanced DNS Services

If I want to customize DNS settings beyond what Google makes possible with its simplified interface, or if I want to add third-party services that necessitate DNS modifications, I need to log in to Go Daddy (or eNom if I'd used that instead) and make those changes.

From the Google Apps Control Panel, I go to Domain Settings, choose the Domain Names tab, and then click the Advanced DNS Settings link, which indicates in a note under it that it will allow me to go to Go Daddy to alter my DNS. When I click it, I end up at a page on which Google provides me with a sign-in name (really a string of numbers), a password (a lengthy string of letters and numbers), a customer service PIN, and the email for Go Daddy's customer service. Under all that is the link to Go Daddy's DNS Console.

After I'm at Go Daddy, I see a page, shown in Figure 2.25, that lists all the domains that I registered through Google. However, it does not show the accounts I registered through Go Daddy that were not registered through Google. In other words, if you've been following along in this chapter, you know that I registered heavymetalmassage.com through Go Daddy, but not through Google, even though I later went ahead and changed the DNS records to point to Google's services. That domain does not show up in Figure 2.25.

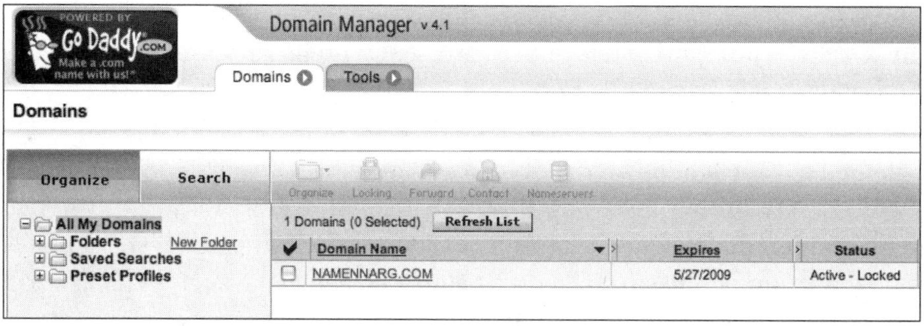

FIGURE 2.25   I can see only the domain I registered through Google, but not any other Go Daddy domains. Boo!

After I choose namennarg.com, I can change contact info, transfer ownership to another registrar (which would remove the automated configuration and require me to manually create CNAMEs and MX records), and change the DNS any way I'd like.

It's nice that Google's partnership with Go Daddy doesn't limit your ability to get your hands dirty with the DNS records of the domain you registered.

Should You Purchase Your Domain Through Google?

My short answer: probably not.

My longer answer: If you know anything at all about DNS or are a person who can read instructions and make changes without freaking out, you should probably not purchase your domain through Google and its registrar partners.

As you've seen throughout this chapter, it really isn't that difficult to manually change your DNS records to match what Google requires. I've been using Go Daddy, but I've also used DynDNS and a few other registrars, and they're all about the same. Google has gone out of its way to provide instructions for most of the top registrars, as well as generic steps to go through, so you can more than likely do it on your own. It's so easy to do that it's just not worth it to have Google do it for you.

On top of that, there is no way to change the username and password assigned to you when you purchase a domain through Google and Go Daddy (or eNom). Add to that issue the problem that this domain and its account at Go Daddy is separate from my already existing Go Daddy account, and registering a domain through Google turns into a major hassle. In fact, for me, it's a deal breaker. I don't want to have to remember some long string for a username when I already have a Go Daddy username that I know and like, and I certainly don't want to have to write down or save an incredibly long string for a password when I already have memorized a great password (although, in its defense, the automatically generated password is a pretty good one, just hard to remember). Worse, I'd prefer to centralize management at Go Daddy in one account, not two.

You can centralize management, but you have to transfer the domain from the Google-created account to your preexisting Go Daddy account. Yes, that's from Go Daddy to Go Daddy, but that's how it works. According to ICANN rules (ICANN is the organization that oversees the rules for domain names), however, you have to wait 60 days after purchasing a domain before you can make such a change. Arrgh!

To transfer the domain, I'd log in to my Google Apps Control Panel, go to Domain Settings, choose the Domain Names tab, and then click the Advanced DNS Settings link, which takes me to a page listing my Go Daddy sign-in name and password. Enter those, submit the data, and I'm on the Go Daddy page listing my domain. I click namennarg.com, which takes me to the Details page, shown in Figure 2.26.

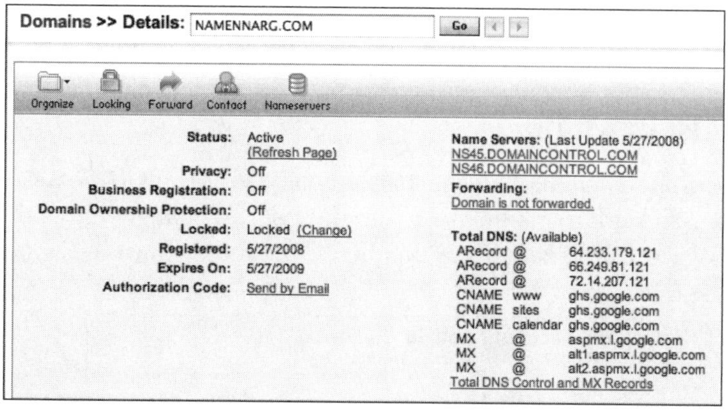

FIGURE 2.26   The Details page for namennarg.com at Go Daddy.

My domain is listed as Locked, which is a good thing because this prevents unauthorized transfers. However, it also means that I can't transfer it when I want to, so I need to click the word Change next to Locked. On the next page, I can unlock the domain. After I've done that, back on the Details page, I see the Send by Email link next to Authorization Code. I click that, and Go Daddy will email me the information I need to transfer the domain—back to another account at Go Daddy— or, if I wanted, to a completely different registrar. Nothing is forcing me to stay at Go Daddy except for that ICANN-mandated 60-day waiting period, and I can move if I so desire.

> **⚠ WARNING**
>
> Again, keep in mind that if you change or move this account, the automatic configurations of DNS for Google Apps will stop working, and you will have to make changes manually.

If you don't mind the different account, and you really don't want to have to make DNS changes yourself, buying a domain name through Google can make a lot of sense. But for most people, I'd recommend against it.

CREATING USERS

So far you have one user: an administrator. But what about other users? Unless you run an extremely small organization, you're going to have to eventually add more than one user. Google Apps provides two ways to do so: manually and in bulk.

Adding Users Manually

Adding users one at a time is easy, but tedious. Go to your Dashboard and either click the Create More Users link or select the User Accounts button; then click the Create a New User link. Either way, you'll see the form shown in Figure 2.27.

Bulk account update (step 1 of 3)
Create and update many accounts at once.

1. **Make a list of user accounts**

   You'll need to create a CSV (comma separated value) file with the user accou
   and edit CSV files.

   Your CSV file should be formatted as a table and must include a header, or fir
   name, last name, password.

   Example:

	A	B	C	D
1	username	first name	last name	password
2	picasso	Pablo	Picasso	59h731
3	claude.monet	Claude	Monet	6d8945
4	lilies	Georgia	O'Keeffe	319w56

2. **Choose update options**

   For each row in your file, this update will:
   ☑ **Create new accounts** for usernames that do not yet exist.
   ☑ **Update existing accounts** with new names and passwords.
   ☐ **Require a password change** when new or updated users sign in.

3. **Upload list of user accounts in CSV format**

   (Choose File) no file selected

FIGURE 2.27 Add a single new user with this form.

It's pretty self-explanatory—fill in a first name, last name, and username (also an email address at yourdomain.com). You'll notice in Figure 2.27 that Google has autogenerated a temporary password for the user (and not the greatest one, in my opinion). If you're happy with that, press Create New User, and you now have another user at your domain, ready to use Google Apps.

If you don't like the temporary password, and you either want to assign one that you've created or one that the user herself has created, click Set Password, and you'll see what's visible in Figure 2.28.

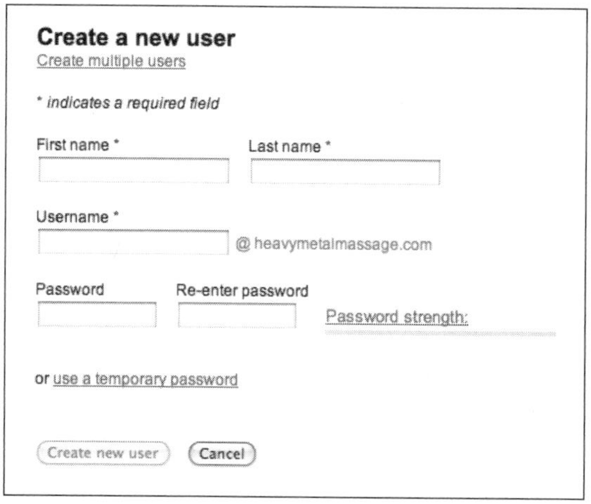

Create a new user
Create multiple users

* indicates a required field

First name *   Last name *

Username *

@ heavymetalmassage.com

Password   Re-enter password

Password strength:

or use a temporary password

(Create new user)   (Cancel)

FIGURE 2.28   If you don't want to use Google's temporary passwords, feel free to use your own.

Enter a password, enter it again to make sure it's the same thing, and press Create New User. Bam!

Adding Users in Bulk

As I said, it's a simple thing to add new people by filling out the Create a New User form, but it quickly gets very old when you have more than a tiny number to add. If you find yourself facing a long list of new users to add to Google Apps, or you are simply enamored of automation, you need to instead look into adding users in bulk.

Go to your Dashboard and either click the Create More Users link and then click the Create Multiple Users link or select the User Accounts button and then the Upload Many Users at Once link. You should have in front of you what you see in Figure 2.29.

The easiest way to proceed is to create a spreadsheet using your favorite spreadsheet-creating software—Excel, for example, or better yet, OpenOffice.org's Calc. (You could use Google Docs, but I'm pretending that you don't yet know much about it!) Create four header columns: username, first name, last name, and password. Fill out the spreadsheet and enter the correct data into each cell, something like the examples in Table 2.3.

NOTE

All passwords must be at least six characters long. Nope, 1234 won't work.

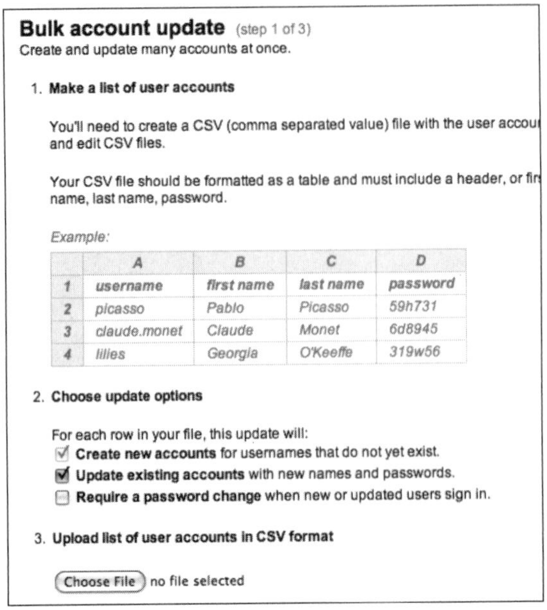

FIGURE 2.29 Instead of creating one user at a time, upload a spreadsheet with as many as you'd like.

TABLE 2.3 User Data in a Spreadsheet Formatted for Upload to Google Apps

USERNAME	FIRST NAME	LAST NAME	PASSWORD
jcarter	John	Carter	DotarSojat
dthoris	Dejah	Thoris	Carthoris
ttarkas	Tars	Tarkas	Jeddak

When you've finished entering the data, save the spreadsheet as a CSV (comma-delimited) file. If you don't do this, you will not be able to upload your data to Google, so make sure that it's a file that ends in .csv, not .xls or .xlsx or .ods or anything else.

Next, before you've actually uploaded the spreadsheet, you need to tell Google how you want it to process the new data you're going to provide it. You have three check boxes:

```
Create new accounts for usernames that do not yet exist.
Update existing accounts with new names and passwords.
Require a password change when new or updated users sign in.
```

The first option is automatically checked, and you cannot uncheck it. If someone is new on your spreadsheet, he will be added as a new user to your Google Apps account.

The second option is great if you want to change passwords or usernames for several people at once.

The third option is something you definitely want to use if you created temporary passwords for your users ("Hey, everyone—you all have the password of "widgetinc," so log in to Google Apps and change it!") and expect them to create their own when they start using the service.

Press the Choose File button, select your CSV file, and then press Upload and Continue. On the next screen, Google shows you the results of the parsed file so you can review it to make sure everything looks copacetic. If it does, press Confirm and Run Update; if it doesn't, press the Back button on your web browser, edit your CSV file, and try again.

On the final screen, Google informs you that it's processing the update, and a report will be mailed to your email account. If it's not too huge an addition, you can probably head back to your Dashboard and already see that your new users are in place.

Syncing with Your Active Directory or LDAP Server

If you're using an Active Directory or LDAP Server to manage user accounts, you can use Google's free LDAP Synchronization Tool, available at http://code.google. com/p/google-apps-for-your-domain-ldap-sync/. It's quite a sophisticated program, with several key features:

- Automatic detection or new, renamed, or removed users
- Automatic detection of attribute changes
- Scheduled syncing of deltas, to reduce traffic flow

You'll need Python 2.4 or later, as well as the Python client of the Google Apps Provisioning API and the python-ldap library. All the requirements are laid out for you at the previous URL.

Google provides detailed documentation for those who are interested in using the LDAP Synchronization Tool at http://code.google.com/p/google-apps-for-your-domain-ldap-sync/wiki/HowToUseIt.

CANCELING GOOGLE APPS

Some of you may decide that Google Apps isn't right for you. If Google isn't right for you, you can cancel Google Apps—most of the time, that is. There are a few little issues you should know about before you try to cancel.

- If you're using the Premier Edition, like the Mafia, you can't just leave. If you're still using the free trial, you have to cancel the free trial (instructions at www.google.com/support/a/bin/answer.py?answer=60755), and then you can cancel. If you paid for the Premier Edition, you have to wait until your year expires before you can cancel (don't freak—you can change your DNS settings so you're not forced to use Google Apps).

- If you purchased your domain name from Google through one of Google's partners, you need to transfer your domain name to another registrar before you can cancel Google Apps.

- If you have multiple user accounts, you can't delete Google Apps. Instead, you have to delete all users (instructions at www.google.com/support/a/bin/answer.py?answer=33314) except for the Administrator.

If you're able to delete Google Apps after all that and you still really want to do so, log in to your Control Panel and select Domain Settings, Account Information. You can now click Delete Google Apps for Your Domain. You'll be warned and asked to confirm your actions. Do so, and five days later, your Google Apps account is like the passenger pigeon: gone.

> **⚠ WARNING**
>
> Keep in mind: All data inside those user accounts will be irrevocably gone. Make sure you've backed everything up (see Appendix A for details) before you say bye-bye to Google Apps!

SOLVING COMMON PROBLEMS

Nothing in life is perfect, so you might run into a few issues as you're setting up Google Apps. Here are some solutions.

I Can't Get Back to the Control Panel!

You signed up for Google Apps and got as far as the Control Panel, but then you were distracted by something else. Now you can't get back to the Control Panel.

If you can remember it, go to www.google.com/a/mydomain.com (using your domain name, of course). If you can't, no problem: you can instead go to www.google.com/a/ and click the link in the top right that reads Returning User, Sign in Here.

When you do, you'll be prompted to enter your domain name and choose your destination after your login is successful. Because you're an administrator, at this early stage you probably don't have any services set up completely, so click the drop-down menu and choose Manage This Domain, as in Figure 2.30.

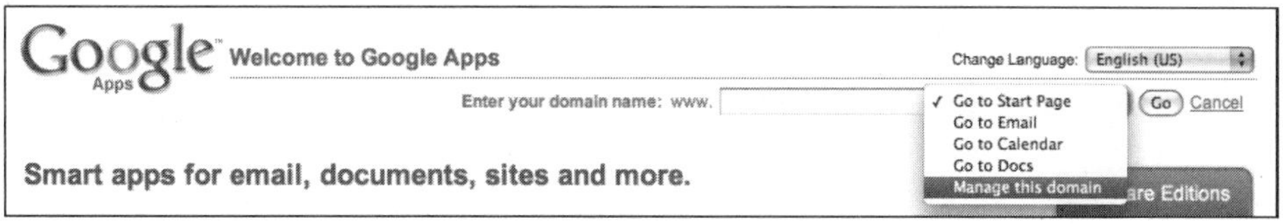

FIGURE 2.30 It might seem as if the Control Panel is hidden, but you can always get back to it pretty easily.

Press Go, log in, and you'll be back on your Control Panel. Don't forget to bookmark it this time, OK?

I Lost the Admin Password!

To make your life easy in case you do lose or forget the Admin password, prepare ahead of time by opting in to the password reset feature of Google Apps. Go to your Control Panel, to Domain settings, and then to Account Information. Find the Secondary Contact section and check the box next to In Case of Forgotten Administrator Password, Send Password Reset Instructions to Secondary Contact.

Assuming you did that, it's time to reap the benefits of your forward thinking. Open your browser and go to https://www.google.com/a/mydomain.com (using your domain name, of course). Click I Can't Access My Account. You'll need to type in some numbers and letters to prove you're a human being and not a spambot. Do so and then press Submit. Go to the secondary email account you provided to Gmail, and you should see an email from Google. In that email is a link you need to click. On the resulting page, select Administrator Account to Change in the drop-down menu. Enter your new password and press Save New Password to activate it.

If you never checked the box that tells Google it can send password reset instructions, or if you have more than 500 active accounts in your domain, you're going to have to contact Google directly and request a password change. Go to www.google.com/support/a/bin/answer.py?answer=33561 and scroll to the bottom, where you'll see Troubleshoot the Problem. Click that link, make the appropriate choices on the next page, and your password will get changed eventually. It's much quicker if you automate the process by checking that box, however, so I recommend doing that.

CONCLUSION

It might seem like there's a lot to consider and perform when you're setting up Google Apps, but that's really a function of the fact that you're dealing with five different editions, with multiple services available within each addition. If you've ever tried to set up an email or groupware server before, you know how complicated it can be—so Google Apps is among the simpler examples of that software species. Nonetheless, you need to plan thoroughly, read carefully, and work meticulously to get Google Apps set up the way you want it. Now let's move on to migration, in which you move users and data you've already created in other programs over to Google Apps.

FURTHER READING

There's always more to learn, so here are some resources that you might find handy if you want to learn more about setting up Google Apps:

- Quick Steps to Get You Started:
  www.google.com/a/help/intl/en/admins/resources/setup/
- How To Manage A Successful Deployment:
  google.com/support/a/bin/answer.py?answer=67774
- Google Knol on Google Apps for Admins—Demos and Guides:
  knol.google.com/k/google-apps-admin-help-center/google-apps-for-admins-demos-and-guides/1p0i914w5kwkv/21
- All Help topics on one page:
  www.google.com/support/a/?fulldump=1
- Setup screencast:
  www.google.com/a/help/intl/en/admins/resources/setup/setup_video.html
- Signing Up
  - Signing Up For Google Apps:
    http://services.google.com/apps/resources/overviews/welcome/topicWelcome/page16.html
  - Train Signal's Google Apps Signup HOWTO video:
    www.youtube.com/watch?v=nkSIF7RFsu4

- Users
  - Managing Users screencast:
    http://services.google.com/apps/resources/admin_breeze/ManagingUsers/
  - Train Signal's Google Apps Bulk User Upload HOWTO video:
    www.youtube.com/watch?v=ocEWcCego4Y
  - LDAP Sync discussion group: http://groups.google.com/group/google-apps-for-your-domain-ldap-sync
- For developers
  - SAML-based Single Sign-On (SSO) API:
    www.google.com/support/a/bin/answer.py?answer=60224&topic=10717
  - Google Provisioning API Developer's Guide:
    http://code.google.com/apis/apps/gdata_provisioning_api_v2.0_reference.html
- Control Panel
  - Help Topics: www.google.com/support/a/?hl=en
  - Google Apps Control Panel – YouTube playlist:
    http://www.youtube.com/view_play_list?p=445899A1305C271C
  - Train Signal's Google Apps Management Page HOWTO video:
    http://www.youtube.com/watch?v=UD7ATyjuKNk
- Verifying your domain
  - Verifying Your Domain:
    http://services.google.com/apps/resources/admin_breeze/VerifyingYourDomain/index.html
  - Train Signal's Google Apps Domain Verification HOWTO:
    www.youtube.com/watch?v=i_8QUrhI5fQ
  - Train Signal's Google Apps Email Verification HOWTO video:
    http://www.youtube.com/watch?v=BI4zdxsSz48
- DNS
  - Creating CNAME Records:
    https://www.google.com:443/support/a/bin/answer.py?answer=47283&topic=9196 and www.google.com/support/a/bin/answer.py?answer=47283&topic=9204
  - Configuring MX Records:
    www.google.com/support/a/bin/answer.py?answer=33352&topic=9196
  - Train Signal's Google Apps Easy URLs HOWTO video:
    www.youtube.com/watch?v=6gmWYyrXC0U
  - SPF Tools for testing SPF records: www.openspf.org/Tools

- Salesforce.com integration
  - Salesforce for Google Apps: http://googleblog.blogspot.com/2008/04/posted-by-scott-mcmullan-google-apps.html
  - Google And Salesforce.com Integrate Apps To Penetrate Enterprise, Duel Microsoft: http://searchengineland.com/080414-090939.php
- Email
  - Email gateway: www.google.com/support/a/bin/answer.py?answer=60730
  - Email routing: www.google.com/support/a/bin/answer.py?answer=77182
- Support options: www.google.com/a/help/intl/en/admins/support.html
- Known Issues: www.google.com/support/a/bin/request.py?contact_type=known_issues

CHAPTER 3

Migrating Email to Google Apps

You've set up your Google Apps account, and you've added users, so you'd think everyone is ready now to start using Google Apps. It may not be that simple, however. If your users have been using other programs and services for their email, contacts, and calendar, they most likely have a mass of data already in those programs that they'll want to use in Google Apps. In those cases, you're going to have to migrate that data into Google Apps, which isn't always as obvious as you might think.

In this chapter, you're going to learn how to migrate email. I'm going to first give you the generic instructions, and then I'll focus on major programs that should help most users.

 NOTE

Google provides some advice for conversion from many programs, and it's adding more all the time. Searching at www.google.com/support/a/?hl=en and http://mail.google.com/support/?hl=en for the program from which you need to extract data is a good start.

Email is one of the most important functions in businesses today, and many people have built up a huge warehouse of saved messages that they refer to constantly. On the one hand, your users are going to love the super-powerful search capabilities built into Gmail; on the other hand, you have to first get all that email onto Google's servers before those users can start accessing it.

> ### ⚠ WARNING
>
> Throughout this part of the chapter, I'm going to reference copying your emails from the current client or system you're using into Gmail. You could move the emails, of course, but better safe than sorry. Not to mention, if you try to move mail and a network issue interrupts things, you'll be left in a messy state that could result in lost mail. Copy first, verify that everything is working correctly, and only then delete—or better yet, archive—your old email from your current client.

Keep in mind that to perform a migration, you first have to have set up your users' email accounts in Google Apps so that they're working correctly. I cover setting up Gmail in Chapter 7, "Setting Up Gmail," so you may want to skip ahead there and make sure things are up and running before returning to this chapter.

> ### 📝 A NOTE ON TECHNICAL TERMS
>
> This chapter contains some technical jargon. Let's review a few key terms that are going to appear again and again:
>
> **POP**—An Internet protocol defining how email clients retrieve email from remote email servers. Clients move the email messages from the remote servers to the clients. For more info, see http://en.wikipedia.org/wiki/Pop3.
>
> **IMAP**—A newer, more feature-rich Internet protocol defining how email clients access email on remote email servers. Clients view email on remote servers without actually moving it to the clients. For more info, see http://en.wikipedia.org/wiki/Internet_Message_Access_Protocol.
>
> **Microsoft Exchange**—Microsoft's email server, extremely popular in medium and large businesses. Exchange can use both POP and IMAP, but by default, it uses its own proprietary protocol, MAPI (Messaging Application Programming Interface). For more info, see http://en.wikipedia.org/wiki/Microsoft_Exchange_Server and http://en.wikipedia.org/wiki/MAPI.
>
> **mbox**—A widely used format for storing email messages in which all the messages in a folder—or mailbox—are concatenated into a single file. For more info, see http://en.wikipedia.org/wiki/Mbox.
>
> **Maildir**—A widely used format for storing email messages in which each message is stored in a separate, unique file. For more info, see http://en.wikipedia.org/wiki/Maildir.

PLAN CAREFULLY BEFORE MIGRATING

Before migrating, you need to think about several key matters, and more importantly, you need to plan. Don't just blindly jump into an email migration, or you could have a disaster on your hands that will take days to clean up or fix and very unhappy clients. The three matters you need to consider before you migrate are

- Molding your email folder structure into the one used by Gmail (they are most likely very different!)
- Processing new emails arriving during the migration
- Dealing with emails you send during the migration

Let's walk through these issues one by one.

Molding Your Email Folder Structure into the One Used by Gmail

It's important that you understand a key aspect of how Gmail works: You can have folders (actually labels, which I discuss in depth in Chapter 8, "Things to Know About Using Gmail," but for now let's just call them folders), and you can have folders inside folders, but that's it. In other words, you can have two levels of folders, but no more. So Friends as a top level folder is OK, and Alice and Jackie as subfolders inside Friends are OK (because they're the second levels), but Project A, First Strike, and SuperCop as subfolders of Jackie are not OK (because they would be third-level folders).

This turns into a headache if you or your users have done what so many people do, which is to create folders inside folders inside folders inside folders inside folders, down level after level after level. One friend of mine had his folders in Outlook nested ten levels deep, and I know he's not uncommon.

Before you migrate your email, whether you do it manually or automatically, you need to change your folder structure so that it matches what Gmail can handle. I know that many of you reading this are freaking out right now. You're thinking, "But I have to have my folders within folders within folders! That's the only way I can organize or find anything! I have very carefully created those subfolders over the span of several years, and I must have them that way!"

No, you don't.

You really don't. Studies have shown that folders actually make it harder to find things (see Farhad Manjoo's "Too Much of a Good Thing" at http://dir.salon.com/story/tech/feature/2004/07/16/e_mail/index2.html) and can be woefully inefficient. When I see hundreds of folders in someone's email account, that usually spells an enormous amount of work that may not result in better organization. Quantity doesn't always spell quality, after all.

Also when you file a message into a folder, that's it—it's now secreted into one single location. Many of the messages I get, however, could just as easily go into several places or at least have several reference points. For instance, I might want to reference an email I get from my business partner Jans about the new calendar widget we developed for the Saint Louis Zoo website in three folders: Jans, Calendar, and STLZoo. I could copy the email, but that's crude, and most people wouldn't even think to do that. Instead, I'd like to associate that email with Jans, the calendar widget, and the Zoo, which Gmail makes possible.

Finally, with folders, you still have to remember where you filed a message and then manually go find it. Too often, this is difficult, and you end up spending valuable time clicking through folders looking for that one message you need. Gmail's super-powerful, highly-configurable search options, built around the amazing Google search engine, obviate the need for manually pawing through hierarchical folders. When you want to find a message, search for it!

> **NOTE**
>
> Yes, I know that many mail clients provide you with the capability to search your email. By and large, those are slow, clunky, and inefficient. Gmail's search is fast, powerful, and "just works." Once you use it, you'll never want to go back to your client's search.

My advice is to accept Gmail's constrictions and live within them. Simplify your email with a set of top-level folders that contain a single level of subfolders. Search to find messages. You'll soon find that it's a better, more efficient way to approach your email.

If you're really feeling daring, move all your old email into the Gmail Inbox. Don't use any folders at all. That's an option a surprising number of people have chosen to adopt.

Here's an example of how another business partner of mine, Jerry, dealt with his rampant folder growth in Outlook before he moved over to Google Apps. First, look at Figure 3.1 to see what just a section of his folder tree looked like in Outlook.

In Figure 3.1, you can see three subfolders under Inbox (although in reality, there were many more that you can't see): Bryan Consulting, Civic, and JLB. Under Civic, Jerry has eight subfolders, one for each of the groups in which he's active, with the Alzheimer's Association leading the list. Under the Alzheimer's subfolder,

Jerry has three more subfolders (now sub-sub-subfolders), and one of those, Local, itself has four sub-sub-sub-subfolders. And Jerry is pretty good; as I said, my buddy Rich's subfolders went ten levels deep!

My advice to Jerry went as follows:

FIGURE 3.1   Jerry has nested folders several levels deep in Outlook, and this is nothing compared to other users!

After you move to Gmail, your Inbox will become its own separate thing, and you can't put any subfolders under it. You can keep Bryan Consulting, Civic, and JLB as top-level folders, but understand that you can have only one level of subfolders under each. In the case of Civic, you can keep Alzheimer's, CEA-CSD, Grand Center, and so on down the list.

However, you cannot keep the subfolders that you currently have under Alzheimer's. But really, do you need those? Why not just lump everything together in Alzheimer's? Won't it be obvious by searching a FROM, a TO, a SUBJECT, or the body of a message, if the message relates to your local chapter or the national office? And if it's from the local chapter, and it has to do with fundraising, won't that be searchable pretty easily?

Going even further, do you really need all those subfolders under Civic? Why not throw everything into the Civic folder and skip the subfolders altogether? It should be pretty easy to search for messages and distinguish between Grand Center, Parkway Schools, Missouri Baptist Medical Center, and Washington University in St. Louis, shouldn't it?

Look a bit further down. Do you really need separate subfolders under Friends, one for each family? Combine all emails from friends together in a Friends folder and be done with it. Searching for Bachmann, Benton, or Deering, and getting the right set of emails, should work like a charm.

Jerry took my advice. It was an adjustment, sure, but it wasn't that hard for him to make, and Gmail's powerful search capabilities made it almost painless. I know that it seems almost like you're jumping off a cliff to give up your masses of subfolders, but it's eminently doable, and it really is where email is headed. In five years, when we've all got tens of thousands of emails archived, we won't be relying on folders to provide our organization. We'll be way past that. Instead, it will be searching and tagging. Best to get started now.

> This happened to my friend Rich (the one with ten levels of subfolders in Outlook), so be careful. He used an automatic migration tool that transferred all his email from Outlook to his new Google Apps Gmail account. The tool didn't warn him that his levels upon levels of subfolders wouldn't transfer and ended up moving an enormous amount of email over, apparently with no problems.
>
> But then he noticed that search didn't really find very many emails, certainly not the ones he expected to find. The problem was that his emails hadn't really transferred over. The lesson is clear—plan out your new folder structure ahead of time. And if you're going to use an automatic tool to migrate your email, make sure that your folder structure on your client matches as closely as possible what you will end up with at Gmail.

Processing New Emails Arriving During the Migration

Don't forget that new emails will be arriving as you're migrating your old mail. If you don't do something about them before you begin the process, you're quickly going to face a "mell of a hess," as my Mom likes to say, as new mail mixes in with the old mail and you have to keep trying to remember if you've moved a particular message or not. Ugh.

If you've already switched over MX records so that mail sent to you@yourcompany.com is now settling nicely into Google's mail servers, you don't need to worry about new mail intermixing in with old mail on your old server. You can just open your email client that contains your storehouse of old mail and start transferring it using the method you've chosen.

However, many people actually use the move to Google's servers as a chance to put new email addresses into play. Their old email address was @sbcglobal.net, for instance, or @aol.com. Now they've purchased a domain and plan to use @yourcompany.com going forward. In those cases, they're going to continue receiving email at the old address while setting up and migrating old email to the new Gmail account.

Before you start the migration process, then, set up an autoforward rule for all incoming mail that sends it along to your new Google Apps email address. As email comes in to fiona@sbcglobal.net, then, it automatically heads right on to fiona@iloveanimals.com. Ideally you can set this forwarding up on the server so that it never hits the email client on your machine, a process that will be cleaner and more efficient.

If you have to use your client, then you have to. In those cases, however, try to redirect instead of forward so that the email headers (From, CC, Message-Id, and Date) are more closely preserved.

For instance, if Fiona at fiona@sbcglobal.net receives an email from jans@web-sanity.com and then autoforwards it to her new address at fiona@iloveanimals.com, the email's headers will indicate that it came from fiona@sbcglobal.net, not jans@websanity.com, and the date will conform to the time Fiona forwarded the mail, not the original time Jans sent it.

If, on the other hand, Fiona redirects that email message to fiona@iloveani-mals.com, the email will show up in that mailbox as coming from jans@websanity.com, with the original date and time that Jans sent it.

Just to make things confusing, some email clients call this capability a "redi-rect," whereas others call it a "resend" or even a "bounce" (although I generally use "bounce" to refer to sending an email back to a sender as though it didn't arrive because of a bad address, a technique sometimes used with organizations that continue sending me email after I've unsubscribed from them). Table 3.1 contains a list of some popular email clients and their support for redirection.

TABLE 3.1   Email Clients and Their Support for Redirection

Client	Support for Redirection
AOL	None
Apple Mail	Message, Redirect
Eudora	Message, Redirect
Evolution	Actions, Forward, Redirect
Gmail	None (access Gmail with a client that supports redirection)
Hotmail (Windows Live Mail)	None (access Hotmail with a client that supports redirection)
KMail	Message, Forward, Redirect
Outlook	Actions, Resend This Message

TABLE 3.1 Continued

CLIENT	SUPPORT FOR REDIRECTION
Outlook Express (Windows Mail)	None
Thunderbird	Install the free Mail Redirect extension (https://addons.mozilla.org/en-US/thunderbird/addon/550)
Yahoo	None (access Yahoo Mail with a client that supports redirection)

If you have a bunch of email sitting around in mbox files, and you're running Linux or Mac OS X, you can use the following command in your terminal to redirect every message in a particular mbox file:

```
$ formail +1 -i "To: me@newaddress.com" -i Cc: -f -ds /usr/sbin/sendmail
-t -oi < /path/to/mbox
```

 TIP

If you don't like the options I've presented, or you're using a client (such as Outlook Express) that doesn't support redirection, search Google for **"Windows redirect email"** and start examining the solutions you find.

And here's one final bit of advice concerning redirection of your email. We're going to discuss labels, the use of a "+" for email aliases, and filters later in Chapter 7 ("Setting Up Gmail") and Chapter 8 ("Things to Know About Using Gmail"), but for now, know that you can redirect all your emails from your @sbcglobal.net address to me+sbcglobal@newaddress.com. As a result, you will be able to set up a filter to autolabel those emails as you see fit (maybe as "sbcglobal" or "old" or "home"). Redirect emails from a different account to me+aol@newaddress.com with a different autolabeling filter ("AOL" or "old" or "personal"). Use your computer to automate your tasks—it's what computers do best.

Dealing with Emails You Send During the Migration

While you're migrating, you may still be using the old account or the old client to send email. You could, assuming everything is set up correctly, direct your client to use your new Google Apps account as your SMTP server. But maybe you aren't ready to make that cutover yet.

In those cases, go ahead and send email using the old server but put your new Gmail address into the BCC field. Even better, if your client supports automatic BCC, use that. Table 3.2 contains a list of some popular email clients and their support for automatic BCC.

TABLE 3.2   Email Clients and Their Support for Automatic BCC

CLIENT	SUPPORT FOR AUTOMATIC BCC
AOL	None
Apple Mail	See "Adding Automatic BCC to Apple Mail" in the following section
Eudora	Create a Stationery with your address in BCC and set it as your default (Tools, Options, Composing Mail)
Evolution	Edit, Preferences, Mail Accounts, [Account] , Edit, Defaults
Gmail	On Firefox, install Greasemonkey (https://addons. mozilla.org/en-US/firefox/addon/748) and the Gmail Auto BCC Greasemonkey script (http:// userscripts.org/scripts/show/2255)
Hotmail (Windows Live Mail)	None
KMail	Settings, Configure KMail, Identities, Modify, Advanced
Outlook	See "Adding Automatic BCC to Outlook" later in the chapter
Outlook Express (Windows Mail)	See "Adding Automatic BCC to Outlook Express" later in the chapter
Thunderbird	Tools, Account Settings, Copies and Folders
Yahoo	None

Some of the more popular email clients have a few peculiarities when it comes to automatic BCC, or they make users jump through hoops or even require the purchase of third-party software. The following sections contain a look at a few of those clients (Apple Mail, Outlook, and Outlook Express).

In the same way I recommended using a "+" for email aliases in the previous section when it came to redirecting your email, I recommend you do that for mail you send via automatic BCC. Instead of simply BCCing to me@newaddress.com, use me+sent@newaddress.com and then create a filter that autolabels those emails with "Sent" (the same thing as moving them all into the Sent folder at Gmail).

Adding Automatic BCC to Apple Mail

Apple Mail is a bit complicated to set up for automatic BCC, but it can be done in a two-step process. First, go to Preferences, Composing, shown in Figure 3.2.

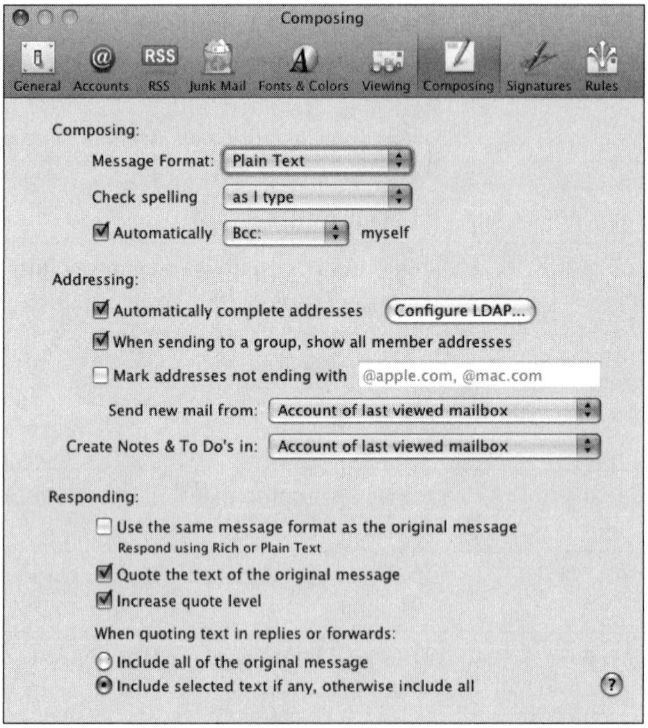

FIGURE 3.2 Tell Apple Mail to automatically BCC yourself on every message sent.

Check Automatically Cc: Myself and change Cc: to Bcc:. Then go to Preferences, Rules and create a new rule, shown in Figure 3.3.

Title the new rule something like **Redirect Mail I Send** and change any to All in If All of the Following Conditions Are Met. Add two new conditions: if a message comes in *from* your old address (fiona@sbcglobal.net in Figure 3.3) and if the message is *to* your old address (again, fiona@sbcglobal.net in Figure 3.3). If those conditions are met, set up an action that redirects the message to your new Google

Apps account (fiona+sent@iloveanimals.com in Figure 3.3). Press OK to create the rule.

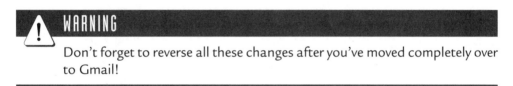

FIGURE 3.3   Using some clever rules, you can redirect email to your new Google Apps account.

Notice that I used the "+sent" in the example because I would set up a filter at Gmail that assigns any mail bearing that alias with the Sent label (thus placing it in the Send "folder" at Gmail).

⚠️ **WARNING**

Don't forget to reverse all these changes after you've moved completely over to Gmail!

Alternatively, if you're not afraid to use the Terminal on Mac OS X, you can run this command, replacing "me+sent@newaddress.com" with your address, (and you don't need to use the "+sent," but it sure might help you set up a filter that puts email coming into that address in the Sent folder by default):

```
$ defaults write com.apple.mail UserHeaders '{"Bcc" =
"me+sent@newaddress.com"; }'
```

There's one little problem with this method, however: If you type a different address into the BCC field, it will be automatically replaced with the address you specified in this command, which could be a major pain. Then again, if you rarely use BCC, it won't matter at all during the migration.

Adding Automatic BCC to Outlook

Incredibly, Outlook—Microsoft's flagship email program and Personal Information Manager—doesn't natively support automatic BCC. If you know how to code or are comfortable working with other folks' VBA code, you can head over to www.out-lookcode.com/article.aspx?id=72 and grab what's there.

If you'd be more comfortable with buying someone else's software, the Office Add-ins website has a review of some of the more popular choices at www.office-addins.com/plugins-reviews/outlook-cc-bcc/.

Adding Automatic BCC to Outlook Express or Windows Mail

Outlook Express (and its big Vista brother, Windows Mail) doesn't support auto-mated BCC, but you can add it with other software. Your best bet is to search Google for "**Outlook Express automatic BCC**" or "**Windows Mail automatic BCC.**"

Although I've never used it, AJ Systems' OE Quick Tools (www.ajsystems.com/oequicktools/qt.html) does get a few mentions from apparently satisfied users when it comes to providing automatic BCC and quite a number of other upgrades and missing features that Outlook Express should have but doesn't. It's $30, but if you're looking to kiss Outlook Express goodbye, that may be a price you're willing to pay.

MANUALLY MIGRATE EMAIL USING IMAP

- Operating Systems: Windows, Mac OS X, Linux
- Email Clients and Services: All desktop clients that support IMAP
- Google Apps Editions: Standard, Premier, Education and Nonprofit, Partner

NOTE

I'll be repeating the three lines you see preceding this note throughout this chapter where appropriate to help you know if a section speaks to your situation or not.

This method is the simplest, but it's also the most tedious. Basically, you add your Google Apps account in your email client using IMAP as the connection, and then you copy messages from your old accounts into your new Google Apps account. You can drag or copy entire folders, or you can create new folders under your Google Apps account and then drag selected messages into those folders.

There are definite advantages to this method:

- Your messages' original metadata—senders, recipients, dates, and more—are all preserved.

- You'll know what's happening throughout the entire process.

- You can easily centralize all your saved email from across all your accounts by copying it into your Gmail account.

- Gmail automatically labels your messages according to the folder into which you copied them or the folder you transfer. It doesn't matter if you create a folder at Gmail called ABC Project and then drag messages into it or if you copy the ABC Project folder over from your old email into your new Gmail account within your client. All the messages in the ABC Project folder will receive the Gmail label ABC Project.

You should also be aware of the disadvantages:

- It could take a loooooong time. If you have thousands and thousands of messages, be prepared to wait a while. And if you're on a slow Internet connection—well, my advice is to go find a fast one.

- It's manual, so it's tedious. As in copy, wait, wait, wait, wait, wait, done. Select next folder or messages, copy, wait, wait, wait, wait, wait, done. Repeat, ad infinitum. Open Solitaire or your favorite book or turn on the TV. You're going to need something to distract you.

- If you're not careful and you copy over the same mail more than once, you could end up with duplicate messages that you will have to remove.

And finally, you should be aware of something that could really confuse you.

When you import mail from your current client into Gmail, it will collapse threads of messages into what Google calls "conversations." In other words, suppose you and two other pals sent 12 emails back and forth, all with subjects containing the words "Facebook must be destroyed." When you import those messages into Gmail, it will appear as a single conversation that happens to contain 12 components.

So if you're transferring 5,000 emails but Gmail reports that you have 2,000 conversations, don't freak. You didn't lose any mail. You can verify that you still have 5,000 messages by viewing the folders you copied in your desktop client. No clients that I'm aware of understand Google's conversations, so they simply report the total number of email messages.

Outlook-Specific Settings

- Operating Systems: Windows
- Email Clients and Services: Outlook
- Google Apps Editions: Standard, Premier, Education and Nonprofit, Partner

I know that I could walk through many other email clients, but I wanted to focus on Outlook because it is so widely used.

If you use Outlook, you can copy your messages from your local PST file using a variety of methods.

- Select the folder or messages you want to transfer and then go to Edit, Copy to Folder.
- Right-click the folder you want to copy (let's call it the "old folder") and select Copy Folder. In the window that opens, select the folder on your Gmail account to which you want to copy the old folder and press OK.
- Select the folder(s) or messages you want to duplicate. Hold down the Control key as you drag the selected items to the place in which you want them to go in your Gmail account. Outlook asks you if you want to Copy or Move the items; I recommend you choose Copy.

Whichever method you use, pretty soon (depending on how much email you're transferring), your Outlook email will appear inside the Gmail folder into which you copied it.

Automatically Import from IMAP Servers Using Google's IMAP Migration Tool

- Operating Systems: N/A
- Email Clients and Services: Any supported IMAP server
- Google Apps Editions: Premier, Education & Non-Profit

Sure, you can move your mail manually, but if you have tens of thousands of emails, that's not likely to happen. Or if you have quite a few accounts in your organization, and you're the person tasked with taking care of the migration? Manual moving just ain't gonna happen. Time to bring in the automation!

If your mail is already on IMAP servers, you can use Google's built-in automatic migration tools. There are some big advantages to this method:

- The original data associated with each message—sender, recipient, date—is preserved.
- The folder structure is preserved.
- It's automated.

However, there are also a few gotchas that you should know about.

- Google's tool is available for only the Premier and Education Editions.
- The "old" server from which you are transferring messages must support IMAP. This might seem obvious, but often, Microsoft Exchange server admins turn on MAPI only, even though Exchange servers will support IMAP quite well.
- Any message whose text and attachments total more than 20MB will not be transferred. Time to have users clean up those messages that are hogging their email boxes!
- If a user has more than 25GB of email in her account, Google will stop transferring mail after it hits that ceiling.
- Messages that contain viruses aren't allowed into Gmail. No surprise there, and a good thing to boot.
- If a user has somehow amassed more than 1,800 folders (how, I have no idea), she will be skipped, and you will have to use another method.
- For this process to work, you're going to have to provide Google with a list of the usernames and passwords on the "old" IMAP server. Of course, you're going to shortly be trusting Google with names and passwords after everyone is moved to Google Apps, so this shouldn't be a big deal.

- Google needs access to the "old" IMAP server, so you need to make sure that any firewalls protecting that server allow the following IP addresses access to the box (this list comes from www.google.com/support/a/bin/answer.py?hl= en&answer=61369, in case you want to check for updates):

  216.239.56.0/23

  64.233.160.0/19

  66.249.80.0/20

  72.14.192.0/18

  209.85.128.0/17

  66.102.0.0/20

- If your organization uses Microsoft Exchange Server 2003, you need to make sure that your users have not used forward slashes ("/") in their folder names. If they have, their messages will not be migrated. Instead, change those slashes to some other character, like a hyphen.

Google supports migration from the following servers:

- Microsoft Exchange Server 2003
- Cyrus IMAP Server
- Courier-IMAP
- Dovecot

If your IMAP mail is on one of those servers, and the caveats are not killers, great—keep reading. If there's a problem, skip ahead to the next section.

> ⚠ **WARNING**
>
> Be patient and ultra-careful and test this process out with a few accounts before you turn things loose on all your user accounts!

To begin the process, go to your Dashboard and select the blue Advanced Tools tab. In the section labeled Email Migration, click the Set Up Mail (IMAP) Migration link. Step 1—Set Server Connection—will load, showing a screen you can see in Figure 3.4.

For Name This Server Connection, use something meaningful to you, like **HR Dept** or **St. Louis Division**.

For Type, you don't have a choice, so IMAP it is. Maybe this will change some day, but for now…

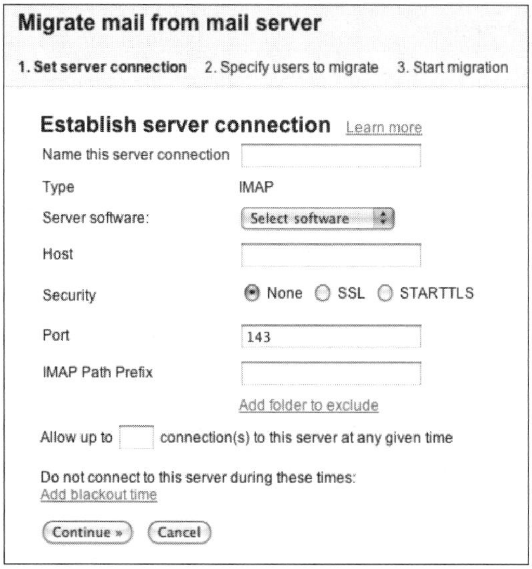

FIGURE 3.4   Step 1 in setting up
Google's automatic IMAP migration tool.

For Host, enter the domain name or IP address of your IMAP server from which you're importing mail.

For Security, you should choose SSL or STARTTLS because that will mean that you're protecting your users and your IMAP server with encryption. Otherwise, it's None.

For Port, type in the port number clients need to access your IMAP server. If you're not using encryption, that's most likely 143. If you are using encryption, it's probably 993, but it could be anything (within reason). You just need to find out.

IMAP Path Prefix could be tricky, but it's important, or Google won't know where the email it's going to import is kept. You should definitely look at your IMAP server's config files to find out what this value is. You're looking for the path in which user email folders are stored on the server.

You can also look at the email clients that your users currently have and try to deduce the IMAP Path Prefix from that. The problem is that each email client seems to call the IMAP Path Prefix something different. Google provides a helpful list of examples for you to use.

- Thunderbird: IMAP server directory
- Outlook Express: Root folder path
- Pine: Name of Inbox Server

- Kmail: Prefix to folders
- Apple Mail: IMAP path prefix

The link Add Folder to Exclude allows you to do just that: tell Google which folders should be ignored during the email migration. For instance, you may have IMAP folders containing newsgroups or info about the server that you wanted all your users to see in a shared mailbox. Or if you're running a Microsoft Exchange server, you'll definitely want to skip those folders that contain contacts and calendar info, such as these:

- Calendar
- Contacts
- Deleted Items
- Public Folders
- Tasks
- Notes
- Journal

> **⚠ WARNING**
>
> Now do you see why you need to test the process first? Excluding or including the wrong folders could result in one huge mess for you and your users.

Finish the sentence in Allow Up to ___ Connection(s) to This Server with a number that works for your server based on its capabilities and your network connectivity. When in doubt, go low. It's better for the transfer to take longer than for it to overwhelm your IMAP server. In other words, 1 or 2 might be just fine.

If you want to set up times during which Google will not contact your IMAP server, so that your server can continue to operate as normal, click Add Blackout Time and enter those times. For each blackout time, you'll need to enter Time Zone, Day of the Week, Hours of the Day.

> **NOTE**
>
> Keep in mind that this is IMAP, so mail that has been transferred to Google's servers will still be on the old server as well, and your users will still be able to access that mail as long as their email clients are configured to do so.

When you press Continue, Google will test the server connection. If things don't work, you'll be informed of that and asked to fix things; if things do work, you'll proceed to the next step.

Step 2 is Specify Users to Migrate, and that's exactly what you'll do here, as you can tell in Figure 3.5.

Select how you want to specify user accounts for migration

○ **Specify a few user accounts**
   Specify user accounts individually if you only need to transfer a few users. Use this to test out the process.

○ **Specify many user accounts via file upload**
   Upload a list of user accounts if you need to transfer mail for many users at once.

« Back | Continue » | Cancel

FIGURE 3.5   You have a choice when it comes to creating accounts.

You'll be able to add accounts either manually or in batches. If you have only a few users to migrate, manually will probably be OK, depending on your acceptance of this sometimes tedious process. If you have a bunch of users to migrate, by all means use the batch process.

WARNING

Keep in mind that you must have already created user accounts in Google Apps for each of the accounts you're planning to migrate, or Google will not process the transfer.

If you select Specify a Few User Accounts and press Continue, you'll be taken to a page on which you can enter as many accounts as you'd like, which you can see in Figure 3.6.

Migrate mail from mail server

1. Set server connection   **2. Specify users to migrate**   3. Start migration

Enter user accounts to migrate

Username	Source username	Source password	Retype password	
@acmesystemsinc.com				Add

Source usernames may require a domain eg. susan@acmesystemsinc.com Learn more

FIGURE 3.6   It's not hard to add users one at a time—it's just tedious.

The Google Apps Username is obvious and easy. The next field, Source Username, is where the complexity begins. If your mail server required you to enter usernames as complete email addresses, you'll need to enter that. Many servers, however, want just a username (the part before the @ sign). And if you're using Microsoft's Exchange, the username looks like `[Domain]/[Admin]/[User]`, with substitutions as follows:

- [Domain] is the Microsoft Exchange domain name
- [Admin] is a user with rights to the user's mailbox that you're migrating
- [User] is the name of the user you're migrating

For Source Password, enter the user's password. If you're using Exchange, that needs to be the password of the person you specified in [Admin].

NOTE

It may be a heck of a lot easier—and more secure—to just assign users a temporary password during the migration process. Be sure to tell them, though, or they may freak out. Because you're moving them over to Google Apps, this may be a great time to get everyone to change those old, insecure passwords into something a bit safer.

After you complete entering data for a user, press Add if you want to migrate more accounts at this time. If you're finished with this group, press Continue to review what you've entered.

NOTE

If you use the Dovecot IMAP server, be sure to read Dovecot's own advice on master users and passwords, at http://wiki.dovecot.org/Authentication/MasterUsers.

If you instead earlier selected Batch Upload User Accounts and pressed Continue, you can now create a list of accounts you want to add in bulk. This process is very similar to creating new Google Apps users in bulk, as I outlined in Chapter 2. You're going to create a CSV file and then upload it so that Google can parse it and then follow your instructions.

> **⚠ WARNING**
>
> Make sure that your CSV file is correct before you turn it loose on Google. If things are out of whack, you could import Bob's email into Alice's new Google Apps account, and you know that wouldn't be good. Or it may not work at all. Test with a few users first, and then let 'er rip!

You can use OpenOffice.org or Excel or any spreadsheet program to create your CSV, but it must be formatted according to Google's specifications. You must make sure that the first row is set up as headers that define the columns, and you must have only three columns: Google Apps Email Address, Source Username, and Source Password. The results will look something like Table 3.3.

TABLE 3.3   A Sample CSV File for Adding Multiple User Accounts

GOOGLE APPS EMAIL ADDRESS	SOURCE USERNAME	SOURCE PASSWORD
jcarter@barsoominc.com	john.carter	WarlordOfMars
dthoris@barsoominc.com	dejah.thoris	PrincessOfMars
ttarkas@barsoominc.com	tars.tarkas	JCarterIsMyBFF

For the Source Username, you have to use whatever your current IMAP server uses for a login, which you can determine by looking at an email client such as Outlook or Thunderbird that is currently accessing mail at your server. In other words, instead of a username, you may need to insert an actual email address. Again, test thoroughly!

When your CSV looks good, upload it and then press Continue.

Now you've told Google about your IMAP server and the accounts you want to transfer—whether that's one or 10,000—so Google asks you to confirm everything before it actually goes to work.

If everything looks correct, press Start Transfer, and Google begins (unless you're doing so during a scheduled blackout time). You'll be taken to the Migration History page, which shows you the date you started, the number of migrating users, the current progress in terms of a percentage, and the current state (complete, aborted, or in progress). If you want to see the status of a particular user, just click on the user's item in the list of accounts. If for some reason you want to stop the transfer, press Abort.

After everything has been transferred, you can begin the process with a new batch of users, or if you're completely finished with all accounts, you can turn off your current IMAP server and begin using Google Apps.

> **NOTE**
>
> According to Google, more than 100,000,000 (yes, 100 million) messages have been migrated using this tool since it was released. Wow!

Automatically Migrate from Exchange Server

- Operating Systems: Windows
- Email Clients and Services: Exchange Server
- Google Apps Editions: Premier, Education and Nonprofit

Microsoft Exchange servers support IMAP, so one solution to migrating from Exchange to Google Apps is to enable IMAP access to your server so that Google can access it. Unfortunately, many Exchange administrators don't want to enable IMAP for various reasons (not all of them good), which means that they need to investigate other solutions.

> **NOTE**
>
> Not sure how to enable IMAP support on your Exchange Server? Check out Microsoft's TechNet article at http://technet.microsoft.com/en-us/library/bb123880.aspx.

Persistent Systems makes a software package called "e2GMigrator" that runs on a Windows server running Exchange 2000 and later (the fact that it supports older versions of Exchange is really nice). It costs $15 per user, with volume discounts available, but it performs a bulk movement of email, contacts, and calendars to Google. It's powerful and has a lot to offer the Exchange admin. You can read more about it at www.persistentsys.com/ttm_mt.html, and you can see a video of the software in action at www.persistentsys.com/products/downloads/e2gmigrator/e2gmigrator.htm.

> **NOTE**
>
> Other companies and products do roughly the same thing. If you're in need of a tool to help move from Exchange to Google Apps, check out MailShadowG by Cemaphore Systems (www.cemaphore.com/mailshadow_g.php) and gMigrate Premier by CompanionLink (http://gmigrate.com/products/gmigrate-premier.html). At the time of writing, gMigrate supports transferring everything *but* email from Exchange to Google; hopefully, mail will be supported as well by the time you're reading this.

DEVELOP YOUR OWN POP TOOLS WITH GOOGLE'S EMAIL MIGRATION API

- Operating Systems: Windows, Mac OS X, Linux
- Email Clients and Services: Any that supports POP
- Google Apps Editions: Premier, Education and Nonprofit, Partner

Google's IMAP Migration Tool has been very successful and widely used, but it doesn't help organizations that don't already use IMAP to serve their email. As an answer to groups who rely on POP to serve email, Google released the Google Apps Email Migration API, a set of specifications that allows developers to create custom software that can satisfy most other groups interested in migrating email to Google Apps.

There are a few caveats:

- It works only with the Premier, Education, and Partner Editions of Google Apps.
- You're going to have to be a developer, have developers available, or use a third-party tool that will probably cost some money.

If this sounds good to you, and you want to oversee the actual development yourself, head over to the Google Apps Email Migration API Developer's Guide at http://code.google.com/apis/apps/email_migration/developers_guide_protocol.html and the Google Apps Email Migration API Reference Guide at http://code.google.com/apis/apps/email_migration/reference.html and start reading.

MANUALLY MOVE MESSAGES FROM A PREEXISTING MBOX FILE OR MAILDIR STORE

- Operating Systems: Windows, Mac OS X, Linux
- Email Clients and Services: Any that generates mbox files or a Maildir store
- Google Apps Editions: Standard, Premier, Education and Nonprofit, Partner

This is the same method ultimately as that covered earlier in "Manually Migrate Email Using IMAP," except that the source of the email to be migrated comes from an mbox file or a Maildir storehouse of archived messages.

Essentially, you open the mbox file with your favorite email client and then add your Google Apps account in the same email client using IMAP as the connection. At that point, you can copy messages from your old mbox file into your new Google Apps account.

If you have mbox files sitting around on your computer, you presumably have an email client available that can read them. If you're not sure, Thunderbird, which runs on Mac OS X, Windows, and Linux, makes an excellent choice for this job because it opens mbox files with aplomb. In fact, MozillaZine has very complete instructions for that process at http://kb.mozillazine.org/Importing_and_exporting_your_mail. If you use Linux, KMail imports mail from an astonishing number of sources, including mbox files, as you can read at http://kontact.kde.org/kmail/tools.php.

If you're using Maildir to store your mail, it would probably be easiest to convert your Maildir store to the mbox format because so many more clients support it (I still prefer maildir for local mail storage, however, so I'm not putting down mbox). Here are some places you can look for that information:

- www.macosxhints.com/article.php?story=20051002175356349 contains a bash shell script that should work on Mac OS X and Linux boxes; note that there are corrections to the original script in the reader comments.
- If you have Python on your box, the script at http://yergler.net/Maildir_to_Mbox might do the trick for you.
- If your system has formail on it (part of the procmail package that all Linux machines can download), this simple shell script takes care of things: http://does-not-exist.org/mail-archives/mutt-users/msg05250.html.
- Finally, a Google search for **`convert maildir to mbox`** will turn up something.

AUTOMATICALLY MOVE MESSAGES FROM A PREEXISTING MBOX FILE

- Operating Systems: Windows, Mac OS X, Linux
- Email Clients and Services: Any that generates mbox files
- Google Apps Editions: Standard, Premier, Education and Nonprofit, Partner

If you have an mbox file containing archived messages, and you want to automate the moving of those messages to your Google Apps account, and you're running Linux or Mac OS X and can therefore run Ruby scripts from the command line, you may be in luck. A script called "2gmail.rb" will take of your needs.

Download the Ruby script from http://blog.tquadrado.com/wp-content/uploads/source/2gmail.rb and make it executable (`chmod u+x 2gmail.rb`). It's ready to run immediately if you're using Debian or Ubuntu. If you're using a different Linux distro or Mac OS X, check line 1 or prepend a path to your Ruby interpreter when you run the command.

> **NOTE**
>
> For more information about the Ruby script, read the post at http://blog.tquadrado.com/?p=166.

The basic structure of the command is

```
$ 2gmail.rb mbox GmailFolder [StartingMessage]
```

If you want to transfer every message in an mbox file named Sent to a Gmail folder named Sent Mail, you'd run the following:

```
$ 2gmail.rb Sent "[Gmail]/Sent Mail"
```

In this code, Sent Mail already exists because it's a default Gmail folder that you can't change or remove. If you'd instead specified a folder named WebSanity Clients that didn't exist, the script would create that folder for you.

If you have problems, check the 2gmail.log file that is created in the directory you're in when you run 2gmail.rb. In particular, the log file will indicate the last message successfully sent by the program. If you want to restart again from that message, provide the message number:

```
$ 2gmail.rb Sent "[Gmail]/Sent Mail" 707
```

NOTE

If you search for automatic programs to upload mbox files and Maildir stores, you may run across GMail Loader, available at www.marklyon.org/gmail/. It was one of the first, if not *the* first, automatic scripts to upload email to Gmail, and I remember using it years ago.

However, it has one big problem that prevents me from recommending it to you: Every message you upload ends up with the date you added the message to Gmail, losing the original date in the process. You can still search for the original date in the body of the message, but Gmail displays the date of upload to Google, not the original date you received the mail.

AUTOMATICALLY MOVE MAIL FROM A CLIENT WITH THE GOOGLE EMAIL UPLOADER

- Operating Systems: Windows
- Email Clients and Services: Outlook, Outlook Express, Windows Mail, Thunderbird
- Google Apps Editions: Premier, Education and Nonprofit, Partner

If you have a ton of email in your Outlook, Outlook Express, or Thunderbird client, and you use Windows XP or Vista, you're in luck: You can automatically transfer all your email (and contacts, but we'll cover that later) to your Google Apps Gmail. Google provides the Google Email Uploader, a free download from https://mail.google.com/mail/help/email_uploader.html.

NOTE

What's really cool about the Google Email Uploader is that it's an open source project, so you can download the source code and change it to fit your organization's needs.

The Google Email Uploader won't work unless admins enable the Email Migration API first. To do so, they need to go to the Dashboard, Advanced Tools and then click the box in the User Email Uploads section next to Allow Users to Upload Mail Using the Email Migration API. In addition, users wanting to use Google Email Uploader must also log in to their Gmail accounts and accept the Terms of Service so their accounts are activated.

Before you start the Google Email Uploader, close your email programs. After that, start the Google Email Uploader and press Next to get past the first screen. On the following screen, enter your Google Apps email address and password and press Sign In. After you're authenticated (over a secure connection, by the way), you'll see the screen shown in Figure 3.7.

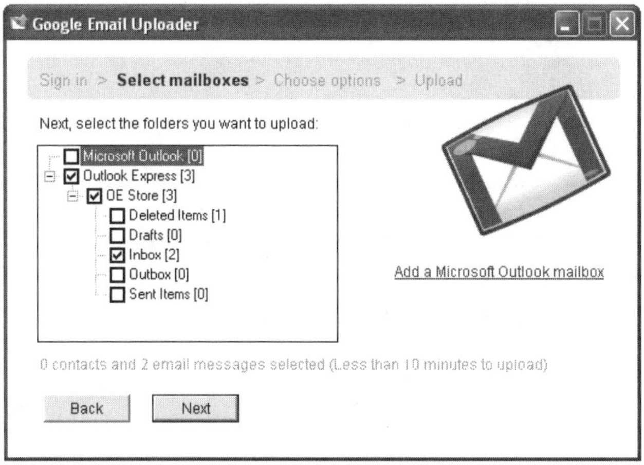

FIGURE 3.7 The Google Email Uploader is smart enough to know what email programs you have installed.

The Google Email Uploader detects whether you have Outlook, Outlook Express, or Thunderbird running on your computer and displays the list accordingly. Select the folders you want to transfer to Google by checking the box in front of them. If you want to select every folder used by a program, check the box next to the program. If you want to add a PST file that isn't currently open and used in Outlook, click Add a Microsoft Outlook Mailbox and choose the file. After you've made all your selections, press Next, and you should see Figure 3.8.

If you want your folders to become labels that are applied to your messages (and remember that labels look like folders in your email clients), check the box next to Create Labels from Folder Names. If you want to skip the Inbox and just archive everything (and I'll discuss what that means in a lot more detail in Chapter 8, "Things to Know About Using Gmail"), check the box next to Archive Everything. Press Upload, and the Google Email Uploader starts its work, presenting you with a progress bar as it churns through your messages.

When the Google Email Uploader is finished, it informs you that the upload is complete. Press the OK button to close the program. All done!

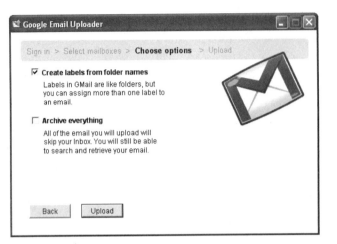

FIGURE 3.8 Answer a few simple queries, and the Google Email Uploader goes to work.

If something bad happens and the program or Windows crashes, feel free to restart the Google Email Uploader and start the process over. It will not upload mail if it's already been transferred, so don't worry about duplicates.

That doesn't mean, however, that you can start moving mail, kill the program, move a bunch of folders, download some new email messages, and otherwise change your email in a significant way, and then restart the Google Email Uploader and expect that it will run smoothly. If you accidentally make a bunch of changes to your email between sessions of running the Google Email Uploader, find the program's directory (probably at C:\Program Files\Google\Google Email Uploader) and delete a file named UserData.xml. Next time you restart the Google Email Uploader, you'll have to walk through the configuration process again so everything is clean and the Uploader doesn't get confused.

When you log in to Gmail or check it with your client, your new mail should appear, although Google warns that it could take up to 48 hours for it to appear. If you chose to convert your folder names into Gmail labels, those labels/folders should appear for your messages. In addition, all your emails transported via Google Email Uploader will have a label of Imported as well. You could, however, search for all emails with the label of Imported and apply a new label to them, such as Outlook or Thunderbird, as a reminder to you of the origin of those emails.

TIP

If you need help with the Google Email Uploader, check out the "Google Email Uploader User Guide" at http://code.google.com/p/google-email-uploader/wiki/UserGuide or buzz on over to the Google Group for the software, at http://groups.google.com/group/google-email-uploader.

AUTOMATICALLY TRANSFER MAIL FROM THUNDERBIRD WITH THE MAIL REDIRECT EXTENSION

- Operating Systems: Windows, Mac OS X, Linux
- Email Clients and Services: Thunderbird
- Google Apps Editions: Standard, Premier, Education and Nonprofit, Partner

Thunderbird users are lucky because their email program has a seemingly endless list of extensions available for it that can add an amazing variety of cool and useful features. In particular, the Mail Redirect extension allows Tbird users to redirect instead of forward emails (if you're not sure what redirection is, check out "Processing New Emails Arriving During the Migration" earlier in this chapter), thus preserving the original dates and other important metadata.

Get the Mail Redirect extension at https://addons.mozilla.org/en-US/thunderbird/addon/550 and install it in Thunderbird (instructions are on that web page). When you restart Thunderbird, you should probably go to View, Toolbars, Customize and then drag the Redirect icon to your Thunderbird toolbar so it's easy to access. Press Done to close the Customize Toolbar window, and you should see something like Figure 3.9 (of course, your Redirect icon could be somewhere else, depending on where you placed it).

FIGURE 3.9 For some reason, the Redirect icon doesn't quite fit in with the default Thunderbird theme on Mac OS X.

Select the messages you want to redirect to your Gmail account and press Redirect. You should see something like Figure 3.10.

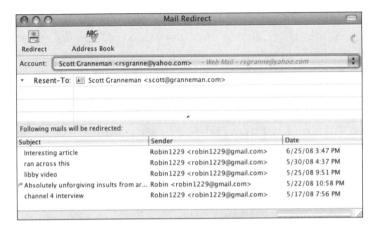

FIGURE 3.10 The Mail Redirect extension makes it easy to transfer mail from Thunderbird to Google.

Enter the address to which you want to send the mail next to Resent-To and press Redirect. Depending on how many emails you've selected, the process could take a very long time. At the end of the process, your old email will be in your new account with the dates and other essential data intact.

> **TIP**
>
> By default, the Mail Redirect extension keeps five SMTP connections open at the same time. If you want to (carefully) increase or decrease that number, go Tools, Add-ons, Mail Redirect, Preferences and change the number next to Number of Concurrent SMTP Connections.

Migrate Mail from Gmail to Google Apps Premier Edition

- Operating Systems: N/A
- Email Clients and Services: Gmail
- Google Apps Editions: Premier

If you're already using a non-Google Apps Gmail account and you want to move mail from it into a Google Apps Premier Edition account, you're in luck: You can use the IMAP Migration Tool discussed earlier in this chapter. Your settings should include the following:

- Host: imap.googlemail.com
- Security: SSL
- Port: 993
- IMAP Path Prefix: Leave blank

Best of all, your messages, headers, and even your labels will be preserved, which will vastly reduce the work you have to do.

MANUALLY MIGRATE FROM HOTMAIL (OR LIVE MAIL) USING THE MICROSOFT OFFICE OUTLOOK CONNECTOR

- Operating Systems: Windows
- Email Clients and Services: Hotmail, Outlook
- Google Apps Editions: Standard, Premier, Education and Nonprofit, Partner

So you've been using Hotmail (or the newly rebranded Live Mail) and now you want to move over to a web-based email system that's far more powerful and useful? No problem. You'll need Outlook 2003 or 2007 running on Windows XP or Vista, but everything else is free.

You need to download the Microsoft Office Outlook Connector, which is available at www.microsoft.com/downloads/details.aspx?FamilyID=7aad7e6a-931e-438a-950c-5e9ea66322d4&displaylang=en (Great URL, eh? I'd recommend searching Google for **"Microsoft Office Outlook Connector"** and going from there). Install it, and then the next time you open Outlook, you'll be prompted to configure the Outlook Connector by entering the information you can see in Figure 3.11.

The E-mail Address and Password are those you use to access Hotmail, whereas the Name is what you want to appear in the Outlook folder list. When Outlook finishes opening, you should see your new Hotmail account in the folder list on the left.

Now that you can easily access all your Hotmail messages inside Outlook, go ahead and configure Outlook to also access your Google Apps account using IMAP (for details on that process, see Chapter 7, "Setting Up Gmail").

After you can get to both your Hotmail and your Google Apps accounts, it's a simple matter of dragging your Hotmail messages into the appropriate folders in your Google Apps account. The time this will take depends on the number and size of your messages. When you're finished and everything is copied over, you can say goodbye to Hotmail.

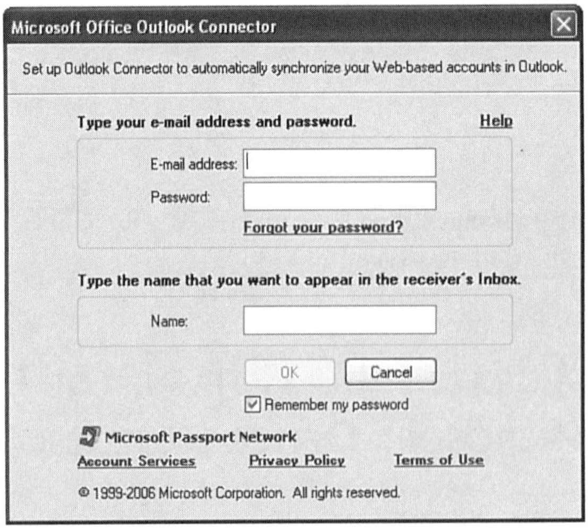

FIGURE 3.11 You're automatically prompted to fill in the required info when you start Outlook

MIGRATE FROM WEB-BASED EMAIL SYSTEMS USING THUNDERBIRD AND THE WEBMAIL EXTENSION

- Operating Systems: Windows, Mac OS X, Linux
- Email Clients and Services: Thunderbird, Hotmail, Yahoo, Lycos, Mail.com, Gmail, AOL, and others
- Google Apps Editions: Standard, Premier, Education and Nonprofit, Partner

In other sections in this chapter, we've looked at ways you can move your mail from your current host or client into Google Apps. In all those cases, you could easily access your mail. Nowadays, however, many people use web-based email systems such as Yahoo or Hotmail (or Gmail, for that matter, but as you'll see, Google makes it easy to get mail out of Gmail). Unfortunately, most web-based email systems make it difficult to easily extract emails out of them using POP without forcing you to pay fees (if they even allow you to download mail at all). Yahoo, for instance, charges $20 per year to allow users to access and download email via POP clients—and don't even think about IMAP. So how do you download your emails from those services without spending some cash?

Fortunately, there's a free solution that works well. You'll need to start with Thunderbird, but that's free and runs on everything that matters. Next you'll need to install the WebMail extension, which you can find at http://webmail. mozdev.org/installation.html. To install it, you must first right-click the link to the extension and save the file to your hard drive (at the time I'm writing this, it's web-mail-1-3-2.xpi). In Thunderbird, go to Tools, Add-ons, and then drag the xpi file into the Add-ons window. When prompted, tell Thunderbird to go ahead and install the extension and then restart the program.

Now go back to http://webmail.mozdev.org/installation.html in your web browser and download the components you need for the webmail service from which you want to grab your mail. Currently, these are supported: Hotmail, Yahoo, Lycos, Mail.com, Gmail, Libero, and AOL. In my case, I right-clicked the Yahoo component and saved the file to my hard drive (currently yahoo-1-3-2.xpi). Again, go to Tools, Add-ons in Thunderbird and drag the new xpi to the Add-ons window to install it. Restart Thunderbird, and let's grab some Yahoo mail!

NOTE

I'm demonstrating how to set things up for Yahoo Mail. Other services, such as Hotmail and AOL, are similar but can be slightly different. Still, it's not that hard to figure things out to get them to work, and at the end of this section I will provide you with some places you can go for help if you're stumped.

To configure the WebMail extension, go back to Tools, Add-ons, and press Preferences for WebMail. There are three buttons in the prefs: Servers, Domains, and Logging.

Servers is the most important because problems here mean that you will not be able to use the extension and access your mail. The WebMail extension works by creating its own POP server on your machine that talks to the webmail service from which you want to download (it also creates an SMTP and an IMAP server, but those don't concern us here). You need to make sure that the POP server is running, so you want to see a green light and the word "Running" under POP.

If you don't, it probably means that your firewall is blocking access. Try fiddling with your firewall so that port 110 is open (the default port for POP) and then press the "+" to turn the POP server on. If the green light appears, great; if not, you may need to set the port number somewhere north of 1024. I used 4000, and the POP server started up immediately, as you can see in Figure 3.12.

Domains isn't important until you've configured the Yahoo component. After that's working, if you choose Domains, the WebMail extension shows you the various domains that Yahoo uses for mail and whether they support POP, IMAP, and SMTP.

FIGURE 3.12 A few notable ports have to be open for the WebMail extension to work.

You can turn on logging by pressing the cleverly named Logging button. Why do that? If you have problems and want to troubleshoot, logs will help tremendously. Check the box next to Enable Logging, press the Browse button, and find a place into which you want the logs to go (and pick a good one, preferably inside its own folder called something like WebMail Logs because this extension generates a lot of logfiles!), and close the Prefs window. Time to restart Thunderbird again!

Okay, it's running again. In Thunderbird, go to File, New, Account. For the type, select Web Mail and press Continue. Enter the correct data in Your Name (for example, **Scott Granneman**) and Email Address (because we're working with Yahoo here, I'd put **rsgranne@yahoo.com**) and press Continue. For Incoming User Name, you need to ignore what Thunderbird tells you. The program encourages you to just put a username in, like **rsgranne**, but that won't work with the WebMail extension. Instead, you must enter in the complete email address, such as **rsgranne@yahoo.com**, and then press Continue. The final screen reviews what you've entered. Verify everything, uncheck Download Messages Now because we're not quite ready to do that, and press Done.

The new account should now appear in your list of accounts in the left-most pane of Thunderbird. Right-click the account (in my case, Thunderbird gave it the name of "Web Mail – rsgranne@yahoo.com") and select Properties. Under the account, choose Server Settings, shown in Figure 3.13.

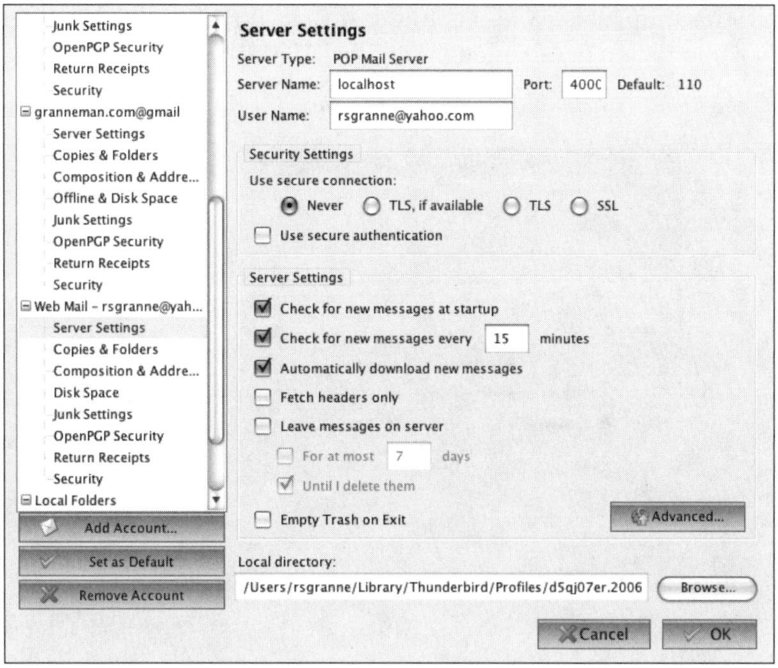

FIGURE 3.13   Set up your webmail account like you would any other POP or IMAP account.

Make sure that the Server Name is localhost and the Port corresponds to the port you set on the Servers tab in the WebMail preferences.

By default, Leave Messages on Server is checked. This might sound like a good idea, and you may want to leave this checked while you're still trying to figure out how this thing works. But you very well may need to uncheck that box. When I used this extension with my Yahoo account, it would download only 65 emails—the most recent 65—and that was it. Of course, those same 65 remained behind on Yahoo's servers. After I unchecked Leave Messages on Server, I was able to download my email from Yahoo's server, albeit 65 messages at a time.

In other words, I would download 65 messages from Yahoo to my local copy of Thunderbird. If I then checked my Yahoo mail using a browser, those most recent 65 messages were gone from Yahoo. I could then repeat the process again and download the next 65. I had only a few hundred messages on Yahoo, so it wasn't bad at all. If I had thousands and thousands, it would be time to play some Solitaire or Mahjong while I went through a very tedious process (or pursued an automated solution).

Now it's back to Tools, Add-ons (the last time, I promise!), but this time you want to click the Preferences button next to WebMail—Yahoo. You'll see the results in Figure 3.14.

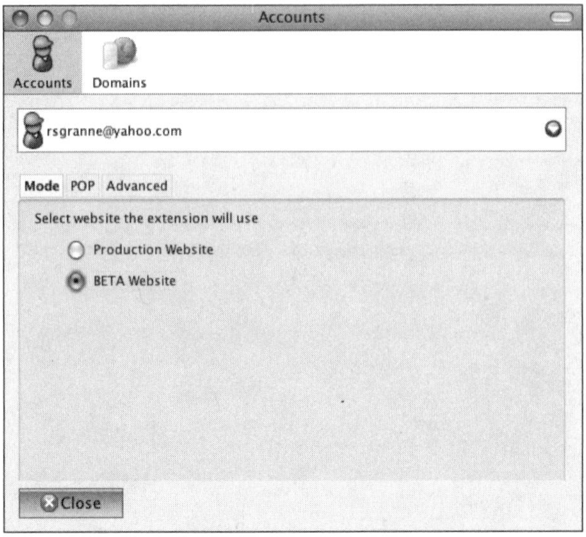

FIGURE 3.14   Choose the version of Yahoo Mail that works best with your setup of Thunderbird.

You should see the email address of the new account you created (in my case, rsgranne@yahoo.com). On the Mode tab, you can choose either Production Website (which corresponds to the old, pre-AJAXy version of Yahoo Mail) or BETA Website (which is for the shiny new AJAXy version of Yahoo Mail). I experimented and went back and forth on the Yahoo Mail website between the old and new versions and found that I had to choose the new version on the website and BETA Website here in order for things to work.

On the POP tab, check Download Unread Emails Only if you want to do that. Because you're performing a migration, I can't imagine you'd want to make that choice. If you chose earlier, while setting up the Yahoo Mail account in Thunderbird, to actually download all mail and not leave any on the server, it really doesn't matter whether you check Mail Emails as Read on Server because they're not going to be on the server when you're finished. Finally, only a masochist would select Download Junk Mail, so don't do that.

If you want to grab other folders besides the Inbox, add those folders on this screen as well.

On the Advanced tab, you can go ahead and check Use Short ID if you want, but in my experience, even though you're warned that all of your email will be downloaded, causing repeats, it didn't happen; in other words, all my email was not downloaded, and I was instead still getting just 65 at a time.

> **NOTE**
>
> What is a "short ID" anyway? It turns out that Yahoo tends to change the hidden IDs on emails about once a week or so. When Thunderbird sees that new ID using the WebMail extension, it sees a new email message and downloads it again, even if it was previously downloaded. By checking Use Short ID, you're telling Thunderbird to ignore that part of the ID that changes, thereby using a shortened ID number.

Check Reuse HTTP Session Data if you want to slightly speed up your login process by reusing Yahoo Mail's cookies from the last time you logged in.

You can now press Close to put this window away, and you should now be able to download your email from Yahoo Mail.

In Thunderbird, I would go to File, Get New Messages For, Web Mail, rsgranne@yahoo.com. You will need to pick the account you created. A few moments later, mail—65 messages at a time—began flowing into Thunderbird from Yahoo Mail, without my paying a cent. Soon I could see what is shown in Figure 3.15.

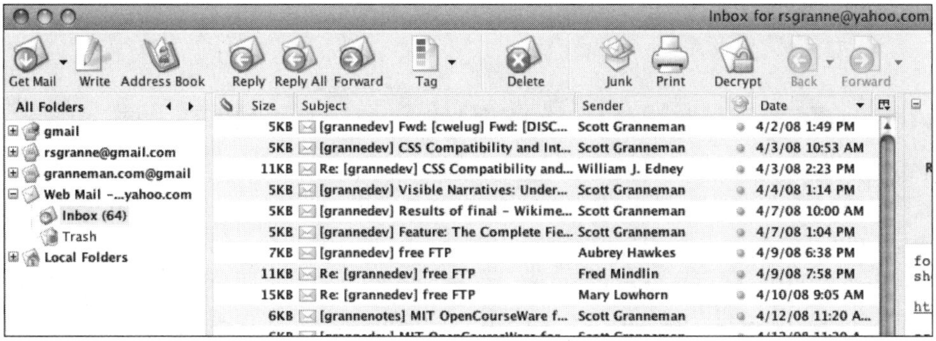

FIGURE 3.15 Emails from a few Yahoo Groups I administer show up in Thunderbird thanks to the WebMail extension.

Remember, you'll have to acquire your messages 65 at a time. If you get some error message about "negative vibes" from Yahoo (actually, you may see it from some other webmail services, like Hotmail), you need to fiddle with your settings in the WebMail—Yahoo preferences in Thunderbird Add-ons. If you still can't get it to work, you should first head over to the official website of the WebMail extension, at http://webmail.mozdev.org, and look there. The problem is that there's not a huge amount of info there, so you'll probably end up at the Thunderbird Webmail Extension discussion group, at http://groups.google.com/group/thunderbird-webmail-extension, where you can look at past discussions or ask for help.

After my mail from Yahoo is in Thunderbird, it's a simple matter of creating an IMAP-based Google Apps account and then manually moving mail over, as detailed earlier in this chapter. If you don't want to do it manually, you can use the Redirect Mail extension or access the mbox files containing your downloaded webmail and work with those directly, both of which were discussed previously.

> **NOTE**
>
> To find out where the heck Thunderbird has placed your mbox files, go to Tools, Account Settings, find the account in the list on the left, select Server Settings under it, and then look for the path next to Local Directory.

The WebMail extension is a powerful, incredibly useful piece of software that can help you liberate your mail from the clutches of email providers that want to hold your stuff hostage. If you're making the move to Google Apps, this could be the extension that helps you get things transferred over.

MIGRATE FROM WEB-BASED EMAIL SYSTEMS

In the previous section, I covered one method of acquiring messages stuck in web-mail systems that either force you to pay to have POP access to your mail or, even worse, don't allow you POP access at all. The WebMail extension for Firefox runs a POP daemon that acts as a mail proxy on your local computer and then talks to your webmail provider, allowing your POP client to access your webmail. Very clever.

However, other software packages do similar things, without requiring Thunderbird. In fact, if you set up any of the following on your computer, you can use any email client you want, such as Outlook, Apple Mail, Outlook Express, or whatnot. I'm not going to go through each one in depth, or this book would be the size of the New York telephone book, but I'll give you some information that you can pursue if one sounds interesting to you.

> **NOTE**
> For a list of even more programs than the ones I cover in this section, see http://ypopsemail.com/links/42-similar-apps.

FreePOPs

- Operating Systems: Windows, Mac OS X, Linux
- Email Clients and Services: AOL, Lycos, Excite, Gmail, Hotmail, NetZero, Juno, Mail.com, Netscape, Yahoo, and many others
- Google Apps Editions: Standard, Premier, Education and Nonprofit, Partner

FreePOPs (http://www.freepops.org/en/) is free and open source and runs on Windows (95 through Vista, which is nice), Mac OS X, and Linux. You can get it at www.freepops.org/en/download.shtml, and after it is installed, you can download email from a staggering number of webmail services, including all the big ones and an enormous list of smaller services in use around the world. The entire list is viewable on www.freepops.org/en/viewplugins.php. Then, after you have your webmail safely inside your email client, you can manually or automatically transfer your messages to Google Apps using the methods outlined earlier in this chapter.

Full details about configuring and using FreePOPs can be found in the manual, and you can talk to other users of the program in the forums; links to both can be found on the documentation page at www.freepops.org/en/doc.shtml. The program is well-maintained and has a sizable community around it—all good signs for an open source project.

MacFreePOPs

- Operating Systems: Mac OS X
- Email Clients and Services: AOL, Lycos, Excite, Gmail, Hotmail, NetZero, Juno, Mail.com, Netscape, Yahoo, and many others
- Google Apps Editions: Standard, Premier, Education and Nonprofit, Partner

MacFreePOPs (http://www.e-link.it/macfreepops/) is a Mac-specific and Mac-friendly version of FreePOPs and includes nice touches such as automatic updates and integration with the Mac OS user interface. It's free but does not appear to include source, even though it is based on the open source FreePOPs (hmmmm…). If you're a Mac user, this is the program you may want to use.

The program's website is mostly in Italian, however, and although it's a beautiful language, that's not going to be particularly helpful for the majority of users. Fortunately, instructions for setting up and using MacFreePOPs can be found at http://email.about.com/od/macosxmailtips/qt/et_free_yahoo.htm.

YPOPs

- Operating Systems: Windows, Mac OS X, Linux
- Email Clients and Services: Yahoo
- Google Apps Editions: Standard, Premier, Education and Nonprofit, Partner

YPOPs (http://ypopsemail.com) is like FreePOPs, but it focuses solely on Yahoo Mail. There is an official release for Windows, but because it's an open source program, other volunteers recompile it to run on Linux (a Mac OS X version exists, but users complain long and loudly about it, so I'd avoid it, and besides, MacFreePOPs is probably what you want anyway). You can download the Windows version at http://ypopsemail.com/download; if you're a Penguinista, you should head over to the Linux forum for YPOPs at http://forums.ypopsemail.com/ypops-linux-f3.html and poke around there for a binary suitable to your distro. Of course, you could download the source code from http://sourceforge.net/cvs/?group_id=52835 and compile it yourself.

Documentation for configuring various email clients, including Outlook, Thunderbird, Outlook Express, Eudora, and many others, as well as help on several other matters, is at http://ypopsemail.com/documentation. If you want to talk to developers or other users, head over to the forums, found at http://forums.ypopsemail.com/.

A nice step-by-step illustrated guide to install YPOPs on a Windows machine and then configure Thunderbird to work with it is available at http://opensourcearticles.com/thunderbird_15/english/part_10. It was written for version 1.5 of Thunderbird, but it should still apply just fine to the latest versions of the software.

SOLVING COMMON PROBLEMS

As with everything, you'll find that a few problems crop up as you're migrating email. Here are some problems you might run into and their solutions.

Why Can't I Use Gmail's Mail Fetcher to Import Email?

If you're in Gmail and you go to Settings, Accounts, Get Mail from Other Accounts, you'll see a really neat feature known as the Mail Fetcher. Basically, it allows you to specify up to five other email accounts that you can pull into Gmail via a POP connection. In other words, if you can access an email account using POP, you can pull all of that account's emails into your Gmail account and centralize all your email in one place.

Some people on the Net recommend using the Mail Fetcher as a way to migrate your email from your old POP accounts to your new Google Apps account. The problem with this idea has to do with the nature of POP. Remember, in the vast majority of cases, a POP email client moves email from the mail server to the email client, leaving nothing behind on the server. Obviously, then, the Mail Fetcher will get only new email, not anything that was previously moved.

If you have been leaving all your POP mail on your mail server, perhaps the Mail Fetcher would work. But this is extremely unlikely, so it's also extremely unlikely that the Mail Fetcher will help you migrate old email to your new Google Apps account.

I Want to Pay for Software or Hire Someone to Do the Work for Me! Where Do I Look?

If you're more interested in finding software that you can simply acquire and use or service providers that you can hire for custom development and support, you really should go to the Google Solutions Marketplace, at www.google.com/enterprise/marketplace/ and search around there.

CONCLUSION

Writing about migrating email is a complex task because of the vast variety of email protocols, software, and services. When it comes to the admins out there who have to actually perform the migration, things are most likely a bit simpler because you know which protocols, software, and services you're using and have to deal with. Still, migration is a task that you have to approach with care and precision. People rely on their email nowadays, and any interruption in service will drive your users batty and result in trouble for you. Be careful, plan ahead, and test, test, test.

FURTHER READING

There's always more to learn, so here are some resources that you might find handy if you want to learn more about migrating email to Google Apps:

- Migration guides
  - IMAP Mail Migration:
    www.google.com/support/a/bin/answer.py?answer=61369&query=migration
  - Best Approaches for Large Migrations:
    www.google.com/a/help/intl/en/admins/pdf/google_apps_imap_migration.pdf
    - Migrating email screencast:
      http://services.google.com/apps/resources/admin_breeze/MigratingEmail/
- Google Email Uploader
  - Software page:
    http://mail.google.com/mail/help/email_uploader.html
  - Google Email Uploader User Guide:
    http://code.google.com/p/google-email-uploader/wiki/UserGuide
  - Google Email Uploader open source project page:
    http://code.google.com/p/google-email-uploader/
  - Google Email Uploader discussion group:
    http://groups.google.com/group/google-email-uploader
- Email redirection
  - Jerry Peek's "Great Email Features (You've Never Heard Of)" at *Linux Magazine*:
    www.linux-mag.com/id/1698
  - SpamAssassin's "Resending a Mail Message While Preserving the Headers": http://wiki.apache.org/spamassassin/ResendingMailWithHeaders
- List of software similar to YPOPs and FreePOPs:
  http://kb.mozillazine.org/Using_webmail_with_your_email_client. Scroll down to the "Add-ons" section
- For developers
  - Google Apps Email Migration API Developer's Guide:
    http://code.google.com/apis/apps/email_migration/developers_guide_protocol.html
  - Google Apps Email Migration API Reference Guide:
    http://code.google.com/apis/apps/email_migration/reference.html

CHAPTER 4

Migrating Contacts to Google Apps

I'm a big fan of most things Google—otherwise I wouldn't be writing this book—but I'm also honest. And here's my honest opinion: Google Contacts stinks. It has too many limitations (which you'll be reading about shortly), it's under-featured, the user interface is awkward and badly needs a redesign, and the new version that appeared in the past year actually manages to be a step backward in several key ways!

Nonetheless, you have to use Google Contacts if you plan to use Gmail or many other Google services. And if you're like most people, you've accumulated over the years quite a collection of people, phone numbers, email addresses, and other data in an address book stored on your computer. This chapter covers how to get that mass of information into Google Contacts.

> **NOTE**
>
> If you're more interested in finding software that you can acquire and use or service providers that you can hire for custom development and aid, you really should go to the Google Solutions Marketplace at www.google.com/enterprise/marketplace/ and search around there.

In essence, you have two methods to get your addresses into Google: a manual import via a CSV file (the only format Google accepts for this task) or a two-way synchronization between your current address book and Google. It might not seem obvious, but a migration doesn't have to involve a one-way transfer of data from another program into your Google Contacts. Software packages exist that provide syncing between Google Contacts and other address books; if you start with no addresses in your Google Contacts, syncing will result in copying your addresses into Google Contacts as surely as if you exported and moved them.

Both techniques have their purposes, although, as you'll see, I favor synchronization for several reasons.

> **⚠ WARNING**
>
> Before you sync any of your data, it is vitally important that you back up whatever it is you're planning to sync. Do not proceed without making a good backup first. Do not put this off—you want to be prepared in case disaster (or at least Murphy's Law) strikes!

PREPARING TO MIGRATE CONTACTS

Before you attempt to migrate your existing address book into Google Contacts, you should be aware of some rules that may cause you headaches unless you first prepare for them:

- **Records must have unique email addresses**. If Alice's email address is info@widgetco.com and Bob's email address is info@widgetco.com, you're going to have problems because whoever gets uploaded last "wins." Make sure that every entry in your address book has a unique email address. Yes, I know this is tedious and virtually impossible to tell with most address book programs. If, however, you export your address book into a CSV file and then sort by email address, it will be a lot easier to detect duplicates.

- **All characters must be in English**. For most people reading this book, it's not a big deal. As Google attempts to expand Apps to an international audience, this requirement will surely change.

- **You can import a maximum of 3,000 contacts at a time.** Again, this is not a huge deal. If you have more than 3,000 contacts, it will take you multiple importing sessions to get everyone into Google Contacts. However, it appears that 3,000 is not a hard and fast number; rather, it's an approximation. Instead, file size is more of an issue. If you're a diligent note taker, you may be able to manually upload only a few hundred contacts at a time. My buddy Rich, for instance, records every phone call and interaction with his clients in the Notes field of his address book and has for years. Some contacts have hundreds of lines in the Notes. In his case, there is no way he'll be able to upload even 1000 at a time. Experimentation and flexibility are the keys here.

- **You can't transfer email groups or distribution lists**. Sure, you can create them after all your contacts are in Google, but you can't copy groups that already exist. Yes, this is a pain in the posterior if you have a lot of groups. If, as I discuss later in this chapter, you're automatically syncing Google Contacts with your desktop address book, and you plan to continue using your desktop address book and email client, it won't be that big of a deal.

Those are the things you need to look out for as you begin to migrate your existing address book to Google Contacts. Before we continue to the details of the various programs and methods for contact migration, however, I want to share some hard-earned experience with you in the following sidebar.

MY ADVICE AFTER HARD-EARNED EXPERIENCE

If it were my account, I would begin migrating contacts by first erasing all Google Contacts if any already exist. If you're worried that you may lose someone's email address that you don't have anywhere else, export your Google Contacts first and then erase them.

I would then find some program that automatically syncs your client address book of choice with Google Contacts. In my case, I use Spanning Sync on my Mac, which I have found reliable, effective, and unobtrusive (and which is discussed later in this chapter under "Automatically Syncing Apple Address Book and Google Contacts with Spanning Sync"). There are many other syncing programs for most of the major address books out there; some I cover in this chapter, and others I will mention.

I sync my Apple Address Book with Google Contacts, which means initially that all the folks in my Apple Address Book are copied up to Google. After that, I never manually change anything at Google. All changes are made on my Mac and are then automatically synced with Google. I do this for a couple of reasons.

As I said earlier, Google Contacts is pretty bad. However, it's also what the web-based version of Gmail (as well as some other Google services) uses. So I have to use it, even if I'd rather not. This doesn't mean, though, that I have to make it the master for all my contacts. I'd rather use something more full-featured, such as the Apple Address Book (or even Outlook, if I were on Windows) to store the data I need on the people with whom I interact and then push that data out to Google Contacts when it changes.

Because I'm syncing, I'm looking at a two-way transfer. Unfortunately, this means I'm going to end up with some messiness in my address book because

Gmail automatically adds anyone I reply to as a contact. When I sync, I'll move changes from my computer's address book into Google, but I'll also add the random email address from Google to my computer's address book. I'll just have to regularly parse through my Apple Address Book, looking for new contacts and verifying that I want to keep them and then fixing them if I do so that they conform to the rest of my data or deleting those I don't want.

Why sync? I don't want to constantly mess with CSV files, with importing and exporting manually. I'd rather automate the whole process so that it just happens in the background with as little of my involvement as possible. In this case, lazy is good—and more productive in the long term.

TIP

You can't erase more than 20 contacts at a time with the new, updated version of Gmail, which is now the default for all new accounts. This limitation is outrageously ridiculous, and I hope that Google removes it soon. Fortunately, there's a way around this straightjacket: At the top of your Gmail web page, you'll see a link to Older Version. Click it, go into your Contacts, scroll to the bottom and select all contacts, and then scroll back to the top of the page and delete everyone. After you've done that, click Newer Version to revert back. With the exception of the ridiculous limitation on removing Contacts, the newer version of Gmail is better in every way.

MANUALLY IMPORTING A CSV FILE INTO GOOGLE CONTACTS

- Operating Systems: Windows, Mac OS X, Linux
- Address Book Clients and Services: All compatible
- Google Apps Editions: Standard, Premier, Education and Nonprofit, Partner

NOTE

I repeat the three lines you see preceding this note throughout this chapter where appropriate to help you know if a section speaks to your situation or not.

Perhaps you don't want to automatically sync contacts between your address book of choice and Google Contacts. You may plan to use Gmail with your desktop client and hardly ever, if at all, via the Web, so it doesn't matter what's stored at Google Contacts. Perhaps you email with only a very small, select group of people, so you can afford to perform a one-time upload of people into Google Contacts via a CSV file and then forget about it. If you want to manually import a CSV file, you'll find out how to do it here.

In general, it's a pretty simple process to import names and contact info into Google Contacts: You log in to your Google Apps email, click Contacts, click Import, press Browse to select a comma-separated values (CSV) file on your computer, and then press Import. A few moments later, depending on how many contacts you're importing, you'll see the results in Google Contacts.

That's simple enough, but the key to getting contacts *into* Google is first getting them *out* of the client or service you've been using, in a format that Google can import. In this section, I first discuss the format of the CSV file that Google requires, and then I walk through several of the major address book clients and services and explain how to get your contact data out of them.

Working with the CSV File

Google allows the import of contacts in only one format: a CSV, or comma separated values, file. You might be thinking that this is great because you know your address book of choice exports data in CSV format, but don't count your chickens before they're hatched. Google will try to work with a variety of common headers produced by your favorite address book's export program, but things may not ultimately appear in Google Contacts in the places you'd like. Therefore, it is imperative that you test importing a CSV file using a few records from your address book—and the more data in those records, the better.

⚠️ **WARNING**

I'm repeating it again here so that everyone sees this: It is absolutely imperative that you test importing a CSV file using a few records from your address book—and the more data in those records, the better.

Export or generate a CSV file from your address book of choice. If you can, export just a few records—10, for instance—that contain a variety of data in various fields. If you can't export just a few records, export everything, open the CSV file in a spreadsheet, and then remove all but 10 or so data-rich records. Now you have a file you can upload to Google Contacts and thereby check the results. You may be very happy with the import, meaning that Google parses your program's CSV file with a minimum of bother. In that case, proceed with the full export of all your contacts from your address book of choice.

More likely, you may find that you're unhappy with the places in which Google decides to place data. As a general rule, if Google can't figure out how to map one of your labels to Google Contacts, that particular data item gets shoved into Notes. In those cases, you're going to have to massage the exported data in a CSV file to help it conform more with what Google wants (although, again, Google is quite liberal in what it accepts).

At its most basic, your CSV file needs just two columns:

- Name
- Email

That's it. If you create a CSV file with just names and email addresses, Google will happily import it into your Contacts. If you'd prefer to split up the name, you can do this:

- First Name
- Last Name
- Email Address

You can add Middle Name, or Middle Initial, if you'd like. Note that you can use Email or Email Address as your header; Google isn't picky.

If, on the other hand, you are picky and want to adhere as closely as possible to Google's own headers and CSV structure, there's an easy method to view "the Google way" of ordering your contacts in a CSV file: Create one person in Google Contacts, fill in every bit of data you can imagine, and then export that contact as a CSV file.

TIP

Don't know how to export your contacts from Google? See "Exporting Contacts from Gmail" later in this chapter.

Open the CSV file you exported in a spreadsheet program like Excel or OpenOffice.org (or even the Google Docs spreadsheet component) to see how Google sets up a CSV file. You'll find that Google uses the following headers and columns, in the order given here.

- Name
- E-mail
- Notes
- Section 1—Description
- Section 1—Email
- Section 1—IM
- Section 1—Phone
- Section 1—obile
- Section 1—Pager
- Section 1—Fax
- Section 1—Company
- Section 1—Title
- Section 1—Other
- Section 1—Address
- Section 2—Description
- Section 2—Email
- Section 2—IM
- Section 2—Phone
- Section 2—Mobile
- Section 2—Pager
- Section 2—Fax
- Section 2—Company
- Section 2—Title
- Section 2—Other
- Section 2—Address
- Section 3—Description
- Section 3—Email
- Section 3—IM
- Section 3—Phone
- Section 3—Mobile
- Section 3—Pager
- Section 3—Fax
- Section 3—Company

- Section 3—Title
- Section 3—Other
- Section 3—Address

You may immediately notice that Google doesn't have some headers you might expect, such as Work Email and Home Email, for instance. Instead, it provides for three Sections. Which one is work, which one is personal, and what's the third for? And in what order should they go?

Google actually allows you quite a bit of flexibility. It doesn't matter what order you place data pertaining to home and work, as long as you label the data using the Section # - Description column. You have three choices for what you put in those columns:

- Work
- Personal
- Other

This means you could do something like what is shown in Table 4.1, and it would import without issue into Google Contacts (I'm cutting out most of the columns to keep things comprehensible):

TABLE 4.1   A Sample CSV File Showing How the Description Header Works

NAME	SECTION 1— DESCRIPTION	SECTION 1— EMAIL	SECTION 2— DESCRIPTION	SECTION 2— EMAIL	SECTION 3— DESCRIPTION	SECTION 3— EMAIL
John Carter	Work	jcarter@ barsoominc. com	Other	dotarsojat@ yahoo.com	Personal	warlord@ gmail.com
Dejah Thoris	Personal	princess@ gmail.com	Work	dthoris@ barsoominc. com	Other	tarasmom@ aol.com
Tars Tarkas	Other	fourarms@ hotmail.com	Personal	tharkme@ gmail.com	Work	ttarkas@ barsoominc. com

Remember, you don't have to use the "official" Google headers in your CSV file because Google will endeavor to parse whatever you provide to it. But things undoubtedly will go a heck of a lot smoother if you use that long list of headers I listed.

> **TIP**
>
> Google provides a page in its Help Center titled "Creating or Editing CSV Files" (https://mail.google.com/support/bin/answer.py?answer=12119), but it's so sparse as to be virtually useless. It doesn't even list all the fields found in a standard CSV export from Google! C'mon Google—hire some writers!

Exporting Contacts from AOL

AOL doesn't include the capability to export your AOL Address Book, which is pretty bad. You can print your Address Book into an HTML report and then parse it, but that's a lot of work. It's yet another reason not to use AOL.

You can also sync your AOL contacts via Plaxo, discussed later in this chapter in "Automatically Syncing Contacts with Plaxo."

Exporting Contacts from Apple Mail

Unfortunately, although Apple allows you to easily export your contacts, it does so in only two formats: a backup of the Address Book or vCards. Neither works directly with Google Contacts.

All is not lost, however. Google itself recommends a free, open source program named A to G, available at http://bborofka.com/atog/. Unzip it, run it, and you'll see the ultrasimple program shown in Figure 4.1.

Press the button labeled Export to Desktop and a few moments later, a new file will show up on your desktop: Contacts for Gmail.csv. A to G does a

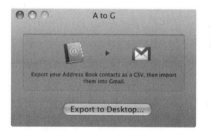

FIGURE 4.1 A to G is about as stripped down and simple as it gets.

pretty good job converting everything, but you'd still be wise to open up that CSV file in a spreadsheet app and check it out first.

You can also sync your Apple Address Book via Plaxo, discussed later in this chapter in "Automatically Syncing Contacts with Plaxo."

Exporting Contacts from Eudora

Open your Eudora Address Book and go to File, Save As. Choose CSV as the file type. Now open the file in OpenOffice.org or the equivalent spreadsheet program and get to work editing and changing.

Exporting Contacts from Evolution

If you use Evolution on your Linux box, you actually have a little-known program available to you that you can use to export your contacts: evolution-addressbook-export. Simply run the following in your terminal:

```
$ evolution-addressbook-export —format=csv —
output=~/Desktop/EvolutionContacts .csv
```

Soon enough, depending on the number of your contacts, you'll have a file named EvolutionContacts.csv on your desktop. Open that file in OpenOffice.org and double-check it before importing it into Google.

Exporting Contacts from Gmail

If you want to get your contacts out of a standard Gmail account and into your new Google Apps account, you're in luck—you won't need to do any reformatting because you're moving from Google to Google.

Go to your Gmail account's Contacts page and click the Export link in the upper right. Choose which contacts you want to free from the clutches of your Gmail account—all or just those in a particular group—and then, for the format, select Google's CSV format, which is helpfully described as "for importing into another Google account." Press the Export button, and your browser will download a file named contacts.csv. You can now import that into your Google Apps Contacts without an issue.

Exporting Contacts from Hotmail and Windows Live Hotmail

Before you can import your Hotmail contacts into Google Apps, you first need to export your contacts from Hotmail. Log in to Hotmail and click Options, Export Contacts. Press the Export Contacts button and save the file named WLMContacts.csv on your hard drive. You're still going to need to open the CSV file with Excel or some other spreadsheet program in order to massage it to Google's liking.

You can also sync your Hotmail and Windows Live Contacts via Plaxo, discussed later in this chapter in "Automatically Syncing Contacts with Plaxo."

Exporting Contacts from KAddressBook

When it comes to supporting a variety of formats for export and thereby not locking you in at all, KAddressBook, the KDE contact manager, takes the cake. Select File, Export, and you'll have quite the choices for a format: vCard 2 and 3, LDIF, GMX, Bookmarks, GeoData, and the one we need, CSV. Choose CSV, and then open the resulting file in OpenOffice.org or your spreadsheet of choice to edit the results to fit Google's needs.

Exporting Contacts from Outlook

Microsoft makes it pretty easy to get your contacts out of Outlook and into a CSV file. Go to File, Import/Export, Export, Comma Separated Values (Windows), Contacts, and then save the exported file on your hard drive. Don't trust this file, however—open it in Excel and go over it to make sure it conforms to what Google Contacts expects.

You can also sync your Outlook Contacts via Plaxo, discussed later in this chapter in "Automatically Syncing Contacts with Plaxo."

Exporting Contacts from Outlook Express

So you've decided to quit using Outlook Express—wonderful! Let's get those contacts out of OE. Select File, Export, Address Book, select Text File (Comma Separated Values), and finally, click Export. I know this isn't a surprise, but you're going to need to open that CSV file in your fave spreadsheet program and rejigger it to work with Google.

You can also sync your Outlook Express Address Book via Plaxo, discussed later in this chapter in "Automatically Syncing Contacts with Plaxo."

Exporting Contacts from Thunderbird

Thunderbird is a great email program, but its Address Book is still something of a joke (at least it's supposed to get better when version 3.0 comes out). Thank goodness you can get your info out of the Thunderbird Address Book easily.

Open Thunderbird, then the program's Address Book, choose the Address Book you want to rescue from Thunderbird, and select Tools, Export. Enter a name for the file—ThunderbirdContacts.csv would be an appropriate choice—and change the

Format to Comma Separated. After you have the file, open it in the Google Docs spreadsheet component and fix it up so that you can safely import it into Google Contacts.

Exporting Contacts from Yahoo!

Log in to Yahoo Mail and go to your contacts. Click the Import/Export link and on the following page, scroll down to the Export section. You can export in a variety of formats, but the one you want is Yahoo! CSV. You should end up with a file named yahoo_ab.csv.

If you import the yahoo_ab.csv without massaging it at all, you'll find that your phone numbers came over just fine, as did your email addresses, titles, and companies. But addresses don't come over at all, and IM handles, dates, and notes all end up in Google's Notes field. If you export contacts from Yahoo, expect to spend some time in a spreadsheet app fixing the data.

You can also sync your Yahoo Contacts via Plaxo, discussed later in this chapter in "Automatically Syncing Contacts with Plaxo."

DEVELOPING YOUR OWN CONTACT MIGRATION TOOLS WITH GOOGLE DATA APIS

- Operating Systems: Windows, Mac OS X, Linux
- Address Book Clients and Services: Any compatible
- Google Apps Editions: Standard, Premier, Education and Nonprofit, Partner

Earlier in this chapter I pointed out that if you were so inclined, you could use Google's APIs to build your own email migration tool. The same point is true when it comes to transferring contacts—Google provides a pretty comprehensive set of APIs that enable developers to build their own software and services for synchronizing address book data with Google Contacts.

If you want to learn all you can about Google's Contacts Data API, you can find the Developer's Guide at http://code.google.com/apis/contacts/developers_guide_protocol.html and the Reference Guide at http://code.google.com/apis/contacts/reference.html. An official blog titled the "Official Google Data APIs Blog" is available at http://googledataapis.blogspot.com/. Although it covers far more than just working with Google Contacts, it would still be extremely useful to developers interested in developing their own solutions. Finally, for an example of a program that works with the Google Contacts Data API, check out a Mac-centric blog post at http://googlemac.blogspot.com/2008/03/new-frontiers-with-google-data-apis-and.html.

AUTOMATICALLY MIGRATING FROM EXCHANGE SERVER

- Operating Systems: Windows
- Email Clients and Services: Exchange Server
- Google Apps Editions: Premier, Education and Nonprofit

In Chapter 3, "Migrating Email to Google Apps," in the section titled "Automatically Migrate from Exchange Server," I discussed Persistent Systems' e2Gmigrator, which allows Windows servers running Exchange 2000 and later to bulk migrate email, contacts, and calendars to Google Apps for only $15 per user (volume discounts are available). For more information about e2Gmigrator and a few similar programs, see that earlier section.

AUTOMATICALLY SYNCING CONTACTS WITH PLAXO

- Operating Systems: Windows, Mac OS X, Linux
- Address Book Clients and Services: AOL, Apple Address Book, Gmail, Hotmail, Outlook, Outlook Express, Windows Mail, Yahoo
- Google Apps Editions: Standard, Premier, Education and Nonprofit, Partner

Plaxo is an interesting service that has shifted directions a few times; even so, a lot of folks swear by the company and its services. The one that interests us here is the service that synchronizes contacts among different services and even devices, including the following:

- AOL
- Apple Address Book
- Google
- Hotmail/Windows Live Hotmail
- Outlook
- Outlook Express
- Plaxo
- Windows Mail
- Yahoo
- Many different models of cell phones

If you're interested in signing up, go to http://www.plaxo.com and register a Plaxo Basic account (you don't need the $50 a year Plaxo Premium account for our purposes). It's free and easy, and when you're finished you can start adding various sync points, which are the various services and software you want to join together. It all works pretty seamlessly, especially with your Google Apps account, and it is free, so many people might find it very attractive.

The one downside is that you have to provide Plaxo with your logins and passwords to the various services you want to sync, as you can see in the case of AOL in Figure 4.2.

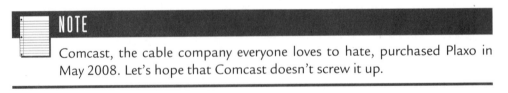

Sync with AOL / AIM

First, we'll connect to your AOL / AIM account and check your address book.

Screenname:

Password:

Your data is safe with us. Privacy Policy

Passwords are encrypted using Secure Socket Layer (SSL)

FIGURE 4.2 Plaxo even syncs with AOL— impressive because AOL doesn't even allow for contact export.

In Plaxo's defense, I haven't heard of any privacy or security breaches involving the passwords its users have provided, so that's a good sign.

> **NOTE**
>
> Comcast, the cable company everyone loves to hate, purchased Plaxo in May 2008. Let's hope that Comcast doesn't screw it up.

AUTOMATICALLY SYNCING WITH OUTLOOK USING OGGSYNC

- Operating Systems: Windows
- Clients: Outlook
- Google Apps Editions: Standard, Premier, Education and Nonprofit, Partner

OggSync is a program originally designed to sync Google Calendars with Outlook and Windows Mobile devices. However, a beta version in development at the time I'm writing this promises to sync contacts as well. If you're using Outlook 2003 or 2007, this could be a good fit for you.

After you install the program, you'll see an icon for OggSync in your System Tray (next to the clock) that automatically loads when you start Windows. As you work, OggSync automatically keeps everything in sync in the background, so you don't really have to think about it. In fact, Outlook doesn't even need to be running for syncing to occur.

There's a free version, which should be adequate for an initial sync of contacts to Google, and a pro version that costs $30 per year, which gives you automatic syncing (volume purchase plans are available). If you're planning to use OggSync only once, or manually, to copy everything between Outlook and Google Contacts, the free version may be enough. If you're planning to use OggSync on a daily basis, however, the pro version may be best for you (we'll look at OggSync again in Chapter 10, "Integrating Google Contacts with Other Software and Services," and Chapter 13, "Integrating Google Calendar with Other Software and Services").

For more about OggSync, head over to the home page (which also contains a blog with the latest news and updates) at http://oggsync.com. An FAQ concerning Outlook syncing is at http://oggsync.com/index.php/documentation-for-outlook-add-in/faq-for-outlook/.

AUTOMATICALLY SYNCING YOUR APPLE ADDRESS BOOK AND GOOGLE CONTACTS

- Operating Systems: Mac OS X
- Address Book Clients and Services: Apple Address Book
- Google Apps Editions: Standard, Premier, Education and Nonprofit, Partner

Here's some news a lot of people may not know: If you use Apple's Address Book, you can now sync it with Google Contacts. Well, kind of. I have some good news and some bad news about that syncing. First, the good news: syncing your Apple Address Book and your Google Apps Contacts is now built in to Apple's operating system. Now the bad news: you have to be using Mac OS X 10.5.3 or later, and you need to have an iPhone. Apple doesn't have to require iPhone ownership for this syncing to work, so we can all hope that it removes that requirement in the future.

If you're interested, and you meet the requirements, open your Apple Address Book, go to the application's Preferences, and select the General screen, shown in Figure 4.3.

Check the box next to Synchronize with Google and press the Google button. You'll be prompted for your Google Account (your email address, in other words, such as scott@granneman.com or jcarter@barsoominc.com) and that account's Password. Enter them, press OK, and then close your Address Book Preferences.

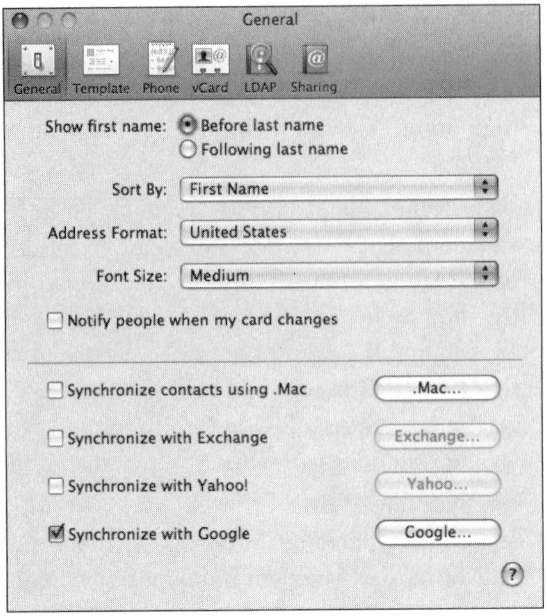

FIGURE 4.3   Ever since Mac OS X 10.5.3, Address Book supports syncing with Google Contacts.

Next time you sync your iPhone with your Mac, your Address Book will automatically update Google Contacts, and vice versa. It all happens in the background, meaning no fuss for you.

Even though I use a Mac and Apple's Address Book, I don't rely on this feature to sync my Address Book with Google Contacts. In my experience, it was creating duplicate contacts and doing other weird things, so I turned it off. However, it's a brand-new feature at the time of this writing, and I'm sure the bugs will get squashed given a little time. In the meantime, I'm a happy customer of Spanning Sync, discussed next.

TIP

You don't have to own an iPhone to get this feature of Apple's Address Book to work. If you don't mind mucking around a bit in some system files, you can make a small setting that fools your Mac into thinking you use an iPhone, even though you don't. Instructions can be found at www.zaphu.com/2008/05/29/how-to-enable-mac-address-book-syncing-with-googles-gmail-contacts-without-an-iphone-or-mac/.

AUTOMATICALLY SYNCING APPLE ADDRESS BOOK AND GOOGLE CONTACTS WITH SPANNING SYNC

- Operating Systems: Mac OS X
- Address Book Clients and Services: Apple Address Book
- Google Apps Editions: Standard, Premier, Education and Nonprofit, Partner

Instead of using the built-in support in Apple's Address Book for syncing with Google Contacts, I've been relying on Spanning Sync. Originally designed solely to sync Apple's iCal with Google Calendar (more about that later in Chapter 5's "Automatically Syncing with Apple iCal Using Spanning Sync"), it now also supports syncing Address Book and Google Contacts.

Information about Spanning Sync is available at www.spanningsync.com. To keep up with the latest developments, I've been visiting the Spanning Sync Beta Blog, which can be found at http://betablog.spanningsync.com. New versions are coming out almost daily, as development heats up.

Spanning Sync isn't free, but it's reasonably priced at $25 for a one-year subscription or $65 for a permanent license. You have 15 days to try it out before you buy it.

You decide how often Spanning Sync should talk to Google, as you can see in Figure 4.4.

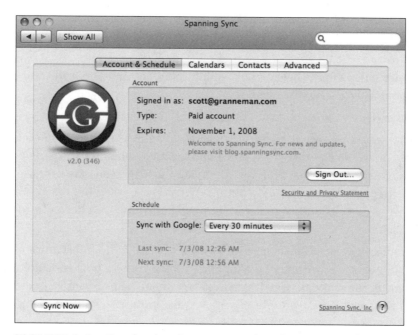

FIGURE 4.4   Set the time between synchronizations.

You can sync every 10 minutes, 30 minutes, hour, day, week, or manually. By default, Spanning Sync is set to one hour. However, the beta has introduced a new feature called "Trickle syncing," which automatically syncs changes in Apple's Address Book (and iCal, for that matter) to Google as those alterations are made.

You can also determine which contacts are synced, as shown in Figure 4.5.

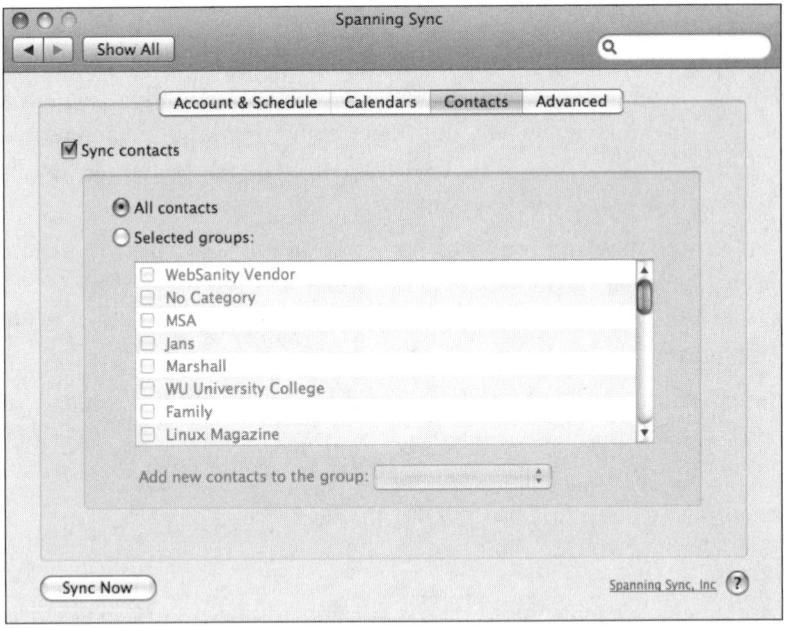

FIGURE 4.5   Sync only the contacts you want.

I prefer All Contacts because it's simpler, but you may instead want to select certain groups.

Finally, there's the Advanced tab, displayed in Figure 4.6.

If you want to see what Spanning Sync is doing as it copies contact data back and forth, press the Open Log Window button, which shows a surprising amount of useful information. The first time you run Spanning Sync, you may very well want to press the Replace Data on Google button. Why? I discussed the reasons earlier in "What's My Advice?" Suffice to say, it may make the process a heck of a lot cleaner and simpler.

Spanning Sync does some very smart things and is quite full-featured, even for a product in beta. For instance, it supports syncing contact photos, which is a nice touch, and it automatically ignores contacts without names (which, remember, is required by Google), instead offering to use email addresses in the Name field as well. In addition, it detects duplicate email addresses (a big no-no for Google Contacts, remember) and notifies you of those contacts. Overall, it's a very good choice if you're looking to sync your Apple Address Book and Google Contacts.

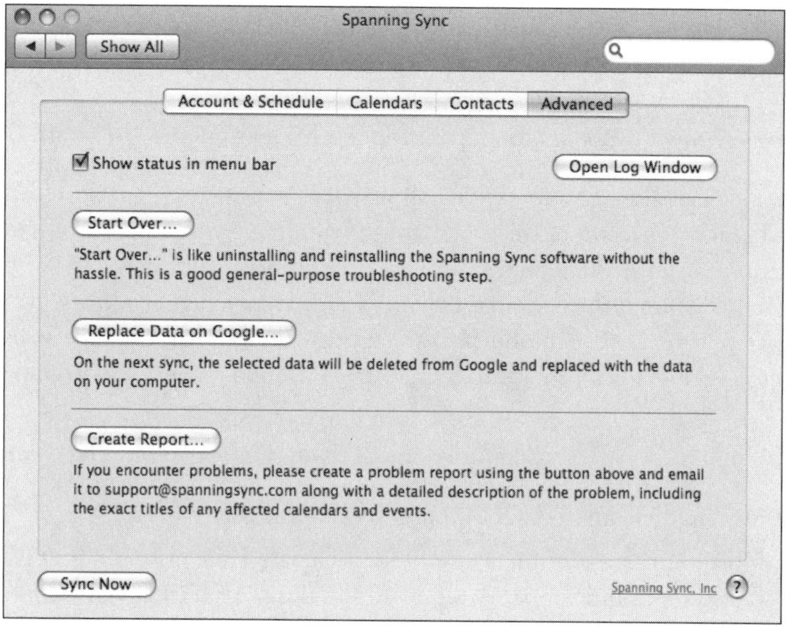

FIGURE 4.6   Spanning Sync includes some useful tools on the Advanced tab.

NOTE

Although I haven't used it, a lot of people swear by BusySync (www.busy-mac.com), a competitor to Spanning Sync. The difference between the two products is in their initial orientations: Spanning Sync was created to link Google Calendar (and now Contacts) with your Apple desktop productivity apps, whereas BusySync's original goal was to share calendars between multiple Macs and users on a LAN, although it is now integrated with Google Calendar.

Automatically Syncing Your Thunderbird Personal Address Book and Google Contacts with Zindus Thunderbird Contact Sync

- Operating Systems: Windows, Mac OS X, Linux
- Address Book Clients and Services: Thunderbird
- Google Apps Editions: Standard, Premier, Education and Nonprofit, Partner

In the previous section, I showed you software that syncs Apple's Address Book and Google Contacts. Of course, this software—Spanning Sync—works only on Macs. Thunderbird, however, runs on all three major platforms: Windows, Mac OS X, and Linux. Zindus Thunderbird Contact Sync is an extension that allows users on all three platforms to sync Thunderbird's Address Book with Google Apps over a secure https connection, providing a nice way for almost everyone to transfer contacts.

A few limitations exist to Zindus Contact Sync that you should be aware of:

- Mailing lists and contact groups aren't synced.
- Multiple values for the same field at Google have only the first transferred to Thunderbird. In other words, if a person in Google Contacts has two mobile phone numbers, Zindus copies only the first one into Thunderbird.
- Only the following fields in Google Contacts map to Thunderbird: Name, Email, Phone Numbers, IM Handles, Company Name and Title, Notes.
- If you have the same email address in more than one contact (info@ widgetco.com, say), Zindus Contact Sync will prompt you with a conflict. You'll need to resolve it by either changing the email address in all but one of the conflicting contacts or by giving each contact a unique email address.

Download the Thunderbird extension at www.zindus.com/download-extension/ and install it. The next time you start Tbird, go to Tools, Zindus to open the extension's settings, starting with the first screen, Server Settings, shown in Figure 4.7.

Select Google, type in your Email Address and Password, and press Test Connection to Server. If everything is good, go to the Preferences tab, which you can see in Figure 4.8.

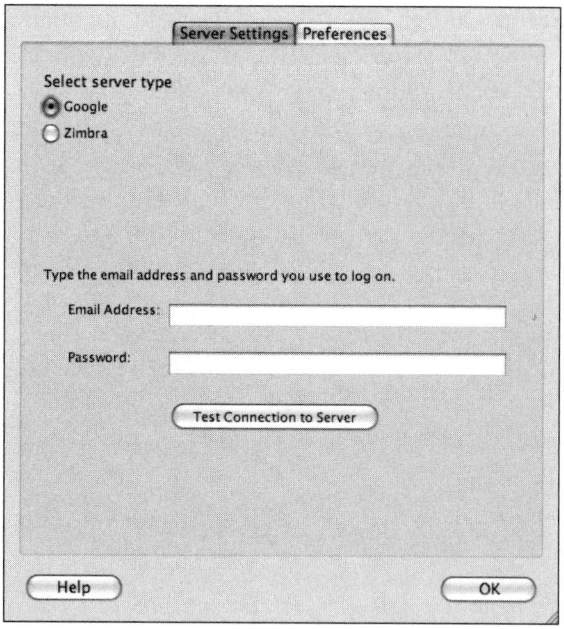

FIGURE 4.7   You can use the Zindus extension with Google or Zimbra, but all we care about here is Google.

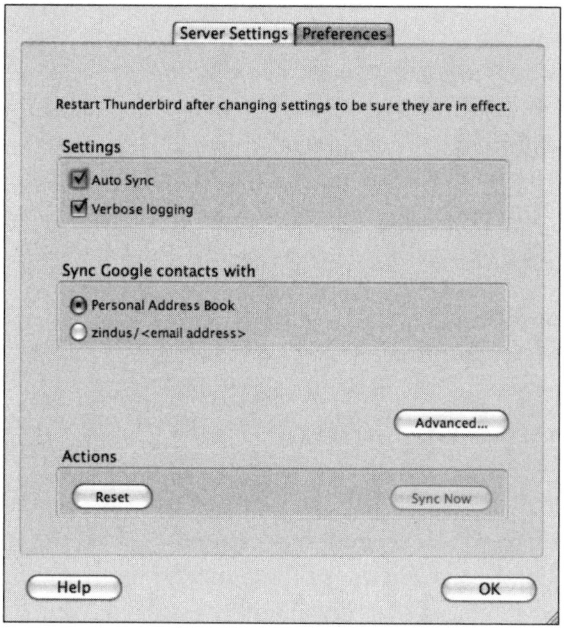

FIGURE 4.8   The settings for the Zindus extension are simple, which is just fine.

The settings are pretty obvious—do you want to automatically sync? Do you want more detail in the extension's logs? Do you want to sync Google Contacts with your Thunderbird Personal Address book (I hope that one's obvious)? Press Reset if you want to start from scratch and grab contacts from Google and merge them with Thunderbird's. Sync Now does just what it says and would be required as the only way to sync if you don't have Auto Sync checked. Finally, the Advanced button, if pressed, presents you with the screen shown in Figure 4.9.

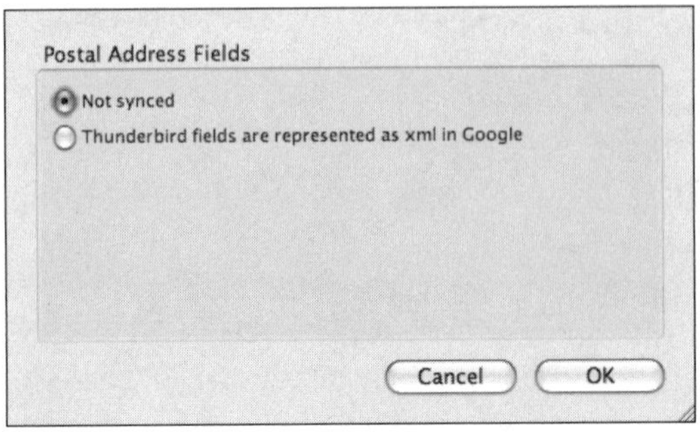

FIGURE 4.9 Syncing street addresses can get a little complicated.

According to Zindus, syncing street addresses between Thunderbird and Google Contacts is a tricky business at best (granted, other syncing solutions appear to have it working). You can either choose not to sync addresses—which seems OK only if you plan to use your Google Contacts for email—or you can sync addresses, but end up with XML in your Google Contacts. In other words, if you choose Thunderbird Fields Are Represented as XML in Google and then sync the two programs, addresses at Google might look like this:

```
<address>
<street> 1610 S. Big Bend Blvd. </street>
<city> St. Louis </city>
<country> US </country>
<otheraddr> Stuff that was in Google prior to syncing </otheraddr>
</address>
```

I don't mind looking at XML, but I can see how a lot of people might find it confusing or even ugly. But problems can occur if you go the XML route. If you log on to your Google Contacts, you'll see that next to each address is a link to Google Maps, unless you have XML around your addresses. In those cases, Google can't provide the right link because it doesn't understand the XML. Finally—and this is the most dangerous gotcha of all—if you edit the XML in your Google Contacts and accidentally break the syntax, Zindus will think that you've removed the address from Google. The next time you sync, it will remove the address from Thunderbird as well!

Still, nice features with Zindus make it worthwhile. For instance, if a conflict occurs when you change a contact in Thunderbird's Address Book and at Google Contacts, Zindus follows some rules that determine how it handles the conflict. For more about conflicts and what Zindus does when it finds one, see www.zindus.com/faq-thunderbird/#toc-what-are-conflicts.

If you want to learn more about Zindus Thunderbird Contact Sync, check out the home page at www.zindus.com, which also includes a blog, but then make sure you view the FAQs at www.zindus.com/faq-thunderbird-google/. If you understood the good and bad aspects of Zindus Thunderbird Contact Sync, you may find that it's a useful tool in your migration arsenal.

> **TIP**
>
> If you're looking for another tool you can use with Thunderbird, check out gContactSync, available at http://gcontactsync.mozdev.org. Don't neglect watching the video at http://pirules.net/gcontactsync/tutorial/index.html because it contains some important information.

AUTOMATICALLY COPYING ADDRESSES WITH THE GOOGLE EMAIL UPLOADER

- Operating Systems: Windows
- Address Book Clients and Services: Outlook Contacts, Windows Address Book, Windows Contacts, Thunderbird Address Book
- Google Apps Editions: Standard, Premier, Education and Nonprofit, Partner

Earlier in Chapter 3, in "Automatically Move Mail from a Client with the Google Email Uploader," I went over using the free Google Email Uploader to move mail from Outlook, Outlook Express, Windows Mail, or Thunderbird to your Google Apps account. One of the side benefits of the Google Email Uploader is that it will also transfer contacts from those apps to Google Contacts. This is a nice way to move both email and contacts at the same time, with a minimum of fuss.

SOLVING COMMON PROBLEMS

Nothing in life is perfect, so you might run into a few issues as you're migrating contacts to Google Apps. Here are some solutions to some of those problems.

While Importing into Google Contacts, I Keep Getting This Error Message: "Error saving data: Cannot have more than one contact with email address." Why?

Earlier in "Preparing to Migrate Contacts," I went over the (somewhat annoying) fact that you can't have two or more contacts at Google with the same email address. However, some people report getting an error message about more than one contact sharing an email address and then searching for a contact with the duplicated email address and coming up with nothing. In other words, only one contact has the email address in question—so where is the other contact with the conflicting address?

The solution is to revert back to the Older Version of Gmail by clicking the link in the upper right of Gmail's web page. Find the contact there, edit or delete it, and then change back to the Newer Version. Your problem should now be solved.

CONCLUSION

Some people may not want to move contacts to Google because they'll be using a desktop email client and address book. It's still wise to try to sync your contacts between your desktop software and Google, however, because you never know when you'll need to use the web interface to Gmail. Fortunately, a variety of software packages exist that can help make migration from your old address book to Google Contacts relatively painless. Just be careful, back your data up regularly, and be patient as you perform the migration.

CHAPTER 5

Migrating Calendars to Google Apps

In this chapter, we cover migrating existing calendar data to Google Calendar. I'm going to first give you the generic instructions for the two data types Google accepts if you're doing a manual import, and then I look at ways to automatically sync your data with Google Calendar for a faster approach.

TIP

If you're more interested in finding software that you can acquire and use or service providers that you can hire for custom development and aid, you really should go to the Google Solutions Marketplace at www.google.com/enterprise/marketplace/ and search around there.

PREPARING TO MIGRATE CALENDARS

Before you do anything else, back up your existing calendars. If you don't know how to do so already, read the Help files for your favorite calendar app or service and make sure all your valuable data is safe in case there's a problem. You'll be glad you took the time to do so.

After that, change your Google Calendar's time zone to match the one in the calendar you're currently using. Log in to Google Calendar and click Settings in the upper-right corner. Choose the General tab if it isn't already active and then look next to Your Current Time Zone to see what the current time zone is. Change it with the drop-down menu to match the one you need and then scroll to the bottom of the page and press Save.

Now, let's talk about the kinds of data that Google will accept if you are manually migrating calendars from your current software or service to Google Calendar. You have two choices: ICAL or CSV (comma-separated values). Basically, you export your current calendar data into one of those two formats and then import it into Google Calendar. Let's walk through ICAL and CSV so that you understand what each is and how it works.

WARNING

I'm going to be referring to editing ICAL and CSV files in the next two subsections, and when I said "text editor," I meant text editor. Not Word and not any other word processor because those have a tendency to chew up text files—like iCal and CSV—in very bad ways that cause huge headaches during migrations. Instead, Windows users can try Notepad, or better yet, the free NoteTab Light (www.notetab.com/ntl.php). Mac OS X has Text Editor, but I prefer BBEdit or BBEdit's free cousin, TextWrangler (www.barebones.com/products/bbedit/ and www.barebones.com/products/textwrangler/, respectively). Linux users have the largest number of choices of all, but I'm a vim man myself. No matter what you use, make sure you save as a text file and make sure your extension stays `.ics`—don't let your text editor change it to `.txt`.

ICAL

An ICAL (which is short for iCalendar, but I don't know anyone who actually says "iCalendar," so let's stick with ICAL) file is a standard way to organize calendar data for interoperability between programs. Typically these files end with the `.ics` extension.

NOTE

Want to learn more about the iCal standard? Check out http://en.wikipedia.org/wiki/ICalendar.

Yes, I know Apple calls its calendar program iCal, which kind of makes sense because it uses ICAL files, but it's annoying in the same way that Microsoft database server is named SQL Server, when pretty much every database server is a SQL server. It's just confusing, and that's never helpful for anyone. So to make things more clear, if I'm referring to the type of file, I'll use ICAL, but if I'm referring to Apple's program, I'll use iCal.

ICAL files must be formatted a certain way to work. The first line must be BEGIN: VCALENDAR, for instance, and the last line must be END: VCALENDAR. Between those two lines, all the events appear, with BEGIN:VEVENT and END:VEVENT surrounding each one. After BEGIN: VCALENDAR, but before the first BEGIN:VEVENT, you may see a bunch of header information generated by your calendar program. It's perfectly okay to leave that in if you'd like.

> ⚠ **WARNING**
>
> It's all right to open your ICAL file in a text editor if you want to edit the file or just eyeball it, but be careful: If you accidentally delete or alter a header (such as BEGIN:VEVENT) or a footer (such as END:VEVENT), that event will not import into Google.

Here's a sample ICAL file with one event in it. I've included a lot of the header info, but not all of it. In addition, I indented the various elements in the ICAL file so you could read everything a bit easier; normally, every line is left-aligned, and there is no indenting.

```
BEGIN:VCALENDAR
        METHOD:PUBLISH
        CALSCALE:GREGORIAN
        VERSION:2.0
        BEGIN:VTIMEZONE
                TZID:US/Central
                BEGIN:DAYLIGHT
                        TZOFFSETFROM:-0600
                        TZOFFSETTO:-0500
                        DTSTART:19460428T020000
                        RRULE:FREQ=YEARLY;UNTIL=19730429T080000Z;BYMONTH=4;
                BYDAY=-1SU
                        TZNAME:CDT
                END:DAYLIGHT
                BEGIN:STANDARD
                        TZOFFSETFROM:-0500
                        TZOFFSETTO:-0600
                        DTSTART:19551030T020000
                        RRULE:FREQ=YEARLY;UNTIL=20061029T070000Z;BYMONTH=10
                ;BYDAY=-1SU
                        TZNAME:CST
                END:STANDARD
        END:VTIMEZONE
        BEGIN:VEVENT
                SEQUENCE:0
                TRANSP:OPAQUE
```

```
            UID:767B26B5-79E4-4C13-BD72-E47D028406A0
            DTSTART;TZID=US/Central:20080726T190000
            DTSTAMP:20080710T183915Z
            SUMMARY:Dinner with Hedy
            CREATED:20080713T031035Z
            DTEND;TZID=US/Central:20080726T200000
        END:VEVENT
END:VCALENDAR
```

Fortunately, most every good calendar program today supports exporting data as an ICAL file, so you should be in good shape.

CSV

We've already met CSV files in the previous chapter, "Migrating Contacts to Google Apps." If you don't remember or if you skipped that chapter, CSV stands for "comma-separated values," and it's a common way to transfer data back and forth between programs and services. There's nothing special or required about CSV files when it comes to calendar data, and they're not a standard in the same way that ICAL files are. If you have a choice, ICAL is a better way to go because it is a standard and the data will therefore be more regularly formatted, making migration easier. But if your current calendar program supports only CSV, then CSV it must be.

Fortunately, Google Calendar will import the CSV files generated by most calendar programs without much of a fuss. However, the headers at the top of the CSV files must be correct. The simplest possible headers would consist of these three fields:

```
Subject, Start Date, Start Time
```

However, Google Calendar supports a much larger range of headers, such as the following:

```
Subject, Start Date, Start Time, End Date, End Time, All Day Event,
Reminder On/Off, Reminder Date, Reminder Time, Meeting Organizer,
Description, Location, Private
```

For instance, if I export a calendar from Yahoo with one event, the resulting CSV file looks like this:

```
"Subject","Start Date","Start Time","End Date","End Time","All day
event","Description"
"Dinner with Gabe","7/12/2008","06:00 PM","7/12/2008","08:00
PM","false","His favorite restaurant"
```

WARNING

It's all right to open your CSV file in a text editor if you want to edit the file or just eyeball it, but be careful: If you accidentally delete or alter the field headers, or the fields on an event's line, that event—or even the whole file—will not import into Google.

There's one gotcha when it comes to CSV files: Your recurring events may not be recognized when you import the CSV file into Google. Instead, you'll end up with a series of individual events. In other words, if you create an event in Outlook for June 1 and indicate that it occurs once a week for three more weeks, you'll end up with four events in your CSV file and therefore in Google Calendar as well. Not a disaster, but something you should be aware of nonetheless.

EXPORTING CALENDAR DATA FROM SOFTWARE AND SERVICES

So now you know what ICAL and CSV files are and how to import them into Google after you have one on your computer. Now let's look at how to get ICAL or CSV files out of common calendar software and services.

Exporting Calendars from AOL

Log in to your AOL mail account and then click the Calendar link on the left side of the screen. In your calendar, click the Action menu and choose Export, as you can see in Figure 5.1.

On the following screen, select the calendar you want to export (if you have more than one), enter the dates you want to export, and then press Export, all of which is shown in Figure 5.2.

Save the ICAL file on your computer. You're now ready to import it into Google Calendar.

FIGURE 5.1   AOL may make it impossible to export contacts, but exporting calendars is a different matter.

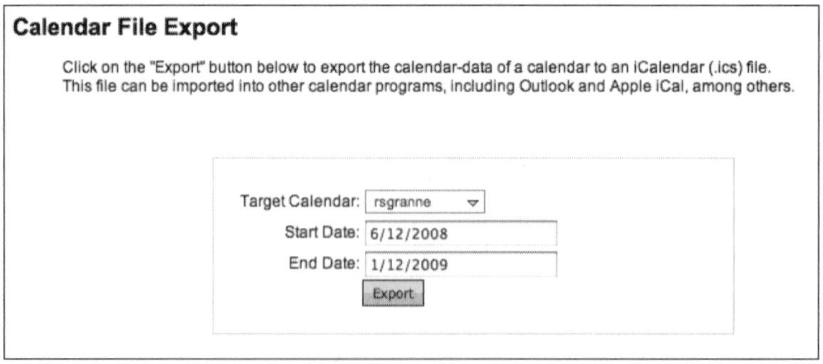

Calendar File Export

Click on the "Export" button below to export the calendar-data of a calendar to an iCalendar (.ics) file. This file can be imported into other calendar programs, including Outlook and Apple iCal, among others.

Target Calendar: rsgranne

Start Date: 6/12/2008

End Date: 1/12/2009

Export

FIGURE 5.2   Just a few simple choices and a mouse click, and your calendar is exported.

Exporting Calendars from Apple iCal

Apple's iCal program allows you to have multiple calendars. If you have more than one calendar, select each calendar you want to export one at a time and follow the next step. If you have only one calendar, that makes things a tiny bit easier.

When the calendar you want to export is selected, go to File, Export. Select where you want the resulting ICAL file to go on your Mac, give it a name if you don't like the default, and press Export. That's it!

> ## 💡 TIP
>
> Google supports importing ICAL files created using versions 2.0 and later of Apple's iCal program.

Exporting Calendars from Evolution

Unfortunately, Evolution doesn't have an export feature, so instead you have to find the ICAL file that Evolution creates and uses. On most systems, it will be in

`/home/[user]/.evolution/calendar/local/system/calendar.ics`

Replace [user] with the user's name, of course.

It's even more unfortunate that, because Evolution doesn't provide an export feature (and why in the heck is that, by the way—it's 2008), if your ICAL file doesn't meet your needs, you'll have to edit it manually, which isn't a disaster, but is definitely annoying.

> ## 📝 NOTE
>
> A bug has been filed about the lack of an export, which you can view at http://bugzilla.gnome.org/show_bug.cgi?id=356551. If you're interested in this feature, check in with that bug periodically to see if there's been any progress.

Exporting Calendars from Google Calendar

If you've been using a Google Calendar on a non-Google Apps account and you now want to switch it entirely over to your new Google Apps account, you're going to find it quite easy.

Go to the non-Google Apps calendar and press the triangle next to the calendar name. A small menu will appear, as shown in Figure 5.3, and you should click Calendar Settings in that menu.

On the following page, scroll to the bottom of the page, to the Private Address section, which you can see in Figure 5.4.

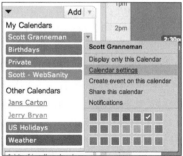

FIGURE 5.3   It can be a little tricky to find the Calendar Settings link.

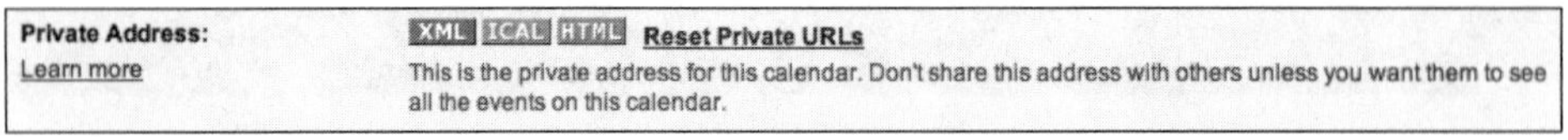

Private Address:	XML ICAL HTML Reset Private URLs
Learn more	This is the private address for this calendar. Don't share this address with others unless you want them to see all the events on this calendar.

FIGURE 5.4 Google allows you to get to your data in a variety of formats.

Right-click the ICAL button (if you're using a Mac without a two-button mouse, hold down the Ctrl key and click) and save the link to the ICAL file onto your computer. The resulting ICAL file can be imported into your new Google Apps calendar.

Exporting Calendars from Hotmail and Windows Live

The so-called classic version of Windows Live Hotmail doesn't allow you to export the Windows Live Hotmail Calendar, which is completely ridiculous. The new whiz-bang beta version of Windows Live Calendar allows you to import ICAL files from different services and software but also doesn't let you export your data. The lesson: do not use Windows Live Hotmail Calendar.

Exporting Calendars from KOrganizer

KOrganizer, part of KDE's PIM (Personal Information Manager) Kontact, makes it super easy to export your calendar to an ICAL file. Go to File, Export, iCalendar, and then provide a name and location for the resulting ICAL file. Press OK, and you're done.

That will export everything in the selected calendar. If you want to publish only selected events, you'll need to set up filters in KOrganizer. More info about that can be found at http://docs.kde.org/kde3/en/kdepim/korganizer/filters-view.html.

Exporting Calendars from Outlook

Microsoft being Microsoft, the way you export your Outlook calendar, and the resulting format you get for import into Google, depends on the version of Outlook you're using.

If you're using pre-Office 2007 versions of Outlook, you need to go to File, Import and Export, Export to a File. Choose Comma Separated Values (Windows) as the format (if you're required to install a translator at this point, go ahead) and then select the calendar you want to export. Choose the location in which you're going to save it and its name, press Next, and then press Finish. After Outlook finishes whirring, you'll have your file ready for importing to Google. Unfortunately, it will be a CSV file, but that's what older versions of Outlook use.

These steps will export the entire calendar. If you want to export a range of dates instead, select them first, and then begin the process.

If you're using Outlook 2007, you're in luck because you can export your calendar to an ICAL file. Select the calendar you want to export and then go to File, Save As. In the File Name box, enter a name for the ICAL file you're going to generate. Next to More Options, you'll see a summary of the data you're going to export. You will definitely want to change what Outlook is going to export, even if it's not obvious at this point, so press More Options, and you'll see the dialog box shown in Figure 5.5.

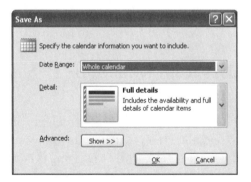

FIGURE 5.5 Microsoft's User Interface design isn't the best, but you can eventually get your task done.

By default, Date Range shows that you will export the entire calendar. If you instead want to select from a range of dates, click the drop-down menu next to Date Range and choose Specify Dates.

When you first open the settings, Detail has Availability Only chosen, which means that your exported calendar will not contain details about your calendar items, only that you are free or busy at selected times! Needless to say, it's your calendar, so that would be pretty useless. The solution is to change Detail to Full Details, as shown in Figure 5.5.

NOTE

If for some reason you want to show more than availability but not your full event info, choose Limited Details.

Now click Show next to Advanced (horrible User Interface design, isn't it?) to dig down even further into these settings.

If you don't change anything, none of your private items will find their way into your ICAL file either—again, pretty useless—unless you check the box next to Include Details of Items Marked Private. If you don't want private items imported into Google, leave this unchecked. If for some reason you have Detail set to Availability Only, you can't include private items.

Finally, if you have attachments in your events and you want to export them, check the box next to Include Attachments Within Calendar Items. This most likely will not work perfectly with Google Calendar, so you probably should leave it unchecked. Regardless, it will work only if you earlier set Detail to Full Details.

Press OK to close More Options, press OK again, and then Save. When Outlook finishes, you'll have an ICAL file that Google can process.

Exporting Calendars from Sunbird or Thunderbird with Lightning

Sunbird and Lightning are essentially the same calendar program and both come from the Mozilla Foundation, the group that gave us Firefox and Thunderbird. However, Sunbird is a standalone program, while Lightning is an extension for Thunderbird.

To export your entire calendar from Sunbird, go to File, Export Calendar. Select the calendar you want to export (you'll have to repeat this process for each one if you have multiple calendars) and press OK. Next to Save As, provide a filename for your exported data; choose a location to which the exported file will go; change Format to iCalendar; and press Save. Done.

If you want to export a range of dates, select them, go to File, Export Selection and repeat the rest of the process delineated in the previous paragraph.

If you're using Lightning, the process is the same as with Sunbird—just make sure you've selected Calendar before you start.

Exporting Calendars from Windows Calendar

Microsoft makes it easy to export data out of Vista's new Windows Calendar. In the program, go to File, Export to see the dialog box shown in Figure 5.6.

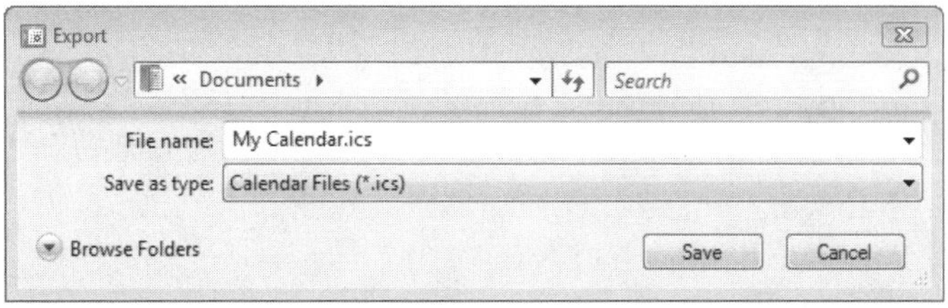

FIGURE 5.6   Windows Calendar makes it surprisingly easy to export calendar data.

Choose a location, enter a filename, leave Save As Type set to Calendar Files (*.ics), and press Save. Told you it was easy!

Exporting Calendars from Yahoo!

Log in to your Yahoo calendar and then click Options, Import/Export. Scroll down to the Export to Outlook section and press the Export button. Save the resulting file, named Yahoo.csv, on your computer. It's a simple process, except that you end up with a CSV file, which is too bad. However, Google can handle it with aplomb.

MANUALLY IMPORTING CALENDAR DATA

- Operating Systems: Windows, Mac OS X, Linux
- Address Book Clients and Services: Any from which you can export data
- Google Apps Editions: Standard, Premier, Education and Nonprofit, Partner

> **NOTE**
>
> I repeat the three lines you see preceding this Note throughout this chapter where appropriate to help you know if a section speaks to your situation or not.

Taking the calendar data you exported in the previous section, "Exporting Calendar Data from Software and Services," and then importing it into Google couldn't be easier: You log in to Google Calendar and then look to the left, where there's a list of your calendars, as shown in Figure 5.7.

At the top of the list is a button with an arrow on it facing down and the word Add, which you can see in Figure 5.7. Click that button and select Import Calendar. On the following page, you'll be prompted to choose a calendar by pressing the Browse button. Press it, navigate to your ICAL or CSV file, and press Open. Choose the Google Calendar into which you'd like to import your events and click Import.

FIGURE 5.7 The Add button allows you to do several cool things, including calendar imports.

You're finished manually importing your calendar data.

DEVELOPING YOUR OWN CALENDAR MIGRATION TOOLS WITH GOOGLE DATA APIS

- Operating Systems: Windows, Mac OS X, Linux
- Address Book Clients and Services: Any applicable
- Google Apps Editions: Standard, Premier, Education and Nonprofit, Partner

Earlier, in Chapter 3, "Migrating Email to Google Apps," I pointed out that if you were so inclined, you could use Google's Application Programming Interfaces (APIs) to build your own email migration tool. The same point applies when it comes to transferring calendar data. Google provides a pretty comprehensive set of APIs that enable developers to build their own software and services for synchronizing calendar data with Google Calendar.

If you want to learn all you can about Google's Contacts Data API, start at http://code.google.com/apis/calendar/. You can find the Developer's Guide at http://code.google.com/apis/calendar/developers_guide_protocol.html and the Reference Guide at http://code.google.com/apis/calendar/reference.html. An official blog titled the "Official Google Data APIs Blog" is available at http://google-dataapis.blogspot.com/. Although it covers far more than just working with Google Contacts, it would still be extremely useful to developers interested in developing their own solutions.

AUTOMATICALLY SYNCING USING SCHEDULEWORLD

- Operating Systems: Windows, Mac OS X, Linux
- Clients: Sunbird (or Thunderbird with Lightning), iCal, Evolution
- Google Apps Editions: Standard, Premier, Education and Nonprofit, Partner

ScheduleWorld is a great, far-reaching service that seeks to sync almost any device, software, or service you could imagine. When it comes to migrating your calendar data to Google Calendar, if you use Outlook, Sunbird (or Thunderbird with the Lightning extension), or Evolution, ScheduleWorld may be the solution for you.

ScheduleWorld is a big project, with lots of information available because it covers so many options for syncing. For the sake of brevity, I'm going to provide the links you need to sync various software packages to ScheduleWorld and, ultimately, to Google Calendar.

- Evolution: http://wiki.scheduleworld.com/wiki/Evolution_Configuration and http://www.estamos.de/projects/SyncML/
- Outlook: http://wiki.scheduleworld.com/wiki/Outlook_Configuration
- Sunbird or Thunderbird with Lightning: http://wiki.scheduleworld.com/wiki/Thunderbird_Configuration
- Google Calendar: http://wiki.scheduleworld.com/wiki/How_Do_I_Sync_Google_Calendar and http://wiki.scheduleworld.com/wiki/Google_Calendar_Interoperability

In addition, a blogger named Eric wrote an article titled "The Holy Grail of Synchronization" at http://internetducttape.com/2006/08/11/the-holy-grail-of-synchronization-how-to-synchronize-microsoft-outlook-multiple-locations-google-calendar-gmail-ipod-and-mobile-phone-with-funambol-scheduleworld/ (yes, that's a crazily long URL) that covers in great detail how to sync your Outlook Calendar with Google Calendar.

AUTOMATICALLY SYNCING USING GCALDAEMON

- Operating Systems: Windows, Mac OS X, Linux
- Clients: Sunbird/Lightning, iCal, Evolution
- Google Apps Editions: Standard, Premier, Education and Nonprofit, Partner

GCALDaemon is a free, open source project that is mature and full-featured. Although it was created to synchronize calendar data between Google and various desktop calendars, it has grown over time and now includes the capability to read

Google Contacts in desktop address books, grab email from Google and read it in your desktop email clients, and a few other tricks as well.

GCALDaemon installs on Windows (NT, 2000, XP, and Vista), Mac OS X, and Linux (as well as a variety of other UNIX flavors), and on any web server running Apache Tomcat. You can find links to the downloads at http://gcaldaemon.source-forge.net/download.html but be aware that you need a version of the Java Virtual Machine (JVM) at 1.5 or later because GCALDaemon requires Java. Installation guides are available at the following web pages:

- Windows: http://gcaldaemon.sourceforge.net/usage10.html
- Mac OS X: http://gcaldaemon.sourceforge.net/usage12.html
- Linux: http://gcaldaemon.sourceforge.net/usage11.html
- Apache Tomcat: http://gcaldaemon.sourceforge.net/usage15.html

The GCALDaemon website provides very detailed, clear instructions for the desktop calendars that are known to sync with Google Calendar using GCALDae-mon: Sunbird (the calendar project under the aegis of the Mozilla Project and there-fore a cousin to Firefox and Thunderbird), Lightning (Sunbird integrated into Thunderbird using an extension), Apple's iCal, and Novell's Evolution. If you use those calendars, visit the following addresses:

- Sunbird/Lightning: http://gcaldaemon.sourceforge.net/usage.html
- iCal: http://gcaldaemon.sourceforge.net/usage13.html
- Evolution: http://gcaldaemon.sourceforge.net/usage16.html

It can be a bit tricky to set up, but after things are running, you can sync your desktop calendars with Google, making the migration process that much easier.

AUTOMATICALLY SYNCING WITH APPLE iCAL USING SPANNING SYNC

- Operating Systems: Mac OS X
- Address Book Clients and Services: Apple iCal
- Google Apps Editions: Standard, Premier, Education and Nonprofit, Partner

In Chapter 4, in a section titled, "Automatically Syncing Apple Address Book and Google Contacts with Spanning Sync," I walked through Spanning Sync, a reason-ably priced piece of software that synchronizes Apple's iCal and Address Book programs with, respectively, Google Calendar and Contacts. Chapter 4 was all about contacts, but the information in that chapter is just as applicable here.

The only thing unique to this chapter is the preferences pane dedicated to Calendars, which you can see in Figure 5.8.

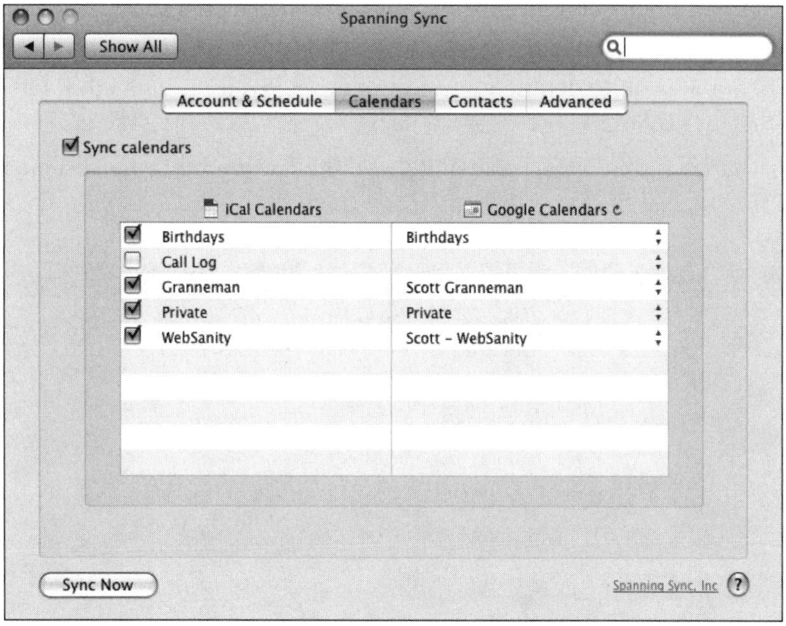

FIGURE 5.8   Spanning Sync contains special preferences for calendars.

As you can see in Figure 5.8, checking or unchecking the box next to Sync Calendars enables or disables calendar syncing. You can also select which calendars on iCal match to calendars on Google. Notice also in Figure 5.8 that the calendars don't have to have the same names, which gives you some useful flexibility.

I use Spanning Sync myself, and I'm a very happy customer.

AUTOMATICALLY SYNCING WITH OUTLOOK USING ICAL4OL

- Operating Systems: Windows
- Address Book Clients and Services: Outlook
- Google Apps Editions: Standard, Premier, Education and Nonprofit, Partner

iCal4OL is an automated syncing program that transfers data between Outlook and Google Calendar. It handles one-way (Outlook to Google) and two-way synchronization. Even better, the sync supports recurrence and even date selections. The software's requirements are actually fairly wide-ranging: Windows 2000 or later, Internet Explorer 5.5 or later, and Outlook 2000 or later. For only 15 Euros (about $23), it's a pretty good bargain, especially when you consider that you can download a 14-day trial at http://ical.gutentag.ch/download.html.

The program is quite detailed, but I want to walk you through a few basic points of setup that you should know.

After you open the Prefs, immediately go the Google tab, which you can see in Figure 5.9.

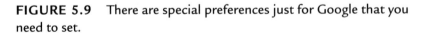

FIGURE 5.9 There are special preferences just for Google that you need to set.

Make sure that Use HTTPS (SSL) is checked because that's good for security. But most important, you have to check Google Apps Support, or it won't work for you. After all, you want to upload to Google Apps, don't you?

The rest of the relevant Prefs are organized in a weird sort of Who-What-How structure. You start with Who, as shown in Figure 5.10.

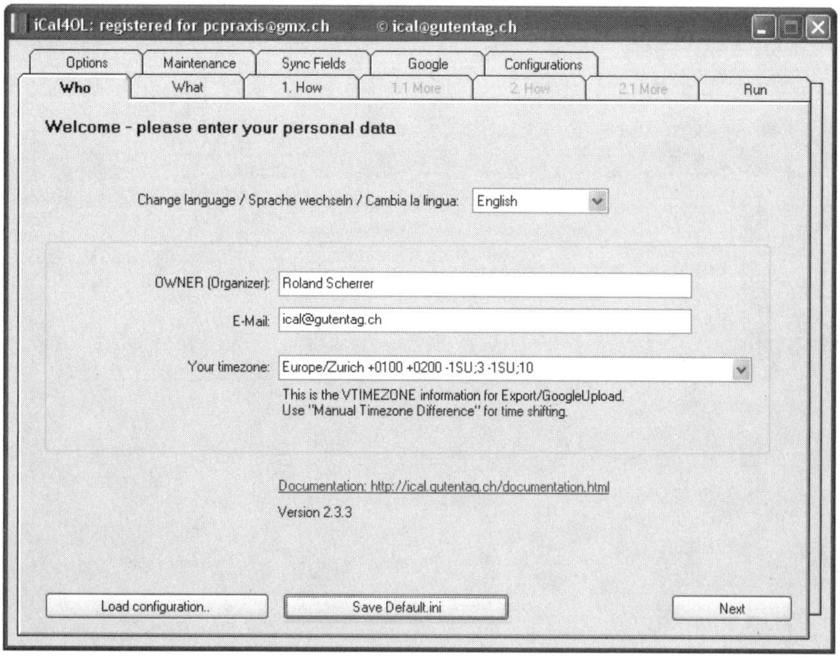

FIGURE 5.10   First is Who...

Enter your personal info, making sure your time zone is correct, and press Next, which brings you to What, displayed in Figure 5.11.

This is the important screen on which you choose the kind of syncing you want to do. Note that you can do either a two-way sync or a one-way sync, in which you upload Outlook's data to Google Calendar. Choose the one you want to perform and press Next, which takes you to How. Which "How" you see, however, depends on the choice you made on What (if this is starting to sound like an old Abbott and Costello routine, I apologize, and urge you to go now to www.youtube.com/watch?v=tPrm6luPmME).

In actuality, both screens look the same, except for the legend at the top of the screen: 1-Way Synchronization or 2-Way Synchronization. For brevity's sake, I'll show you the screen for 1-Way Sync in Figure 5.12.

Enter your Google Apps email address and password, choose a Google Calendar, and press Test. If things are copacetic, fill in the appropriate information in the Outlook section and press Next.

Full documentation is available at http://ical.gutentag.ch/documentation.html, and you really should read it if you want to use the program to its fullest. I haven't gone over all the Prefs, but you now know the key settings needed for Google Apps.

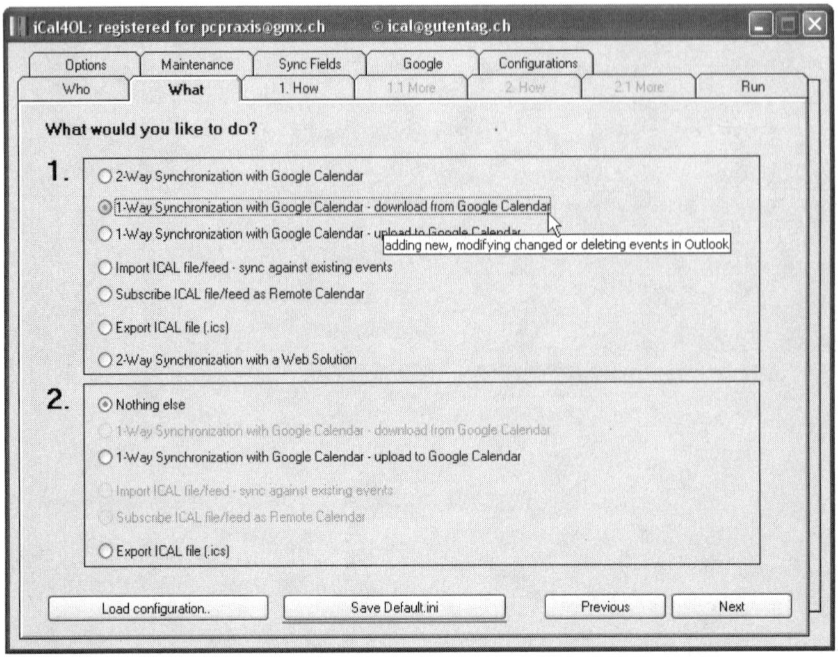

FIGURE 5.11   Second is What...

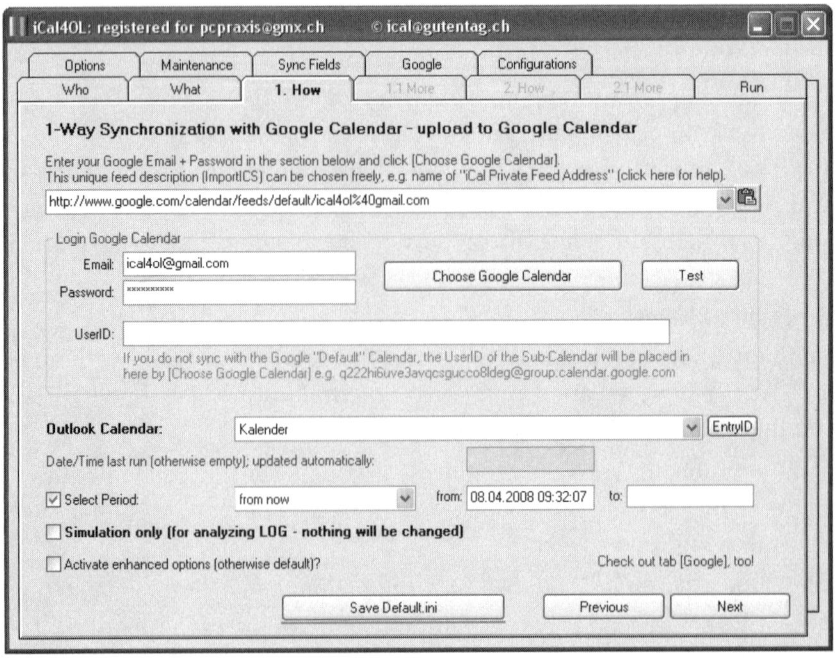

FIGURE 5.12   Third is How...

AUTOMATICALLY SYNCING WITH OUTLOOK AND EXCHANGE USING OGGSYNC

- Operating Systems: Mac OS X, Windows
- Address Book Clients and Services: Outlook and Exchange
- Google Apps Editions: Standard, Premier, Education and Nonprofit, Partner

OggSync is a program that syncs Google Calendars with Outlook (and Windows Mobile device) calendars. A beta version, currently in development as I'm writing this book, will sync contacts as well, so I already discussed OggSync in Chapter 4, in "Automatically Syncing with Outlook Using OggSync." For more information about OggSync, look back at that section in chapter 4. In this chapter, I focus on the calendar-specific parts of the program.

OggSync supports one- and two-way syncing. If you want this to be a one-time process because you want to quit using Outlook (or Exchange), choose one-way syncing, but if you intend to continue using Outlook after you migrate to Google Apps, you'll want to go with two-way syncing. OggSync also detects duplicate events, which is helpful and allows you to sync date ranges if you desire.

As I discussed in Chapter 4, OggSync comes as a free version, which should be adequate for an initial sync of calendar data to Google, and a pro version that costs $30 per year, which gives you automatic syncing (volume purchase plans are available). As in the previous paragraph, if you're planning to dump Outlook, the free version will meet your needs, but if you're planning to stick with Outlook after the big move to Google, you'll probably want to buy the program.

SOLVING COMMON PROBLEMS

As with everything, you'll find that a few problems crop up as you're migrating calendars. Here are some problems you might run into and their solutions.

What Does a "Processed 0 events" Error Message Mean When I'm Importing an ICAL or CSV File?

This usually occurs when you click the Import button more than one time. Your data was imported the first time, but the second time, no data was processed because it was taken care of the first time, so Google reports back that it processed nothing, or "0 events." To verify if this in fact happened, take a look at your newly imported calendar. If you see your dates and times, everything is fine and you can ignore the error.

If you don't see your meetings on your calendar, try again with the ICAL file. If you still get errors, you have two avenues to explore. First, a problem may exist with your ICAL file. Export from your calendar again or open that ICAL file in a text editor and take a look at it for problems. Second, there could be something goofy with the Google Calendar, so create another calendar and try importing into that.

One of those two fixes should take care of the problem.

What Does It Mean That My ICAL or CSV Files Are Too Big to Import into Google Calendar?

If you're going to import ICAL or CSV files into Google, you should try to keep those files below 1MB in size. If your ICAL or CSV file is larger than that, select a smaller range of events in your calendar program and export the ICAL or CSV file (whichever your program supports), import that into Google, and then select a different range of events and repeat the process.

If your calendar program doesn't allow you to specify a range of time for exporting, you're going to need to go ahead and export the whole furshlugginer thing, and then open your ICAL or CSV file in a text editor, divide it up manually—preserving the headers and footers required by the file——and then import those separate files into Google Calendar. And then kiss any program that won't let you specify a range of time for exporting goodbye.

Why Are All My Imported Events Showing Up at the Wrong Time?

If you imported events and they're all displaying at the wrong times, don't panic. It's probably because you had one time zone in your original calendar and haven't set the time zone yet in your new Google Calendar.

You can check your Google Calendar's time zone by logging in to Google Calendar and clicking Settings in the upper-right corner. Choose the General tab if it isn't already active and look next to Your Current Time Zone to see what the current time zone is. If it doesn't match the time zone in the exported ICAL or CSV file, go ahead and change it with the drop-down menu and then scroll to the bottom of the page and press Save.

Why Won't My CSV File Import at All?

Remember, it's a CSV file, as in *comma* separated values. If your CSV file uses semicolons (;) or colons (:) or anything else to separate fields, it won't work with Google.

CONCLUSION

We've now walked through migrating the three kinds of data you or your users may already have created: mail, contacts, and calendars. It turns out that calendars aren't that difficult to migrate because most good calendar solutions already support iCalendar, the standard for the interchange of event-driven data. Because of this, your own calendar migration should go pretty smoothly. Now it's time to explore the settings of Google Apps themselves.

CHAPTER 6

Managing Google Apps Services

Like most every program with just a smidgen of complexity, Google Apps has a control panel, or administrator interface, that lets the people in charge of an organization's Google Apps account make some choices about how they want their implementation to behave. In this chapter, I walk you step by step through the highlights of your Google Apps control panel. We're not going to cover everything because much of it is obvious from the labels that Google provides, but we take a look at some very useful and sometimes contentious settings you can make.

To log in to your control panel, go to www.google.com/a/yourdomain.com. Google will take you to a much longer address that is protected with https so that you can log in and make changes securely.

DASHBOARD

The first thing you'll see when you log in to your domain's control panel is the Dashboard. The Dashboard is useful, but it doesn't contain anything that you can't find elsewhere in the admin interface of Google Apps, with one exception.

In the right of the big box at the top of the Dashboard, you'll see a small graph of active email accounts over the last 90 days, as you can see in Figure 6.1.

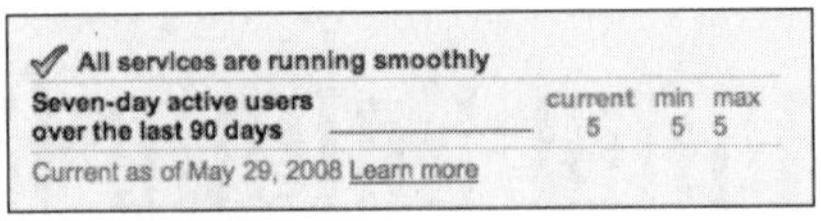

FIGURE 6.1 With one glance, you can see a graph of active email accounts.

At the top of the graph, you can see if all services are working well. That's nice to review.

Then you see the numbers of 7-day active user accounts over the past 90 days, expressed as current, minimum, and maximum. Below that is the date on which the data was last updated; if it says Stay Tuned, the data is being compiled while you wait.

As for the rest of the Dashboard, if you click around, you'll quickly figure out where each link takes you. It's well designed and really easy to use.

USER ACCOUNTS

You have two tabs in User Accounts: Users and Settings. Users is where you view, add, or remove users, and Settings controls how users interact with each other.

Users

Many of the links on this page take you to other areas of the admin interface. I covered what happens when you click Create a New User and Upload Many Users at Once in Chapter 2's "Creating Users," and Email Addresses and Create Email List are discussed later in this chapter in "Email."

If you need more accounts added to Google Apps, click Request More Users. On the following page, enter the number of additional accounts you'd like and provide a reason why Google should give them to you. Google will review your request, and when it's approved (and I can't imagine why it wouldn't be unless you enter something crazy like 500,000), you'll get an email letting you know you now have some new accounts.

The centerpiece of this page is a table listing all your Google Apps accounts. A sample is shown in Figure 6.2.

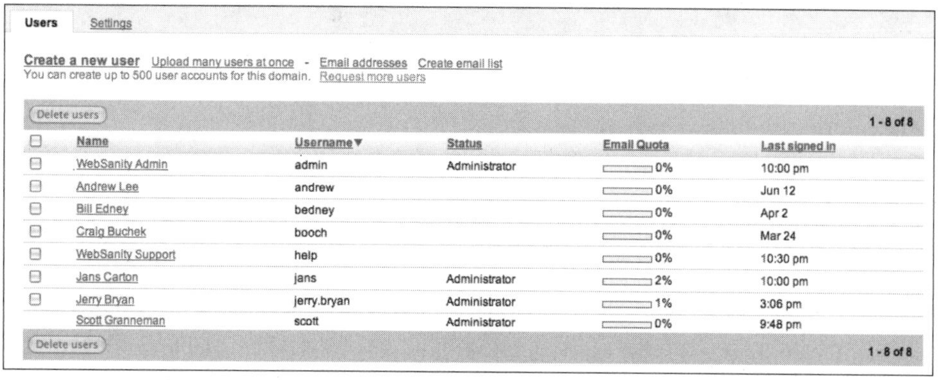

Users Settings

Create a new user Upload many users at once - Email addresses Create email list
You can create up to 500 user accounts for this domain. Request more users

Delete users 1 - 8 of 8

Name	Username ▾	Status	Email Quota	Last signed in
WebSanity Admin	admin	Administrator	0%	10:00 pm
Andrew Lee	andrew		0%	Jun 12
Bill Edney	bedney		0%	Apr 2
Craig Buchek	booch		0%	Mar 24
WebSanity Support	help		0%	10:30 pm
Jans Carton	jans	Administrator	2%	10:00 pm
Jerry Bryan	jerry.bryan	Administrator	1%	3:06 pm
Scott Granneman	scott	Administrator	0%	9:48 pm

Delete users 1 - 8 of 8

FIGURE 6.2 A handy table lists all your Google Apps accounts.

You can sort by any column, in either A to Z or Z to A order. If you click a user's name, you get a page that allows you to change that user's account in your edition of Google Apps, including the following:

- Change the user's name
- Suspend her account if she goes on vacation or temporary leave
- Delete the user if necessary
- Change the user's password or require a password change next time she logs in
- Make the user an administrator of the Google Apps account
- View how much of her email quota she's using
- Add a nickname—another email address people can use to email the user
- Add her to an email list

Settings

At this point, Settings in User Accounts doesn't have much in it. At some time, more will undoubtedly appear here.

For now, you can select one of two option buttons: Enable Contact Sharing or Disable Contact Sharing. You probably should choose Enable Contact Sharing. If you do, every new user is automatically added to a global address book that everyone can access. This does not mean that Fiona's personal Google Contacts are available to Gabe, and vice versa. Instead, it means that users within the same Google Apps domain can email each other without having to actually have every user in their personal address books.

SHARING CONTACTS

Disappointingly, it's kind of a pain to actually get to those email addresses. Here's the process:

1. In Gmail, start composing an email.

2. Click Choose from Contacts. Either a new tab or a pop-up window opens, depending on your browser's configuration.

3. In Choose from Contacts, start typing the person's first, last, or username into the Search box, which will produce a list of users matching the letters you entered. You can see the process in action in Figure 6.3.

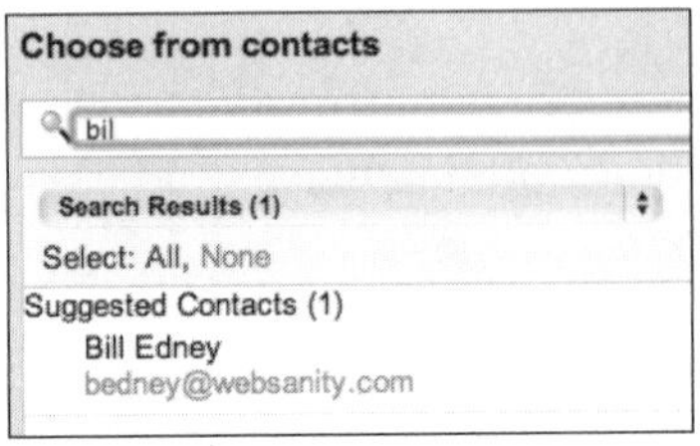

FIGURE 6.3   Just like with Gmail, start typing a few letters, and Google will match what you're looking for.

4. When the user appears who matches what you typed, click him, and his name and address will appear in the To field of your email, shown at the bottom of the window.

5. Repeat this process as many times as you'd like until all of your coworkers' addresses appear in To.

6. Press Done to close the tab or pop-up window and go back to the email you're composing in Gmail.

It would be much easier if those addresses appeared in the normal composition interface and didn't require you to click Choose from Contacts first. It would be great if Google adds that feature someday.

Domain Settings

You have four tabs in Domain Settings: General, Account Information, Domain Names, and Appearance. Most of the items on each tab are obvious, so I'll just point out the interesting or important things you should address.

General

Most of the choices on the General tab are self-explanatory. However, you may want to ponder two sections on this page.

In the section labeled New Services and Features are two boxes you can check: Automatically Add New Google Services and Turn On New Features.

If you check Automatically Add New Google Services, whenever Google launches a new service connected to Google Apps (like it recently did with Google Sites), it will be automatically enabled for your users. Most likely, unless you are very adventurous, or unless the number of users in your Google Apps domain is very small, you want to leave this box unchecked.

If you check Turn On New Features, you will get the opportunity to try new consumer features in Google Apps before other Google Apps accounts. As you probably know, Google periodically adds new features to Gmail, Google Calendar, and the other Google Apps services that consumers use without having to sign up for a Google Apps account. Google usually adds those features first to the consumer-facing versions of those programs, and then after a delay, it adds them to Google Apps. If you want to get those features at the same time consumers do, check this box. I usually check the box because the new features tend to alleviate annoyances and solve problems, but if you're paranoid and want to take your time, leave this box unchecked.

In the section labeled Control Panel, you have a choice: Do you want the Current Version or the Next Generation version of the Google Apps admin interface? If you're using Google Apps in a language other than English, at this time you have no choice—you have to use the Current Version. If you bought your domain name through Google and its partners, or if you signed up for the Premier Edition, you're using the Next Gen UI automatically, and you can't switch to the Current Version.

If you have a choice, I recommend selecting the Next Gen interface. Any new features it introduces aren't that disruptive and may actually prove helpful, and it's the direction that Google Apps is headed anyway, so you might as well embrace it now.

Account Information

This page is pretty clear as to what you can do on it:

- Upgrade your edition of Google Apps
- Delete Google Apps (which I covered in Chapter 2, "Canceling Google Apps")
- Provide a secondary email address
- Enable password reset instructions to be emailed to a secondary email address (which I covered in Chapter 2, "I Lost the Admin Password!")
- Receive email notifications about updates to Google Apps
- Agree to be contacted to provide feedback about Google Apps

The one area I'll direct your attention to is in Admin Support. In that section you'll see your Customer PIN, which is a string of letters and numbers you'll need if you want to contact Google Apps support about an issue. You can write it down for safekeeping somewhere, but the problem is that Google changes it periodically for security reasons—without notifying you!

I guess you could check every couple of days to see if it has changed, but really, you'll just have to log in and see what the PIN is before contacting Google. This becomes a bit difficult if you can't even log in, which happened to one of our clients a few months ago. We were able to call Google Apps support using a Premier Edition account and talk to someone who helped us out of that jam on Google's end. Good thing we had a Premier Edition account!

Domain Names

This page is pretty bare bones. Your domain name is listed, but you can assign domain aliases here as well. In Chapter 2 I revealed that I own heavymetalmassage.com and walked through creating a Google Apps account with that domain name. What if I also owned speedmetalmassage.com and thrashmetalmassage.com and wanted everything to link together under the aegis of heavymetalmassage.com? This is the place to go to solve that problem.

Click Add a Domain Alias, and you'll be prompted to enter the domain name and verify that you own it. If you followed along in Chapter 2, in "Signing Up for the Various Google Apps Editions," you'll know exactly how to do that. You'll need to make the changes Google asks you to make to your MX records for those domains as well, which I also covered in Chapter 2, in "Configuring DNS."

After I finished the process, I would still have heavymetalmassage.com as my primary domain, but if someone sent an email to scott@speedmetalmassage.com or scott@thrashmetalmassage.com, it would come to the correct address: scott@heavymetalmassage.com.

> ⚠ **WARNING**
>
> If you purchased a domain name through Google and its partners (a process I covered in Chapter 2's "Buying a Domain Through Google," and which I also advised against in the same chapter's "Should You Purchase Your Domain Through Google?"), here's another reason not to do it: You cannot add that domain as an alias to a different Google Apps account.

Appearance

This page is divided into two parts. The bottom, labeled Sign-In Box Color, allows you to select the color users see in the box into which they type their usernames and passwords. Knock yourself out and choose a color appropriate to your organization.

The top half of the page, Header Logos, is far more useful. As you can see in Figure 6.4, you can replace the standard Google logos with your own.

FIGURE 6.4   Brand your version of Google Apps with your organization's logo.

After you upload a custom logo, it will show up on every Google Apps service that you and your users open. This is a great way to brand your Google Apps services for your users, and you really should take advantage of this setting.

You should be aware of a few limitations, however. Your image can be in a JPEG, GIF, or PNG format, but it should be no bigger than 143×59 pixels and around 20KB or less. As to the logo itself, stick to your organization's own branding. Don't include any of Google's logos or any words about Google or its services, with one exception: you can use "Powered by Google," but that's it. And don't use anything illegal or with copyrights you don't own—that's a big no-no.

If you ever change your logo again, it may take up to an hour for the new one to appear because of Google's caching of the image. If it's been an hour and you still don't see the new logo, do a force refresh with your web browser by holding down the Shift key while pressing your browser's Reload button.

ADVANCED TOOLS

Advanced Tools is a single page at this time—no multiple tabs of pages here! There are two sections on this page, both of which I have already covered.

- **Bulk Upload** (which allows you to add several user accounts at one time)— Chapter 2, "Adding Users in Bulk"
- **User Email Uploads** (really just a link to the Google Email Uploader)— Chapter 3, "Automatically Move Mail from a Client with the Google Email Uploader" and Chapter 4, "Automatically Copying Addresses with the Google Email Uploader"

SERVICE SETTINGS

No page exists for Service Settings itself; instead, it's a drop-down menu of the various services you've enabled for Google Apps. Let's walk through your choices under Service Settings, looking at each one in turn.

Start Page

The second and third sections allow you to change the URL associated with your organization's Start Page (which I addressed in Chapter 2, "Creating Custom URLs") and disable the Start Page service, if you so desire (see Chapter 2, "Enabling Additional Services").

The first section, cleverly named Start Page, provides a Customize link. Click it, and an administrator can customize the organization's Start Page so there is a consistent appearance and standard content for everyone.

When you click Customize, you'll be taken to a new interface that has five (six if you created your Google Apps account before November 2007) tabs across the top of the page. You can jump directly to any tab, or if this is the first time you're setting things up, you can go in order from the first to last. Let's proceed through each tab, learning how we can customize the Start Page for all our users.

Get Started

There's not much here except an overview of the customization process. The first place you can actually start making decisions is on the next tab, so let's go there.

Layout

If you created your Google Apps account or added the Start Page service after November 19, 2007, you won't see this tab at all because the feature was removed on that date. If you don't have it, skip ahead to Colors; otherwise, read this section.

This page allows you to choose how much freedom your users will have in moving content around on their Google Start Pages, as you can see in Figure 6.5.

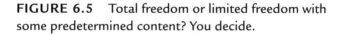

Choose a page layout

Personalized start page content will be organized into three columns. Select additional options below:

○ **Fully customizable**
Users can change any default content.

○ **Locked column**
Lock the content in the first column only (for example, company announcements and news). Your users are free to change the remaining two columns.

FIGURE 6.5   Total freedom or limited freedom with some predetermined content? You decide.

The Start Page always has three columns. The question is, do you want to lock down what's in the first column, or do you want to allow your users to put any content anywhere they want?

My advice for an organization of any size is to select the Locked Column option. That way, you can put company announcements and other important, nonremovable content there, while allowing users to do what they want on the rest of the page.

On the other hand, you may want to choose Fully Customizable because that's where Google has gone since November of 2007.

Colors

This page enables you to set the colors for several elements of your organization's Start Page, including

- Page header background
- Search box background
- Search box link text
- Main page background
- Footer link color
- User section title bar
- User section title text
- User section background
- User section link text
- User section border

Select the page element and then either click a color or enter the hex code for a specific color that isn't included by default. As you make your choices, the preview on the bottom of the page changes to reflect what you've done—a nice bit of feedback.

Header and Footer

Want to customize the header and footer that all your users will see when they're using their Google Start Pages? This is the place.

The interface for editing the header is shown in Figure 6.6.

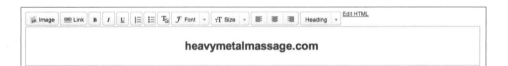

FIGURE 6.6 Editing the Start Page's header is a simple—almost too simple—affair.

You have the standard Google rich text editor available for editing. You can add text, do some basic formatting to it, and even insert images and links.

The images can either be uploaded to Google, or you can point to the URL of an image that's already been uploaded to a website.

Links can point to either web pages (or ftp sites, or really anything as long as you specify the protocol, such as ftp://, webcal://, or feed://) or email addresses. If you want text to appear that is different than the link—as you probably do—you can add that as well.

If you know HTML, click Edit HTML to make changes manually, without the rich text editor. Most HTML elements are supported, with the following exceptions, which will be stripped from your code: APPLET, FRAMESET, HEAD, OBJECT, SCRIPT, STYLE, and TITLE.

Here are some ideas for your header:

- Your company's logo
- Seasonal images
- Navigation links to key websites or pages on websites

The interface for editing the footer is shown in Figure 6.7.

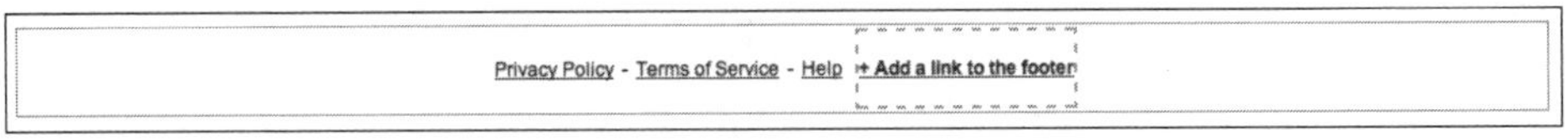

FIGURE 6.7   The Start Page's footer is important, so don't overlook it.

You cannot remove the three links that Google provides by default: Privacy Policy, Terms of Service, and Help. You can, however, change the order in which they appear by hovering your mouse over them, as you can see in Figure 6.8.

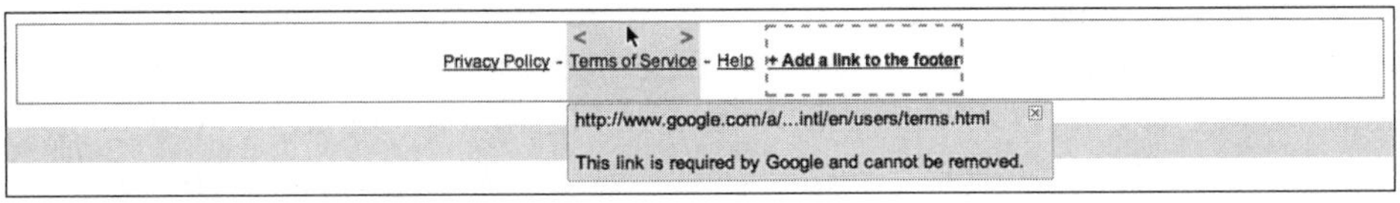

FIGURE 6.8   Click the little blue lesser-than or greater-than symbols to move Google's default links.

The little blue lesser-than and greater-than symbols allow you to move links to the right and left into an order that satisfies you.

You can also add your links by clicking Add a Link to the Footer. Like those that Google puts in, you can position them with the little blue symbols; unlike Google's, you can edit and also delete them by rolling your mouse over them.

Here are some ideas for your footer:

- Contact information or links to contact pages
- Copyright information
- Help link for your organization's own help site

Content

Now it's time for the fun stuff: content. By default, Google includes a wide number of small modules that it calls *gadgets*. Naturally, many of them are related to Google Apps, but you don't need to leave them where Google put them or even keep them at all. The default gadgets include

- Email
- Google Calendar
- Google Talk
- Google Docs
- Reuters Top News
- Weather
- Sticky Note
- Dictionary.com Word of the Day

To move things around, click the title bar of a gadget and drag it to a new location on the page. To delete a gadget, click the X in its upper-right corner.

To add new gadgets, click Add Stuff in the upper-right corner of the page. Before we start adding content, keep in mind that anything you place will be shown on new users' Start Pages by default. You can add as many modules as you want, but don't go hog wild and overwhelm people. Pick the essentials and let individuals customize things as they see fit. And keep in mind that your users will be able to delete modules you placed on the default Start Page if they want.

TIP

Remember that if you registered for Google Apps before November 2007, you can lock the left column, preventing your users from moving or deleting any modules you place there.

Click the links in the column on the left, which sorts new gadgets into categories such as Popular, News, Tools, Communication, Finance, and Technology.

When you find a gadget that looks good and that you want to add to your default Start Page for your users, press Add It Now. If the list on the left isn't precise enough, use the search box at the top to search for gadgets.

WARNING

Unfortunately, Google includes gadgets in its directory that would be completely inappropriate to the vast majority of businesses. Here are just a few examples:

- Hot Girls, Hot Babes, Asian Girls, Hot Chicks—HottestBlogger.com
- Free PSP Wallpapers, Backgrounds, Themes, and Skins
- Babes and Beer
- Nude Women Photo Pool
- Nude Beach World Guide

Even worse, your users will be able to find these and add them to their Google Start Page. Granted, most people in your organization will never engage in such inappropriate behavior because it could get them in a lot of trouble. But Google needs to come up with a way to hide this stuff from their gadgets directory if a Google Apps admin indicates that he wants it hidden.

If you know the URL of a gadget that's out on the Web but is not in Google's directory, press the Add by URL link next to the search box, and you can enter the URL there.

You can also add your own modules by clicking Create Custom Content in the upper right. As you can see in Figure 6.9, the new custom content can be in three formats:

- **Static text, images, and links**—Content that doesn't change or update.
- **Frequently updated content**—Content that comes from regularly updated RSS or ATOM feeds.
- **Google Gadget**—Create your own Google Gadget.

After you create the new custom content, it will appear on the left, in the list of sections, within an area with the default title of Custom Section. Anything you create will appear in there by default. To add your new custom gadget, press Add It Now. It is now on your users' Start Pages by default (but remember, they can always remove it).

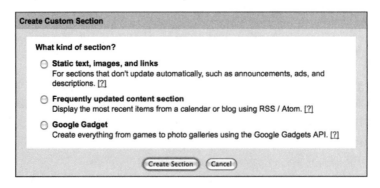

FIGURE 6.9 Adding your own custom content helps make your organization's Start Pages unique and useful.

Now that you know what to do with it, let's quickly look at how to create each kind of custom content.

CREATING A STATIC TEXT, IMAGES, AND LINKS SECTION

If you choose Static Text, Images, and Links, you'll see the fields shown in Figure 6.10.

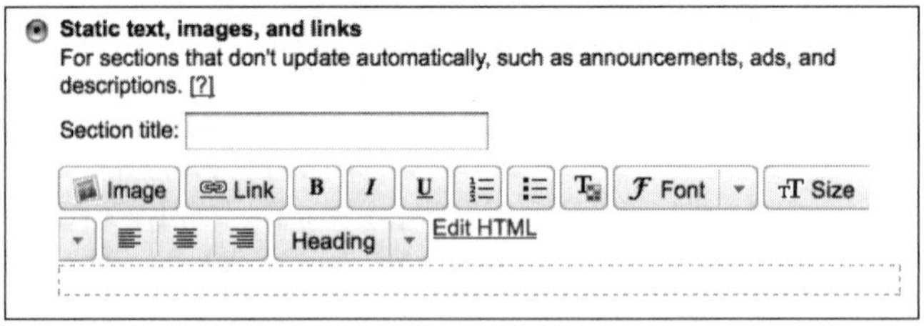

FIGURE 6.10 Editing static content is a lot like editing the Start Page's header and footer.

Enter a title for this section and then start filling in the content. If this looks like what you did earlier in Header and Footer, it should because it's pretty much the same standard Google rich text editor. Using it, you can add text, do some basic formatting to it, and even insert images and links.

The images can either be uploaded to Google, or you can point to the URL of an image that's already been uploaded to a website.

Links can point to either web pages (or ftp sites, or anything as long as you specify the protocol, such as ftp://, webcal://, or feed://) or email addresses. If you want text to appear that is different than the link—as you probably do—you can add that as well.

If you know HTML, click Edit HTML to make changes manually, without the rich text editor. Most HTML elements are supported, with the following exceptions, which will be stripped from your code: APPLET, FRAMESET, HEAD, OBJECT, SCRIPT, STYLE, and TITLE.

Some of the things you could put here include

- Logos and other trademarked images that you want your users to have available
- Advertisements
- Short and simple policies and procedures

CREATING A FREQUENTLY UPDATED CONTENT SECTION

If there's an RSS or ATOM feed you want your users to view as it regularly updates, this is the section for you. Maybe you know of one already out there that would be perfect for your organization. If you want to create one yourself, pretty much any of the free blogging services will do the trick, such as WordPress (http://www.word-press.com) or Blogger (http://www.blogger.com).

> **NOTE**
>
> Don't know what RSS or ATOM is? Wikipedia to the rescue! See http://en.wikipedia.org/wiki/Rss and http://en.wikipedia.org/wiki/Atom_ (standard). You can find out more at Google's online RSS/ATOM aggregator (the best feed reader, in fact), Google Reader, available at http://reader.google.com. Why it's not already a part of Google Apps is beyond me.

If you choose Frequently Updated Content Section, you'll see the choices shown in Figure 6.11.

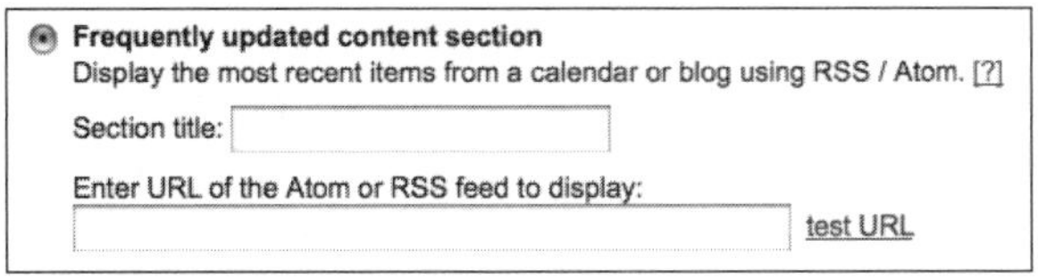

FIGURE 6.11 Two simple fields and you just made a new gadget your users can add to their Start Pages.

Enter something informative in Section Title and the URL pointing to the RSS or ATOM feed in Enter URL. Press Test URL to do just that. If it works, press Create Section, and it's created. If your users subscribe to this gadget, they'll automatically see new content every time the feed is updated, which is a great way to keep up with the latest news and information.

CREATING A GOOGLE GADGET SECTION

If you choose Google Gadget, you'll see the fields shown in Figure 6.12.

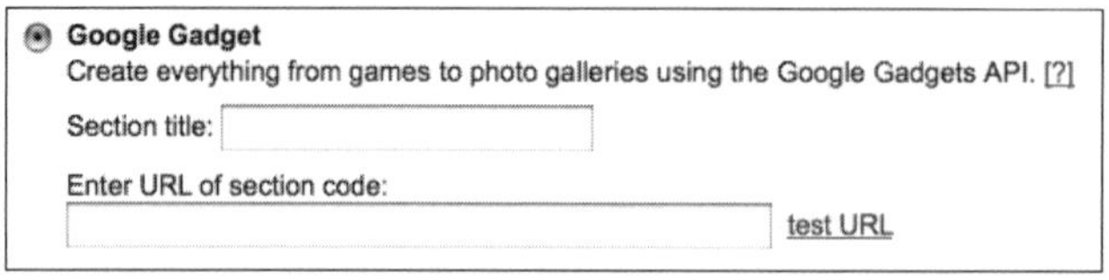

Google Gadget
Create everything from games to photo galleries using the Google Gadgets API. [?]
Section title:
Enter URL of section code:
test URL

FIGURE 6.12 It takes technical skills to create a Google Gadget, but adding it to the Start Page is easy.

Section Title is simple enough; it's what your users will see when they add this gadget to their Start Pages. Enter URL is also obvious because it's the URL for the gadget that your organization or someone else created.

The technical part is in actually creating the new gadget. That subject is way beyond the scope of this book, but you can find out more about the Google Gadgets API at http://code.google.com/apis/gadgets/docs/overview.html.

Publish

This page allows you to publish your finished work on your organization's Start Page. After you're satisfied that everything is set up correctly, press Publish Updates. If you don't like the URL at which it will appear, remember that you can change it (I went over how to do so in Chapter 2, in "Creating Custom URLs").

Email

There are two tabs in the Email settings: General, and Email Addresses. General allows you to change some very general things about your email service (surprise!), whereas Email Addresses provides a list of email addresses and accounts and allows you to create email lists.

General

The General tab has four items on it, three of which we've already covered:

- **Web Address** (the URL users type in to access email)—See "Creating Custom URLs" in Chapter 2
- **Email Activation**—See "Setting Up MX Records for Email" in Chapter 2
- **Disable Service** (no more email for anyone!)—See "Enabling Additional Services" in Chapter 2

The one new item on this tab is Catch-All Address. Suppose I have email addresses set up for scott@heavymetalmassage.com, gabe@heavymetalmassage.com, and fiona@heavymetalmassage.com. What happens when an email comes in addressed to a nonexistent address like info@heavymetalmassage.com?

I can either tell Google to toss it by choosing Discard the Email on this page, or I can instead have it delivered to a set email address, such as scott@, by choosing Forward the Email. Frankly, unless you're absolutely terrified of missing an errant message, I'd select Discard the Email. 99.999% of wrongly addressed email is spam, and it belongs in the Phantom Zone (as do the spammers). Why clutter your inbox even more?

Email Addresses

The Email Addresses tab at first glance may seem like it is simply a table showing each configured email for your Google Apps account, along with the type of address and the recipients. But it's actually a bit more complex than that.

To understand how this page functions, however, you need to know that Google recognizes three kinds of email addresses: accounts, nicknames, and lists, as you can see in Figure 6.13.

info @ websanity.com	Email list	3 recipients Jans Carton,Scott Granneman,Jerry Bryan
jans @ websanity.com	User account	Jans Carton
jerry @websanity.com	Nickname →	Jerry Bryan
jerry.bryan @ websanity.com	User account	Jerry Bryan

FIGURE 6.13 Google allows three kinds of email addresses, and that can be confusing.

Accounts are obvious—they're the usernames you create when you add new users. In Figure 6.13, those are jans and jerry.bryan.

Nicknames are other addresses' links to account addresses. They're additional email addresses tied to an existing user, and that means that nicknames can point only to Google Apps accounts within your domain. You create nicknames by going to your admin interface and clicking User Accounts, Users, selecting a user, and then Add a Nickname. In Figure 6.13, jerry is a nickname that points to the account of jerry.bryan.

Lists allow you to create email addresses at your domain, such as info@mydomain.com. When email is sent to those addresses, it is delivered to the email addresses you specified. This is sort of like nicknames, except that you can specify one or more email addresses, and those addresses don't all have to exist at your Google Apps domain (although they can).

For instance, I signed up for the Premier Edition of Google Apps for granneman.com, but with only one actual paid account: scott@granneman.com. I wanted my brother to have an email address at granneman.com, but didn't want to have to pay $50 per year for the privilege. I created a list with a name of gus@granneman.com, pointing to his work email at the New York Jets. In Figure 6.13 the info@ is a list that points to three user accounts.

Now that you know about the three kinds of email addresses Google uses, this page should make a bit more sense. At the top of the page is a link: Create an Email List. That's now obvious. Below that is a drop-down next to Show; you can choose All Addresses, User Accounts, Nicknames, or Email Lists. After that is the table of email addresses, which allows you to sort on any column, in either A to Z or Z to A direction. Finally, at the bottom of the page you can download the list of email addresses as a CSV file containing columns for Username, First Name, Last Name, Last Login, First Login, and Quota.

> **TIP**
>
> If you look carefully at the note at the bottom of this page, you'll see that Google automatically monitors abuse@ and postmaster@ email addresses for your domain so that you don't have to. If, however, you want copies of mail sent to those addresses, create an email list for either one and make yourself or others recipients.

Chat

As you're going to learn in Chapter 18, Things to Know About Using Google Talk," Google has a bit of a split personality when it comes to chat. This page focuses on the downloadable Windows client for Google Talk and provides a link for that software at the top. (Don't worry—users of other operating systems can still chat with those using Windows and the official Google client, as you'll see in Chapter 18.

The bottom of the page allows you to disable chat if you so desire. That process was covered in "Enabling Additional Services," found in Chapter 2.

Between these two sections are some settings that govern how much information your users provide to other Google Apps users and whether they can communicate with those outside Google's IM networks.

Notice that you cannot prevent your users from IMing other Google Apps users because Google does not provide a way for you to turn that capability off. If you want them to be warned every single time they start to chat with someone who's not in your domain, however, check the box next to Warn Users When Chatting Outside This Domain. I wouldn't do that, though, unless you feel like really annoying your users and training them to click OK in dialog boxes without reading them.

If you want to discourage chatting with others outside your Google Apps domain, a better tack might be to uncheck the other box next to Display Users' Chat Status Outside This Domain. If people at other organizations can't see their statuses, maybe your people will get IMed less. But again, this may just lead to user annoyance. It's definitely something for you to ponder long and hard before you do anything.

> **TIP**
>
> However, you could block Google chat by blocking DNS lookups to both talk.google.com and talkx.l.google.com. In that case, why did you enable the service in the first place? Disable it!

At the end of this middle section is a mention of editing SRV records in DNS if you want your users to be able to chat with people using other IM networks. I covered how to do that in "Setting Up SRV Records for Google Talk Federation," which you can find in Chapter 2.

Calendar

Most admins will see just the General tab, but Premier and Education Edition admins will also see a Resources tab.

General

The General tab has three items on it, two of which we've already covered:

- **Web Address** (the URL users type in to access email)—See "Creating Custom URLs" in Chapter 2

- **Disable Service** (no more email for anyone!)—See "Enabling Additional Services" in Chapter 2

In the middle of the page is a new section: Sharing Options. In this section, admins decide how much their users can share calendars both within and outside your Google Apps domain.

SHARING CALENDARS OUTSIDE YOUR DOMAIN

You have three choices when it comes to your users sharing their calendar data with people not using your edition of Google Apps, from most to least restrictive:

- **Only free/busy information (hide event details)**—People outside your domain can find out if a user is free or busy at a certain time but have no idea exactly what is going on during that time.
- **Share all information, but outsiders cannot change calendars**—People outside your domain can find out about the events your users have scheduled, including any information they have included in the calendar listing (guests, location, and description, for example).
- **Share all information, and outsiders can change calendars**—People outside your domain cannot only view the full information about the events your users have scheduled, but, if the users have given them permission, can also add events to their calendars.

Before you panic, keep in mind that you are simply specifying the maximum allowed privileges on this web page; your users can dial back privileges on their own calendars as they want. In other words, even if you choose Share All Information, and Outsiders Can Change Calendars, an individual user can specify Only Free/Busy Information for sharing his calendar with those outside your organization; the reverse, however, is not true because that would be elevating privileges.

For some people with families, it really helps if they can give a significant other access to their calendars so that scheduling busy lives can be better coordinated. As you'll find out, Google Calendar supports multiple calendars on the same individual's account, so a person could have one calendar for work and one for home life, all accessible through the same Google Apps Calendar interface.

On the other hand, your attitude may be that if someone wants to use a personal calendar, they can simply sign up for a free Google account and create a shared calendar there. It comes down to your organization and how you run things.

SHARING CALENDARS INSIDE YOUR DOMAIN

You have three choices when it comes to your users sharing their calendar data with people inside your domain and using your edition of Google Apps (in other words, people who work together):

- **No sharing**—Coworkers by default can't see fellow employees' calendars at all.

- **Only free/busy information (hide details)**—Coworkers can find out if a fellow employee is free or busy at a certain time, but have no idea exactly what is going on during that time.

- **Share all information**—Coworkers can find out about the events fellow employees have scheduled, including any information they have included in the calendar listing (guests, location, and description, for example).

In the previous section, "Sharing Calendars Outside Your Domain," you were setting the maximum allowable privileges, and although users could choose to be more restrictive, they couldn't choose to be less restrictive. In this section, however, users are free to change these settings on their calendars at will. Even if you say the default is No Sharing, a user can still pick Share All Information for a calendar and thereby say that everything in it is shared with anyone else in your Google Apps domain.

Also, even if someone has Share All Information chosen, the user can still make particular events private so that no one else knows about them or even mark them as busy and keep the actual details hidden.

If you're using the Premier or Education Edition and have resource sharing enabled, you probably shouldn't choose No Sharing. If you do, your users won't be able to find out if resources are available unless you share each resource manually, which will quickly grow to seem tedious and life sapping.

In fact, I recommend setting the default to Share All Information and be done with it. We're talking about coworkers, after all!

Resources

Normally, only people can have calendars at Google Calendar, which means that it's possible to schedule meetings only with people. But if you're a Google Apps Premier or Education admin, you can also create a calendar for nonhuman things that your users can then schedule—things such as conference rooms, projectors, and vehicles. Google calls those *resources*, and you set them up, naturally, on the Resources tab.

To start, click Create a New Resource. You're asked to fill in three things, only one of which is required:

- **Resource Name (required)**—Describe the resource with something like "Conference Room 101" or "Ford Van" or "Flip Video Camera."
- **Resource Type**—A generic term for what the resource is, such as "Conference Room" or "Automobile" or "Electronics."
- **Description**—A short description of the resource so that users know exactly what it is or how it is to be used.

When you're done writing, press Create Resource. You're now back on the Resources tab, with a table listing your resource(s) on the page. You can sort the table, in both A to Z and Z to A order, by clicking the table headers.

To edit a resource, click the resource's name. When you do so, you'll see that Google has assigned a unique email address to the resource, which is what you'll use to share it with your users.

To share a resource, copy the unique email address for the resource and then log in to your calendar account (located at http://calendar.yourdomain.com, if you followed my advice in Chapter 2, "Creating Custom URLs"). Click the little drop-down next to Add, above your list of calendars. Choose Add a Friend's Calendar. When the page loads, enter the email address you copied for the new resource into the field next to Contact Email and press the Add button. A moment later, the calendar for that resource shows up in your list of calendars.

Click the little drop-down arrow to the right of your new calendar and select Share This Calendar. Make sure that Share This Calendar with Others and Share This Calendar with Everyone in the Domain are checked and the drop-down next to the latter is See All Event Details. Your users can now see and use this resource's calendar.

Web Pages

The settings page for Web Pages has three items on it, two of which we've already covered:

- **Web Address** (the URL users type in to access the web pages)—see "Creating Custom URLs" in Chapter 2
- **Disable Service**—See "Enabling Additional Services" in Chapter 2

The new item is Service Setup, which has one link in it: Edit Your Web Pages. Click it, and you're taken to the Google Page Creator, where you can start editing web pages.

> **TIP**
>
> I wouldn't worry too much about Web Page—Google has essentially killed the service in favor of the very similar Sites. More about that in Chapter 17's "Thinking About How Google Sites Fits Into Google Apps."

Docs

The settings page for Google Docs has three items on it, two of which we've already covered:

- **Web Address** (the URL users type in to access Google Docs)—See "Creating Custom URLs" in Chapter 2
- **Disable Service**—See "Enabling Additional Services" in Chapter 2

The new section is Sharing Options, and it governs whether users can share documents with people outside their Google Apps domain. There is no setting governing sharing within your Google Apps domain because that is always allowed. As the administrator, however, you can set the highest level of sharing allowed; your users, of course, can select a lower level on a case-by-case basis. In other words, even if you say users can share docs outside their Google Apps domain, a user can still choose not to share an individual document.

Your choices are as follows:

- **Users cannot share documents outside this domain**—Only coworkers can access documents.
- **Let users receive documents from outside this domain**—This is a check box that gets activated only if you enable the previous option. It allows your users to work on documents shared with them by folks in other organizations but prevents them from offering their own work up for collaboration.
- **Users can share documents outside this domain but will receive a warning each time**—This will quickly grow tedious to your users, and it will only teach them to press OK as fast as possible to dismiss the warning, which is bad security behavior.

- **Users can share documents outside this domain (without any warning)**—Unless you're really paranoid about security, I'd just go with the last option and let your users share docs with people who don't work at your organization. Talk to your users about what should and should not be shared. The vast majority of people understand how to collaborate responsibly with people outside their company.

One of the best features about Google Docs is that it makes collaboration super easy for its users, so think long and hard about limiting the collaboration that your users will be able to enjoy when they use Google Apps.

Message Security and Discovery

The settings page for Message Security and Discovery has three items on it, one of which we've already covered: Disable Service, which you can read more about in the section in Chapter 2 titled, "Enabling Additional Services."

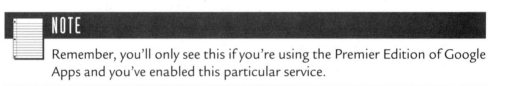

> **NOTE**
> Remember, you'll only see this if you're using the Premier Edition of Google Apps and you've enabled this particular service.

The new items are About the Service, which provides a link to Customize Your Email Policies, and Terms of Service. The latter is easy to dispense with; it's a link to Google's terms and conditions for using this special service.

If you click to Customize Your Email Policies, you'll be taken to a new page at http://login.postini.com. Log in with the email address and password you provided Google's Postini service (discussed in the section in Chapter 2 titled "Enabling Message Security and Recovery") and you can configure this service. That specific subject is beyond the scope of this book, but you can learn more at www.google.com/support/a/bin/topic.py?topic=12977.

Sites

There are two tabs in the Sites settings: General and Web Address Mapping. The General tab is just that—big picture stuff about the wikis you create within Google Sites—whereas Web Address Mapping makes it easy to apply your own domain name to the sites you create.

TIP

If you don't see Sites as an option, it's because your Google Apps control panel (the admin interface) isn't set to display in United States English and you're not using the Next Generation interface for the control panel. To change the control panel language to U.S. English, change to the Next Generation interface by logging in to your control panel, clicking Domain Settings, General and then changing Control Panel from Current Version to Next Generation. Press the Save Changes button, and you can now add sites using the method I covered in "Enabling Additional Services," found in Chapter 2.

Even though the control panel for Google Apps and the interface for Google Sites has to be in English, you can put whatever non-English content you want on your Google Sites.

General

The settings page for Sites has three items on it, two of which we've already covered:

- **Web Address** (the URL users type in to access Sites)—See "Creating Custom URLs" in Chapter 2
- **Disable Service**—See "Enabling Additional Services" in Chapter 2

The new section is Sharing Options, and it governs whether users can share wiki sites with people outside their Google Apps domain. There is no setting governing sharing within your Google Apps domain because that is always allowed. As the administrator, however, you can set the highest level of sharing allowed; your users, of course, can select a lower level on a case-by-case basis. In other words, even if you say users can share sites outside their Google Apps domain, a user can still choose not to share an individual site.

Your choices are as follows:

- **Users cannot share sites outside this domain**—Only coworkers can access your users' wiki sites.
- **Users can share outside this domain but will receive a warning each time**—This could very easily grow tedious to your users, and it will only teach them to press OK as fast as possible to dismiss the warning, which is bad security behavior.

- **Users can share sites outside this domain (without any warning)**—Your users can invite other people outside your organization to view sites they create.

- **Users can make Sites public**—This option relies on the previous one being chosen first. If you enable this, your users can publish sites to the general Internet so that anyone can view them, including search engines.

Unless you're really paranoid about security, I'd just go with the third option and let your users share sites with people who don't work at your organization. The fourth option—which, remember, depends on the third being enabled first—may be appropriate to your organization. Talk to your users about what should and should not be shared. The vast majority of people understand how to collaborate responsibly with people outside their company.

> **TIP**
>
> If you find out that one of your users has published content that isn't appropriate (for whatever reason), as an administrator you can edit or remove it by viewing a list of all your domain's sites at https://sites.google.com/a/mydomain.com (substitute mydomain.com with your domain, of course), selecting the necessary site, and editing the problematic content.

Web Address Mapping

Normally, a wiki one of your users creates will be found at http://sites.google.com/a/yourdomain.com/sitename. However, many organizations would like to use their own domain so that a site appears at http://wiki.yourdomain.com for example.

> **NOTE**
>
> You can change URLs only for sites that are public, a process we discussed in the previous section. If you attempt to set up a URL for a private site, anyone attempting to go to the mapped URL will end up at the "real" URL instead. In other words, you can set up a URL for http://private.yourdomain.com, but anyone going there will be redirected to http://sites.google.com/a/yourdomain.com/private. Keep in mind that this may not be a bad thing for users of that private wiki, as the shorter URL may be easier to remember!

To change this behavior, and use a URL at your domain, click Add a New Web Address. You'll be taken to a new page, where you're asked to provide two items:

- **Site location**—Fill in the blank at the end of http://sites.google.com/a/your-domain.com/_____. Don't use spaces or special characters, except for the hyphen to separate words, and use only lowercase letters. In other words, *New Products* won't work, but *new-products* will.

- **Web Address**—Fill in the blank at the beginning of http://_____.yourdomain.com. Standard DNS rules apply, so no spaces or special characters, except for hyphens.

When you type a new subdomain in Web Address, Google attempts to figure out if it's already in your DNS. If it's not, Google will provide instructions for altering your DNS records to work with your new domain name.

In essence, you need to add a CNAME pointing your new subdomain to resolve to ghs.google.com. In other words, if you add a new Web Address of "products," Google will tell you to create a CNAME at your DNS provider that points "products" to ghs.google.com. If you followed along in "Configuring DNS" in Chapter 2, this should be old hat by now.

After you've configured your DNS, press the button labeled I've Completed These Steps on the bottom of the instructions page. Google goes ahead and makes the necessary changes on its end, which can take up to 24 hours to go through.

> **TIP**
>
> This process does not actually create the wiki site. You still need to do that manually, either before or after you map the site's DNS. We'll discuss how to create a new Google Site in Chapter 16, "Setting Up Google Sites."

After you've created at least one domain mapping, going to this tab will show you a list of your existing mapped sites with sortable columns. To delete a mapping (but not the site itself), check the box next to the address and press Delete Mapping(s). You'll be prompted to make sure you really want to go through with it; if you're sure, press Delete Mapping(s) again and poof! It's gone.

SOLVING COMMON PROBLEMS

Nothing in life is perfect, so you might run into a few issues as you're managing Google Apps. Here are some solutions to some of those problems.

Why Do Administrators See Every Calendar My Users Have Created?

Admins always have full access to every user's calendars, so they always show up by default under the admins' My Calendars section in the list of calendars on the left side of Google Calendar. Although you can't remove those calendars—which could, admittedly, grow outrageously long if you have even a decent number of users—you can hide them.

Click the tiny Manage Calendars link you'll see at the bottom of the calendars list. You should then find yourself on the Calendars tab of Calendar Settings. To the right of each of your users' calendars is a Hide link. Click it, and the calendar is hidden from your calendar list. To bring it back, click Show.

CONCLUSION

This chapter brings us to the end of Part I, in which we got started with Google Apps. Now that we've finished configuring things from the administrative end, it's time to dive into the individual apps themselves and really get to know them. Next stop: Gmail!

FURTHER READING

There's always more to learn, so here are some resources that you might find handy if you want to learn more about managing Google Apps:

- Overview of admin features:
  www.google.com/a/help/intl/en/admins/admin_features.html
- Glossary: http://google.com/support/a/bin/answer.py?answer=60058
- Google Apps for Admins All Help topics on one page: www.google.com/support/a/?fulldump=1
- Control Panel
  - Control Panel: www.google.com/support/a/?hl=en
  - Control Panel YouTube video:
    www.youtube.com/view_play_list?p=445899A1305C271C
- Known Issues:
  www.google.com/support/a/bin/request.py?contact_type=known_issues

Part II

Gmail

CHAPTER 7

Setting Up Gmail

To many users, Gmail is one of the most important programs in Google Apps, if not the most important. With a good understanding of Gmail's settings, it's possible to customize how this powerful and innovative program works in a way that's most productive for you.

To customize Gmail, click Settings in the upper-right corner of the program. When you go to Gmail's Settings, you should see the following tabs: General, Accounts, Labels, Filters, Forwarding and POP/IMAP, Chat, and Web Clips. You might also see Labs if your Google Apps administrator has enabled it (and we'll talk about how to enable it later in this chapter, at "Labs," if it's not already enabled).

Keep in mind that after you start playing with Gmail Labs, you may see different sections on some of the tabs, and you may even see new tabs. For instance, if you turn on the Superstars feature in Labs, a new Superstars section appears on the General tab, so be prepared for some differences between what I'm describing and what you may be seeing.

I'm not going to cover every section on every tab, by the way, because some of them are obvious, but I will take a look at some of the more interesting, notable, or puzzling sections.

GENERAL

This page contains more than ten sections. They're all useful in one way or another, but I'm going to skip a few of them.

Maximum Page Size

You get to use a drop-down to fill in a blank here: Show _____ Conversations Per Page, with your choices being 25, 50, or 100. The default is 50, and that's a good number to start with. If you have a slow connection, change it to 25; if you have a super-fast connection and you don't mind some scrolling, change it to 100.

Keyboard Shortcuts

You have two choices here:

- Keyboard Shortcuts Off
- Keyboard Shortcuts On

Make sure that you turn on keyboard shortcuts because they will vastly increase your speed and productivity using Gmail. You'll learn a lot more about keyboard shortcuts in Chapter 8, "Things to Know About Using Gmail."

Snippets

You have two choices here:

- Show Snippets
- No Snippets

Figure 7.1 shows Gmail with snippets on:

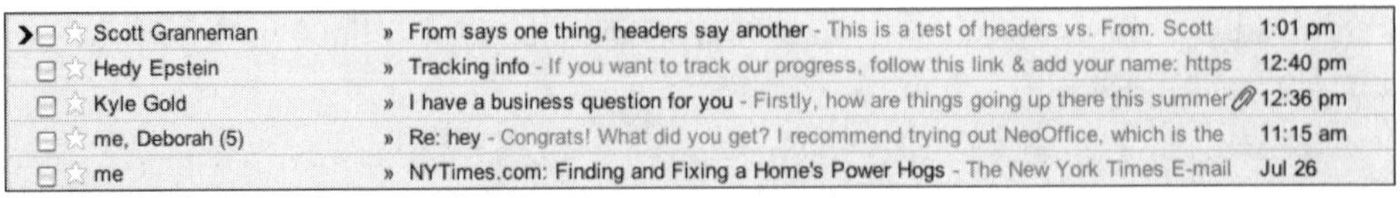

Scott Granneman	» From says one thing, headers say another - This is a test of headers vs. From. Scott	1:01 pm
Hedy Epstein	» Tracking info - If you want to track our progress, follow this link & add your name: https	12:40 pm
Kyle Gold	» I have a business question for you - Firstly, how are things going up there this summer	12:36 pm
me, Deborah (5)	» Re: hey - Congrats! What did you get? I recommend trying out NeoOffice, which is the	11:15 am
me	» NYTimes.com: Finding and Fixing a Home's Power Hogs - The New York Times E-mail	Jul 26

FIGURE 7.1 Snippets show you the first few words of the email message.

Figure 7.2 shows Gmail with snippets off:

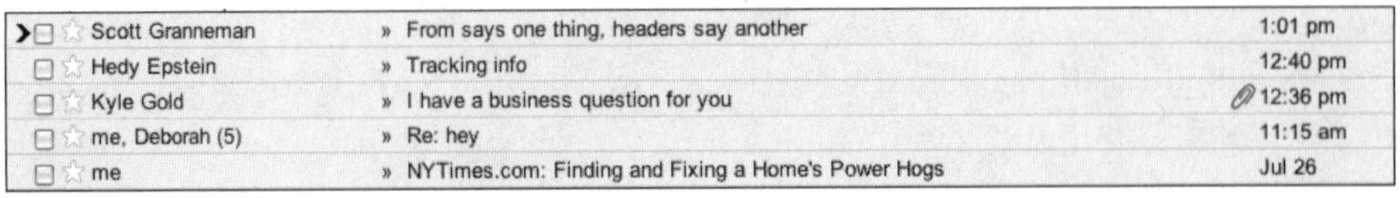

Scott Granneman	» From says one thing, headers say another	1:01 pm
Hedy Epstein	» Tracking info	12:40 pm
Kyle Gold	» I have a business question for you	12:36 pm
me, Deborah (5)	» Re: hey	11:15 am
me	» NYTimes.com: Finding and Fixing a Home's Power Hogs	Jul 26

FIGURE 7.2 How barren and less useful Gmail looks without snippets. Bring back the snippets!

Clearly, unless you think snippets introduce too much clutter, Gmail is far more usable with snippets on.

Vacation Responder

Also known as "Out of Office" replies, this section allows you to send an automated reply to people who send you email while you're on vacation, at a conference, or busy for a period of time.

One of the reasons I hate these things is because of the number of replies I get on the mailing lists I run. For example, someone will go on vacation and set a response to be automatically sent by Outlook or Thunderbird or whatever. Every single time someone sends mail to the list, Mr. Vacationer's email program sends a message back to the list letting us all know that he's gone for a week. Truly annoying.

Google solves this issue by letting you know in little tiny type in this section that "If a contact sends you several messages, this automated reply will be sent at most once every 4 days." Once every four days is still annoying, but it's a lot less annoying than every single message. Thank you, Google.

Outgoing Message Encoding

You have two choices here:

- Use Default Text Encoding for Outgoing Messages
- Use Unicode (UTF-8) Encoding for Outgoing Messages

If your mail mostly consists of characters in English, Spanish, French, or other "Western" languages, the default text encoding is just fine. But if you send messages in Arabic, Chinese, or other "non-Western" languages, choose UTF-8 instead.

NOTE

Want to learn more about UTF-8? Check out Wikipedia's article on the subject at http://en.wikipedia.org/wiki/UTF-8 or read Joel Spolsky's "The Absolute Minimum Every Software Developer Absolutely, Positively Must Know About Unicode and Character Sets (No Excuses!)" at http://www.joelonsoftware.com/articles/Unicode.html.

Browser Connection

You have two choices here:

- Always Use Https
- Don't Always Use Https

If you choose the first option, your login and your mail are all transferred over secure HTTP, which means that anyone sniffing your traffic at a wireless coffee shop will end up with encrypted gibberish instead of your emails.

My advice is to check Always Use Https immediately. If you go to your mail at an http address, Google will automatically redirect you to the more secure https version.

The only downside is a tiny slowdown as your computer has to decrypt your mail, a slowdown so minor that you wouldn't even notice it.

TIP

At the time I'm writing this, Google just rolled out this feature. The company is promising that administrators of the Premier Edition will be able to set HTTPS in the Control Panel for all their users. It's not there yet, but it should be there soon.

ACCOUNTS

This tab contains three sections: Send Mail As, Get Mail from Other Accounts, and Change Password. Actually, the first two are in the wrong order because it only makes sense to configure Send Mail As after you've set up Get Mail from Other Accounts. For that reason, I'm looking at these two sections in the order in which they *should* appear, not their actual order on the web page.

Get Mail from Other Accounts

This feature, commonly known as the Gmail Mail Fetcher, allows you to retrieve email from other email accounts using POP3 and display the messages in your Gmail Inbox. Google allows you to specify up to five accounts here.

TIP

Don't remember what POP3 is? Check out the introduction in Chapter 2, in which I define the term.

To get started, click Add Another Email Account. Enter the email address you want to fetch, and you'll go to a page that looks like Figure 7.3.

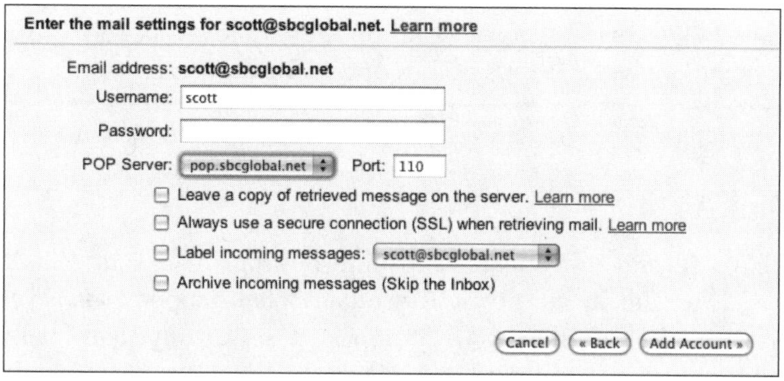

Enter the mail settings for scott@sbcglobal.net. Learn more

Email address: **scott@sbcglobal.net**
Username: scott
Password:
POP Server: pop.sbcglobal.net   Port: 110
☐ Leave a copy of retrieved message on the server. Learn more
☐ Always use a secure connection (SSL) when retrieving mail. Learn more
☐ Label incoming messages: scott@sbcglobal.net
☐ Archive incoming messages (Skip the Inbox)

Cancel   « Back   Add Account »

FIGURE 7.3   Google gives you some nice options when you grab your email from other accounts.

Enter your username and password, select the correct POP server, and change the Port if necessary (110 is most likely just fine). Then you have four check boxes:

- **Leave a copy of retrieved message on the server**—Want a copy in your Gmail Inbox and another copy back on the original POP server? Then check this.

- **Always use a secure connection (SSL) when retrieving mail**—If your POP server supports this, by all means, check it. Added security is a good thing (if you do, you'll probably have to change the Port to 995).

- **Label incoming messages**—Select a label for those messages coming in from a different account. Use one of your existing labels or one that Google offers to create based on your POP email address or create a new one from scratch.

- **Archive incoming messages (Skip the Inbox)**—Get the mail but don't clutter your Inbox.

Make your choices and press Add Account. If problems exist, Google will tell you.

You have no control over how often Google checks your other accounts. Instead, Google will adjust its fetch rates based on previous attempts.

> ### TIP
>
> Some people are so annoyed by the time it takes Google to check their external POP accounts that they stop using this feature and have all mail sent to their other POP accounts forwarded on to their Gmail addresses. Some POP providers, notably Yahoo, don't allow this behavior unless you pay them, however, so it's not an option for everyone.

Send Mail As

Now you have several other email accounts flowing in to your Gmail account, thanks to what we did in the previous section. What happens when you reply to one of those emails? In other words, suppose I set up my heavymetalmassage. com Gmail account to use POP to grab email sent to heavymetalmassage@ gmail.com. An email sent to heavymetalmassage@gmail.com comes to me at scott@ heavymetalmassage.com, and I want to reply to it. I could do so in one of two ways:

- Make the reply look like it's coming from heavymetalmassage@gmail.com, thus keeping up the illusion that I'm using that account.
- Make the reply come from scott@heavymetalmassage.com, the address I want everyone to switch to.

If I do nothing and leave things the way they're displayed in Figure 7.4, any email I send out or reply to, no matter the address to which it was originally sent, will come from scott@heavymetalmassage.com.

Send mail as: (Use Heavy Metal Massage Mail to send from your other email addresses) Learn more	Scott Granneman <scott@heavymetalmassage.com>	edit info
	Add another email address	
	When I receive a message sent to one of my addresses: ○ Reply from the same address the message was sent to ⦿ Always reply from my default address (currently scott@heavymetalmassage.com) (Note: You can change the address at the time of your reply. Learn more)	

FIGURE 7.4 The default is to send all messages as your "real" address.

In Figure 7.4 the choices under When I Receive a Message Sent to One of My Addresses are grayed out—if you have only one address listed in this section, you have no choice as to which address is used when you reply to emails.

If you want to change the default behavior—if, in other words, you want one of the following:

- The ability to receive emails sent to different addresses (scott@heavymetal-massage.com and heavymetalmassage@gmail.com) but then manually choose which address sends the reply (scott@heavymetalmassage.com *or* heavymetalmassage@gmail.com)

- The ability to receive emails sent to different addresses (scott@heavymetal-massage.com and heavymetalmassage@gmail.com) but have all replies automatically come from the same address (scott@heavymetalmassage.com)

- The ability to receive emails sent to several different addresses but have replies sent from the address to which the mail was sent (mail to heavymetal-massage@gmail.com is replied to by heavymetalmassage@gmail.com, and mail to scott@heavymetalmassage.com is replied to by scott@heavymetal-massage.com)

You make that change here in this section.

To start the process, click Add Another Email Address. Enter your name and the other email address on the following page (in my case, heavymetalmassage@gmail.com). If you want to use a custom Reply-To address, click Specify a Different Reply-To Address, enter the email address, and press Next Step. The next page informs you that Google needs to verify that you own the address you provided, which makes sense, so press Send Verification.

The next page tells you that an email has been sent to the address you provided to Google. You can either click the link in that email or enter the confirmation code on this page. I'm lazy, so I'd just click the link.

When I go back to the Accounts tab in Settings, I see what is shown in Figure 7.5.

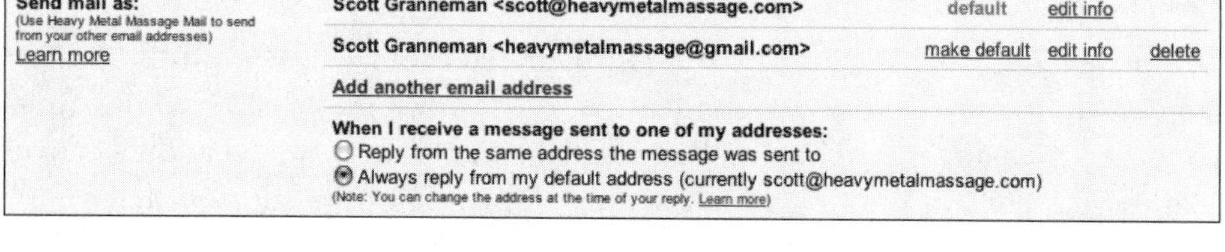

FIGURE 7.5   Bingo! Now I can send as either of two addresses, and I could add more.

In Figure 7.5, scott@heavymetalmassage.com has Default next to it, which means that any email to which I reply, no matter the original address to which it was sent, will by default say it's coming back from scott@heavymetalmassage.com. If I want to change that automatic behavior to a different address, it's a simple matter of clicking Make Default next to the address I want to elevate.

This still means that I can manually change the From when I'm composing a new email message or a reply, however. As you can see in Figure 7.6, Gmail provides a drop-down menu that allows you to select on-the-fly which address you want to send from.

FIGURE 7.6   You can change the From address on a per email basis. Flexibility is nice, isn't it?

Back in Figure 7.5, the choices under When I Receive a Message Sent to One of My Addresses are no longer grayed out; because I now have more than one address listed in this section, I have a choice as to which address is used when I reply to emails. By default, Always Reply from My Default Address (currently scott@heavymetalmassage.com) is chosen, which means that scott@heavymetal-massage.com will be automatically chosen for me. However, as I pointed out in the previous paragraph, you can always change this behavior when composing an individual email.

My other choice here is Reply from the Same Address the Message Was Sent To. If an email comes in to heavymetalmassage@gmail.com and I reply to it, that address will be used in the From (although I can change it manually if I desire); if an email comes in to scott@heavymetalmassage.com and I reply to it, that address is used instead in the From (although I can change it manually as well).

The choice really depends on how strongly you want to keep up the different addresses. In my case, I decided to just consolidate everything under scott@heavymetalmassage.com. When I reply, I want that to be the address anyone emailing me uses in the future. If you want to maintain the illusion that you are actively using several addresses, Gmail allows you to do that.

There's one gotcha with this whole feature, however, and there's not a lot you can do about it (in fact, it's a good thing). Even if you're sending an email as heavymetalmassage@gmail.com, and the From says that, buried in the email's headers (normally hidden from view but easily accessible with a command in virtually every email program out there today) is the real email address used to send the email message: scott@heavymetalmassage.com.

An example will make this clear. I'm logged in to Gmail as scott@heavymetal-massage.com, and I send an email to scott@granneman.com, but I tell Gmail to mark the From as heavymetalmassage@gmail.com. The email arrives, and the basic view of the headers, which is the default in Apple's Mail, looks like Figure 7.7.

> From: Scott Granneman <heavymetalmassage@gmail.com>
> Subject: **From says one thing, headers say another**
> Date: July 27, 2008 1:01:47 PM CDT
> To: Scott Granneman

FIGURE 7.7   The mail says it's from heavymetalmassage@gmail.com. No problem, right?

Then I go to View, Message, Long Headers (remember, every email program is different—this is just how Apple's Mail does it), and suddenly I see the mass of detail shown in Figure 7.8.

FIGURE 7.8   Look carefully, and you can see that scott@heavymetalmassage.com shows up!

Even though the From says heavymetalmassage@gmail.com, scott@ heavymetalmassage.com still shows up several times in the headers in Return-Path and Sender and even in Received-Spf and Authentication-Results.

Why is this? For spam prevention. Your email message is being honest with the various email servers it passes through, letting them know what's really going on, and because it is doing so, because it's not trying to hide anything or pull any funny business, it's allowed to move along without being marked as spam.

At least in most cases. Some organizations have misconfigured email servers that actually mark emails like this as spam. I read a complaint from one user at Ball State University who said that his school's email servers were throwing out emails in which the From and the Sender didn't match. The only thing to do then is complain to your email administrators and try to get the policy changed or put more robust spam filters in place.

The only other problem comes if someone using Outlook or Thunderbird receives your email (and there may be others that have this issue, but those are the two that I know engage in this behavior). Some versions of Outlook, for instance, may display "From heavymetalmassage@gmail.com on behalf of scott@heavymetalmassage.com." This can be a bit confusing, if the person reading the email even notices it in the first place.

So with these problems, should you ignore Send Mail As and avoid it? No. Go ahead and use it. Just be aware of the two issues I've raised in case you have to deal with them. But on the whole, it's a great feature that's a strong plus to using Gmail to manage your email.

Change Password

This one is obvious. But I wanted it to show up in the book's index so that people looking for it there would find the place they need to go to change their Gmail password (which actually changes the password they use throughout all of Google Apps, not just that used by Gmail).

LABELS

We're going to look further at labels in Chapter 8, "Things to Know About Using Google." In this chapter, I simply want to point out that this is the tab on which you manage your labels and then give you a little experienced advice about creating your labels.

To make a new label, enter it into the Create box and press Create. To rename a label, press Rename; to delete it, press Remove. To see all the email conversations using a label, click the label itself. Finally, notice that Gmail shows you how many conversations are using a particular label, as you can see in Figure 7.9.

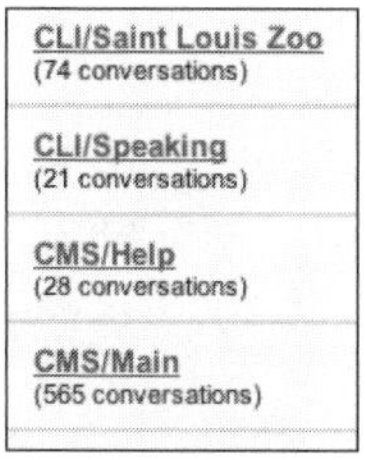

CLI/Saint Louis Zoo
(74 conversations)

CLI/Speaking
(21 conversations)

CMS/Help
(28 conversations)

CMS/Main
(565 conversations)

FIGURE 7.9 You can easily see how many conversations are attached to a particular label.

Now let's chat about what your actual labels should consist of. First, go back and reread "Molding Your Email Folder Structure into the one Used by Gmail" back in Chapter 3. Remember that your labels look like folders if you're accessing Gmail with a desktop client such as Outlook, Mail, or Thunderbird. If you create a label in Gmail using your web browser, it will look like a folder when you access your Gmail account with Outlook, and if you create a folder in Thunderbird, it will look like a label when you access your Gmail account using your web browser.

Although "normal" email accounts allow you to create and nest folders as many levels deep as you'd like in an email client—in other words, Fiona Inc. inside Missouri inside Clients inside Work—you can't do the same for Gmail labels. In fact, when you use Gmail, you're limited to two levels whether you access it via the Web or your desktop client.

> **⚠ WARNING**
>
> If you try to create folders that have more than two levels of labels, Gmail will quickly display weirdness that you don't want, so you're going to have to stick to two levels.

This means that in both the Gmail interface and your desktop email client you can create single-level labels like this:

- Clients
- Personal
- Work

That's simple enough. But what if I want to create labels that look like nested folders (at a max of two levels deep, remember!) in Mail, Outlook, Thunderbird, or any other email app? It's quite simple, really. I use Apple's Mail on my Mac to access Gmail through IMAP, and my folders look like what you see in Figure 7.10.

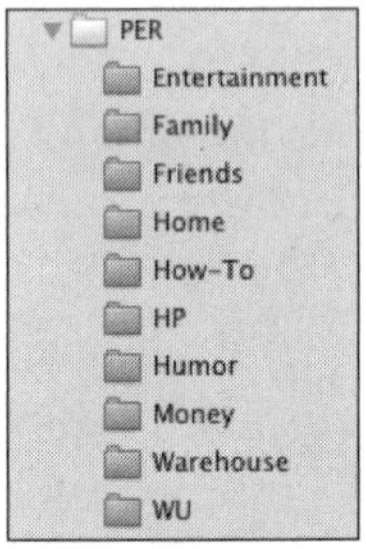

FIGURE 7.10   In Apple's Mail, PER is a top-level folder that contains ten subfolders.

However, Figure 7.11 shows what those same folders look like when they're viewed as labels in Gmail.

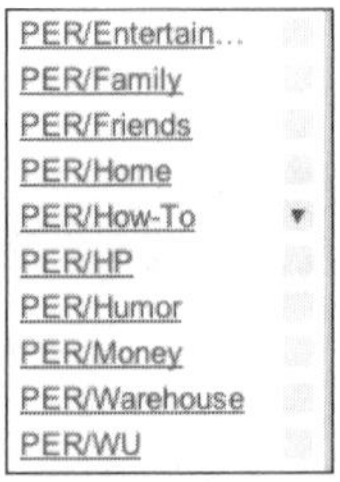

FIGURE 7.11   In Gmail, the subfolders don't appear nested inside a top-level folder.

And if I go to the Labels page in Settings, I see what you see in Figure 7.12.

PER/Entertainment (38 conversations)	rename	remove
PER/Family (209 conversations)	rename	remove
PER/Friends (55 conversations)	rename	remove
PER/Home (3 conversations)	rename	remove
PER/How-To (2 conversations)	rename	remove
PER/HP (129 conversations)	rename	remove

FIGURE 7.12   A simple list of labels.

You've probably figured it out by now: To create the illusion of nested folders in your desktop client, use a forward slash ("/") between the words that will become folders. In other words, at Gmail I see PER/Friends and PER/Home, but in Apple's Mail I see PER as a top-level folder containing subfolders named Friends and Home (and eight others as well).

TIP

If it bothers you that PER is repeated over and over in Gmail's labels, never fear—in Chapter 9 I show you a nifty Firefox extension that creates the illusion of nested folders at Gmail!

Because you get only two levels, that means that PER/Friends is fine, but PER/Friends/Gabe isn't. And don't create a label with a slash in it unless you intend to create a folder and a subfolder as well. In Outlook, Dogs/Cats might be a fine folder name, but if you try to use that as a label name in Gmail and then view the results in Outlook, you'll end up with a top-level folder Dogs, with a subfolder Cats.

NOTE

Again, I cannot emphasize enough that you go back and re-read "Molding Your Email Folder Structure into the One Used by Gmail" in Chapter 3 because it covers some issues you need to keep in mind when working with labels.

Closely tied to the folder/subfolder issue is another piece of advice: Don't go label crazy and overly segment your email where generalities would work better. Remember that Gmail is backed by the best-of-breed Google search engine, so plan to use Search to find emails you want to view, not by clicking around on folders and labels.

In other words, notice that I used PER/Friends, into which all emails from friends go. I didn't create Friends/Jans, Friends/Denise, Friends/Sarah, Friends/Fiona, and so on. That route would lead to a huge number of unnecessary labels. I used PER, as in "Personal," and then created the following labels:

- PER/Entertainment
- PER/Family
- PER/Friends
- PER/Home
- PER/How-To
- PER/HP
- PER/Humor
- PER/Money
- PER/Warehouse
- PER/WU

When I look at my email in Apple Mail, I see a top-level folder named PER, with ten subfolders. Additional top-level folders visible in Mail are CLI, CMS, LIST, WRI, and WS, and each of those has between "just a few" to "many" subfolders. By doing this, I get the benefits of nested folders and subfolders in my desktop email client and the benefits of intelligent labels in Gmail.

One final note about my label names, however: why did I use PER instead of Personal? The same practice informs my other choices. CLI is short for Clients, CMS for Content Management System, LIST for Email Listservs, WRI for Writing, and WS for WebSanity (my company). So why the abbreviations?

When I first started using Gmail, I used Personal, WebSanity, Clients, and so on. But it turns out that the labels column is a fixed width, and my labels were cut off, so that I saw Personal/Entert, Personal/Wareho, and Clients/Saint L. Not very helpful. By shortening the top level names, I get consistency, and I can easily read most of my labels when I'm logged in to Gmail.

Why the all-caps for the top level names? Consistency. That's it.

Filters

We're going to delve into filters in Chapter 8, "Things to Know About Using Gmail." In this chapter, I want to point out that this is the tab on which you manage your filters.

A filter is another word for what Outlook and other email programs call "rules"—the automated tasks your email program performs on your mail before you actually see it. Do you want all messages from coworkers to get labeled as "Work" or all messages with a subject of "Jones Project" to be forwarded to your boss? Filters are the answer.

To make a new filter, scroll to the bottom of this page and click Create a New Filter or click the Create a Filter link next to the search box at the top of every page. I'm going to cover the actual filter creation process in Chapter 8, so for now just understand that this is where you start.

To change a filter, press Edit; to delete it, press Delete.

Forwarding and POP/IMAP

You may very well want to move your mail out of Gmail's interface for a variety of reasons. Fortunately, Google makes that easy.

Forwarding

Unlike some other webmail services that charge to forward emails, Gmail makes it easy and free. If you want to forward your email, select Forward a Copy of Incoming Mail, enter the email address, and then indicate what you want Gmail to do with the mail it forwards:

- Keep a copy in your Inbox
- Keep a copy but archive it so it's not in your Inbox
- Delete it

Easy-peasy, as my British cousin Joe says.

POP Download

Unlike some other webmail services that charge to download your email messages (Yahoo, I'm glaring at you), Gmail makes it easy and free. If you want to enable POP access, you have to make a decision about which messages you want:

- **Enable POP for all mail**—This will download all mail that's currently in Gmail and any future messages.
- **Enable POP for mail that arrives from now on**—Current mail in Gmail will stay there, but any mail that arrives in the future will be downloaded by your POP client.

After that, you have to indicate what you want Gmail to do with the mail that you grab with your POP client:

- Keep a copy in your Inbox
- Keep a copy but archive it so it's not in your Inbox
- Delete it

Google provides instructions for accessing your email via POP in a variety of POP clients. We will look at some of those clients in Chapter 9, "Integrating Gmail with Other Software and Services," but if you want to see Google's directions, just click Configuration Instructions.

IMAP Access

IMAP is a far better option than POP for a number of reasons. If you want to enable IMAP, do it here by selecting Enable IMAP.

NOTE

Don't know what the difference is between POP and IMAP and why IMAP is better? Google explains it all for you at http://mail.google.com/support/bin/answer.py?hl=en&answer=75725, or you can read a white paper titled "Message Access Paradigms and Protocols" and available at http://www.imap.org/imap.vs.pop.html. It was written more than a decade ago, but it's still accurate.

Google provides instructions for accessing your email via IMAP in a variety of IMAP clients. We will look at some of those clients in Chapter 9, "Integrating Gmail with Other Software and Services," but if you want to see Google's directions, just click Configuration Instructions.

Chat

As you'll learn in Part VI, "Google Talk," Google has several chat programs. This section, however, sticks to the chat integrated into Gmail (no surprise because these settings are found in Gmail).

TIP

How do you block people? It's not here! Instead, you have to go into your Google Contacts, choose the person you want to block, and then select Block next to Show In Chat List. To unblock someone, change Show In Chat List to Always or Auto.

Chat History

As you chat with people in Gmail, the program by default saves your conversations in Chats, accessible with the other default links along the top-left side of the Gmail window, as you can see in Figure 7.13.

FIGURE 7.13   Chats is another built-in link that you can't change.

You have two possible settings in Chat History (because I'm logged in to my Heavy Metal Massage account, I see it mentioned; you would see your organization's name instead):

- Save Chat History in My Heavy Metal Massage Mail Account
- Don't Save Chat History in My Heavy Metal Massage Mail Account

If you save your chats, you can access your conversations later and even search for words in them; if you don't save your chats, you lose those capabilities.

> **TIP**
>
> If you don't save chats, however, that still doesn't stop another Gmail user from saving your chats in Gmail. If you say no, but I say yes, and we chat, then I keep a copy even if you don't.

However, this could really concern you. If you want to make sure that a conversation isn't saved by either you or the person with whom you're chatting, you need to go "off the record." If you go off the record, Google doesn't store the chat anywhere. It is lost forever with that person unless you go back on the record with them.

To stop recording chats, click the down arrow at the top right of your chat window and select Go Off the Record. To go back on the record, click Cancel at the top of your chat window or choose Stop Chatting Off the Record in your chat window's Options menu.

Realize, however, that if you're chatting with someone who's not using Gmail—an AIM user, for instance—choosing Off the Record will not stop them from recording your chat.

Just to make things confusing for you, your choice here to save or not save chats also affects how the Windows client for Google Talk behaves, and if you make a change in Google Talk, it will affect how Gmail chats work. So remember that you can't engage in one behavior one place and in a different one elsewhere.

Chat List Location

It's a simple choice: Show the chat box above or below your Labels. By default, Gmail has this set to Above. If you use chat a lot, or even some of the time, this could make sense; if you never or rarely use chat, change this to Below.

Auto-Add Suggested Contacts

You have a choice between two options here:

- Automatically Allow People I Communicate with Often to Chat with Me and See When I'm Online
- Only Allow People That I've Explicitly Approved to Chat with Me and See When I'm Online

By default, Google has the first option chosen, which means that if you email someone "frequently"—and the meaning of "frequently" is left up to Google, not you—Google automatically adds them to your chat list. This also means that you will be able to see when they are available, and they will be able to see the same about you.

Does that bother you? It sure bothers a lot of folks. If you're among them, choose the second option now.

AIM

Gmail chat allows you to sign in to the AOL Instant Messenger (AIM) network if you have an account so that you can chat with all your AIM buddies from within Gmail. To get started, click Sign Into AIM, enter your AIM screen name and password, and press Sign In. If you don't have an AIM account, you can sign up for one as well.

> **NOTE**
>
> To find out more about Gmail and AIM, read Google's help page at http://mail.google.com/support/bin/answer.py?hl=en&ctx=mail&answer= 61024. Ignore the sentence at the bottom of the page that says you can't use AIM if you use Google Apps.

WEB CLIPS

You have one check box on this tab: Show My Web Clips Above the Inbox. By default, it's checked.

So what's a Web Clip? It's just the output of RSS or Atom feeds, which appears randomly at the top of your Inbox. A sample is shown in Figure 7.14.

Engadget - Fujitsu's Lifebook U2010 gets new pics, specs - 15 hours ago   Web Clip < >
(Archive) (Report Spam) (Delete) (More Actions ▼) Refresh   **1 - 100** of **267** Older › Oldest »
Select: All, None, Read, Unread, Starred, Unstarred

FIGURE 7.14 It's easy to use Gmail every day and never even notice the Web Clips.

You can go back and forward through the Web Clips by clicking the < and > on the right side of the area in which they appear.

Web Clips are so innocuous that I know many people who have used Gmail for years and never even noticed they were there. Sounds like a good enough reason to turn it off to me. That, and the fact that the Web Clip area is taking up a few pixels of vertical screen real estate.

If you do want to keep Web Clips on, notice that by default, Google provides more than 20 preselected Web Clips, all listed on this settings page. Don't like one? Click Remove next to it. Want to add one? Browse or search for clips on the left side of this settings page and click Add when you find something you like. If you want to add something that's not in Google's index, enter the URL to a specific RSS or Atom feed in the Search box and press Search.

In fact, an administrator might want to remove every Web Clip except those provided through his organization's RSS feeds, like a tip of the day, for example. That could be handy—if his users ever notice them.

Labs

Think about Labs from Google's perspective: You have a lot of smart programmers who have some neat ideas for quirky, interesting features for Gmail. Some of these features are great, some are good, and some are wacky. How can Google make them available to Gmail users in a controlled way so that people interested in trying out something new can, while your more conservative users can stick to the tried and true Gmail they love? The answer: the Labs tab in Settings.

 NOTE

Your administrator must enable Labs by logging in to your Google Apps control panel, going to the Domain Settings tab, and checking Turn On New Features. I discussed this process in "Domain Settings" in Chapter 6.

Head over to Labs and you'll see 16 features you can enable for Gmail (by the time you read this, there may be more than 16, or there may be fewer if one or two have been retired). Turn on the ones that interest you and give them a whirl. If you like it, cool. If you don't, turn it off again and try another.

Over time, Google may make a feature that proves popular in Labs into an official feature in Gmail. Conversely, a feature that no one uses in Labs may get voted off the island. If you want to talk to the developers who came up a particular feature, and other users as well, you can press the Send Feedback link next to the feature and go to a Google Group where you can praise, complain, and discuss.

TIP

If you have a great idea for a feature that should appear in Labs, surf over to http://groups.google.com/group/gmail-labs-suggest-a-labs-feature/topics and write a post.

I'm not going to go through all 13 features in Labs, but I would like to focus on a few of the more interesting or useful things you'll find there.

WARNING

Google warns users that Labs features may break or otherwise cause issues with Gmail. Granted, I haven't had that happen to me, nor have I read any complaints about problems due to Labs, but it could happen. You can turn a new feature in Labs off as easily as you turned it on by choosing Disable instead of Enable. If you want to temporarily disable Labs entirely due to a hiccup, have your domain admin go to the Domain Settings tab in your Google Apps control panel and uncheck Turn On New Features.

Quick Links

I like to view all my unread messages in Gmail so I can quickly dispense with things that have just arrived in my account. Unfortunately, Gmail doesn't provide any links or buttons that I can click to view only unread items. Sure, I can search for `is:unread`, but I get tired of having to type that all the time. Quick Links to the rescue!

After you enable Quick Links, you'll see a small box to the bottom of the left side of your Gmail interface. It's empty except for a link that says Add Quick Link.

After you perform a search in Gmail, if you click Add Quick Link, you're prompted to enter a name defining that search. Press OK, and that name shows up in the Quick Links box. In Figure 7.15, you can see two Quick Links I've created for my own usage:

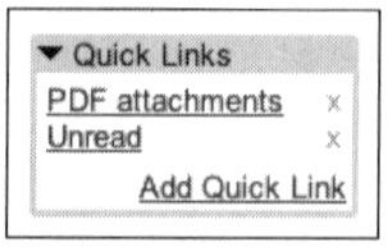

FIGURE 7.15 Quick Links is a great time-saver for searches you perform often.

You can add as many Quick Links as you want. To delete one, click the little X to the right of the Quick Link you no longer want.

Basically, if you can generate a URL to an item in Gmail, you can create a Quick Link to it. That expands its use way beyond searches, to encompass labels and even individual messages.

We'll learn a lot more about searching Gmail in Chapter 8, "Things to Know About Using Gmail," but for now, here are a few searches for which you might like to create Quick Links:

- `is:unread`
  Finds all unread messages everywhere in Gmail.

- `is:unread in:inbox`
  Finds all unread messages in your Inbox.

- `filename:PDF`
  Finds all messages with PDF attachments

- `http://www.youtube.com/watch?v=*`
  Finds all messages with links to YouTube videos.

- `filename:{mov wmv wm mp4}`
  Finds all messages with movie attachments—perfect for clearing up space!

- `filename:{mp3 wav m4a wma}`
  Finds all messages with music attachments—more space cleaned out!

I have only one request for Quick Links: Let me move it just below the Contacts link and above Labels, so it's even easier for me to access it. Other than that, this is an essential feature.

> **NOTE**
>
> Update! As this book was going to press, Google came out with three new items in Labs. One of them, Navbar Drag and Drop, allows you to move and arrange Labels, Chat, and Quick Links into any order you want! Yay!

Superstars

The gold star has been with Gmail since the beginning, and it's tremendously useful. With the Superstars feature, you can go way beyond that simple gold star. After you enable this feature, go to the General Settings tab in Gmail to see 11 new images you can use, which you can view in Figure 7.16.

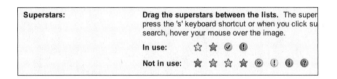

FIGURE 7.16   Stars, checks, punctuation marks, and in variety of colors to boot!

To add a star (I'll call them stars, even though they're not all in that shape) to the In Use category, just drag it from Not In Use. To remove a star, drag it from In Use to Not In Use.

Now that you have your list of stars you want to use, you can view them in your emails. Normally you enable a gold star by clicking the blank star or by pressing "s" on your keyboard (assuming you have keyboard shortcuts turned on). Now you rotate between the stars you've selected by clicking repeatedly on the blank star or by pressing "s" repeatedly. When you find the one you want, stop clicking or pressing. If you pause a second and then click or press again, you will turn the star off and go back to the blank star. This gives you the new stars and the original capability to toggle stars on and off.

You can search for stars using the following list (if the "l:^ss_sy" and so on looks weird, just wait until Chapter 8, and it will become clearer). You can find out the name of a star by hovering over it on the General tab in Settings.

- has:blue-star (or l:^ss_sb)
- has:red-star (or l:^ss_sr)
- has:orange-star (or l:^ss_so)

- has:green-star (or l:^ss_sg)
- has:purple-star (or l:^ss_sp)
- has:red-bang (or l:^ss_cr)
- has:yellow-bang (or l:^ss_cy)
- has:blue-info (or l:^ss_cb)
- has:orange-guillemet (or l:^ss_co)
- has:green-check (or l:^ss_cg)
- has:purple-question (or l:^ss_cp)

You might have noticed that the yellow star isn't in the list. If you search for has:yellow-star, nothing comes up. If you search for is:starred, all the stars show up in the results. At this time, you'd have to create a search like this (the "-" means "don't include this"):

```
is:starred -has:yellow-bang -has:green-check -has:purple-question
```

Of course, for the -has, use only the stars you've enabled.

This is tedious, but if you combine it with the Quick Links feature I just discussed, it becomes a bit easier to find the classic yellow star, or any other star for that matter.

Fixed Width Font

If you enable this feature in Labs, a new entry will appear in the Reply menu that shows up when you're reading an email message: Show in Fixed Width Font. In Figure 7.17 you can see what that menu looks like before and after you enable this feature:

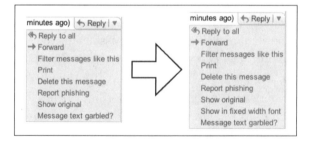

FIGURE 7.17 Before enabling the Fixed Width Font feature and after.

If you receive an email that contains a table, for instance, and you want it to display correctly, use this feature.

Custom Keyboard Shortcuts

Enable this feature, and a new tab appears in Gmail's settings: Keyboard Shortcuts. By default, Google includes a large number of keyboard shortcuts that you can use to make yourself faster and more productive (we'll learn more about those in Chapter 8). If you don't like one, or you're used to a shortcut from another program and want to use that instead of Google's default, use this page to make your changes.

Mouse Gestures

If you're a mouse-centric kind of person, you'll love this. Enable it, and you get three new ways to move your mouse and control Gmail:

- **Right-click and drag your mouse up**—Go to your Inbox
- **Right-click and drag your mouse left**—Go to the previous conversation
- **Right-click and drag your mouse right**—Go to the next conversation

Google's note on this feature says that it "Works best on Windows," but you should be fine on a Mac or Linux box as long as you have a mouse with two or more buttons.

Signature Tweaks

This useful feature does two things:

- When you reply, your signature goes before the quoted text, not at the very end.
- It removes the "—" line that automatically appears before your signature.

One caveat: if you remove the two hyphens that precede your signature, you may cause problems with other email software that use those signature dashes as a way to automatically distinguish and then mark up or even remove the signature as needed. For more information, see http://en.wikipedia.org/wiki/Signature_block.

Keep in mind that you can't use this feature and the Random Signature feature, discussed next, at the same time.

Random Signature

If you like to put quotations or other random information into your signatures, enable this feature. After you do, go to the General tab of Gmail's Settings, scroll down to the Signature section, and you'll see a new check box: Use Random Signature from Feed. You'll need to select the option button next to the sig box *and* check the box next to Use Random Signature for this new feature to work.

For your random quote to work, place a blank line at the end of the sig box, as you can see in Figure 7.18.

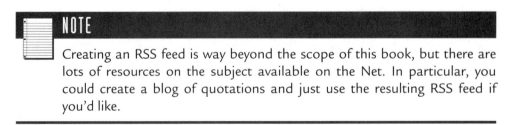

FIGURE 7.18   The cursor is flashing where you should have a blank line.

By default, Random Signature uses an RSS feed from BrainyQuote.com, resulting in a new email with a signature like Figure 7.19:

> Hi Mom!
>
> --
> Scott Granneman
> scott@granneman.com
>
> Pablo Picasso - "Computers are useless. They can only give you answers."

FIGURE 7.19   Boy, my Mom agrees with the first half of that quotation.

If you don't want to use BrainyQuote.com, feel free to insert your own link to an RSS feed.

> **NOTE**
>
> Creating an RSS feed is way beyond the scope of this book, but there are lots of resources on the subject available on the Net. In particular, you could create a blog of quotations and just use the resulting RSS feed if you'd like.

Keep in mind that you can't use this feature and the Signature Tweaks feature, discussed previously, at the same time.

Custom Date Formats

If you want a little more control over Gmail's display of dates and times, enable this feature. Afterward, go to the General tab of your Gmail Settings, and you'll see two new sections, shown in Figure 7.20.

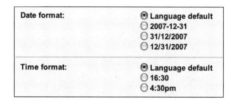

FIGURE 7.20 Change the date and time display with a couple of different options.

You can't come up with your own formats—maybe that will appear down the road—but you can select from a few reasonable options.

CONCLUSION

After reading this chapter, you should have a good understanding of Gmail's various settings and how you can tailor them to your liking. Take some time and explore the options. Test them out and see what works for you. And if you can, definitely play in Gmail Labs—you may find something there that is the perfect fix to an annoyance you're facing.

CHAPTER 8

Things to Know About Using Gmail

Gmail is fantastic, maybe the best aspect of Google Apps. On the one hand, I've found that it's remarkably easy to use, so much so that almost anyone can just sit in front of it and start using it. On the other hand, some aspects of it could use some elucidation, and that's what I intend to provide in this chapter.

Keep in mind that in this chapter, I'm focusing entirely on using Gmail in a web browser. In the next chapter, I look at accessing Gmail using a desktop email client such as Outlook, Apple Mail, or Thunderbird. With that in mind, let's look at five things you absolutely need to know about Gmail to use it more effectively.

SEARCHING FOR THE EXACT MESSAGE YOU NEED

Gmail is a product of Google, after all, so it's no shocker that it has excellent search capabilities. Unfortunately, many Google Search users just type a word or two into the search box and get good results, when they could get great results if they knew some advanced search operators. A similar situation exists with Gmail—most users simply search for a word or two, and they probably get good results, but if they learned a few advanced search operators, they could get great results.

So what's a search operator? Basically, it's just a word or symbol that modifies your search queries. There are oodles of search operators. Some of them are in your email headers, as shown in Table 8.1.

TIP

Here are two ways in which Google Search and Gmail's search are different. If you search Google and misspell a word, Google will suggest a correct spelling; Gmail, however, does not do so. Additionally, if you search Google for a word, Google will find that word and related plurals (searching for "dog" also brings up results with "dogs," for instance); again, Gmail does not do so.

TABLE 8.1 Search Operators for Email Headers

SEARCH OPERATOR	MEANING	EXAMPLES
to:	Messages sent to you or someone else	to:me to:Jans Carton to:jans@websanity.com
cc:	Messages CC'd to you or someone else	cc:me cc:Jans Carton cc:jans@websanity.com
bcc:	Messages you sent via BCC to someone else (not those BCC'd to you)	bcc:jans@websanity.com
subject:	Words in the Subject	subject:Project A subject:"Chapter 8"
from:	Messages sent to you by someone else	from:Jans Carton from:jans@websanity.com

Other search operators are based on searching for attachments or even the types of files that make up the attachments. Table 8.2 shows some of those search operators.

Other filenames you can search for include (this is by no means an exhaustive list):

- **Movies**—avi, mov, mp4, mpg, wmv
- **Sound**—wav, wmv
- **Images**—bmp, gif, jpg, png, tiff
- **Documents**—csv, odt, ppt, rtf, txt, xls

TABLE 8.2   Search Operators for Attachments

SEARCH OPERATOR	MEANING
has:attachment	Messages that have attachments
filename:pdf	Messages with PDF attachments
filename:doc	Messages with Word attachments
filename:mp3	Messages with MP3 attachments

Google relies heavily on labels (which we look at in the next section), and you can use search operators that target specific labels, as demonstrated in Table 8.3.

TABLE 8.3   Search Operators for Labels

SEARCH OPERATOR	SHORTCUT	SHORTERCUT	SHORTESTCUT	MEANING
label:inbox	in:inbox is:inbox	l:inbox	l:^i	Messages in the Inbox
label:starred	in:starred is:starred	l:starred	l:^t	Starred messages
label:chats	in:chat is:chat	l:chats	l:^b	Archived chats
label:sent	in:sent is:sent	l:sent	l:^f	Sent messages
label:drafts	in:drafts is:drafts	l:drafts	l:^r	Draft messages
label:spam	in:spam is:spam	l:spam	l:^s	Junk messages
label:trash	in:trash is:trash	l:trash	l:^k	Messages in the Trash
label:unread	in:unread is:unread	l:unread	l:^u	Unread messages
label:read	in:read is:read	l:read		Read messages
label:anywhere	in:anywhere is:anywhere	l:anywhere		Anywhere in Gmail, including Spam and Trash (which are normally ignored)

You can also search by time, as you can see in Table 8.4. However, dates must always be expressed in yyyy/mm/dd format.

TABLE 8.4 Search Operators for Time

SEARCH OPERATOR	MEANING	EXAMPLES
after:	After, but not including, the specified date	after:2008/12/17
before:	Before, but not including, the specified date	before:2008/12/17

Things get really interesting, however, when you learn to construct more complex queries. Let's start with Boolean search terms and the various symbols you can use to build powerful queries, as displayed in Table 8.5.

TABLE 8.5 Boolean Search Terms and Symbols You Can Use to Devise Complex Queries

SEARCH OPERATOR	SYMBOL EQUIVALENT	EXAMPLES	NOTES
AND	[space]	Jans AND Carton Jans Carton	Word must be in all caps; AND is the default because spaces are its symbol.
OR	|	Jans OR Carton Jans | Carton	Word must be in all caps.
NOT	–	Jans NOT Carton Jans–Carton	Word must be in all caps; no space after the hyphen.
	" "	"Gmail address book" subject: "Saint Louis Zoo"	Search for exact phrase; capitalization ignored.
	()	subject:(Zoo PRSA) from:(Jans | Jerry)	Groups different terms together.
	{}	{from:jerry from:jans}	Group ORs together.

Now that you know all the information contained in the previous tables, let's combine the various operators in Table 8.6 for some complex queries.

TABLE 8.6 Some Complex Queries and Their Meanings

Search Query	Meaning
`to:me l:^u in:inbox` OR to:me l:(unread inbox)	Messages in the Inbox to me that are unread.
from:jans subject:(zoo | prsa)	Messages from Jans with a subject of zoo or prsa.
l:unread from:jans after:2008/06/10	Unread messages from Jans sent after 6/10/2008.
from:jans filename:pdf -subject:zoo	Messages from Jans with PDF attachments that do not have zoo in the subject.
in:chat from:jans flickr	Chats with Jans in which Flickr is discussed.
l:^k from:jans before:2008/06/10 subject:zoo	Messages from Jans sent before 6/10/2008 with zoo in the subject, but now in the trash.
subject:zoo in:anywhere	A message with zoo in the subject that could be anywhere, including Trash and Spam.
filename:{mov wmv pdf tiff} before:2006/01/01	Look for any old messages with any of several kinds of large attachments, so I can delete them to free up space.
`-label:inbox` OR -l:^i	Messages not in the Inbox.

Really, the best way to learn about searching Gmail is to practice and record the ones that work for you the best. If you use the Quick Links features from Gmail Labs (discussed in Chapter 7's "Quick Links" section), you can save those searches and easily return to them later.

In fact, if you often search for a particular label, you can use your browser's bookmarks to quickly return to it later. For instance, if I created a label named "Todo" and I wanted to quickly see all the messages to which I've given that label, I can just bookmark https://mail.google.com/a/heavymetalmassage.com/#label/todo (of course, change the domain name and label to fit your particular case).

LIVING WITH LABELS

I discussed labels in Chapter 7's "Labels" section, but I want to emphasize here just how important they are to Gmail. There are no folders in Gmail. None. Instead, Gmail uses labels to organize email, which are far better and more useful than folders. Why?

Suppose you receive an email from your coworker Bob about the Zoo project you're doing in cooperation with the Yog-Sothoth firm. You have four folders set up in your email program: Bob, Work, Zoo Project, Yog-Sothoth. Into which folder do you file the message? After you pick one, that's it—even though the email has to do with all four subjects, it can go into only one folder. If you want to find it in the future, you either have to remember which folder it's in, or click one at a time on each folder, or search. The first requires a superhuman memory if you get a ton of mail, the second is silly, and the third can be dog slow on desktop clients.

If you use Gmail, you can assign as many labels as you'd like to a message. In the example in the previous paragraph, you could assign Bob, Work, Zoo Project, and Yog-Sothoth to the message. If you wanted to find it later, you could click any of those four labels, or search—and searching Gmail is *fast*. If you learn the search operators I just covered in the previous section, it's even more efficient.

So learn to live with labels. They can be tremendously helpful. But, as I've discussed before (in Chapter 3's "Molding Your Email Folder Structure into the One Used by Gmail" section), don't go label crazy. With Gmail's powerful and fast search, you may find that the fewer labels you use, the better. Before adding a label, first ask yourself if you absolutely need it. And don't be afraid to remove labels down the road and consolidate. Instead of Work/PRSA, Work/Science Center, and Work/Zoo, just create a label titled Work and dump everything in there. After that, search becomes your friend. Try it—you may love it.

FILTERING MESSAGES EFFECTIVELY

Filters were discussed in Chapter 7's "Filters" section, where they were explained as the automated tasks that Gmail performs on your email before you ever see it. For instance, if you're sick of stupid joke emails from your Uncle Gussie, you could set up a filter that sends any email that is from Gussie and also has "joke" or "humor" in the subject to the Trash so you'll never even have to see it.

The "Filters" section of Chapter 7 focused on setting up filters. In this section, I'd like to talk about some uses for filters. To begin with, let's understand what aspects of an email are filterable. You can search for the following criteria and then use them to create your filters:

- **From**—Can be a full name (Jans Carton), part of a name (Jans), an email address (jans@websanity.com), part of an email address (websanity.com), or "me."

- **To**—Can be a full name (Jans Carton), part of a name (Jans), an email address (jans@websanity.com), part of an email address (websanity.com), or "me."

- **Subject**—You can search for an exact phrase by using quotation marks ("blogs to wikis").

- **Has the Words**—You can search for an exact phrase by using quotation marks ("blogs to wikis").

- **Doesn't Have**—You can search for an exact phrase by using quotation marks ("blogs to wikis").

- **Has Attachment**—A check box you can toggle.

To make sure your search criteria are correct, click Test Search, and review the results. If they're what you want, click Next Step. On the next screen you choose the actions you'd like to perform on messages that match your criteria. Those actions are the following, any of which you can check:

- **Skip the Inbox (Archive It)**—You won't see it in your Inbox; instead, it goes into All Mail. This is a good box to check along with others in this list.

- **Mark as Read**—If you check this along with Skip the Inbox, it's archived and won't stick out because it won't be bold or listed as unread.

- **Star It**—If it's important or needs action, star it!

- **Apply the Label**—Choose an existing label or create a new one. This action, when combined with Skip the Inbox, is equivalent to automatically filtering into folders with other email programs. A very common two-fer.

- **Forward It To**—Enter an email address to which you'd like the message to go; don't forget that you can create email lists so that you can enter one address that sends it to several people (covered in Chapter 6's "Email Addresses" section).

- **Delete It**—For the worst offenders.

- **Never Send It to Spam**—This makes sure that the important email from your significant other or boss never gets accidentally dumped into Spam by a mistake in Gmail's antispam technology.

After making your choices, click Create Filter to do just that. Next to that button is a check box labeled Also Apply Filter to # Conversations Below, where # is the number of conversations that match your filter's search criteria. Most of the time you're going to want to check that box because it will apply your filter's actions to email that has already arrived, thus making sure that your mail is nicely organized.

With the filter process in mind, here are a few of my favorite filters. What's shown in Table 8.7 is there to give you ideas, but you can search Google for others. And, of course, the best way to find a filter that works for you is to experiment.

TABLE 8.7   Some of My Favorite Gmail Filters

Filter Criteria	Filter Action	Meaning
From: me To: me	Apply the label: Me	Easy to find emails I've sent myself as reminders.
From: scott@websanity.com	Apply the Label: WebSanity	Emails I've sent from my work address.
Has the words: ("serial number" OR "product key" OR "activation code" OR "license key" OR regsoft	Skip the Inbox (Archive It) Apply the Label: Serial Numbers	Serial numbers for software I've bought (thanks to Micah Diamond, who wrote in to Lifehacker).
Has the words: (В OR И OR Ж OR И OR ל)	Skip the Inbox (Archive It) Delete It	I don't speak Russian or Hebrew, so this is spam (that в isn't a capital B, it's a Russian veh).
Has the words: filename:jpg {photo photos pic pics picture pictures attachment attached}	Apply the Label: Pictures	Finds messages with photo attachments (you can do the same kind of thing for movies, documents, and music).
to:(stlwebdev.org OR to:wwwac.org OR from:userland.com)	Skip the Inbox Apply the Label: LIST/WebDev	Note that you can combine to: and from: in your filter. from:(System Administrator)
subject:("log sizes" OR subject:"disk usage report")	Skip the Inbox Apply the Label: WS/Reports	Look for messages with a certain From and certain phrases in the Subject.

One final note about filters: after you've created one, you may want to add on to it later. For instance, suppose you create a filter that takes any mail from truthout.org, eff.org, or maal.org and labels it LIST/Politics. If you view your list of filters (by going to Settings, Filters, or by clicking Create a Filter and then Show Current Filters) you'll see that it looks like this:

```
Matches: from:(truthout.org OR from:eff.org)
Do this: Skip Inbox, Apply label "LIST/Politics"
```

If you want to add another from:—this one for moabolition.org—you would click Edit and change it to this:

```
Matches: from:(truthout.org OR from:eff.org OR from:moabolition.org)
Do this: Skip Inbox, Apply label "LIST/Politics"
```

And so on. These filters can get quite long—one of mine is 25 addresses and counting, and I've never had an issue. But what you may not know is that you can introduce other criteria that don't match the original set.

Suppose I want to find email sent to ydgsl@yahoogroups.com and also apply the LIST/Politics label to it. I could create a brand new filter for to: ydgsl@yahoogroups.com, but that's kind of silly because I already have a perfectly good filter in place that labels mail with LIST/Politics. Instead, I edit the already existing filter so that it now reads this way:

```
Matches: from:(truthout.org OR from:eff.org OR from:moabolition.org OR
to:ydgsl@yahoogroups.com)
Do this: Skip Inbox, Apply label "LIST/Politics"
```

Even though the Matches line starts with from:, and everything following is in parentheses, you can still put a to: inside the parentheses, and the filter will work just fine and dandy. In fact, you can sneak a from: or a subject: in there without an issue.

> ⚠ **WARNING**
>
> You must use OR between your filter criteria. Not "or" and not "Or." It must be OR. Google says.

SPEEDING THINGS UP WITH KEYBOARD SHORTCUTS

Gmail is eminently usable with a mouse, but if you learn the key commands that Google thoughtfully provides, you can use Gmail far faster and more efficiently.

> **TIP**
>
> Before you can use the advice in this section, you have to have turn on keyboard shortcuts in Gmail's Settings, a process I mentioned in Chapter 7's "Keyboard Shortcuts" section.

I'm not going to go through all the keyboard shortcuts that Gmail possesses because you can find the complete list at the Gmail Help Center, at http://mail.google.com/support/bin/answer.py?answer=6594. In addition, I highly recommend the printable cheat sheet that you can find at http://r.evhead.com/hodgepodge/gmail-shortcuts.html. It's good.

Table 8.8 lists some of the shortcuts that I use all time, so I recommend them wholeheartedly. In addition, check out the links I just gave you because you are sure to find others that are just as useful.

TABLE 8.8 Some of My Favorite Gmail Keyboard Shortcuts

KEYBOARD SHORTCUT	MEANING
Working with Messages	
c	Compose in current window
r	Reply (only works in conversation view)
a	Reply to all (only works in conversation view)
f	Forward (only works in conversation view)
r ESC a	Change from reply to reply to all (only works in conversation view)
Change a Message or Conversation's Status	
x	Selects current conversation so you can work with it
s	Star (or unstar) message or conversation
!	Report spam
#	Delete message; if in conversation view, deletes and returns to list view
]	Archive and move to next conversation
Moving Around Gmail's Interface	
k	Move to newer conversation (works in list or conversation view)
j	Move to older conversation (works in list or conversation view)
u	Return to list view from conversation view
o OR Enter	Return to conversation view from list view
/	Place your cursor in the search box

Keyboard Shortcut	Meaning
g c	Go to Contacts
g i	Go to Inbox
.	Open More Actions drop-down menu

Remember, these are just a few of the many keyboard shortcuts that you can use. Check out the links I provided at the beginning of this section for more. One final thought: it's not vital that you learn all the shortcuts, as there probably isn't a person alive who has them all memorized. Instead, learn the ones that will be of most use to you.

Securing Your Email

Email is one of the primary ways bad guys get into Windows boxes, which are still the majority of desktop computers out there. Fortunately, Google has placed several smart protections into Gmail in an effort to minimize the security risks of its email.

Checking for Viruses

Google has virus checking built in to Gmail, which is a very good thing (it's not so much necessary for Linux or Mac OS X boxes, but it's really nice for the Windows users). Attachments you send and receive are scanned for malware every time you open the message containing the attachment.

If Google finds a virus in a message sent to you, it will try to clean the file so that you can still use it, but if the file can't be cleaned, it's off limits to you. Again, a good thing. If Google has a problem scanning the file, for whatever reason, it will notify you with a small alert. At that point, you can wait or go ahead and download the file at your own risk. That's not a good idea, in my opinion, unless you know you have really good antivirus protection on your PC.

If Google finds a virus in a message you're trying to send, it displays an alert to you, but it won't clean the file. That's up to you. Google does give you an option to Remove Attachment and Send, but that may not be what you want because the attachment may be vitally important to the message. Hopefully, though, a virus-laden attachment isn't vitally important to the message.

Even with the virus scanning, however, Google doesn't allow certain file types to be sent or received at all, including (but not limited to):

- .exe
- .dll
- .ocx
- .com
- .bat

NOTE

If you don't know what those file types are, check out Wikipedia for each of the filename extensions or go to a massive list at http://en.wikipedia.org/wiki/List_of_file_formats_(alphabetical) or check out the enormous database at http://filext.com.

If you try, you'll see the following error message: "This is an executable file. For security reasons, Gmail does not allow you to send this type of file."

You might think that you can just zip up the attachment and sneak it past Google that way, but that won't work. Google scans the compressed file, figures out that it contains a verboten file type, and puts up a stop sign. Other compression formats, such as TAR, TGZ, Z, and GZ, don't work either. For some weird reason, though, RAR is allowed.

Industrious Gmail users have figured out a few ways to get around the restriction against sending executable files, however. I'm not saying that you should do any of these, although some are a lot safer than others, but here are a few ideas:

- Rename the file extension from .exe to .123, or from .bat to .bat.removeme. Of course, tell your recipients in your email message that they need to change the extension.

- Zip the file, then zip the Zip file, and password-protect the container ZIP file.

- Use compression software that creates RAR files. Google is your friend.

- Perhaps the easiest solution is using something like YouSendIt (www.yousendit.com), Box.net (www.box.net), or any of the others listed at http://en.wikipedia.org/wiki/One-click_hosting. If you don't know about them, check them out—you'll find them quite useful, and they complement Gmail well.

Stopping Image Spam

Gmail does an excellent job detecting spam, but a few can get through. One of the most annoying types of spam is image spam, in which a spammer has nothing but a picture in the body of the email. By using an image, spammers hope that it will be harder for Gmail's antispam tools to detect their come-ons. Here's a good way to make sure none of that junk gets into your Inbox.

Create a filter with these criteria:

- Has the Words: type "multipart/related.gif"
- Check the box next to Has Attachment

For the filter's actions, use these:

- Skip the Inbox (Archive It)
- Apply the Label: Image Spam

You may get false positives, which is why you're applying a label to the message. Check the messages in that label every once in a while to make sure there's nothing in there that you want and also to delete junk in there permanently.

Another way to help make spam more obvious when you look at the list of conversations in the Image Spam label is to use the Personal Level Indicators. To turn them on, in Gmail, go to Settings, General, Personal Level Indicators, and select Show Indicators. After you do so, a single right-pointing angle quotation mark (›) appears in front of messages in which your email address is in the To or CC field, and a right-pointing double angle quotation mark (») appears in front of messages sent only to you.

If you see a message that has a › or » in front of it, it's less likely that it's spam and more likely that's it's legit, but if you see a message without either symbol in front of it, it's more likely that it's spam and less likely that it's legit.

Finding Out Who's Accessing Your Gmail Account

If you think someone may have hacked into your Gmail account, you now have a way to tell, thanks to a feature recently added by Google. Scroll to the bottom of the main page, and you'll see text that says something like this:

```
This account is open in 1 other location at this IP (76.211.85.91). Last
account activity: 1 minute ago.
```

This lets you know if another computer is accessing your Gmail account. In my case, it's perfectly okay that my account is open in two locations at my IP address because I'm looking at Gmail in two browsers (I'm writing a book on the subject, after all!).

If you want to know more, click the Details link. On that page, you'll see all recent activity, including the type of access (browser, POP, IMAP, or SMTP), the IP address of the accessing device, and the time of access. If one of the items listed freaks you out, click the Sign Out All Other Sessions button to do just that. In a flash, you're the only one accessing your account.

And then, immediately change your password. As in right now!

Preventing Phishing

Google is now checking any email that says it comes from paypal.com or ebay.com using a technology known as DomainKeys. If the email doesn't come from either of those two domains, it's rejected silently, behind the scenes, and you'll never even know a scammer was trying to trick you. That's fantastic and a great way to protect users.

NOTE

Don't know anything about DomainKeys? Hie thee to Wikipedia, at http://en.wikipedia.org/wiki/DomainKeys.

Limiting How Many Emails You Can Send

To prevent spam and abuse, Google limits how many emails you can send a day. If you go over that limit, your account is temporarily suspended from sending mail.

If you're using the Standard Edition of Google Apps, you can send email to up to 500 addresses outside your domain each day. If you use the Premier or Education Editions of Google Apps, you can send mail to up to 2,000 addresses outside your domain each day. These email addresses can be anywhere in To, CC, and BCC fields.

What if you're an administrator? How do you send email to all your users if the total number of users is greater than the number of addresses to which you're allowed to send mail? Google suggests that you create multiple accounts, such as Admin1 and Admin2. If you do that, each account can send 500 messages, for a total of 1,000 if you're using the Standard Edition; the number is larger if you're using the Premier or Education Edition.

SOLVING COMMON PROBLEMS

As with all things in life, you're going to find little gotchas. Here are a few of those and their solutions.

What the Heck Is a "Lockdown in Sector 4?"

If you have the misfortune to find that you can't access Gmail any longer, and now you get a web page that says there's been a "Lockdown in sector 4!" you were probably doing something that triggered alarms at Gmail. For instance, you may have been doing one of the following:

- Using a third-party program to access Gmail that didn't behave. In particular, software that turns Gmail into a file storage system can cause problems, as well as programs that repeatedly log in to Gmail.

- A huge amount of POP-based email activity (grabbing or deleting) in a short period of time.

- Sending lots of bounced, invalid email messages (often a sign of a spammer).

- Continuous failed attempts to access your Gmail account.

No matter what the cause, you have three choices:

- Wait a while. Usually within 24 hours your access is restored. During this time you can still grab your email via IMAP or POP with a desktop client (for more on that, check out the next chapter, which is all about that subject).

- Try to figure out what you were doing that may have caused the problem and disable or uninstall that program or activity.

- Follow the provided link to fill out a form and request that Google take a look at your problem.

Receiving a lockdown in sector 4 can be tremendously irritating. I should know because I've received one myself. But be patient, give it time, figure out what may have been causing it, and all should be restored soon enough.

How Do I Troubleshoot Gmail Problems?

If you're having trouble accessing Gmail at all—the page is blank, or it never finishes loading, for instance—first check your network connection. Make sure everything is working correctly when it comes to the Net.

If that all looks fine, then try the following, in no particular order:

- Clear your web browser's cache and cookies (you'd be surprised how often that fixes things).

- Open Gmail in its Basic HTML (in other words, nonfancy) view at http://mail.google.com/mail/h/. After that loads, try switching to the Standard View.

- Open Gmail in Mobile View at http://m.gmail.com.

- If Google says that it doesn't like your web browser, but there's no reason it shouldn't, you can always bypass the check that Gmail does to make sure your browser will work. Go to http://mail.google.com/gmail?nocheckbrowser and see if that displays.

- Finally, check out Gmail Known Issues at https://mail.google.com/support/bin/static.py?page=known_issues.cs&hl=en&topic=12878, which contains problems and solutions in the following categories: Logging In, Chat and Contacts, Composing and Reading Mail, and POP and IMAP.

CONCLUSION

In this chapter, I looked at five things you should know about if you're using the web-based version of Gmail: search, labels, filters, keyboard shortcuts, and security. The more you can learn about each, the more effectively you'll be able to use Gmail. In the next chapter, we examine how to integrate Gmail into desktop and mobile email programs. Some of the things we've learned in this chapter will apply, but there's a ton of new information, too. In the same way that Gmail is constantly improving and adding new and exciting features, there's always more to learn!

FURTHER READING

There's always more to learn, so here are some resources that you might find handy if you want to learn more about Gmail:

- Overviews and high points
  - Gmail overview: www.google.com/a/help/intl/en/users/gmail.html
  - 10 reasons to use Gmail: http://mail.google.com/mail/help/about.html

- Getting Started Guide:
  http://mail.google.com/support/bin/answer.py?answer=90877&topic=12925

- Email Quick Facts:
  www.google.com/support/a/bin/answer.py?answer=60761&topic=11543

- Google Apps for Admins

  - Help Topics: www.google.com/support/a/bin/topic.py?topic=9202

  - All Help topics on one page: http://mail.google.com/support/?fulldump=1

  - Email Switch Guide:
    http://google.com/support/a/bin/answer.py?answer=48237

- Google Apps for Users Help Topics:
  http://mail.google.com/support/?ctx=ausers&hl=en

- Interactive Video Guides

  - Gmail Welcome: http://services.google.com/apps/resources/overviews/welcome/topicWelcome/page05.html

  - Gmail tutorials: http://services.google.com/apps/resources/overviews/welcome/topicMail/index.html

- Gmail videos from the Google Apps YouTube Channel:
  www.youtube.com/view_play_list?p=8A0C9023238F7724

- Video product overviews and tours

  - Overview of Gmail in Google Apps:
    www.youtube.com/watch?v=9JJDugn4RoQ

  - User testimonials: http://mail.google.com/mail/help/yourstory.html

- PDFs for training support staff

  - Login: http://services.google.com/apps/training/user_support/Mail/MailUserSupportModule2LoginIssues.pdf

  - Reading and Sending: http://services.google.com/apps/training/user_support/Mail/MailUserSupportModule3ReadingAndSending.pdf

  - Delivery: http://services.google.com/apps/training/user_support/Mail/MailUserSupportModule4DeliveryIssues.pdf

  - POP: http://services.google.com/apps/training/user_support/Mail/MailUserSupportModule6POPIssues.pdf

- Discussion groups

  - Gmail Help Discussion Group: http://groups.google.com/group/Gmail-Help-Discussion

- Gmail-Users: http://groups.google.com/group/Gmail-Users
  - APIs: http://groups.google.com/group/google-apps-apis
- The Official Gmail Blog: http://gmailblog.blogspot.com
- News and Announcements: http://mail.google.com/mail/help/about_whatsnew.html
- Known Issues
  - http://mail.google.com/support/bin/static.py?page=known_issues.cs
  - Google Apps Frequently Reported Issues: www.google.com/support/a/bin/request.py?contact_type=known_issues
- Support options: http://mail.google.com/support/bin/request.py?contact_type=contact_policy

CHAPTER 9

Integrating Gmail with Other Software and Services

As great as Gmail is when used in a web browser, you don't have to access it that way. In fact, you can access Gmail in three ways: in a web browser, such as Firefox, Safari, or Internet Explorer; POP access via a desktop email client or device; and IMAP access via a desktop email client or device.

The previous chapter, "Five Things to Know About Using Gmail," looked at the essentials when using Gmail in a web browser. In this chapter I examine using Gmail via a desktop client or mobile device, but I focus almost entirely on IMAP, for a variety of reasons that I'll explain shortly. In addition, I look at software tools that allow you to extend and change the web interface for Gmail, taking it in new, exciting, and even more useful directions.

A NOTE ON ADDING SCRIPTS TO YOUR WEB BROWSER

At different points throughout this chapter, I refer to various userscripts that you can install in your web browser. Most of those grow out of Greasemonkey, an awesome Firefox extension that allows developers to write scripts that change websites in new and interesting ways. A short example will make this clearer.

Suppose that I visit two sites regularly, www.foo.com and www.bar.com, each with its own annoyances. The columns for text are too narrow at www.foo.com, and www.bar.com features lots of tables that would be far easier to read if they used zebra striping (one row white, one row dark, and so on). I install Greasemonkey in Firefox, and then I go to http://userscripts.org and search around. I find that someone has written a userscript that solves each site's annoyances, so I install those into Greasemonkey. Now when I visit foo.com, the columns for text are as wide as my browser, and when I go to bar.com, all the tables use zebra striping.

> **NOTE**
>
> To learn more about Greasemonkey and userscripts, read Wikipedia's article on the subject, at http://en.wikipedia.org/wiki/Greasemonkey.

Many of the techniques people use to fix problems with Gmail, extend its capabilities, or even change how it looks, rely on Greasemonkey, but you can use other similar technologies. Some work with Firefox, and some do not. Here's a partial list of tools that you may want to familiarize yourself with:

- **Greasemonkey (https://addons.mozilla.org/en-US/firefox/addon/748)**—One of the essential Firefox extensions. Find scripts at http://userscripts.org.

- **Stylish (https://addons.mozilla.org/en-US/firefox/addon/2108)**—Another essential Firefox extension, this one centered around CSS instead of JavaScript; for more, see http://en.wikipedia.org/wiki/Stylish.

- **IE7Pro add-on (http://www.ie7pro.com)**—An add-on for Internet Explorer that provides some functions similar to Greasemonkey; you can read more at http://en.wikipedia.org/wiki/IE7Pro, and the scripts are at www.iescripts.org.

- **GreaseKit (http://8-p.info/greasekit/)**—Greasemonkey for Safari and other Safari-based apps on Mac OS X.

- **Opera User JavaScript (www.opera.com/support/tutorials/userjs/)**—Opera contains built-in support for Greasemonkey-like scripts, some of which you can find at http://userjs.org.

- A much longer list of software similar to Greasemonkey can be found at http://en.wikipedia.org/wiki/Greasemonkey#Greasemonkey_compatibility_and_equivalents_for_other_browsers.

Keep in mind that many scripts that run on Greasemonkey will run with the other software listed previously, but in virtually all situations you will need to tweak the code, which requires at least some technical knowledge.

Understanding the Implications of POP and IMAP

There are two ways to access email with a client: POP and IMAP. In this section, I talk about the two methods, their advantages and disadvantages, and then drill down on the one that's ideal for Gmail.

IMAP Versus POP

When you access mail using POP, you move messages from the email server to your computer. When you access mail using IMAP, your mail stays on the server always, but you view it and work with it on your computer.

The big advantage of POP is that you can download your mail, disconnect from the Net, and then work with your mail offline. The big disadvantage is that if you use different computers and devices to access your mail, you will very rapidly end up out of sync because each machine downloads the email it sees, ensuring that the next machine can't see it and instead downloads the newest messages.

The advantages of IMAP are multiple:

- IMAP supports connected and disconnected modes, meaning that you can work with your email while you're connected to the Net, or you can disconnect and still work with your mail. When you reconnect, your changes are synced to your IMAP server. Your email client needs to support disconnected mode, however, and not all of them do.

- Your emails and filters are the same on every device and client used to connect to your mail. If you view your email via IMAP at work using Outlook, at home using Thunderbird, and on the go with an iPhone, you will see the same thing everywhere.

- Filters and sorting take place on the server before your desktop client ever accesses your mail, so it's faster and more centralized.

The disadvantages of IMAP are twofold: It requires your email provider to maintain lots of storage because your mail lives permanently on its servers, and it's more difficult for people who program email applications to implement. But those aren't your problems, and Google has taken care of those issues so you don't need to worry about them.

Google's advice and mine intersect here perfectly: In this day and age, POP is a relic that should be abandoned in favor of IMAP. Google wants you to use IMAP, and I do too. If you've never used it before, you're in for a treat; if you're an old hand at IMAP, you'll find that your knowledge should work just fine with Google's email system.

Using POP

I'm not going to focus on POP in this chapter very much because I believe strongly that IMAP is so much better. Google does, too, so it pushes IMAP instead of POP for client access to Gmail. Furthermore, virtually every major email client today supports IMAP (granted, some better than others). Finally, more people are accessing their mail on multiple devices—several computers, a mobile phone, and so on—and IMAP is the definite solution to that issue. In the battle of email protocols, IMAP is the future winner.

However, if you absolutely must use POP, Google provides explanations for configuring POP access for various desktop clients:

- **Apple Mail**—https://mail.google.com/support/bin/answer.py?answer=13275
- **Outlook 2002**—https://mail.google.com/support/bin/answer.py?answer=70770
- **Outlook 2003**—https://mail.google.com/support/bin/answer.py?answer=13278, with an animated demo at http://mail.google.com/mail/help/demos/Gmail_POP/788_Google_Gmail.html
- **Outlook 2007**—https://mail.google.com/support/bin/answer.py?answer=86373
- **Outlook Express**—https://mail.google.com/support/bin/answer.py?answer=13276
- **Thunderbird**—https://mail.google.com/support/bin/answer.py?answer=38343
- **Windows Mail**—https://mail.google.com/support/bin/answer.py?answer=86382
- **Other**—https://mail.google.com/support/bin/answer.py?answer=13287

  Google also explains how to access email via POP on mobile devices:
- **BlackBerry Internet Service**—https://mail.google.com/support/bin/answer.py?answer=14748
- **iPhone**—https://mail.google.com/support/bin/answer.py?answer=72454

If you do use POP to access the same email account from multiple locations, you really must make sure that you're using what Google calls "recent mode." This always grabs the last 30 days of mail, even if you've already accessed that mail from another client. It's kind of like a fake IMAP but without all the other benefits.

If you access Gmail via POP on your BlackBerry, you're automatically signed in using recent mode. Otherwise, you need to change the username you sign in from gabe@redheadeddoofus.com to recent:gabe@redheadeddoofus.com (of course, use your own name and domain, but keep the recent:).

Using IMAP

IMAP is what Google recommends, and I heartily second that. After using it for almost a decade, I'm convinced that it's the best way for most people to work with email, and as more people access mail on multiple computers and devices, IMAP crosses over from nice-to-have to essential. Still, Google's implementation of IMAP takes some getting used to, even for experienced IMAP users. In this section, I try to answer some common questions about Google's IMAP—questions that even experienced IMAP users might ask.

> ## NOTE
>
> In fact, some sticklers have major problems with Google's implementation of IMAP. Google itself lists IMAP features it doesn't support at https://mail.google.com/support/bin/answer.py?answer=78761&topic=12762. You can read complaints about IMAP as done by Google at Tim Alman's "Gmail's Buggy IMAP Implementation" (http://weblog.timaltman.com/archive/2008/02/24/gmails-buggy-imap-implementation) and *Wired's* "IMAP, YouMAP, WeMAP: Mail Protocol's Proponents Argue for Better Support" (www.wired.com/software/webservices/news/2007/10/imap).

What Are All These New Labels and Folders in My Desktop or Mobile Client?

After you set up a new Gmail account and then access it in a desktop or mobile client, you're going to see some folders you probably haven't seen in another email account. A new top-level folder named [Gmail] will be present, and it contains the following subfolders (which are actually labels, remember):

- **All Mail**—All your messages, including Inbox, Sent, and archived. If you move a message from All Mail to Trash, it is deleted for good when you empty the Trash.
- **Drafts**—Messages you started writing but then put off to work on later.
- **Sent Mail**—Messages you've sent.
- **Spam**—Gmail's junk mail holding space, with any message in here automatically deleted after 30 days.
- **Starred**—Equivalent to flagging an email as important in your desktop client.

- **Trash**—Messages you don't want anymore. Kind of. See the next section, "What Happens When I Delete a Message?"

The [Gmail] folder is a special top-level folder inserted by Google. You cannot delete it, nor can you delete any of the subfolders inside it.

> **NOTE**
>
> If you live in certain countries in Europe, you'll see [Google Mail] instead of [Gmail]. Blame court cases involving trademarks.

Issues arise when it comes to Google's advice in regard to these special folders and how you should map your desktop client's folders to Gmail's (even though they're actually labels, your desktop and mobile clients see them as folders, so that's what I'm going to call them here).

If you aren't sure what I mean by "map," understand that many desktop clients automatically create Sent and Trash and other folders when you create a new email account, and those folders will most likely be separate from Gmail's Sent and Trash folders. The end result: two Sent folders, two Trash folders, and so on. And when you delete a message, where does it go? The desktop client's Trash or Gmail's? When you save a draft, where is it? In your desktop client's Drafts folder or Gmail's? To get around that, many—but not all—desktop and mobile clients allow users to map their automatically created folders to the server's, which in this case would be Gmail's.

> **NOTE**
>
> I'll walk you through mapping your desktop client's folders and Gmail's later in this chapter, in "Accessing Gmail in a Desktop Email Program" and "Accessing Gmail on a Mobile Device."

Here's what Google says to do about those special folders under [Gmail], followed by what I recommend:

- **All Mail**—Google doesn't say anything about All Mail beyond how to use it.
- **Drafts**—Google recommends that you map your desktop client's Drafts folder to Gmail's, and I agree. That way, your draft messages are available to you no matter how you're accessing your mail.

- **Sent Mail**—Google recommends that you do not map your desktop client's Sent folder to Gmail's, as it could create duplicates. However, I do it anyway, and I've never seen duplicates. My advice is to go ahead and map desktop Sent to Gmail Sent, and if you do see duplicates, reverse the process.

- **Spam**—Moving a message here teaches Gmail that you consider it spam and that you want Gmail to "learn" about its characteristics so that future messages like it will automatically go to Spam. For this reason, go ahead and map your desktop's Spam folder to Google's. However, do not tell your desktop or mobile clients to use Spam as your Trash!

- **Starred**—Google says nothing about this folder, other than moving messages here is the same as flagging them.

- **Trash**—Because of Google's slightly confusing advice on Trash, I'm going to focus on this label/folder and how your desktop and mobile clients interact with it in the next section, "What Happens When I Delete a Message?"

If you do not map your desktop and mobile clients' folders to Gmail's folders, you may find labels representing your desktop client's folders at Gmail, such as Sent Messages or Junk. In particular, you may see a new top-level folder named [Imap] at Gmail, with subfolders using names similar to Gmail's. The names of these labels will vary according to your clients, and if you decide to go ahead and map folders later, you can safely delete the folders and labels created by your clients.

What Happens When I Delete a Message?

Google really wants you to save all your email and never throw any away. At all. As in, don't ever use the Trash. Just archive—move emails out of the Inbox and label them. Or don't. Either way, save those emails forever!

I find this advice crazy, as do many other people. Sure, one of the really great things about Gmail is that it features huge amounts of storage and an awesomely fast and powerful search engine that makes it easy to find old mails, but that doesn't mean I want to save an announcement for a party that occurred two months ago, or a note from someone on a mailing list that I barely read, or a request to go to lunch with a friend tomorrow. Read 'em, process 'em, delete 'em. Why save 'em too?

The way Gmail works, when you delete a message from a folder other than Trash, you are really stripping the labels (which corresponds to the folder) off of the message, and thus are archiving it. When, however, you move a message to the Trash, you strip away all labels associated with that message, and it is truly in the Trash, where it can be completely deleted (or will be automatically deleted by Google in 30 days).

If you remap your desktop or mobile client's Trash folder to Gmail's Trash, deleting a message on your client moves it to both your client's Trash and Gmail's Trash, thus bypassing the archive function of Gmail. In other words, if you follow my suggestion for remapping the Trash, when you delete an email message, it's gone daddy gone. A copy is not kept in All Mail, as Google would like you to do (remember, Google really doesn't want you to delete any email at all—it would much rather you kept a copy of everything you ever received in your Gmail archives). Instead, it's sent to the Trash, and when the Trash is emptied, any messages in there are thrown away for good.

If you'd rather subscribe to Google's method and not delete any messages, don't do what I recommended previously with the Trash folder. That seems crazy to me, however; with every other system I've ever used, putting something in the Trash means you don't want it any longer. Why should Gmail be any different?

However, let's make sure we understand the situation. Imagine you have a message to which you've applied three labels—Work, Project A, and Project B, for example—and you want to remove the Project B label but keep the other two labels. Realize that in reality, Gmail has only one copy of the message but with three labels attached to it.

If you have *not* mapped your client's Trash to Gmail's Trash, if you delete the message in the Project B folder, Gmail thinks you've stripped the Project B label from the message but left Project A and Work intact.

If, however, you *have* mapped your client's Trash to Gmail's Trash, when you go into the Project B folder and send the message to the Trash, you just told Gmail to remove *all* labels—not just Project B, but also Work and Project A—and move the mail to the Trash, where it will be deleted in 30 days if you don't first empty the Trash manually. Instead of moving the message to the Trash, you'd need to log in to Gmail using your web browser and remove the label for Project B by clicking the little X next to the label you want to remove in the web client of Gmail, as you can see in Figure 9.1.

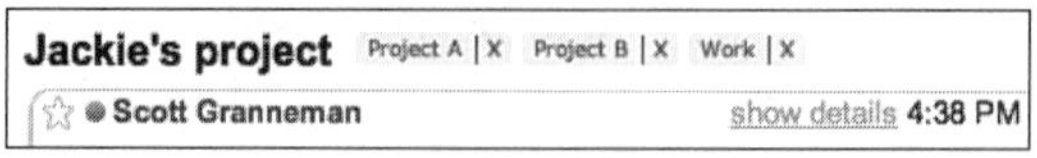

Jackie's project Project A | X   Project B | X   Work | X
☆ ● Scott Granneman   show details 4:38 PM

FIGURE 9.1   Click the little X next to the label you want to remove in the web-based version of Gmail.

This might sound like a terrible annoyance, except for a few factors:

- If you solely use a desktop client, the only way to apply multiple labels to a message is to copy it into multiple folders, which is something the vast majority of desktop client users are never going to do because no other email system supports labels.

- Almost everyone is going to work with a single copy of an email message— it's going to be in the Inbox or another folder. That's it. So if it's deleted, the user wants it gone. The behavior exhibited by Gmail in this case—sending the message to the Trash, where it will be completely removed—is expected and desired.

If any of this makes you nervous, and you're growing worried about losing or accidentally deleting important messages, or if you're a person who likes to save virtually all her email, then the answer is simple: Don't map your desktop or mobile client's Trash folder to Gmail's Trash folder.

> ⚠️ **WARNING**
>
> Throughout the rest of this chapter, I'm operating under the assumption that you want to map your client's Trash folder to Gmail's, so that's the advice I'll be giving. If you don't like that, ignore my advice and do not map the Trash folder.

What About Spam?

Google strongly recommends that you do not turn on your desktop client's spam filters and instead rely on Gmail's. This means that junk mail filtering will happen on the server instead of your client.

This is very good advice, and I completely agree with it for the following reasons:

- Gmail's spam filters are excellent, better than any desktop client's I've ever used.
- It's faster to filter your spam on Google's servers than on your computer or mobile device.
- Some devices, like the iPhone, don't have built-in spam filtering, so it's necessary to rely on Google's.
- If you filter spam at Google and then again on your client, odd results may occur.

A few sections ago, in "What Are All These New Labels and Folders in My Desktop or Mobile Client?" I recommended that you map your desktop's Spam folder to Google's. This is not the same thing, however, as turning on your desktop client's junk filters. Many desktop email programs, such as Thunderbird and Apple Mail, allow you to manually mark emails as spam even if automated spam detection is turned off.

If you map your program's Spam folder to Gmail's, but disable automatic spam filtering, you can still click the occasional junk message that comes through into your Inbox and move it to the Spam folder. Gmail will learn that you consider that message, and others like it, to be junk mail. You get the best of all worlds: really great spam filtering on the server, but the ability to indicate on the desktop client that a message that made it through the spam gauntlet is actually junk—and by indicating that on the desktop, notify the server, too, thanks to IMAP's communication between desktop and server. Nice!

Can I Get Rid of That [Gmail] Top-Level Folder?

You might notice that even after mapping folders like I recommended previously in "What Are All These New Labels and Folders in My Desktop or Mobile Client?" and "What Happens When I Delete a Message?" you're still left with a [Gmail] folder and some subfolders. This doesn't bother me, but some people find it annoying. If you're among that group, go into your email program's Preferences or Options and nose around until you find a field named something like IMAP Path Prefix. After you find that, enter [Gmail], and then save and close Preferences.

Now when you look at your list of folders in your email client, [Gmail] will be gone, and the folders that were formerly under it—probably All Mail and Starred, at least—will now be top-level folders. Even if you don't like those new top-level folders, however, you can't get rid of them. They're there for keeps, as Gmail absolutely requires them. If you mapped any other folders, you may have to remap them at this point as well.

Personally, I don't see the point, so I just leave IMAP Path Prefix (or its equivalent) blank. I'd rather keep the unique Gmail folders that I can't remap under [Gmail] to make it obvious where they belong anyway.

Besides, there's an even worse problem: If you create a new top-level folder in your email program (in my example, I'll use Apple Mail), it shows up fine and dandy in that program, but it's actually a subfolder inside the [Gmail] top-level folder at Gmail (remember, Gmail separates top-level folders and subfolders with a forward slash ("/")! Figure 9.2 makes this clear.

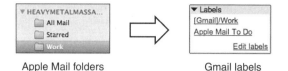

Apple Mail folders   Gmail labels

FIGURE 9.2   Things are not as they seem, and it's all because you changed the IMAP Path Prefix.

When you entered [Gmail] for IMAP Path Prefix in Mail, you told the program that any future folders you created would actually be subfolders under the top-level [Gmail] folder, but to hide it from your view. When you log in to Gmail, the full reality of what you requested is exposed.

If you will *never* log in to Gmail and will *only* use Mail, then you might want to use an IMAP Path Prefix. Otherwise, skip it!

ACCESSING GMAIL IN A DESKTOP EMAIL PROGRAM

Although Gmail in a web browser is an excellent way to read your email, a lot of people choose, at least part of the time, to read their Gmail in desktop email clients like Outlook, Thunderbird, and Apple Mail. Why do clients make sense, at least some of the time?

- Gmail doesn't provide an easy way to sort your messages by size, but it's easy to do in a desktop client. And if you can sort by size, you can figure out where those emails with humongous attachments are so that you can delete them.

- Managing multiple signatures is far easier in a desktop client.

- Although Gmail is blazingly fast for a web-based email client, a desktop client can often be faster.

- You can't read and reply to email with the web client if you're not online, but you sure can with a desktop client. Granted, one day soon Gmail will support Google's awesome Gears project (more info at http://gears.google.com and http://en.wikipedia.org/wiki/Google_gears), which will allow users to work with the web client even if they're offline, but that day isn't here yet.

- Thunderbird in particular has some excellent plug-ins that do things even Gmail doesn't do yet. And Outlook sports things like the LinkedIn toolbar, which heavy users of that social networking service might find indispensible.

For all those reasons and more, we cover how to set up the most popular desktop email clients so they can access Gmail via IMAP. Let's start, however, with the general instructions for setting up IMAP and then get more specific.

> **NOTE**
>
> Throughout the following sections, I use my heavymetalmassage.com account as an example, but you should enter your own info. In addition, make sure you've enabled IMAP access to your Gmail; for instructions, see the section "IMAP Access" in Chapter 7.

Generic Email Configuration for IMAP

If you're using a desktop email program that's not covered elsewhere in this chapter, you can still probably set up IMAP without issue as long as you follow some basic guidelines. Following are the basic settings you'll want:

- Type of Email Account: IMAP
- Incoming Mail Server: imap.gmail.com
- Use SSL: Yes
- Port: 993
- Outgoing Mail Server (SMTP): smtp.gmail.com
- Use SSL (or STARTTLS): Yes
- Port: 465 or 587
- SMTP Authentication: Yes
- User Name: scott@heavymetalmassage.com. Use your full Gmail address.

> **TIP**
>
> Anywhere I mentioned gmail.com, you can also substitute googlemail.com.

As for mapping Gmail's folders to your desktop client's folders, many clients don't allow you to do this. But for those that do, here's my advice:

- **Sent**—Google says not to map your desktop client's Sent folder and Gmail's [Gmail]/Sent Mail folder because it may cause duplicates. In my experience, this has never happened, so I always do it.

- **Drafts**—Google says to go ahead and map your desktop client's Drafts folder with Gmail's [Gmail]/Drafts folder, and I agree with that.

- **Junk**—As I discussed previously in "What About Spam?" I recommend mapping your desktop client's Junk folder and Gmail's [Gmail]/Spam.

- **Trash**—As I discussed previously in "What Happens When I Delete a Message?" I recommend mapping your desktop client's Trash folder and Gmail's [Gmail]/Trash.

Apple Mail

Apple makes it pretty easy to add an email account for Google Apps with its built-in email program, cleverly called Mail. I do, however, recommend a few important changes to Google's instructions at http://mail.google.com/support/bin/answer.py?answer=13275.

 NOTE

The following instructions are for Apple Mail 3.0, found in Leopard. If you still use Tiger, head over to http://mail.google.com/support/bin/answer.py?answer=77663.

Open up Mail, Preferences, Accounts. Click the + button to add a new account. On the Add Account screen, enter the following:

- Full Name: Scott Granneman
- Email Address: scott@heavymetalmassage.com
- Password: 123456 (like I'm gonna tell you guys my real password!)

Click Continue. On the following screen, Incoming Mail Server, enter the following:

- Account Type: IMAP
- Description: heavymetalmassage.com

  You can enter whatever you want here; just make it meaningful to you.
- Incoming Mail Server: imap.gmail.com
- User Name: scott@heavymetalmassage.com
- Password: 123456. Yes, it's annoying to do it twice.

Click Continue. On the following screen, Incoming Mail Security, enter the following:

- Check the box next to Use Secure Sockets Layer (SSL).
- Authentication: Password

Click Continue. On the following screen, Outgoing Mail Server, enter the following:

- Description: heavymetalmassage.com.
  You can enter whatever you want here; just make it meaningful to you.
- Outgoing Mail Server: smtp.gmail.com
- Check the box next to Use Only This Server.
- Check the box next to Use Authentication.
- Username: scott@heavymetalmassage.com
- Password: 123456

Click Continue. On the next screen, Account Summary, review what you've entered. If it looks correct, check the box next to Take Account Online and click Create. If something's bollixed, click Go Back and fix it.

You should now be back on the Accounts tab in Mail's Preferences. The account you just created should be chosen, with the Account Information tab highlighted. Select the Mailbox Behaviors tab and enter the following:

- Check the box next to Store Draft Messages on the Server.
  If you check this box, every machine you use to check email will show the same drafts. However, the downside is that several versions of a draft tend to get saved here when using Apple Mail, and they don't get automatically deleted when you finally send the mail. It's a minor annoyance, but an annoyance nonetheless. If it bothers you, uncheck the box, which means that particular drafts will be stored only on the machine on which you're writing them.
- Check the box next to Store Notes in Inbox.
- Check the box next to Store Sent Messages on the Server.
  If you do this, you may occasionally see multiple copies of a message you sent, but the other copies will shortly disappear.
- Change the drop-down for Delete Sent Messages When to Never.

Obviously, if you want your Sent mail to go bye-bye after a certain time, change this, but why would you?

- Check the box next to Store Junk Messages on the Server.

- Change the drop-down for Delete Junk Messages When to what you're comfortable with.

    Remember that Gmail automatically deletes Junk mail that is 30 days old; if you want it deleted more regularly, change the drop-down here.

- Check the box next to Move Deleted Messages to the Trash Mailbox.

- Check the box next to Store Deleted Messages on the Server.

- Change the drop-down for Permanently Erase Deleted Messages When to what you're comfortable with.

    I usually put Quitting Mail.

We'll come back to the next tab, Advanced, later, but for now, let's click OK to close Preferences and make a few changes to your new account's mailboxes.

If everything has been set up correctly, you should now see your new account in the left pane of Mail. If you charge ahead at this point and start using Gmail, you'll quickly find out that messages aren't necessarily going into the correct default locations. To fix this and get everything synchronized correctly, we need to map Mail's folders to Gmail's.

NOTE

The previous instructions for remapping the folders under [Gmail] came from Derek Punsalan's excellent blog post titled "How-to: Proper Gmail IMAP for iPhone & Apple Mail," available at http://5thirtyone.com/archives/862.

Click the triangle next to the account. If you previously migrated email to Gmail as described in Chapter 3, "Migrating Email to Google Apps," you'll see your old folders and messages. In addition, you'll see a folder named [Gmail] (with the brackets). Expand that folder by clicking the triangle, and you'll see the following subfolders; after each one, I've given you instructions for what to do with it:

- **All Mail**—Do nothing.

- **Drafts**—Click Sent Mail and then choose Mailbox, Use This Mailbox For, Drafts.

- **Sent Mail**—Click Sent Mail and then choose Mailbox, Use This Mailbox For, Sent.

- **Spam**—Click Sent Mail and then choose Mailbox, Use This Mailbox For, Junk.

- **Starred**—Do nothing. Know, however, that if you flag a message in Mail, or drag it into this folder, it will appear as starred at Gmail.

- **Trash**—Click Sent Mail and then choose Mailbox, Use This Mailbox For, Trash.

After you perform the preceding tasks, the [Gmail] folder will have only two subfolders: All Mail and Starred.

> **TIP**
>
> If after doing all of this you're now going nuts because Spotlight searches for email to find duplicate emails, it's because Spotlight finds the email in its original folder *and* in All Mail. This is how Gmail works, and you can't remove the All Mail folder out of Mail, or Gmail—nor would you want to! Instead, tell Spotlight not to index the All Mail folder. Go to your Apple System Preferences, Spotlight, Privacy. Click the + on the bottom left and find your Gmail account's All Mail folder, which is most likely at [Your User Name], Library, Mail, IMAP-scott@heavymetalmassage.com@imap.gmail.com, [Gmail], All Mail.imapmbox and click OK to add it to the list of folders Spotlight should ignore (of course, use your email address instead of mine).

One final word of advice—if you ever see any weirdness with IMAP in Apple Mail, try going to Mailbox, Synchronize, heavymetalmassage.com (you'd choose your account name, obviously). If you want to start from scratch, a much longer process, select the account under Mail's Inbox folder and then go to Mailbox, Rebuild.

Evolution

In Evolution, go to Edit, Preferences, Mail Accounts, and click Add. Click Forward to begin and enter the following information on the Identity screen:

- Full Name: Scott Granneman
- Email Address: scott@heavymetalmassage.com
- Check the box next to Make This My Default Account if that's what you want.

- Reply-To: scott@heavymetalmassage.com
- Organization: Heavy Metal Massage

Click Forward. On the Receiving Email screen, enter the following information:

- Server Type: IMAP
- Server: imap.gmail.com
- Username: scott@heavymetalmassage.com
- User Secure Connection: SSL Encryption
- Authentication Type: Password
- Check the box next to Remember Password (unless you're really paranoid).

Click Forward. On the Receiving Options screen, enter the following information:

- Check the box next to Check For New Messages Every ___ Minutes and set the number to one you like (unless you want to only check manually).
- Check the box next to Check For New Messages In All Folders.

Click Forward. On the Sending Email screen, enter the following information:

- Server Type: SMTP
- Server: smtp.gmail.com
- Check the box next to Server Requires Authentication.
- Use Secure Connection: SSL Encryption
- Type: Login
- Username: scott@heavymetalmassage.com
- Check the box next to Remember Password (unless you're really paranoid).

Click Forward. On the Account Management screen, enter the following information:

- Name: Heavy Metal Massage

Click Forward. On the final screen, click Apply. In a few moments, depending upon how much email you have, your folders and messages should appear in Evolution.

If you want to map Evolution's default folders to Gmail's folders, go back to Edit, Preferences, Mail Accounts, select your Gmail account, and click Edit. On the Defaults tab, click the Drafts button next to Drafts Folder and select the folder at Heavy Metal Massage/[Gmail]/Trash (of course, use your Account Name instead of Heavy Metal Massage). Click OK and then repeat the process for the Send Messages Folder but select Heavy Metal Massage/[Gmail]/Sent Mail. Click OK to close the Account Editor window and then close the Evolution Preferences window.

You're ready to read your Gmail via IMAP in Evolution.

KMail (and Kontact)

In KMail, go to Settings, Configure KMail, Accounts, Receiving; if Kontact is loaded, select E-Mail and then go to Settings, Configure KMail, Accounts, Receiving. Click Add to create a new account. For Account Type, select Disconnected IMAP and click OK (you'll be presented with some warnings about Disconnected IMAP; if those scare you, choose IMAP instead, but I've used Disconnected IMAP for years without issue).

On the General tab, fill in the following information:

- Account Name: Heavy Metal Massage
- Login: scott@heavymetalmassage.com
- Password: 123456
- Host: imap.gmail.com
- Port: 993
- Check the box next to Store IMAP Password (unless you're really paranoid).
- Check the box next to Enable Interval Mail Checking and set the Check Interval to a number you like (unless you want to only check manually).

On the Security tab, make the following choices:

- Encryption: Use SSL for Secure Mail Download
- Authentication Method: Clear Text

Click OK. On the Receiving tab, check the box next to Check Mail On Startup (unless you want to only check manually).

Go to the Sending tab. Click Add to create a new outgoing email account. For Transport, choose SMTP and click OK.

On the General tab, fill in the following information (I'll be using my heavymetalmassage.com account as an example, but you should enter your own info):

- Name: Heavy Metal Massage
- Host: smtp.gmail.com
- Port: 465
- Check the box next to Server Requires Authentication.
- Login: scott@heavymetalmassage.com
- Password: 123456
- Check the box next to Store SMTP Password (unless you're really paranoid).

On the Security tab, make the following choices:

- Encryption: SSL
- Authentication Method: PLAIN

Click OK and then go to Identities. If the account you just added for Google Apps is your only email account, select the Default identity and click Modify; otherwise, click Add to create a new identity.

On the General tab, fill in the following information:

- Your Name: Scott Granneman
- Organization: Heavy Metal Massage
- Email Address: scott@heavymetalmassage.com

Click OK and then click OK again to close the Configure window. In a few moments, depending on how much email you have, your folders and messages should appear in KMail.

If you want to map KMail's default folders to Gmail's folders, go back to Settings, Configure KMail, Accounts, select your Gmail account on the Receiving tab, and click Modify. On the General tab, click the blue folder next to Trash Folder and select the folder at Heavy Metal Massage/[Gmail]/Trash (of course, use your Account Name instead of Heavy Metal Massage). Click OK and then click OK again to close the Modify Account window.

If you want to change the other folders, go back to Identities, select your Gmail account, and click Modify. On the Advanced tab, click the blue folder next to Send-Mail Folder and Drafts Folder. Map them, respectively, to Heavy Metal Massage/[Gmail]/Sent Mail and Heavy Metal Massage/[Gmail]/Drafts (using your Account Name, of course). Click OK after each one, click OK to close the Edit Identity window, and then click OK again to close the Configure window.

You're ready to read your Gmail via IMAP in KMail, which is easily the best Linux-native email client.

Outlook 2003

In Outlook 2003, go to Tools, E-mail Accounts, choose Add a New E-mail Account, and click Next.

On the Server Type screen, select IMAP and click Next. On the Internet E-mail Settings (IMAP) screen, enter the following information:

- Your Name: Scott Granneman
- E-mail Address: scott@heavymetalmassage.com
- Incoming Mail Server (IMAP): imap.gmail.com
- Outgoing Mail Server (SMTP): smtp.gmail.com
- User Name: scott@heavymetalmassage.com
- Password: 123456
- Check the box next to Remember Password (unless you're really paranoid).

Click More Settings. In the Outgoing Server tab of the Internet E-mail Settings window, enter the following information:

- Check the box next to My Outgoing Server (SMTP) Requires Authentication.
- Select Use Same Settings as My Incoming Mail Server.

In the Advanced tab, enter the following information:

- Check the box next to the first This Server Requires an Encrypted Connection (SSL).

  When you do so, Incoming Server (IMAP) should change to 993; change it if it doesn't.
- Outgoing Server (SMTP): 465
- Check the box next to the second This Server Requires an Encrypted Connection (SSL).

Click OK to close the Internet E-mail Settings window. Click Next and click Finish to close the E-mail Accounts window.

You're ready to read your Gmail via IMAP in Outlook 2003.

TIP

If you're seeing duplicate items in your Outlook To-Do Bar when you flag an email in Outlook or star an email in Gmail, check out the How-To Geek's "Prevent Outlook with Gmail IMAP from Showing Duplicate Tasks in the To-Do Bar" (www.howtogeek.com/howto/microsoft-office/prevent-outlook-with-gmail-imap-from-showing-duplicate-tasks-in-the-to-do-bar/) for the fix.

Outlook 2007

In Outlook 2007, go to Tools, Account Settings, E-mail, and click New.

On the Auto Account Setup screen, enter the following information:

- Your Name: Scott Granneman
- E-mail Address: scott@heavymetalmassage.com
- Check the box next to Manually Configure Server Settings.

Click Next. On the Choose E-mail Service screen, choose Internet E-mail and click Next. On the Internet E-mail Settings screen, enter the following information:

- Your Name: Scott Granneman

  This should have been filled in already from the previous screen.
- E-mail Address: scott@heavymetalmassage.com

  This should have been filled in already from the previous screen.
- Account Type: IMAP
- Incoming Mail Server: imap.gmail.com
- Outgoing Mail Server (SMTP): smtp.gmail.com
- User Name: scott@heavymetalmassage.com
- Password: 123456
- Check the box next to Remember Password (unless you're really paranoid).

Click More Settings. In the Outgoing Server tab of the Internet E-mail Settings window, enter the following information:

- Check the box next to My Outgoing Server (SMTP) Requires Authentication.
- Select Use Same Settings as My Incoming Mail Server.

In the Advanced tab, enter the following information:

- The first Use the Following Type of Encrypted Connection: SSL

  When you do so, Incoming Server (IMAP) should change to 993; change it if it doesn't.
- Outgoing Server (SMTP): 465
- The second Use the Following Type of Encrypted Connection: SSL

Click OK to close the Internet E-mail Settings window. Click Next, click Finish to close the E-mail Accounts window, and click Close to close the Account Settings window.

You're ready to read your Gmail via IMAP in Outlook 2007.

Outlook Express

In Outlook Express, go to Tools, Accounts and click Add, Mail. On the Your Name screen, enter the following information:

- Display Name: Scott Granneman

Click Next. Click Next again. On the Internet E-Mail Address screen, enter the following information:

- E-mail Address: scott@heavymetalmassage.com

Click Next. On the E-mail Server Names screen, enter the following information:

- My Incoming Mail Server Is: IMAP
- Incoming Mail Server: imap.gmail.com
- Outgoing E-mail Server Name: smtp.gmail.com

Click Next. On the Internet Mail Logon screen, enter the following information:

- Account Name: scott@heavymetalmassage.com
- Password: 123456
- Check the box next to Remember Password (unless you're really paranoid).

Click Finish.

In the Internet Accounts window, select your new Gmail account and click Properties. In the Properties window, go to the Advanced tab and enter the following information:

- Outgoing Mail (SMTP): 465
- Check the box next to This Server Requires a Secure Connection (SSL).
- Incoming Mail (IMAP) 993
- Check the box next to This Server Requires a Secure Connection (SSL).

On the Servers tab, enter the following information:

- Check the box next to My Server Requires Authentication.

Click OK to close the Properties window and Close to close the Internet Accounts window.

You're ready to read your Gmail via IMAP in Outlook Express.

> **TIP**
>
> Google has a list of some common errors Outlook Express users may see—and their solutions—at www.google.com/support/a/bin/answer.py?answer=57921&topic=10743.

Thunderbird

In Thunderbird, go to Tools, Account Settings, and click Add Account. On the New Account Setup screen, select Email Account and click Continue. On the Identity screen, fill in the following information:

- Your Name: Scott Granneman
- Email Address: scott@heavymetalmassage.com

Click Continue. On the Server Information screen, select IMAP and enter the following information:

- Incoming Server: imap.gmail.com
- Outgoing Server: smtp.gmail.com

This may not appear if you've already entered an SMTP server for another account. If so, we'll take care of that in a moment.

Click Continue. On the User Names screen, enter the following information:

- Incoming User Name: scott@heavymetalmassage.com
- Outgoing User Name: scott@heavymetalmassage.com

This may not appear if you've already entered an SMTP server for another account. If so, we'll take care of that in a moment.

Click Continue. On the Account Name screen, enter the following information:

- Account Name: Heavy Metal Massage

Click Continue. On the Congratulations screen, review the information and click Done if it looks correct.

When the list of Accounts appears, select the name of the account you entered on the Account Name screen; in other words, actually click the name of the account. Enter the following information:

- Reply-To Address: scott@heavymetalmassage.com
- Organization: Heavy Metal Massage

Select Server Settings on the left and enter the following information:

- Use Secure Connection: SSL (This should automatically change Port to 993; if it doesn't, change it manually.)
- Check the box next to Check For New Messages at Startup (unless you want to only check manually).
- Check the box next to Check For New Messages Every ___ Minutes and enter a number you like (unless you want to only check manually).

Select Junk Settings on the left and enter the following information:

- Uncheck Enable Adaptive Junk Mail Controls for This Account.
- Check the box next to Move New Junk Messages To.
- Select Other and choose the folder at Heavy Metal Massage/[Gmail]/Spam (of course, use your Account Name instead of Heavy Metal Massage).

Select Outgoing Server on the left. If you added smtp.gmail.com earlier, select it and click Edit; otherwise, you'll need to create it now by pressing Add. Enter (or edit) the following information:

- Description: Heavy Metal Massage
- Server Name: smtp.gmail.com
- Port: 587
- Check the box next to Use Name and Password.
- User Name: scott@heavymetalmassage.com
- Use Secure Connection: TLS

Click OK to close the SMTP settings. If you'd like this SMTP address to be the default, select it and click Set Default. If you don't, click the name of the account on the left and change Outgoing Server (SMTP) to the one for your Google Apps account. Click OK to close the Account Settings window.

In a few moments, depending on how much email you have, your folders and messages should appear in Thunderbird.

If you want to map Thunderbird's default folders to Gmail's folders, go back to Tools, Account Settings, select your Gmail account, and go to Copies and Folders. Enter the following information:

- Check the box next to Place a Copy In.
- Select Other and choose the folder at Heavy Metal Massage/[Gmail]/Sent Mail.
- For Keep Message Drafts In, select Other and choose the folder at Heavy Metal Massage/[Gmail]/Drafts.

Unfortunately, fixing the Trash folder so it maps to Gmail requires a few more slightly complicated steps. Go to Tools, Options (on a Mac, go to Thunderbird, Preferences), Advanced, General, and click Config Editor. Make the following changes:

- In the Filter box, enter `mail.server.server` and look around until you find your Gmail username (your email address, remember) on the right side in the Value column. To the left of your user name you'll see `mail.server.server#.userName`, where # is a number. That's the number that Thunderbird has assigned your Gmail account. Remember that number.
- Right-click `mail.server.server#.userName` and select New, String.

- Preference Name: `mail.server.server#.trash_folder_name` (for #, enter the number you found earlier) and click OK
- Enter String Value: `[Gmail]/Trash` and click OK

Close the about:config window and restart Thunderbird. When you delete an email now, it's really gone for good, as I explained in "What Happens When I Delete a Message?" earlier in this chapter.

Google also recommends a few tweaks to make Thunderbird access Gmail via IMAP. Go to Tools, Options (on a Mac, go to Thunderbird, Preferences), Advanced, General, and click Config Editor. Make the following changes:

- In the Filter box, enter `browser.cache.memory.capacity`. When you find it, double-click the entry and change the value from 4096 to 31457280 and click OK.
- In the Filter box, enter `mail.server.default.fetch_by_chunks`. When you find it, double-click on the entry to change its value from `true` to `false` and click OK.

Close the about:config window and then close the Options window.

You're ready to read your Gmail via IMAP in Thunderbird.

💡 **TIP**

If you're a huge fan of Gmail's keyboard shortcuts and would like to have them available to you in Thunderbird, download and install the GMailUI Thunderbird extension (https://addons.mozilla.org/en-US/thunderbird/addon/1339). As a bonus, you also gain the ability to use Gmail's search operators (like from:, subject:, and to:, for instance) in Thunderbird's search box.

Windows Mail

In Windows Mail, go to Tools, Accounts, Add. On the Your Name screen, enter the following information:

- Display Name: Scott Granneman

Click Next. On the Internet E-Mail Address screen, enter the following information:

- E-mail Address: scott@heavymetalmassage.com

Click Next. On the Set Up E-mail Servers screen, enter the following information:

- Incoming E-mail Server Type: IMAP
- Incoming Mail Server: imap.gmail.com
- Outgoing E-mail Server Name: smtp.gmail.com
- Check the box next to Outgoing server requires authentication.

Click Next. On the Internet Mail Logon screen, enter the following information:

- E-mail Username: scott@heavymetalmassage.com
- Password: 123456

Click Next to advance through screens until you can click Finish. Now select Tools, Accounts, IMAP Account, Properties, Advanced, and enter the following information:

- Outgoing Mail (SMTP): 465
- Check the box next to This Server Requires a Secure Connection (SSL).
- Incoming Mail (IMAP): 993
- Check the box next to This Server Requires a Secure Connection (SSL).

Click OK to close Properties.

You're ready to read your Gmail via IMAP in Windows Mail.

Accessing Gmail on a Mobile Device

More and more people are using mobile devices like the iPhone and BlackBerry to access their email on the go, and Gmail fits right in with that desire. In this section, I first cover the generic instructions for most mobile devices, and then I look more deeply at today's two most popular smart phones: the iPhone and BlackBerry.

 TIP

If you have a different mobile device and need instructions for it, Google provides help for Windows Mobile 5 (https://mail.google.com/support/bin/answer.py?answer=10149), Windows Mobile 6 (https://mail.google.com/support/bin/answer.py?answer=78886), and Symbian (https://mail.google.com/support/bin/answer.py?answer=78887).

Generic Instructions for Mobiles

In general, if you can access the Web with your phone or mobile device, you can probably read your Gmail on it. After you connect to the Web, go to http://mail.google.com/a/heavymetalmassage.com/ (use your domain name instead of mine). Because a variety of web browsers and screens exist on the hundreds of different phone models out there, your experience with Gmail on your phone may range from great to OK to utterly horrible. You have been warned!

If you use a BlackBerry or any other device that supports J2ME (Java) applications, you can install a specialized program designed for Gmail. Go to http://m.google.com/a and download and install the program. Make sure you get the one titled Mail by Google, which is for Google Apps, and not Gmail. You can tell because the icon for the program is a blue M for Google Apps and a red M for Gmail.

> **NOTE**
>
> For more information about the J2ME program, see Google's help page at www.google.com/support/mobile/bin/topic.py?topic=13545.

Blackberry Internet Service (BIS)

On your BlackBerry, select BlackBerry Set-Up, Personal Email Set-Up (if you're using an older model, the Personal Email Set-Up icon is on the home screen). Accept the Terms and Conditions.

On the Email Account Set-Up screen, enter your Gmail address, but don't fill in a password. Click Next.

On the following screen, BlackBerry will complain, "We are unable to set up your email account." Select I Will Provide the Settings to Add This Email Account and click Next.

Select Internet Service Provider Email (POP/IMAP) and click Next.

Select I Will Provide the Settings to Add This Email Account and click Next.

Your BlackBerry will again complain, this time that "The BlackBerry Internet Service could not configure [your email] account." Select Provide the Settings.

Enter your Gmail username—which is your full email address—and your password and click Next.

For your email server, enter `imap.gmail.com` and click Next, OK. Below the address you just added, choose Edit, Advanced Setting.

Set the port to 993, check that Use SSL is set to Yes, and then select Save.

If everything worked correctly, you should see an icon on your BlackBerry home screen with the name of your Gmail account under it. Open the mailbox icon and then open the menu and select Options, Email Reconciliations. Enter the following information:

- Delete On: Mailbox and Handheld
- Wireless Reconcile: On
- On Conflicts: Mailbox Wins

Click Save. You're ready to read your Gmail via IMAP on your BlackBerry.

iPhone

If you want to access Gmail via the Web, you can with the excellent built-in mobile Safari web browser by going to www.google.com/m/a/yourdomain.com (enter your actual domain instead of yourdomain.com). Although that will work, the built-in email program on the iPhone can be faster and easier to use, so you should probably set it up and play with it before deciding if you'd rather use the Web instead.

On your iPhone, tap Settings and then Mail, Contacts, Calendars. On the following screen, tap Add Account, Other (yes, I know Gmail is there, but don't use it). On the New Account screen, enter the following information (I'll be using my heavymetalmassage.com account as an example, but you should enter your own info):

- Name: Scott Granneman
- Address: scott@heavymetalmassage.com
- Password: 123456
- Description: scott@heavymetalmassage.com

Click Save. On the New Account screen, enter the following information:

- IMAP should be chosen
- Incoming Mail Server
    - Host Name: imap.gmail.com
    - User Name: scott@heavymetalmassage.com
    - Password: 123456
    - This field should already be filled in.

- Outgoing Mail Server
  - Host Name: smtp.gmail.com
  - User Name: scott@heavymetalmassage.com
  - Password: 123456

Click Save. On the Mail, Contacts, Calendars screen, tap the new account you just created and then Advanced. To map the iPhone's default folders to Gmail's folders, make the following changes:

- Drafts Mailbox: On the Server, [Gmail], Drafts
- Sent Mailbox: On the Server, [Gmail], Sent Mail
- Deleted Mailbox: On the Server, [Gmail], Trash

Keep in mind that moving messages on your iPhone can be equivalent to certain actions at Gmail:

- Moving a message to [Gmail]/Starred: Star a message at Gmail
- Moving a message to [Gmail]/All Mail: Archive a message at Gmail
- Moving a message to [Gmail]/Spam: Mark a message as Spam at Gmail
- Moving a message to a folder: Label a message at Gmail
- Trashing a message: Removing all labels from a message and moving it to the Trash at Gmail; in other words, deleting it completely from Gmail (if this bugs you, go back to "What Happens When I Delete a Message?" earlier in this chapter)

When I access my Gmail on my iPhone, I usually do it by going to my Inbox first, taking care of those messages, and then going to the All Mail folder to take care of any messages that were filtered into any other folders and subfolders. When I delete a message from All Mail, it's removed from my account. If I move it to a folder, it's labeled and archived. If I move it to Spam, Gmail now knows that I want it to look for other messages like that one and automatically mark them as junk. If I move it to Starred, it's marked as important. And so on.

NOTE

The best place for instructions about syncing your iPhone and Gmail is at http://5thirtyone.com/archives/862, in an excellent blog post by Derek Punsalan titled "How-to: Proper Gmail IMAP for iPhone & Apple Mail."

RECEIVING NOTIFICATIONS

Information about what's going on with your email can be just as important as information about what's happening on your computer. Even though Gmail is a web-based program, there are still lots of ways you can be notified about changes to your email.

Receiving Notifications About New Emails

Most desktop mail programs can let you know in some way that you have new mail to view, with a sound or pop-up notification, for instance. If you stick to the web-based version of Gmail, and you'd like to know that you've received a new message, you have several options.

NOTE

Yes, many of these are named "Gmail Notifier." They're all different. Some creativity in app naming is needed, people!

If you use Firefox, you can install one of these browser extensions:

- **GMail Checker (https://addons.mozilla.org/en-US/firefox/addon/ 3179)**—Lacks support for multiple accounts, which means it can check only one Google Apps account at a time. Probably not an issue for most people.

- **Gmail Notifier (https://addons.mozilla.org/en-US/firefox/addon/ 173)**—Monitors multiple accounts. Displays notifications on the status bar or a toolbar.

- **Gmail Manager (https://addons.mozilla.org/en-US/firefox/addon/ 1320)**—Monitors multiple accounts. On the Notifications tab of this extension's preferences, you can tell it to show short snippets of new messages or play alert sounds when new mail arrives.

If you use Windows, you can install one of these programs:

- **Gmail Notifier (http://gmailnotifier.net)**—It costs $8, but it comes with a lot of interesting features, and it sure is pretty!

- **Gmail Notifier (http://toolbar.google.com/gmail-helper/notifier_ windows.html)**—The official Google tool.

- **Google Talk (www.google.com/talk/)**—The official Google Talk client also lets you know if you have any new email. If you want it to use https for better security, follow the instructions at http://mail.google.com/support/bin/answer.py?hl=en&answer=9429.

If you use a Mac, you can install this program:

- **Google Notifier (http://toolbar.google.com/gmail-helper/notifier_mac.html)**—The official Google Tool.

If you use Linux, you can install

- **Gmail Notifier (http://gmail-notify.sourceforge.net)**
- **CheckGmail (http://checkgmail.sourceforge.net)**—Or install using your favorite package manager.

Receiving Notifications That Sent Mail Has Been Read

I was once hired by a man who was involved in an ugly child custody case with his ex-wife. Whenever he emailed his former wife about arrangements to see his daughter, his ex would deny that she'd ever received the emails (he wanted a written record of their conversations, so the phone was out). He wanted to know about methods he could use to track whether emails he sent had been received and read.

There are several ways to do this, but the method that I liked comes from a company named RPost (www.rpost.com). To understand what's interesting about this solution, we first need to understand what the legal definition of "delivered" is when it comes to email. It's not when the recipient actually opens the message. Section 15(b) of the Uniform Electronic Transactions Act (UETA), available at www.law.upenn.edu/bll/archives/ulc/fnact99/1990s/ueta99.htm and which "establishes the legal equivalence of electronic records and signatures with paper writings and manually signed signatures," states the following in regard to when an email is considered "delivered":

> Unless otherwise agreed between a sender and the recipient, an electronic record is received when:
>
> (1) it enters an information processing system that the recipient has designated or uses for the purpose of receiving electronic records or information of the type sent and from which the recipient is able to retrieve the electronic record; and
>
> (2) it is in a form capable of being processed by that system.

In other words, an email is considered legally "delivered" when it reaches the email server that collects the recipient's email, not when the recipient reads it. After signing up for an account with RPost, a Gmail user would send a registered email to fiona@iloveanimals.com by changing the email address to fiona@ilove animals.com.rpost.org. The email would go through RPost's SMTP servers, which act as a substitute delivery service in place of the normal Gmail SMTP servers (this means that you will not retain a record of the email at Gmail). RPost retains all SMTP communications performed between RPost's email servers and the recipient's email servers and presents those to the sender as proof of delivery, with "delivery" as defined by UETA, in an Delivery Receipt email that contains the relevant information.

RPost does not alter the content of the sender's email messages except to place a notice alerting the recipient that the email is "Registered" through RPost (see www.rpost.com/site/registered/registered_receiving.htm). RPost does, however, utilize "web bugs," in addition to other methods, to determine when the recipient initially opens the email.

> **NOTE**
>
> A web bug is a tiny, 1 pixel by 1 pixel transparent image that is inserted into an HTML-formatted email message. When the recipient views the email, the invisible web bug imperceptibly loads. Every time the invisible web bug is requested, that request is logged. For more on this technology, see Wikipedia article on the subject at http://en.wikipedia.org/wiki/Web_bug. And by the way: many email clients now block web bugs by default, which is generally a good thing.

If RPost determines that the recipient opened the email after the company has already sent the sender a Delivery Receipt, it will send an Opened Receipt to the sender as well. After that, RPost does not notify the sender if the recipient views the email.

RPost is a good service and has been approved for use by the U. S. government by the United States Postal Service; in addition, many professional organizations recommend it, including the Los Angeles County Bar, the Puerto Rico Bar, the Colorado Bar, and the Council of Insurance Agents and Brokers.

TIP

If you don't want to pay for RPost, you can sign up for a free StatCounter account at www.statcounter.com. After doing so, generate an "invisible tracking button" and paste the resulting HTML inside an HTML email message you create at Gmail. When a recipient opens the email message, a hit will appear in your StatCounter logs. However, this will fail to work if the recipient blocks the downloading of images from the Net in email messages—something that Gmail does automatically, for instance.

SECURING YOUR EMAIL

Even though Google allows you to automatically work with Gmail in your browser over an HTTPS connection (as I discussed in Chapter 7's "Browser Connection"), there's still more you can do to secure your email. In this section, let's look at a couple of problems and their solutions.

Encrypting Your Email

HTTPS is great, and you'd be crazy not to default to it, but what about your email as it traverses its way about the Net? Remember that HTTPS just encrypts the connection between your web browser and Google; it doesn't do a thing for your email as it travels from server to server on its way to its final destination in someone's mailbox. If you're concerned about someone viewing the contents of your message, you need to encrypt it.

An excellent free solution for encrypting email messages (and files on your computer as well) is GnuPG, an open source and free version of PGP. Although GnuPG integrates with desktop email clients, it does nothing with Gmail. You could manually encrypt and decrypt your messages in a text editor and then cut and paste them into and out of Gmail, but that's laborious and unpleasant. Automation is better!

NOTE

Don't know anything about PGP? Check out Wikipedia's article on the subject at http://en.wikipedia.org/wiki/Pretty_Good_Privacy. How about GnuPG? Again, Wikipedia to the rescue, at http://en.wikipedia.org/wiki/GNU_Privacy_Guard.

I'm not going to go into installing and configuring GnuPG for your operating system; you can find guides for that process on the Web (but I suggest you start out at www.gnupg.org, or www.gpg4win.org for Windows and http://macgpg. sourceforge.net for Mac OS X). After you have GnuPG set up, however, you'll need to install FireGPG, an open source extension for Firefox that integrates GnuPG into Gmail, making it easy for you to encrypt, decrypt, sign, or verify the signature of text in your browser. You can get FireGPG in one of these places:

- https://addons.mozilla.org/en-US/firefox/addon/4645
- http://getfiregpg.org

To understand everything you can do with FireGPG, read through the website at getfiregpg.org. However, I want to draw your attention to the new drop-down that appears next to the Discard button, which you can see in Figure 9.3.

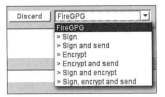

FIGURE 9.3 FireGPG does a nice job integrating GnuPG into Gmail.

As you can see, FireGPG does a great job providing you with the necessary features needed for encrypting and decrypting your email messages, and it does so while integrating into the default Gmail interface in a smart and unobtrusive manner.

> **TIP**
>
> Most desktop email clients support encryption as well, either through a built-in function or plugins.

Backing Up Your Email

Part of security is backup. Google is a huge company with a lot of money and technical experience, but accidents can still happen. You should make sure that your email is backed up so that you can sleep more soundly at night knowing that if an oops happens somewhere in Google's network infrastructure, you're not going to be screaming when you find out.

You can use several programs to back up your Gmail:

- **Getmail (http://pyropus.ca/software/getmail/)**—Free and open source Python program that runs on Linux, Mac OS X, and Windows with Cygwin installed (www.cygwin.com). A nice set of instructions for configuring Getmail are at http://howto.wired.com/wiki/Make_a_Local_Backup_Of_Your_Gmail_Account.
- **Gmail**—Yep, you can open another Gmail account and use the mail fetcher to grab email from your main account. Read more at "Get Mail From Other Accounts" in Chapter 7.
- **The desktop mail client of your choice**—Set up Gmail for POP access as I described in Chapter 7's "POP Download" (don't worry—you can access a Gmail account with IMAP and POP at the same time, as long as you leave mail on the server with POP) and then use Thunderbird, Outlook, or Apple Mail to grab a copy of every email.

CHANGING GMAIL'S APPEARANCE

With userscripts and some other software, you can make changes to Gmail that are purely cosmetic. In the same way that makeup on a woman or a nice haircut on a man can make a big difference, however, some of those purely cosmetic changes in Gmail can make using it a lot more enjoyable.

Giving Gmail a New Skin

Don't like the way Gmail appears? Industrious coders have come up with new "skins" that can change the way Gmail looks in ways that range from small to radical. For example, the Air Skin gives the Gmail interface more room to breathe with a bit more whitespace and some cleaning up. I do find it a bit easier to read my Gmail when I'm using this skin.

On the other hand, you can jump all the way to Gmail Redesigned, which completely changes how Gmail's UI looks, as Figure 9.4 shows:

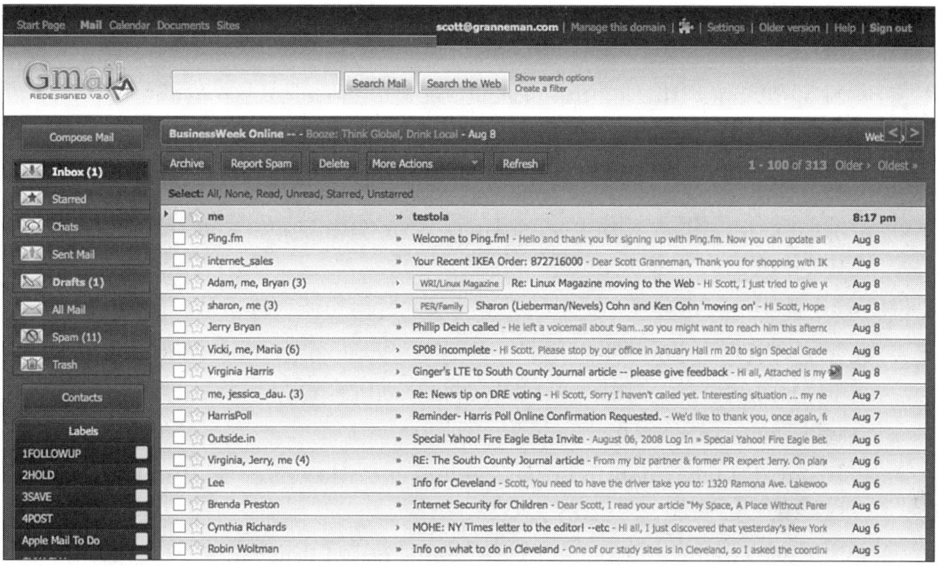

FIGURE 9.4 Now that's a new interface!

I really like it, except for the tiny fonts, which are hard for me to see.

Here are some interesting skins for Gmail you may want to try and how you can get them. After you install the skin, refresh Gmail in your web browser to see the results. If things blow up, don't panic—just reverse what you did and refresh Gmail in your browser again, and you'll be back to normal.

- **Air Skin**
  - Install the userscript found at http://userscripts.org/scripts/show/8833.
  - Works in Firefox with Greasemonkey or with Opera and IE with some tweaking.
  - Install Better Gmail 2 (https://addons.mozilla.org/en-US/firefox/addon/6076).
  - Select Air Skin on the Skins tab of this Firefox extension.
- **Blue Gmail**
  - Install the userscript found at http://pascal.herbert.googlepages.com/bluegmailskin.
  - Works in Firefox with Greasemonkey or with Opera and IE with some tweaking.

- Install Better Gmail 2 (https://addons.mozilla.org/en-US/firefox/addon/ 6076).
- Select Gmail Blue on the Skins tab of this Firefox extension.

- **Gmail Beautifier**
  - Install the userscript found at http://userscripts.org/scripts/show/8212.
  - Works in Firefox with Greasemonkey or with Opera and IE with some tweaking.

- **Gmail Redesigned**
  - Install the userscript found at www.globexdesigns.com/gmail/.
  - Works in Firefox with Greasemonkey, with Stylish, or with Opera and IE with some tweaking.
  - Install Better Gmail 2 (https://addons.mozilla.org/en-US/firefox/addon/ 6076).
  - Select Gmail Redesigned on the Skins tab of this Firefox extension.
  - Install the Google Redesigned extension for Firefox (www. globexdesigns.com/gr/).

- **Grays and Blues Redux**
  - Install the userscript found at http://userstyles.org/styles/6209.
  - Works in Firefox with Greasemonkey or with Opera and IE with some tweaking.
  - Install Better Gmail 2 (https://addons.mozilla.org/en-US/firefox/addon/6076).
  - Select Grays and Blues on the Skins tab of this Firefox extension.

Hiding Ads

If you're paying for the Premium Edition of Google Apps or using the Education Edition, you can turn ads off. But what if you don't like ads and don't want to see them? You can hide them if you'd like, using a variety of methods.

Should you hide them? Well, if you're getting Google Apps for free, remember that it's those ads that make it free for you to use, and many people find them useful. But if you hate them, try one of the following techniques.

If you use Firefox:

- Install the AdBlock Plus extension (https://addons.mozilla.org/en-US/ firefox/addon/1865).

- Install the CustomizeGoogle extension (https://addons.mozilla.org/en-US/ firefox/addon/743).
- Select Remove Ads and Related Pages on the Gmail tab.

If you use Internet Explorer:

- Install the IE7Pro add-on (www.ie7pro.com). It's very full-featured and does a lot more than just block ads.
- Install the Super Ad Blocker add-on (http://www.ieaddons.com/en/details/ Security/Super_Ad_Blocker/).
- Install the Adblock Pro add-on (www.ieaddons.com/en/details/Security/ Adblock_Pro/).
- Check Internet Explorer Add-Ons for more (www.ieaddons.com).

If you use Safari:

- Install Safari AdBlock (http://safariadblock.sourceforge.net). Uses the same patterns as the AdBlock Plus extension for Firefox.

If you use Opera:

- Download the file at www.fanboy.co.nz/adblock/opera/urlfilter.ini. Read the top of the file for instructions about where to place the file on your computer. The file is periodically updated, so look for a new one often.

Making Labels Look Like Nested Folders

In the "Labels" section of Chapter 7, I explained how labels with forward slashes in them at Gmail look like nested folders when they're viewed in desktop clients, as shown in Figure 9.5.

It is kind of silly that I have to repeat PER/ over and over again in my Gmail labels. And wouldn't it be nicer if my labels kind of looked like the folders in my desktop client so that the relationship between top-level and sublevel items was more apparent, kind of like in Figure 9.6?

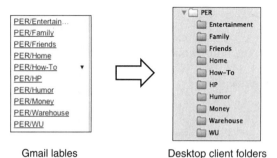

Gmail lables   Desktop client folders

FIGURE 9.5 PER/Family at Gmail becomes a top-level folder PER with a sub-folder named Family in Apple Mail.

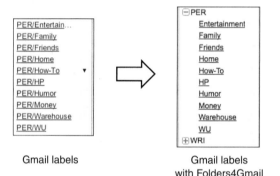

Gmail labels   Gmail labels with Folders4Gmail

FIGURE 9.6 It's labels at Gmail that look like folders! It's... Folders4Gmail!

If this looks good to you, try one of the following methods:

- Install the userscript found at http://userscripts.org/scripts/show/8810 or http://arend-von-reinersdorff.com/folders4gmail/.

  Works in Firefox with Greasemonkey or with Opera and IE with some tweaking.

- Install Better Gmail 2 (https://addons.mozilla.org/en-US/firefox/addon/6076).

  Select Folders4Gmail on the Sidebar tab of this Firefox extension.

Always Showing CC and BCC

Normally, Gmail requires that you click the Add CC link to show the CC field and click the Add BCC link to show the BCC field. If you use CC or BCC constantly and you're tired of having to click those links, install the following:

- Install the Gmail Always Show CC userscript found at http://cache. lifehacker.com/assets/resources/2008/06/gmailalwaysshowcc.user.js.

  Works in Firefox with Greasemonkey or with Opera and IE with some tweaking.

- Install the Gmail Always Show BCC userscript found at http://cache. lifehacker.com/assets/resources/2008/06/gmailalwaysshowbcc.user.js.

  Works in Firefox with Greasemonkey or with Opera and IE with some tweaking.

- Install Better Gmail 2 (https://addons.mozilla.org/en-US/firefox/addon/6076).

  Select Show CC Automatically and/or Show BCC Automatically on the Compose tab of this Firefox extension.

If you're more of a keyboard user and want to be able to use a key combination instead of the mouse, try out these methods:

- Install the Gmail Show CC Key Combination userscript found at http://cache.lifehacker.com/assets/resources/2008/06/gmailshowcc.user.js.

  Works in Firefox with Greasemonkey or with Opera and IE with some tweaking.

- Install the Gmail Show BCC Key Combination userscript found at http://cache.lifehacker.com/assets/resources/2008/06/gmailshowbcc.user.js.

  Works in Firefox with Greasemonkey or with Opera and IE with some tweaking.

- Install Better Gmail 2 (https://addons.mozilla.org/en-US/firefox/addon/6076).

  Select Show CC (Ctrl+Shift+C) and/or Show BCC (Ctrl+Shift+B) on the Compose tab of this Firefox extension.

Highlighting Conversations as You Mouse Over Them

We all like visual cues because they make using our computer easier. When you're looking at the list of conversations in Gmail, sometimes it can be hard to detect the location of your mouse. It would be a lot easier to see where you were if each conversation was highlighted as you moused over it, as in Figure 9.7.

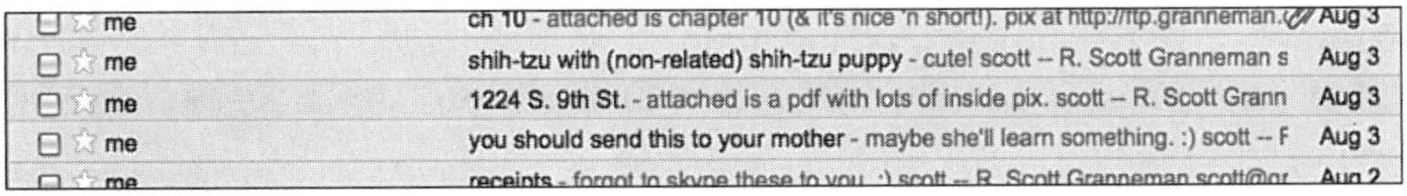

FIGURE 9.7 As you mouse over each conversation, it's highlighted for your convenience.

If you'd like your conversations to be highlighted as you mouse over them, use one of the following methods:

- Install the userscript found at http://userstyles.org/styles/4725.

  Works in Firefox with Greasemonkey, with Stylish, or with Opera and IE with some tweaking.

- Install Better Gmail 2 (https://addons.mozilla.org/en-US/firefox/addon/6076).

  Select Add Row Highlights on the Messages tab of this Firefox extension.

Displaying Attachment Icons

If a conversation has attachments in it, Gmail displays a little paper clip icon. That doesn't tell you what kinds of files are actually attached, however. Wouldn't it be more efficient if Gmail told you what the attachment file types were with just a glance, as in Figure 9.8?

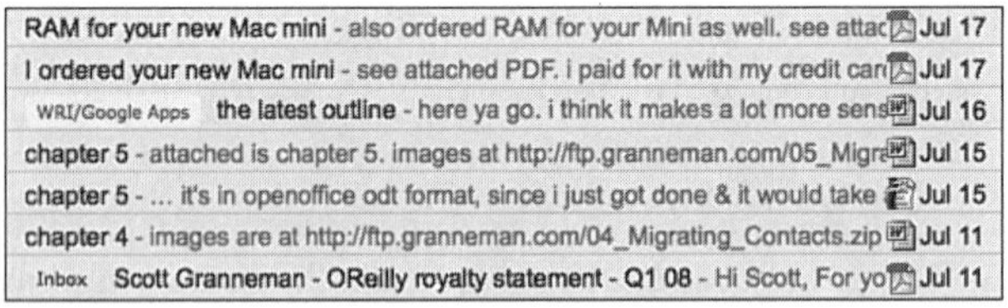

FIGURE 9.8   Word, Excel, Text—the little icons let you know!

If you'd like to get those handy icons, use one of the following methods:

- Install the userscript found at http://userstyles.org/styles/226.

  Works in Firefox with Greasemonkey, with Stylish, or with Opera and IE with some tweaking.

- Install Better Gmail 2 (https://addons.mozilla.org/en-US/firefox/addon/6076).

  Select Attachment Icons on the Messages tab of this Firefox extension.

Hiding the Chat Box

If you never use the built-in chat feature of Gmail, you might as well hide the chat box that takes up space on the left side of Gmail's web interface. You can use the following methods:

- Install the userscript found at http://userstyles.org/styles/7897.

  Works in Firefox with Greasemonkey, with Stylish, or with Opera and IE with some tweaking.

- Install Better Gmail 2 (https://addons.mozilla.org/en-US/firefox/addon/6076).

Select Hide Chat on the Sidebar tab of this Firefox extension.

Displaying the Unread Count First on a Tab or Title Bar

By default, Gmail displays the following information on your browser's title bar and tab:

```
Mail - Inbox (15) - scott@heavymetalmassage.com
```

The number in parentheses after the Inbox is the number of unread messages. That's a useful number to have in front of you, but if you have a lot of tabs open, it can get cut off as your shortened tab shows you this:

```
Mail - Inbox...
```

However, it's easy to switch the order of the information presented to you so that it instead looks like this:

```
15 unread - Mail Inbox
```

Now the most relevant info—the number of unread messages—is right in front. If your tabs get so short that you can't even see that number, you won't be able to see anything on any tab at all.

If you're interested in changing the order in which data is presented on your browser's title bar and tab, install one of the following:

- Install the userscript found at http://userscripts.org/scripts/show/10253.

  Works in Firefox with Greasemonkey or with Opera and IE with some tweaking.

- Install Better Gmail 2 (https://addons.mozilla.org/en-US/firefox/addon/6076).

  Select Inbox Count First on the General tab of this Firefox extension.

Showing Message Details

By default, Gmail doesn't show much info at the top of an email conversation, as you can see in Figure 9.9.

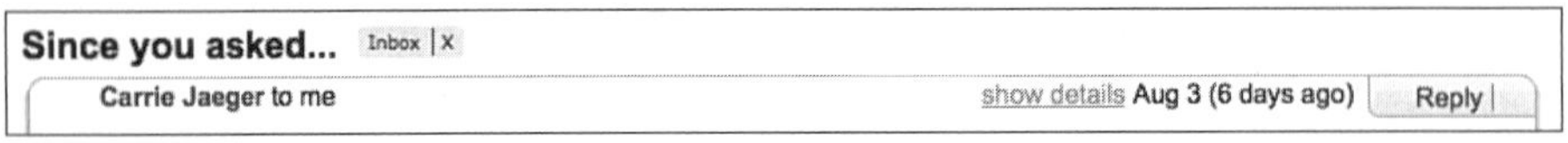

FIGURE 9.9   A name? That's it?

More would definitely be better, as you can see in Figure 9.10:

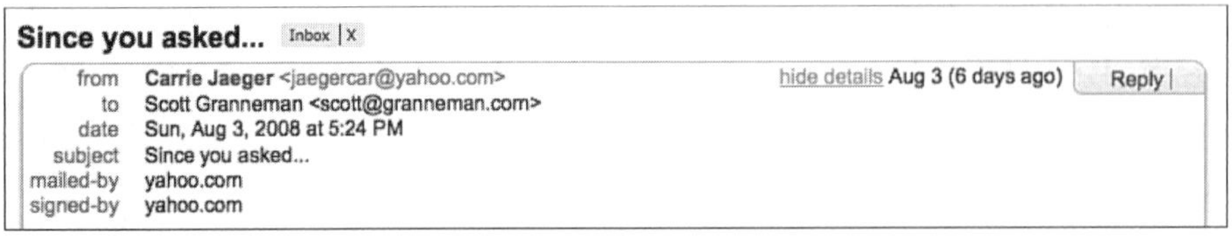

FIGURE 9.10   Now that's more like it!

If you'd like the data shown in Figure 9.10 to appear on the first open message of a conversation in Gmail, use of these methods:

- Install the userscript found at http://userscripts.org/scripts/show/13700.
  Works in Firefox with Greasemonkey or with Opera and IE with some tweaking.

- Install Better Gmail 2 (https://addons.mozilla.org/en-US/firefox/addon/6076).
  Select Show Message Details on the Messages tab of this Firefox extension.

ADDING NEW FEATURES

As awesome as Gmail is, it doesn't do everything. However, clever users and developers have taken it upon themselves to add new features in a variety of ways. In this section I'll call out a few interesting ways to add some cool features to Gmail that you might find useful.

Providing More Keyboard Shortcuts

One of the best things about Google, as I discussed in Chapter 8, "Five Things to Know About Using Gmail," are the program's extensive keyboard shortcuts. As I said there, learning the keyboard shortcuts will make you faster and far more efficient with Gmail.

If you're hungry for even more keyboard shortcuts, you have several options. Unfortunately, they are mutually exclusive. You can choose one set or the other.

First up is Mihai Parparita's work, which you can install using one of the following methods:

- Install the userscript found at http://blog.persistent.info/2007/11/macros-for-new-version-of-gmail.html.

  Works in Firefox with Greasemonkey or with Opera and IE with some tweaking.

- Install Better Gmail 2 (https://addons.mozilla.org/en-US/firefox/addon/6076).

Select Macros (? for Help) on the General tab of this Firefox extension.

As the title of the selection in the Better Gmail 2 extension indicates, if you click ?, you will see a pop-up screen listing all of Gmail's keyboard shortcuts. In addition, Parparita's work introduces some new ones, including those listed in Table 9.1:

TABLE 9.1 Key Commands Provided by Mihai Parparita

KEY COMBO	RESULTS	KEY COMBO	RESULTS
Shift + i	Mark as read	Shift + 8, r	Select read
Shift + u	Mark as unread	Shift + 8, u	Select unread
Shift + 3	Move to Trash	Shift + 8, s	Select starred
Shift + 8, a	Select all	Shift + 8, t	Select unstarred
Shift + 8, n	Select none		

Other keyboard shortcuts are also available, which you can find out about at the link at blog.persistent.info referenced previously.

Second is sewpafly's program, which you can install using one of the following methods:

- Install the userscript found at http://userscripts.org/scripts/show/14189.

  Works in Firefox with Greasemonkey or with Opera and IE with some tweaking.

- Install Better Gmail 2 (https://addons.mozilla.org/en-US/firefox/addon/6076).

  Select Macros Modified (h for Help) on the General tab of this Firefox extension.

As the title of the selection in the Better Gmail 2 extension indicates, if you press h, you will see a pop-up screen listing all of this app's keyboard shortcuts, some of which are listed in Table 9.2 (note that they are case sensitive, so r and R are different):

TABLE 9.2   Key Commands Provided by Sewpafly

Key Combo	Results	Key Combo	Results
E	Mark as read & archive	e	Archive
T	Move to Trash	X, u	Select unread
q	Add Quick Link	X, s	Select starred
r	Mark as read	X, t	Select unstarred
R	Mark as unread		

Other keyboard shortcuts are also available, which you can find out about at the link at userscripts.org referenced previously.

Using Gmail with the Getting Things Done System

If you're a big fan of David Allen's Getting Things Done system for organizing your tasks and your life, you'll be pleased as punch to find out that there's an extension for Firefox that transforms Gmail into a GTD powerhouse. Called GTDInbox, it's available at https://addons.mozilla.org/en-US/firefox/addon/3209, with complete information available at http://gtdinbox.com.

 NOTE

If you don't know anything about Getting Things Done, you should check it out. It's very smart, and lots of folks absolutely swear by it. Start at David Allen's website (www.davidco.com) and then read the Wikipedia article on the subject for a good overview of his method (http://en.wikipedia.org/wiki/Getting_Things_Done).

Posting on the Bottom of Replies

To really understand this feature, take a look at Figure 9.11.

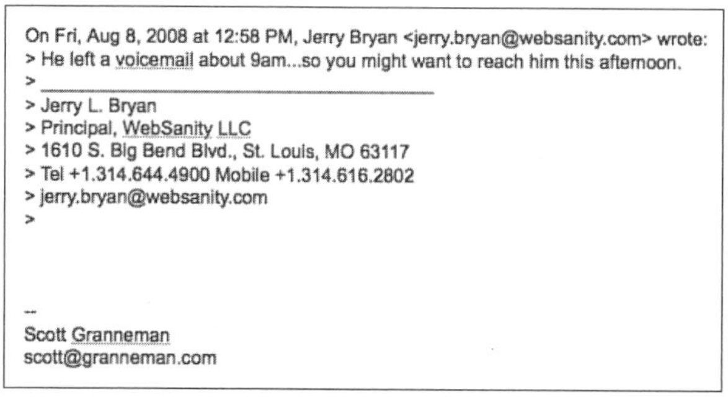

On Fri, Aug 8, 2008 at 12:58 PM, Jerry Bryan <jerry.bryan@websanity.com> wrote:
> He left a voicemail about 9am...so you might want to reach him this afternoon.
>
> _____
> Jerry L. Bryan
> Principal, WebSanity LLC
> 1610 S. Big Bend Blvd., St. Louis, MO 63117
> Tel +1.314.644.4900 Mobile +1.314.616.2802
> jerry.bryan@websanity.com
>

--
Scott Granneman
scott@granneman.com

FIGURE 9.11 Should the cursor go above or below the quoted text?

By default, when you click Reply to a message, Gmail puts your signature at the bottom of the new email, *below* the quoted text, but puts the cursor for your typed reply *above* the quoted text. This behavior drives some people, like my business partner Jerry, absolutely nutso. Instead, Jerry wants his signature at the bottom of the new email, below the quoted text—just like the default—but he wants the cursor to be *below* the quoted text, but *above* the signature, so he can start typing immediately. If this sounds of interest to you, check out one of the following:

■ Install the userscript found at http://userscripts.org/scripts/show/14256.
  Works in Firefox with Greasemonkey or with Opera and IE with some tweaking.

■ Install Better Gmail 2 (https://addons.mozilla.org/en-US/firefox/addon/6076).
  Select Bottom Post in Reply (Plain Text Only) on the Compose tab of this Firefox extension.

Creating More Effective Filters, Faster

Creating a filter for email messages isn't that difficult, as I discussed in Chapter 8. However, the problem is that by the time you're creating a filter, you're somewhat separated from the message that gave you the inspiration for filtering in the first place. If you'd like to make the filtering process a little quicker and more focused on the message that put the idea of a filter in your head in the first place, install the Gmail Filter Assistant userscript using one of these two methods:

■ Install the userscript found at http://userscripts.org/scripts/show/7997.
  Works in Firefox with Greasemonkey or with Opera and IE with some tweaking.

■ Install Better Gmail 2 (https://addons.mozilla.org/en-US/firefox/addon/6076).
  Select Filter Assistant on the Messages tab of this Firefox extension.

After you do so, you'll discover a small addition next to the normal tiny drop-down menu at the upper right of all messages in Gmail: a link to Filter Assistant, as you can see in Figure 9.12.

FIGURE 9.12   The Gmail Filter
Assistant adds a small link at the
top of all Gmail messages.

When you're in a message and you decide that you should create a filter around it, click Filter Assistant, and the fields displayed in Figure 9.13 appear:

Carrie Jaeger to me	show details Aug 3 (6 days ago)	Reply	Filter Assistant	

From: [   ]   Hasword: [   ]
To: scott@granneman.com   Doesn't have: [   ]
Subject: [   ]   ☐ Has attachment:

☐ Skip the inbox (Archive it)
☐ Mark it as read
☐ Star it
☐ Apply the label [1FOLLOWUP]
☐ Forward it to [   ]
☐ Delete it
☐ Apply the filter to existing conversations

More actions...
More actions...
Backup filter&label
Restore filter&label
Consolidate filters

Cancel   Create Filter

FIGURE 9.13   Wow! Filter fields galore, and some extra goodies as well!

Instead of the normal three-step filter process that I discussed in Chapter 8, the Gmail Filter Assistant centralizes everything on one screen. Better yet, the More Actions drop-down allows you to back up and restore your filters and labels, thus enabling you to migrate your filters and labels from one Gmail account to another.

Adding Attachments by Drag and Drop

With every desktop email program I've ever used, I could add attachments to a message by dragging and dropping the files onto the message. This capability doesn't exist in Gmail—or any other webmail app—unless you install the dragdropupload extension for Firefox (https://addons.mozilla.org/en-US/firefox/addon/2190).

After it is installed, if you want to add a file to a message you're composing in Gmail, drag it directly over the blue area of the compose screen. A few moments later, depending upon the size of your attachment, the file will appear as an attachment to your message. You can repeat the process as many times as necessary.

If you'd like more information about this extension, check out the developer's page at www.teslacore.it/wiki/index.php?title=DragDropUpload.

DEFAULTING TO GMAIL

If you grow to depend on Gmail, you'll probably want to take the final step and make it your default for all new emails you'd like to compose. In this section, we look at how to make Gmail the default for different operating systems.

> **TIP**
>
> If you just want to make Gmail the default in Firefox, but not for your operating system as a whole, see Lifehacker's "Set Firefox 3 to Launch Gmail for mailto Links" at http://lifehacker.com/392287/set-firefox-3-to-launch-gmail-for-mailto-links.

Making Gmail the Default for Your Windows PC

If you want to compose your message in Gmail when you click any email link in Windows, try one of the following methods:

- Install Google Talk (www.google.com/talk/).

  The official Google Talk client lets you set Gmail as your default email client.

- Install the official Google Gmail Notifier (http://toolbar.google.com/gmail-helper/notifier_windows.html).

  Check Use Gmail for Internet mailto: Links to set it up systemwide.

- Install gAttach (www.gattach.net).

  Very powerful; free for individuals and inexpensive for organizations.

Making Gmail the Default on Your Mac

The easiest solution is to install the official Google Notifier, available from http://toolbar.google.com/gmail-helper/notifier_mac.html. After you have it up and running on your Mac (you'll see it in your Menu Bar, by your clock), click the Mail icon on the Menu Bar, go to Preferences, choose the Gmail tab, find the Compose Mail In drop-down menu, and choose Gmail as the default program.

TIP

According to a commenter on www.macosxhints.com/article.php?story=200707030100345, all your traffic is encrypted via HTTPS, which is a very good thing. If you have multiple Google Apps accounts and want separate Google Notifiers for each of them, follow the steps given at www.macosxhints.com/article.php?story=20061117161341318.

Making Gmail the Default on Your Linux Box

If you use Linux, you're gonna have to do a bit more work than if you use Windows or Mac OS X. But if you use Linux, you've already understood and accepted that!

NOTE

The following script came from the Gentoo Wiki, at http://gentoo-wiki.com/HOWTO_Open_mailto:_links_in_gmail.

First you need to prepare Firefox. In the address bar, type **about:config**. If you're warned, go ahead and say OK. In the Filter, type in **mailto**. In the resulting list, double-click `network.protocol-handler.external.mailto` so it changes from `false` to `true`. You're now done setting up Firefox. Now on to the script.

Open up your favorite text editor and enter the following (change YOURDOMAIN to your actual Google Apps domain):

```
#!/bin/sh
BROWSER="firefox"

# remove the ? from the uri
uri=`echo "$1" | sed -e 's/subject=/su=/' -e
's/^mailto:\(([^&?]\+\)[?&]\?\(.*\)$/\1\&\2/'`

if [ "$uri" ];
  then exec $BROWSER
"https://mail.google.com/a/YOURDOMAIN/?view=cm&tf=0&ui=1&to=$uri"
fi

exec $BROWSER "https://mail.google.com/"
```

NOTE

If you don't want to type out the script, you can download it from http://ftp.granneman.com/googleapps/gmail_default.sh.

If you have a bin directory in your home directory, great; if you don't, create one. Save the file as **gmail_default.sh in ~/bin** and then open your terminal and type the following to make the new file executable:

```
chmod 755 ~/bin/gmail_default.sh
```

If you use GNOME, go to System, Preferences, Preferred Applications, Internet. In the Mail Reader section, change the drop-down to Custom, and then enter the following into the field next to Command:

```
/home/[your user name]/bin/gmail_default.sh %s
```

Do not check Run In Terminal. Click Close, and if you click a mail link now, it should open in Gmail in Firefox.

If you use KDE, go to System Settings, Default Applications, Email Client. Select Use a Different Email Client and enter the following into the field:

```
/home/[your user name]/bin/gmail_default.sh %t
```

Click Apply, and if you click a mail link now, it should open in Gmail in Firefox.

SOLVING COMMON PROBLEMS

As with all things in life, you're going to find little gotchas. Here are a few of those and their solutions.

Why is Gmail so slow?

If you're using Gmail, and it's unbearably slow and you're a web developer who has the fabulous Firebug installed, you have a conflict. Google advises that you disable Firebug when using Gmail because it can cause glacial access speeds. For more info, see http://mail.google.com/support/bin/answer.py?hl=en&ctx=mail&answer=77355.

How can I check more than one Google Apps Gmail account in the same browser?

You need to install the Gmail Manager extension for Firefox, available at https://addons.mozilla.org/en-US/firefox/addon/1320. It was designed to solve exactly this problem, and it works well.

Why do my non-English folders look funky in Outlook and Outlook Express?

If you're using the English versions of Outlook 2002, 2003, or Outlook Express, but Gmail's web interface is set to a language that contains non-Latin characters, you may find that your folder names look weird or don't display at all.

Unfortunately, there's not much you can do about it except switch to another desktop email program. The problem is with Outlook and Outlook Express, not Gmail.

Why is my desktop email client crashing when I download my email?

The short answer is that you probably have too many email messages. Gmail can store hundreds of thousands of messages on its servers, and looking at them via the Web won't be a problem. But downloading and trying to view tons of messages in your desktop client—especially in the [Gmail]/All Mail folder—can cause extreme slowness and even crashes. The solution: use a more robust desktop client, use Gmail via the Web, or delete some email!

Why am I repeatedly getting prompted for my password?

If you're stuck in "enter your password" hell, you may need to clear a captcha for your email account. A *captcha* is the box with squiggly letters and numbers in it that you have to type in so you can prove you're a human and not a spambot. Sometimes captchas get a little confused and you have to clear things.

> **NOTE**
>
> Don't know what a captcha is? Head over to Wikipedia's article on the subject at http://en.wikipedia.org/wiki/Captcha.

To clear a captcha, close any email clients that may be accessing your Gmail account. On the computer on which you're constantly receiving the password prompts, go to https://www.google.com/a/heavymetalmassage.com/UnlockCaptcha, filling in your domain name for heavymetalmassage.com. Enter your email password and password, fill in the new captcha, and sign in. After you've successfully signed in, start up your desktop client, and you should now be able to download your email without the annoying password prompts.

CONCLUSION

This has been a long chapter, but it's a big subject. As useful and innovative as Gmail's web interface has been, old habits die hard, and lots of people want to access their email in a desktop or mobile client, for a seemingly endless number of reasons. In this chapter we've really delved deep into this subject, but I could actually have gone on for double this length because of the huge number of email programs and ways to extend Gmail via a variety of methods. If you want to learn more, check out some of the resources I mentioned in the Acknowledgements and use Google's search engine. New things appear every day, and many of them are smart and useful.

CHAPTER 10

Integrating Google Contacts with Other Software and Services

Using Google Contacts is pretty easy, so easy that I'm not going to spend any time going over that subject. Instead, I want to focus in this chapter on ways to integrate Google Contacts with other address book software. It's silly to have one set of addresses at Google and another set in a different address book, as that results in confusion and unneeded complexity.

Let's unify those address books and make your life easier.

A QUICK LOOK AT SEVERAL CONTACT SYNCHRONIZATION PROGRAMS

In Chapter 4, "Migrating Contacts to Google Apps," I looked at several programs you can use to sync your local address books with Google Contacts, including the following:

- **Plaxo (www.plaxo.com; free)**—A web-based service that synchronizes contacts among different software, services, and even devices.

- **OggSync (http://oggsync.com; $30)**—Automatic synchronization of your Google Contacts and Outlook.

- **Zindus Thunderbird Contact Sync (https://addons.mozilla.org/ en-US/thunderbird/addon/6095; free)**—A free extension that allows users to sync Thunderbird's Address Book with Google Apps over a secure https connection.

■ **Apple Address Book (www.google.com/support/contactsync/;
free)**—A setting in Address Book that allows users to synchronize their contacts with Google Contacts.

QUERY GOOGLE CONTACTS WITH GCALDAEMON

■ Operating Systems: Windows, Mac OS X, Linux

■ Address Book Clients and Services: Thunderbird, Lotus Notes, Outlook,
Windows Address Book, Kontact, KAddressBook

■ Google Apps Editions: Standard, Premier, Education and Nonprofit, Partner

GCALDaemon is free and open source software that installs on Windows (NT, 2000,
XP, and Vista), Mac OS X, and Linux (as well as a variety of other UNIX flavors), or
you can install it on an Apache Tomcat server for a totally web-based solution.
You'll need a Java Runtime Environment (JRE) of at least version 1.5 or later.

Installation guides for your operating system can be found here:

■ **Windows NT/2000/XP**—http://gcaldaemon.sourceforge.net/usage10.html

■ **Windows Vista**—http://gcaldaemon.sourceforge.net/usage17.html

■ **Mac OS X**—http://gcaldaemon.sourceforge.net/usage12.html

■ **Linux/UNIX**—http://gcaldaemon.sourceforge.net/usage11.html

■ **Apache Tomcat**—http://gcaldaemon.sourceforge.net/usage15.html

The GCALDaemon website provides very detailed, clear instructions, with lots
of screenshots, for connecting Google Contacts to Thunderbird, Lotus Notes, Outlook, and Windows Address Book (however, others have reported that it works with
KAddressBook and Kontact as well). If you use those address books, visit the following addresses:

■ **Thunderbird**—http://gcaldaemon.sourceforge.net/usage4.html

■ **Lotus Notes**—http://gcaldaemon.sourceforge.net/usage5.html

■ **Outlook and Windows Address Book**—http://gcaldaemon.sourceforge.
net/usage6.html

These address books access the data provided by GCALDaemon by querying
an LDAP server that GCALDaemon creates, a relationship spelled out in Figure
10.1.

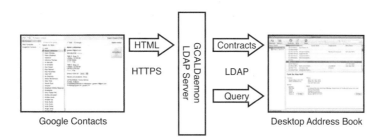

FIGURE 10.1   GCALDaemon creates an LDAP server that sits between Google Contacts and your desktop address book.

Pretty much every major address book can query an LDAP directory nowadays—you just need to figure out where that capability lies in the desktop address book you use.

TIP

Don't know what LDAP is? It's an incredibly complicated topic, one that you really don't have to know much about to use your desktop contacts with GCALDaemon. But if you feel like finding out more about LDAP, Wikipedia's article on the subject is available at http://en.wikipedia.org/wiki/Ldap.

Lifehacker provides a detailed guide to setting up and using GCALDaemon at http://lifehacker.com/software/google-calendar/geek-to-live-sync-google-calendar-and-gmail-contacts-to-your-desktop-251279.php. Check it out if you find this software interesting.

AUTOMATICALLY SYNC APPLE ADDRESS BOOK AND GOOGLE CONTACTS WITH SPANNING SYNC (AND OTHERS)

- Operating Systems: Mac OS X
- Address Book Clients and Services: Address Book
- Google Apps Editions: Standard, Premier, Education and Nonprofit, Partner

I covered Spanning Sync in some detail back in "Automatically Sync Apple Address Book and Google Contacts with Spanning Sync," which you can see in Chapter 4. Spanning Sync is $25 and automatically syncs both Apple's iCal and Address Book with their Google equivalents. It's an excellent way to keep everything in sync. Set the software up and then you can forget it, as everything happens in the background without bothering you.

An added benefit of this method is that my Google Contacts are automatically synced with my iPhone, as Figure 10.2 makes clear:

Google Contacts   Apple Address Book   iPhone

FIGURE 10.2 Google Contacts to Address Book to iPhone—and vice versa!

Spanning Sync makes sure that Apple's Address Book stays in sync with Google Contacts, and because syncing my iPhone keeps the Apple Address Book in sync with the iPhone, ultimately my contacts are the same in all three places.

As I remarked in Chapter 4, Spanning Sync isn't the only software that promises to keep your Apple Address Book and Google Contacts synchronized. Others include the following:

- **BusySync ($25 at http://busymac.com)**—Currently syncs Apple's iCal with Google Calendar, but Address Book and Google Contacts interaction is promised for the future.

- **Syncman ($15 at http://wateree.net/syncman/)**—Supports syncing Name, Company, Title, Notes, Email Addresses, Phone Numbers, and IM Accounts.

- **Soocial (No price set yet at http://www.soocial.com)**—As of August 2008, in closed beta, but invites are available, and the developers promise Outlook and LinkedIn integration as well.

- **GooSync ($40 at http://www.goosync.com)**—For limitations, see http://www.goosync.com/GoogleContactsHelp.aspx.

DEVELOP YOUR OWN CONTACTS TOOL WITH THE GOOGLE CONTACTS API

- Operating Systems: Windows, Mac OS X, Linux
- Address Book Clients and Services: Any you develop for
- Google Apps Editions: Standard, Premier, Education and Nonprofit, Partner

If you have developers on staff, you may want to build your own synchronization tool using Google's Contacts APIs, which you can read about in voluminous detail at http://code.google.com/apis/contacts/. With software built around the API, a program can list, search for, edit, and delete contacts.

In fact, Google frequently introduces new features to the Contacts API. Most recently, they added support for synchronizing contact groups (Work, Family, Friends, and so on) and contact photos and the capability to add new properties unique to your organization's needs. With Google's pace of development, it's likely that more useful capabilities will find their way into the Contacts API soon.

If you're interested in pursuing this subject further, I provided some links in "Develop Your Own Contact Migration Tools with Google Data APIs," which you can find in Chapter 4.

SOLVING COMMON PROBLEMS

As with all things in life, you're going to find little gotchas. Here are a few of those and their solutions.

Why Does Everyone I Email Show Up in my Google Contacts?

This one has been driving people absolutely bonkers for years, ever since Gmail rolled out, in fact. Every time you email anyone—by typing a new address into the To, CC, or BCC fields, or by replying to an email—the email address you send the mail to is added to your contacts. Google said it did this to make it easier to auto-complete email addresses, but most users howled that it was instead resulting in a grotesque bloat in their address books. For years there was absolutely nothing we could do about it.

Google recently fixed the problem. When you log in to your Google Contacts, you'll see that you have three categories for your addresses:

- **My Contacts**—Your main list of contacts, added to by you manually or by importing other address books.

- **Most Contacted**—The people you contact most from those listed in My Contacts.

- **Suggested Contacts**—The new place that Google puts people who are not in My Contacts, but to whom you have sent an email.

In addition, you should see the wording and option shown in Figure 10.3:

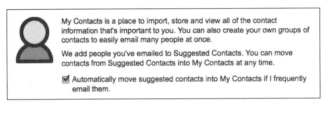

FIGURE 10.3   Google listens to the pleas of its users, eventually.

If you're bothered by a steadily growing list of email addresses in your Google Contacts, uncheck the box next to Automatically Move Suggested Contacts into My Contacts if I Frequently Email Them. If you leave it checked, Google will move addresses from Suggested Contacts into My Contacts if it thinks you've emailed them five or more times. If that number suits you, leave it checked. If, on the other hand, you want to be in charge completely, uncheck the box, periodically check Suggested Contacts, and move over to My Contacts only those that you want to move.

How Can I Quickly Edit Contact Names?

If you want to edit a contact's name super quickly, hover over the person's name in the chat list that appears on the left side of your Gmail window. If the person you want isn't already listed, search for her. Hover your mouse over the person, and the name that appears in the little pop-up is editable. That's all you can edit, however, but at least it's a start.

How Can I Make the Boxes into Which I Enter Info Bigger?

When you add or edit a contact, the text boxes (for those knowledgeable about HTML, the text areas) for Address and Notes aren't resizable. In the case of Address, this isn't a big deal, but when it comes to Notes, it's a real annoyance, as you can see in Figure 10.4.

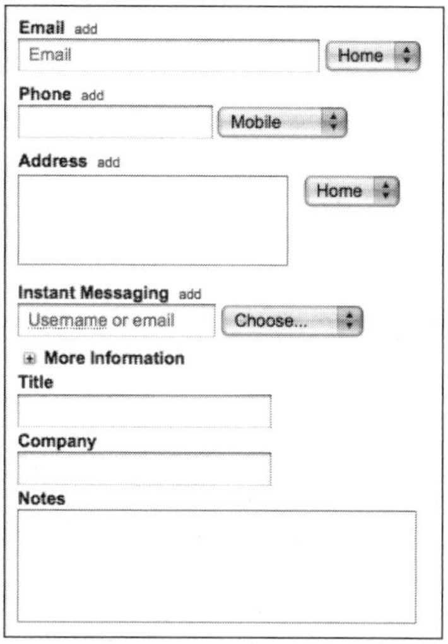

FIGURE 10.4   Jeeminy—
what is that text area for
Notes? Four rows by about 30
columns? A joke!

My buddy Rich, for instance, used the Notes field in Outlook like a mini-CRM (Customer Resource Management) app, keeping records about every phone call and communication he's had with his clients. When he moved to Google Apps and Gmail, he complained loud and long about the dinky little Notes field in Google Contacts.

I proposed a few solutions:

- Use Safari in Leopard, which automatically allows the user to resize any text area.

- Install the Resizeable Textarea extension for Firefox, available at https://addons.mozilla.org/en-US/firefox/addon/3818.

- Some people, however, think that the Text Area Resizer extension for Firefox does a better job. Try them both and make up your own mind! Get it from https://addons.mozilla.org/en-US/firefox/addon/8287.

- Install the wonderful It's All Text! extension for Firefox, which allows you to open the contents of any text area in the editor of your choice, edit there, and then save the contents back into the text area. You can find it at https://addons.mozilla.org/en-US/firefox/addon/4125.

- After you install the fabulous Greasemonkey Firefox extension (https://addons.mozilla.org/en-US/firefox/addon/748), you have your pick of a large number of scripts that work with Greasemonkey to allow for text area resizing, including http://userscripts.org/scripts/show/600 and http://userscripts.org/scripts/show/12970.

- If you install Greasemonkey and then Platypus (https://addons.mozilla.org/en-US/firefox/addon/737), you can use Platypus to set up the text area for Notes the way you'd like and then save the results as a Greasemonkey script.

- If you use IE, hoo boy. There is a port of Greasemonkey for IE available at http://www.gm4ie.com, and you can try working with some of the Greasemonkey scripts I listed previously, but you're going to have to make some modifications. Exactly how to do that is completely beyond the scope of this book, so head over to the Greasemonkey for IE site and start reading.

Is There Any Way I Can View Contacts Without Having to Log In to Gmail?

If you want to access, add, edit, and delete your Google Contacts without having to log in to Gmail first, you can do so by visiting https://docs.google.com/c/ui/Contact Manager. If you look carefully at the URL, you'll notice that it's at your Google Docs account. You use your Google Contacts to send collaboration requests, hence the capability to access your Contacts. There's only one caveat: You need to be signed in to your Google Docs account to view your Contacts in this way. Try it and see.

Help! My Contacts Won't Load!

If after clicking Contacts you see a blank white box and nothing else, it's one of these things:

- An out-of-date web browser. If you're not using a modern web browser—the latest Firefox, Safari, or Internet Explorer (although you should be using Firefox, of course)—get one, pronto.

- A browser cache that needs to be cleared. Each browser is a bit different, so Google for the way to clear your browser's cache.

- A temporary problem on Google's servers. Wait a while and try again.

- At that point, if you're still having a problem, Internet security programs are probably the culprit. Google contains information for resolving this problem with a variety of firewall and antivirus programs, including Kerio, McAfee, Norton, Proxomitron, ZoneAlarm Pro, and many others. Go to https://mail.google.com/support/bin/answer.py?answer=80444&topic=12878, choose your application, and follow Google's instructions.

CONCLUSION

No matter what OS you use, you should be able to find some software package that will synchronize Google Contacts with a desktop address book. Not every address book is supported, and many will never work because of the way they're programmed. But virtually all the major address books will happily synchronize with Google Contacts, which makes going through with it a no-brainer.

FURTHER READING

There's always more to learn, so here are some resources that you might find handy if you want to learn more about Google Contacts:

- Google Apps for Users Help Topics
  - Managing Contacts:
    http://mail.google.com/support/bin/topic.py?topic=12867
  - About the Contact Manager:
    https://mail.google.com/support/bin/answer.py?answer=77259&topic=13291
  - Contact Sync Help Center: www.google.com/support/contactsync/
- Franklin Davis' "How to Enable Mac Address Book to Sync with Google's Gmail Contacts without an iPhone or .Mac":
  www.zaphu.com/2008/05/29/how-to-enable-mac-address-book-syncing-with-googles-gmail-contacts-without-an-iphone-or-mac/
- PDFs for Training Support Staff:
  http://services.google.com/apps/training/user_support/Mail/MailUserSupportModule5ContactsAndChat.pdf
- For Developers
  - Contacts Data API: http://code.google.com/apis/contacts/
  - JavaScript Client Library for the Google Contacts Data API:
    http://googledataapis.blogspot.com/2008/06/javascript-client-library-for-google.html
  - Contacts API Google Group: http://groups.google.com/group/google-contacts-api
- Google Apps Frequently Reported Issues: www.google.com/support/a/bin/request.py?contact_type=known_issues

Part III

Google Calendar

CHAPTER 11

Setting Up Google Calendar

Calendars aren't nearly as complicated as email programs—thank goodness!—so it's no surprise that the settings for Google Calendar aren't nearly as complex as those for Gmail. Still, you should know about a few tricky things, and we'll cover those in this chapter, while leaving out the obvious stuff.

By the time we're done, your Google Calendar will be set up, and you'll be ready to start creating and sharing events and appointments. Organization, here you come!

GENERAL

The Settings page at Google Calendar contains more than 13 sections. They're all useful in one way or another, but I'm going to skip most of them in favor of the essentials.

Your Current Time Zone

Be sure to set your current time zone, and as you travel, feel free to change the time zone to match your current location. When you change the time zone, your appointments will adjust to reflect the new start and end times.

Location

If you plan to enable the weather feature (and why wouldn't you?) you'll need to set your location first so that Google knows which weather to display. You can specify your city and state ("Marshall, MO" or "Hempstead, NY") or give a ZIP code instead (65340 or 11550).

Google Calendar recognizes non-U.S. postal codes, by the way, such as those found in Canada and the United Kingdom. If you find that a postal code doesn't work, try specifying the name of the location instead.

Show Events You Have Declined

If you decline an invitation to an event, by default, Google Calendar shows you the event anyway. Of course, you can still delete it manually, but if you decline events and normally don't want to know about them, manual deletions can quickly grow tedious. If you want declined events off your calendar automatically, change Yes to No.

Automatically Add Invitations to My Calendar

At first, automatically adding invitations to your calendar as soon as you receive them might seem like a good idea. The problem is, as with so many other things in the online world, spammers have ruined a nice feature with their greed, selfishness, and criminality.

Spammers create events in their Google Calendars filled with language hawking their garbage and then invite masses of people to the fake events by adding their email addresses in the Add Guests text box. Because Google by default has Automatically Add Invitations to My Calendar set to Yes, if a spammer invites you to a non-event created purely to sell you junk, it will show up on your calendar without any approval on your part. I've been the victim of this attempted scam, and it's very annoying when you have to clean spammy appointments out of your calendar.

For that reason, it's best to change this setting from Yes to No.

Change Password

If it's time to change your password, for whatever reason, click the Change Password link. Keep in mind that you'll actually be changing your Google Apps account password because everything is tied together.

WARNING

Be sure you understand the implications of what I said in the previous paragraph—if you change your password, you're not just changing it for Google Calendar. You're changing it for all Google Apps!

CALENDARS

This section of Google Calendar's settings is where most of the action is; it's the place where you create and work with the specific calendars that contain data about your appointments. The page is divided into two sections: My Calendars and Other Calendars. My Calendars are those that you create and manage, whereas Other Calendars are those that belong to other people but which you access and use.

The calendars you see listed here also appear on the left side of the main Google Calendars page in blue boxes titled My Calendars and Other Calendars, which you can see in Figure 11.1.

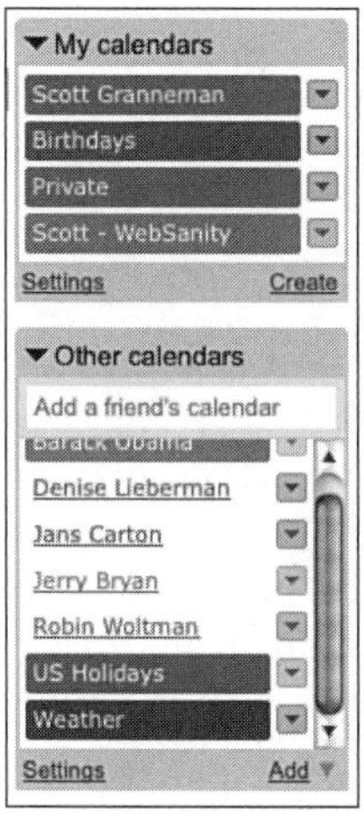

FIGURE 11.1 You can see a list of all your calendars on the left side of Google Calendar's main screen.

In fact, if you click the Settings link at the bottom of either of those blue boxes, you end up on this Settings page, which is a nice shortcut.

My Calendars

When you start using Google Calendar, you have one calendar, titled with your name ("Scott Granneman" in my case). You can add as many calendars as you'd like, resulting in something that may look like Figure 11.2.

My Calendars			
CALENDAR	**SHARING**		
⊞ Scott Granneman	Shared: Edit settings	Notifications	🗑
⊞ Birthdays	Share this calendar	Notifications Hide	🗑
⊞ Private	Share this calendar	Notifications Hide	🗑
⊞ Scott - WebSanity	Shared: Edit settings	Notifications Hide	🗑
Create new calendar			

FIGURE 11.2 I created and manage four calendars at this time.

On this page you can add, edit, and delete calendars. Deleting is easy—just click the trash-can icon on the far right of a particular calendar, acknowledge that you want to remove it, and it's gone. The other two processes—adding and editing—are more complicated, however.

Adding a New Calendar to My Calendars

To add a new calendar, press the Create New Calendar button. On the new page that opens, enter the following information (I'll be using my heavymetalmassage.com account as an example, but you should enter your own info, of course):

- **Calendar Name: Appointments**—You can name the calendar whatever you'd like; just make sure it's meaningful.

- **Domain: Heavy Metal Massage**—You can't change this because it's based on the name of your organization.

- **Description: Client appointments for Heavy Metal Massage**—This is most useful if you're sharing the calendar, so others will know what this calendar is tracking.

- **Location: St. Louis, MO**—If you're going to make your calendar public, a location will help people find your events. Even if you're not making it public, it doesn't hurt to fill this in.

- **Calendar Time Zone: (GMT -06:00)**—Central Time

The sharing features on this page require a bit more discussion.

If you check the box next to Share This Calendar with Others, you are giving others access to your appointments. What that means exactly depends on what you do in the check boxes right after that.

> ### TIP
>
> More information about sharing your calendar is available in an official Google video at http://www.youtube.com/watch?v=G7kniMsskDg.

If you checked Share This Calendar with Others, you can then check the box next to Make This Calendar Public. If you do this, you have two choices about what people can view: See All Event Details or See Only Free/Busy (Hide Details). All Event Details is just that—What, When, Where, and Notes—and everyone in the world will be able to see that information, including Google Search. Free/Busy just says that you're busy during a particular block of time, with no other details. In addition to the ability to see your calendar, people will now be able to add your calendar data to their Google Calendars (or to any other calendars that support iCal or XML feeds). This is great for a truly public calendar but not for personal or business data.

If you checked Share This Calendar with Others, the box next to Share This Calendar with Everyone in the Domain Heavy Metal Massage is automatically checked, and you cannot uncheck it, which makes sense because everyone at Heavy Metal Massage is part of the public. If you check Share This Calendar with Others but then uncheck Make This Calendar Public, you can now uncheck Share This Calendar with Everyone in the Domain Heavy Metal Massage. If this sounds a bit confusing, take a look at Figure 11.3, and it should become a bit clearer.

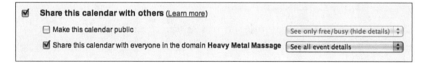

FIGURE 11.3   You have a few choices to make about sharing your calendar.

Again, you have two choices about what people can view: See All Event Details or See Only Free/Busy (Hide Details). You may feel a lot more comfortable sharing All Event Details with everyone in your organization because part of working together is knowing who's doing what and when.

Finally, at the bottom you can share your calendar with up to 75 specific individuals per day by entering each person's email address and then choosing one of four permissions that governs exactly what that person can do with your calendar:

- **Make Changes and Manage Sharing**—The other person can add, modify, and delete events, and share your calendar with others. Don't worry, though—he can't remove you because you're the owner of the calendar.

- **Make Changes to Events**—The other person can add, modify, and delete events but cannot share your calendar with others.

- **See All Event Details**—The other person can see complete information about your events but cannot add, modify, or delete them.

- **See Only Free/Busy (Hide Details)**—The other person can see that you're busy during a particular block of time, with no other details.

To revoke a person's access to your calendar, click the trash can icon on the far right of her email address, acknowledge that you want to remove her, and she's gone.

TIP

More information about sharing your calendar with specific individuals is available in an official Google video at http://www.youtube.com/watch?v=K0l-YuKYuhU.

After you've entered all the appropriate information, press the Create Calendar button. You now have a new calendar for your data.

Editing One of My Calendars

To edit general settings for a calendar, find the calendar in the list on the left side of the your screen, click the drop-down arrow to the right of the calendar's name, and select Settings (you could also go to Settings, Calendars and then click the name of the specific calendar you want to edit). When you do so, you'll see that you can change the following information you entered when you created a calendar: Calendar Name, Description, Location, and Calendar Time Zone. You cannot, however, change the Calendar Owner or Domain, which makes sense.

Further down on the page, you'll see three new sections:

- **Embed This Calendar**—Code that lets you insert your calendar into a website. Keep in mind that it shares all your details, as there is apparently no way to show just free/busy info. To customize the way the calendar looks, click Customize the Color, Size, and Other Options for a surprisingly complete set of options.

- **Calendar Address**—A read-only version of your calendar, available in three formats: XML and iCal, which are suitable for using in other programs, including Google Calendar, and HTML, which is a web page others can access without needing to sign in. Click the buttons to get the specific URLs. These links work only if you've indicated that you want to share your calendar.

- **Private Address**—A read-only version of your calendar that automatically contains all your appointment data. Available in three formats: XML and iCal, which are suitable for using in other programs, including Google Calendar, and HTML, which is a web page others can access without needing to sign in. These links work only if you've indicated that you want to share your calendar. If you accidentally share a Private Address and need to revoke it, click Reset Private URLs to tell Google to issue new URLs.

> **NOTE**
>
> When I refer to iCal in the previous list, I'm not talking about Apple's desktop calendar program, which is named iCal. Instead, I'm referring to the iCalendar standard (which Apple's iCal adheres to, by the way) for sharing calendar data. You can read more about it at http://en.wikipedia.org/wiki/ICalendar.

To edit a calendar's sharing settings—in other words, to add, edit, or remove sharing with particular individuals, organizations, or the world—click Shared: Edit Settings in the row of the calendar you want to change (if you haven't shared it yet, it will say Share This Calendar instead). The page that loads looks exactly like the Sharing section at the bottom of the page you see when you create a calendar, and all the options are the same. To find out more, read the previous section, "Adding a New Calendar to My Calendars."

To set the defaults for how you want Google to remind you about upcoming appointments, click Notifications back on the Settings page. You can first specify how you'd like Google to remind you and with how much advance warning. The method can be through SMS (text messaging), Email, or a Pop-up in your web browser. The times can range from 5 Minutes to 1 Week before the appointment starts. You can set as many as you'd like as defaults; for instance, you might want an email reminder 1 Day prior and an SMS and Pop-up 1 Hour before the event begins.

You can also choose if you'd like to be notified when certain events take place—New Invitations, Changed Invitations, Cancelled Invitations, and Invitation Replies—and if you'd like to receive those notifications through email and/or SMS.

In addition, you can ask Google to send you a Daily Agenda via email every day at 5 a.m. with that day's events on it.

Finally, if you want to receive text messages for any notifications, you first have to verify with Google that you own your cell phone. To do so, click Set Up Your Mobile Phone to Receive Notifications, which takes you to the Mobile Settings page, discussed in a later section in this chapter.

Other Calendars

On this page you can add, edit, and delete calendars that you do not own.

To add another person's calendar, press the Add Calendar button. This takes you to an Add a Public Calendar page, where you can search or browse for other calendars that people have made available.

If you already know the URL of the iCal file and you want to add it directly, look at the top of the Add a Public Calendar page where you'll see a tiny link to Add by URL. Click it, enter the address, and press Add.

Another way to add a calendar is by clicking the Add link at the bottom of the blue Other Calendars box on the front page of Google Calendar. When you do, a small pop-up appears, allowing you to add the following calendars:

- **Add a Public Calendar**—The same as pressing Add Calendar on the Settings page, discussed a few paragraphs ago.
- **Add a Friend's Calendar**—Allows you to enter an email address, but if they don't actually have a calendar, this doesn't help much!
- **Add by URL**—The same as clicking Add by URL on the Add a Public Calendar, discussed a few paragraphs ago.
- **Import Calendar**—We looked at importing calendars in Chapter 5, "Migrating Calendars to Google Apps."

After a calendar has been added, you can change general settings by clicking the calendar's name on the Settings page. You can change the calendar's name as it appears to you, you can embed it in a web page with provided code, and you can access the calendar's data through XML, iCal, or HTML link. All this is similar to your own calendars and was covered in the previous section.

You can set up how you're notified about new events in the other person's calendar by clicking the Notifications link on the Settings page. For more about setting Notifications, see the previous section.

Deleting another person's calendar from your Google Calendar listings is easy—just click the trashcan icon on the far right of a particular calendar, acknowledge that you want to remove it, and it's gone.

MOBILE SETUP

To access reminders on your cell phone, you need to reassure Google that your cell phone's number belongs to you.

To get things set up, enter the following information:

- Country
- Phone Number
- Carrier

After you've filled that in, press Send Verification Code. A few moments later, you should receive a text message from Google with the code in it. Enter those characters next to Verification Code and press Finish Setup. You should now be able to use your cell phone to receive notifications from Google Calendar.

SOLVING COMMON PROBLEMS

As with all things in life, you're going to find little gotchas. Here are a few of those along with their solutions.

When I Share Calendars, Why Am I Limited to Showing Free/Busy Times?

If your only option when you try to share a calendar is See Only Free/Busy (Hide Details), your Google Apps administrator has limited your sharing rights. To change this, your admin will need to go to your domain's Google Apps control panel, Service Settings, Calendar, and change Only Free/Busy Information (Hide Event Details) to one of the other settings.

CONCLUSION

After reading this chapter, you should have a good understanding of Google Calendar's various settings and how you can tailor them to your liking. Take some time and explore the options. Test them out and see what works for you.

CHAPTER 12

Things to Know About Using Google Calendar

Google Calendar is an excellent online calendaring tool, one of the best services in Google Apps. It's easy to use, but I'm going to call out a few features to you so that you can get even more use out of it.

Keep in mind that in this chapter, I'm focusing entirely on using Google Calendar in a web browser. In the next chapter, I look at accessing Google Calendar using a desktop calendar client such as Outlook, Apple iCal, or Sunbird. With that in mind, let's look at the things you absolutely need to know about Google Calendar to use it more effectively.

ADDING EVENTS

When it comes to adding appointments to your calendar, Google gives you a cornucopia of options:

- Click the Create Event link in the upper left of the main Google Calendar window. When you do, you're taken to the detail page for the event immediately, which is nice if you know you have a lot of extra detail to add to the event.

- Click the Quick Add link in the upper left of the main Google Calendar window. When you do, a small pop-up opens into which you can type a short description of your event. Google will do its best to parse what you write and add an event from it. Some examples follow:

  - Meeting with Saint Louis Zoo 10am-noon Thursday at WebSanity office. This correctly fills in the What, When, and Where fields.

- Meeting with Saint Louis Zoo 10am–noon Thursday at WebSanity office jerry@websanity.com. Jerry gets an email inviting him to the event. My only complaint: his email address shows up in the What.

- Breakfast 8–9 a.m. with Gabe & Fiona at Kopperman's one week from today. This does *not* work—it's added to today, not one week from today.

- Breakfast with Gabe & Fiona at Kopperman's 9/3/2008. This does work, with the correct What, When, and Where.

- Vacation in Arrow Rock 9/6-9/7. An all-day event is created covering the weekend, with the right What and Where.

- Gabe's birthday 6/1/2002 yearly. An event is added that recurs yearly.

- On the day you'd like to create the event, click a blank area of your calendar. A pop-up appears into which you can enter data. If you'd like to fill in more information, you can instead click Edit Event Details.

- In Day, Week, or 4 Days view, click and drag in the area of time in which you want to create an appointment—from 2 p.m. to 4 p.m. on Thursday, for instance. After you finish, a pop-up appears into which you can enter data. If you'd like to fill in more information, you can instead click Edit Event Details.

- If you're reading a message in the web-based interface of Gmail that mentions a date and time, Gmail does its best to parse what the sender wrote and then offers, on the column to the right of Gmail, to add it to your calendar. You can see Gmail's offer in Figure 12.1.

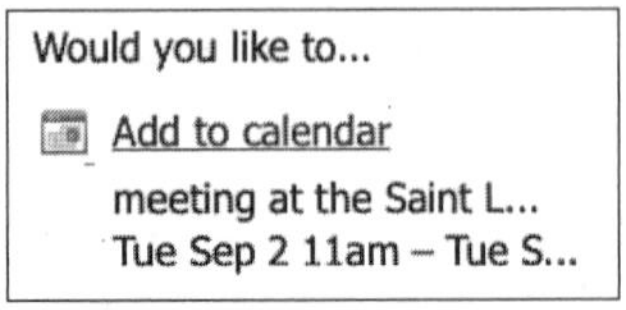

Would you like to...

Add to calendar
meeting at the Saint L...
Tue Sep 2 11am – Tue S...

FIGURE 12.1 Gmail smartly offers to add a meeting mentioned in an email message to Google Calendar.

Use the option that suits you best—if you're in a hurry, Quick Add is fabulous. If you use Gmail all the time, use the note in the right column. I like to click and drag and then fill in the necessary information. No matter what your style is, Google Calendar has you covered.

> **NOTE**
>
> For more on Quick Add, watch the video or read the help page at www.google.com/support/calendar/bin/answer.py?hl=en&answer=36604.

REPLACING EVITE

I like going to parties, but boy do I hate receiving invitations from Evite. Talk about an ad-laden, inefficient, poorly designed website (for more, Google "evite sucks"). Fortunately, you—and your friends—don't have to use Evite. Instead, you can use Google Calendar to plan your next shindig, and you'll find that you don't need Evite and all of its useless bloat.

Create an event—"80s Old Skool Rap Party," let's say—and pay attention to the Guests area. Enter in the email addresses of your guests, separated by commas, or click Choose From Contacts and use the Contact Picker. If you want to duplicate some of the features of Evite, make sure that you check both Guests Can Invite Others and Guest Can See Guest List.

Click Save, and Google Calendar creates your event and sends an email out to your guests. As your guests reply, those responses are added to your Google Calendar. Better still, if your guests use Google Calendar, the event is automatically added to their calendars, and at any time they can click on the event to see details, like who's coming.

If you want to email people with reminders, that's now easier as well. You can select whom to email—those who've said Yes, those who've said No, or even those who've said Maybe and are still on the fence. If you'd rather focus on specific individuals, just click Select Specific People and choose the exact folks you want to email.

Google Calendar doesn't have every bell and whistle when it comes to invitations—after all, it wasn't created to let people know about parties—but it does a very nice job in that department. Give it a try, and you might find that it perfectly meets your needs.

SEARCHING FOR EVENTS

Google Calendar is a product of Google, after all, so it's no shocker that it has excellent search capabilities. It's not nearly as complex or powerful as Gmail's search (which I covered in Chapter 8's "Searching for the Exact Message You Need"), but it has some nice advanced features that you should use.

If you want to perform a basic search, type your query into the search box and click Search My Calendars (if you instead want to search all public calendars, click Search Public Calendars). If you need something more nuanced, click Show Search Options.

When you do, you'll see the following fields:

- **What**—This corresponds to the What field on the Event Details page.
- **Who**—This corresponds to the Who field on the Event Details page.
- **Where**—This corresponds to the Where field on the Event Details page.
- **Search**—Choose which specific calendar you want to search within or choose All My Calendars, All Other Calendars, or All Calendars (the default).
- **Doesn't Have**—Enter words that you do not want to appear in your results.
- **Date From ___ To ___**—A nice pop-up calendar appears, making it easy to pick dates, or you can enter dates in the form of month/day/year.

As I said, this isn't nearly as powerful as Gmail's search operators, but then, it doesn't need to be. If you need to find an event, these search tools will definitely help you.

SPEEDING THINGS UP WITH KEYBOARD SHORTCUTS

Google Calendar is eminently usable with a mouse, but if you learn the key commands that Google thoughtfully provides, you can use Google Calendar far faster and more efficiently.

I'm not going to go through all the keyboard shortcuts that Google Calendar possesses because you can find the complete list at the Google Calendar Help Center, at www.google.com/support/calendar/bin/answer.py?hl=en&answer=37034.

Table 12.1 lists some of the shortcuts that I use all time, so I recommend them wholeheartedly. However, do check out the link I just gave you because you are sure to find others that are just as useful.

TABLE 12.1   Some of My Favorite Google Calendar Keyboard Shortcuts

KEYBOARD SHORTCUT	MEANING
Calendar Views	
w	Go to Week view
m	Go to Month view
Moving Around Google Calendar's Interface	
k	Move to next (newer) date range
j	Move to previous (older) date range
t	Jump to today
/	Place your cursor in the search box
s	Go to Google Calendar Settings
Adding Events	
c	Create event
q	Open Quick Add to create event
Event Details	
Alt+s	Saves event
Esc	
OR	
u	Go back to Calendar view

Remember, these are just a few of the many keyboard shortcuts that you can use. Check out the link I provided at the beginning of this section for more. And one final thought: It's not vital that you learn all the shortcuts. Instead, learn the ones that will be of most use to you.

CONCLUSION

In this chapter I've looked at the things you should know about if you're using the web-based version of Google Calendar: adding events, inviting groups, search, and keyboard shortcuts. The more you can learn about each, the more effectively you'll be able to use Google Calendar. In the next chapter, we examine how to integrate Google Calendar into desktop and mobile calendaring programs.

FURTHER READING

There's always more to learn, so here are some resources that you might find handy if you want to learn more about Google Calendar:

- Google Calendar Tour: www.google.com/googlecalendar/tour.html
- Overviews
  - Google Calendar Overview: www.google.com/a/help/intl/en/users/calendar.html
  - Overview: www.google.com/googlecalendar/overview.html
  - Getting Started Guide: www.google.com/support/calendar/bin/answer.py?answer=97699
- Google Apps for Admins Help Topics
  - Google Apps Admin Help: Calendar: www.google.com/support/a/bin/topic.py?topic=9201
  - All Help topics on one page: www.google.com/support/calendar/?fulldump=1
- Google Calendar Help for Users: www.google.com/support/calendar/?ctx=ausers&hl=en
- Videos
  - Google Calendar Welcome: http://services.google.com/apps/resources/overviews/welcome/topicWelcome/page07.html
  - Google Calendar interactive video guide: http://services.google.com/apps/resources/overviews/welcome/topicCalendar/index.html
  - YouTube Channel: http://www.youtube.com/view_play_list?p=86393B62706987AD
- For Developers
  - Calendar Data API: http://services.google.com/apps/resources/admin_breeze/APIGdataCalendar/
  - APIs discussion group: http://groups.google.com/group/google-apps-apis)

- PDFs for Training Support Staff: http://services.google.com/apps/training/user_support/Calendar/CalendarUserSupportModule2Issues.pdf
- Discussion Groups
  - Official Google Calendar Help Group (http://groups.google.com/group/Google-Calendar-Help
  - Google Calendar Users: http://groups.google.com/group/Google-Calendar-Users
- Google Calendar Help FAQs: http://groups.google.com/group/Google-Calendar-Help/web
- News and Announcements
  - What's New: www.google.com/googlecalendar/new.html
  - Announcements and Alerts: http://groups.google.com/group/google-calendar-help-updates/topics
- Known Issues
  - Google Apps Frequently Reported Issues: www.google.com/support/a/bin/request.py?contact_type=known_issues
  - Google Calendar Known Issues: www.google.com/support/calendar/bin/static.py?page=known_issues.cs
- Support Options: www.google.com/support/calendar/bin/request.py?contact_type=contact_policy&hl=en

CHAPTER 13

Integrating Google Calendar with Other Software and Services

I've used a lot of desktop calendar programs in my day, but Google Calendar beats any of them. It's a marvelous program, and Google should be commended for the excellence they've brought to calendaring.

However, improvements always can be made to software, and on top of that, some people would rather use their tried and true desktop calendaring program— Outlook, iCal, whatever—so in this chapter we look at various ways you can integrate Google Calendar with other software and services. This includes accessing your Google Calendar in different ways and changing how the web version works and looks.

Before we start, though, I need to emphasize three things that you should know before you read the rest of this chapter:

- In Chapter 12, I discussed how Google makes your calendar data available if you click a button labeled ICAL, which provides your data in the standard iCalendar format, often abbreviated as iCal. However, Apple's desktop calendar program is also called iCal. So to distinguish between the two in this chapter, I use ICAL to refer to the button at Google, and iCal to refer to Apple's program.

- Be sure to read Chapter 9's "A Note on Adding Scripts to Your Web Browser" before reading the rest of this chapter. I'll be talking about userscripts and userstyles, and if you want to understand what those are and why they're cool, check out that earlier chapter.

- In this chapter I'm looking at only a few things that the Better GCal extension for Firefox can do. If you're interested in changing Google Calendar in more ways than I cover here, you owe it to yourself to check out the extension at https://addons.mozilla.org/en-US/firefox/addon/5299.

Got all that? Good! Let's start messing around with Google Calendar!

Accessing Google Calendar in a Desktop Calendar Program

Many prominent desktop calendar programs—with perhaps a few surprising exceptions (Outlook 2003, I'm lookin' at you)—allow you to view a remote iCalendar file in them. You can't edit the file, and you certainly can't sync data; instead, you can simply view it, and that's it. For most people, that will be unacceptable, and if that describes you, then jump ahead to "Synchronizing Google Calendar with a Desktop (or Mobile) Calendar Program." If, however, you're fine with looking but not touching, keep reading.

Generic Instructions

The generic instructions are pretty simple: Find the URL of your calendar's ICAL Private Address on the Calendar Settings page and copy it. In your desktop calendar program, find the place in which you enter that URL. Paste it in, save, and presto! Your Google Calendar should now show up in your desktop calendar app.

As I said in the intro paragraph to this section, it's read-only, but if that's all you need, that's just fine and dandy.

Evolution

Before beginning this process, make sure you know your ICAL private address on your Calendar Details page in Google Calendar Settings, as discussed in Chapter 11's "Calendars."

 NOTE

The following instructions are for Evolution 2.22 and later because the new version makes it far easier to connect to Google Calendar. If you haven't upgraded yet, do so—it's free, after all!

In Evolution, go to File, New, Calendar. In the New Calendar window, enter the following information (I'll be using my heavymetalmassage.com account as an example, but you should enter your own info):

- Type: `Google`
- Name: `Heavy Metal Massage`. This can be whatever you'd like, as long as it means something to you.
- Username: `scott@heavymetalmassage.com`
- Refresh: `30 minutes`. You can enter any number you'd like, with intervals of minutes, hours, days, or weeks.
- Check the box next to Use SSL.
- Color: `Orange`. Choose a color you'd like for this calendar's events (I like orange).
- Check the box next to Copy Calendar Content Locally for Offline Operation. This makes good sense; you can access your calendar even if you're not online.
- Check the box next to Mark as Default Folder. Do this only if you want it to be the default for new events.

Click OK. Go to Calendars, find your Google Calendar under Google in the list of calendars, and check the box next to your calendar to activate it. When you do so, you'll be prompted for your password. Enter it and click OK.

You can view your Google Calendar, but you can't add, edit, or delete events. To do that, you'll need to look at GCALDaemon or ScheduleWorld, discussed later in "Synchronizing Google Calendar with a Desktop (or Mobile) Calendar Program."

As for CalDAV support, at the time I'm writing this, Evolution doesn't like the @ sign in a CalDAV URL, so the instructions Google provides for accessing Google Calendar via CalDAV don't work. Give it time, however, and Evolution will be able to use CalDAV with Google Calendar, which means full two-way syncing!

iCal

Before beginning this process, make sure you know your ICAL private address on your Calendar Details page in Google Calendar Settings, as discussed in Chapter 11's "Calendars."

In iCal, go to Calendar, Subscribe. Enter the URL for your ICAL private address next to Calendar URL and click Subscribe. After iCal connects to Google and downloads the initial information, the Info screen opens. Enter the following information (I'll be using my heavymetalmassage.com account as an example, but you should enter your own info):

- Name: `Heavy Metal Massage`
- Description: `Heavy Metal Massage client calendar`
- Subscribed To: (leave the URL alone)
- Uncheck the box next to Remove Alarms. If you don't want to get alarms, leave it checked.
- Uncheck the box next to Remove Attachments. If you don't want to get attachments, leave it checked.
- Check the box next to Remove To Do Items. Google doesn't yet have a to-do program—c'mon Google! Add one!
- Auto-Refresh: Every 15 Minutes. You have six choices; select the one that's right for you.
- Click OK. You're ready to access your Google Calendar in iCal.

KOrganizer (and Kontact)

Before beginning this process, make sure you know your ICAL private address on your Calendar Details page in Google Calendar Settings, as discussed in Chapter 11's "Calendars."

In KOrganizer or Kontact, make sure that Settings, Sidebar, Show Resource View is selected. In the list of calendars on the bottom left of the program, right-click in a blank area and choose Add. From the list that appears, select Calendar in Remote File and click OK.

In the window that appears, enter the following information (I'll be using my heavymetalmassage.com account as an example, but you should enter your own info):

- Name: `Heavy Metal Massage`. This can be whatever you'd like, as long as it means something to you.
- Check the box next to Read-only.
- Download From: https://www.google.com/calendar/ical/scott%40heavymetal-massage.com/private-abcdef1234567890abcdef1234567890/basic.ics.
- Enter your ICAL private address.
- Upload To: Leave this blank.
- Automatic Reload: Regular interval.

- Interval in Minutes: 10. You can enter any number you'd like.

- Automatic Save: Never.

- Click OK. In the list of Calendars, find your Google Calendar and check the box next to your calendar to activate it. When you're prompted for your password, enter it and click OK.

You can view your Google Calendar, but you can't add, edit, or delete events. To do that, you'll need to look at GCALDaemon, discussed later in "Synchronizing Google Calendar with a Desktop (or Mobile) Calendar Program."

As for CalDAV support, at the time I'm writing this, KOrganizer doesn't work with Google Calendar and its CalDAV support. Give it time, however, and KOrganizer will be able to use CalDAV with Google Calendar, which means full two-way syncing!

Outlook 2003

Outlook 2003, unbelievably (or maybe not, given Microsoft's poor history with standards support), does not support iCalendar files. Fortunately for Outlook users (and Microsoft because they'll make money on the upgrade), Outlook 2007 does support ICAL files. So you can upgrade to Outlook 2007, you can use one of the synchronization tools discussed later in "Synchronizing Google Calendar with a Desktop (or Mobile) Calendar Program," or you can use a free, open source program that gives Outlook 2003 the capability to read and write to ICAL files.

If you're interested in the latter option, point your web browser to https://sourceforge.net/projects/remotecalendars/. There you can download RemoteCalendars, which describes itself as "a COM-.NET Add-in for Outlook 2003/2007, written in C#. After installing this plug-in, every Outlook user should be able to subscribe, reload, and delete a generic remote iCalendar (RFC 2445) from Outlook 2003/2007. If you like it, notice that you can continue using it in Outlook 2007. Instructions for using it are at http://remotecalendars.sourceforge.net/help.html.

Outlook 2007

Before beginning this process, make sure you know your ICAL private address on your Calendar Details page in Google Calendar Settings, as discussed in Chapter 11's "Calendars."

In Outlook 2007, go to Tools, Account Settings, Internet Calendars, and click New. Enter the URL for your ICAL private address in the box next to Enter the Location of the Internet Calendar and click Add. At least that's how it's supposed to work. It didn't for me, though it does for some people. If you get an error message from Outlook that it Cannot Verify or Add the Internet Calendar, you need to perform the following rigmarole.

Copy the private ICAL link and then paste it into your web browser's address bar (Firefox works just fine, so don't feel like you have to do this in Internet Explorer).

Change `http://` to `webcal://`, however, and then press Enter. When you do so, your browser should offer to open the URL in an external program. Choose Outlook 2007 and click OK.

Outlook 2007 will offer to Add This Internet Calendar to Outlook and Subscribe to Updates, which is what we wanted in the first place. If you're fine with that, click OK, but instead you should click Advanced, which allows you to enter the following information (I'll be using my heavymetalmassage.com account as an example, but you should enter your own info):

- Folder Name: `Heavy Metal Massage`
- Description: `Heavy Metal Massage client calendar`
- Check the box next to Download Attachments for Items in This Internet Calendar.
- Check the box next to Update This Subscription with the Publisher's Recommendation.
- Click OK to close the Advanced window and then click Yes to add the calendar.

NOTE

Thanks to Daniel Pauly's comment at www.howtogeek.com/howto/ microsoft-office/view-your-google-calendar-in-outlook-2007/ for the solution to this problem. And by the way, it's ridiculous that Outlook has this problem in the first place.

You're ready to access your Google Calendar in Outlook 2007.

Sunbird and Thunderbird with Lightning

Before beginning this process, make sure you know your ICAL private address on your Calendar Details page in Google Calendar Settings, as discussed in Chapter 11's "Calendars."

In both Sunbird and Thunderbird with Lightning, go to Calendars, New Calendar. On the first screen of Create a New Calendar, select On the Network and click Continue.

On the next screen, select iCalendar (ICS), enter your private ICAL address in Location, and click Continue.

On the next screen, enter the following information (I'll be using my heavymetalmassage.com account as an example, but you should enter your own info, of course):

- Name: `Heavy Metal Massage`
- Color: `Orange.` Choose a color you'd like.
- Check the box next to Show Alarms. If you don't want alarms to show up in Thunderbird/Sunbird, uncheck this, but I don't see why you'd want to do that.
- Click Continue and then Done on the last screen.
- When prompted, enter your Google Apps username (your email address) and password.

You're ready to access your Google Calendar in Thunderbird or Sunbird.

Windows Calendar

Before beginning this process, make sure you know your ICAL private address on your Calendar Details page in Google Calendar Settings, as discussed in chapter 11's "Calendars."

In Windows Calendar, click the Subscribe button on the toolbar. On the Subscribe to a Calendar screen, enter the URL of your ICAL address and click Next.

On the Calendar Subscription Settings screen, enter the following information (I'll be using my heavymetalmassage.com account as an example, but you should enter your own info:

- Calendar Name: `Heavy Metal Massage`
- Update Interval: 15 Minutes. You have five choices; select the one that's right for you.
- Check the box next to Include Reminders. If you don't want reminders, don't check the box.
- Don't check the box next to Include Tasks. Google doesn't yet have a to-do program—c'mon Google! Add one!

- Click Finish, and you should see your appointments in Windows Calendar in a moment.

You're ready to access your Google Calendar in Windows Calendar.

WORKING WITH GOOGLE CALENDAR ON A MOBILE DEVICE

With desktop calendar programs that lack synchronization capabilities (which we looked at in the previous section), you're usually constrained to viewing your Google Calendar without being able to edit it. In the case of mobile devices, however, you can usually edit as well as view.

Generic Instructions

The generic instructions are pretty simple: connect to the Web and go to http://calendar.google.com/a/heavymetalmassage.com/m (use your own domain name—and notice the "m" at the end of the URL!). Sign in with your Google Apps username and password. You can now view appointments in your Google Calendar, with a very limited ability to add events, albeit in a teeny-tiny window over what is probably a painfully slow network connection (although things are definitely improving on both fronts).

BlackBerry

If you use a BlackBerry, you should install Google Sync, software made by Google that keeps your Google Calendar and your BlackBerry working together with the same appointments.

To get Google Sync on your BlackBerry, load up your BlackBerry's web browser and go to http://m.google.com/sync. Then click the Download Google Sync link. On the download page, click Download. After the program finishes installing, you'll see an icon for Google Sync on your BlackBerry's home screen.

To use Google Sync, click the icon for the program and then log in with your Google Apps username and password. At the bottom of the Welcome screen, click the Sync Now button. After a few moments, depending on the amount of data in your Google Calendar account, your events will appear in your BlackBerry's built-in calendar.

For each event, you can see the following information:

- Date, Time, Location, and Notes
- Available/Busy Setting
- Reminder Setting

If you'd like to change how Google Sync works, select Options from the program's menu on your BlackBerry. In particular, you may want to change how often Google Sync connects to your Google Calendar. By default, it does so every two hours. If you'd like Google Sync to check more often, you can change it to something less than two hours; if you'd like to check it only when you say so, you can change it to Manual.

> **NOTE**
>
> For more about Google Sync for the BlackBerry, head over to www.google. com/mobile/blackberry/sync/. If you have an issue, see Google's collection of help pages at www.google.com/support/mobile/bin/topic.cs/bin/ topic.py?topic=13626&hl=en.

iPhone

At this time, there's no direct way on the iPhone to access Google Calendar, nor is there a third-party app that does the same thing. That leaves you with two choices:

- Access Google Calendar via the web browser built in to the iPhone at the URL I gave earlier in "Generic Instructions." This isn't so bad, but it's not as smooth as using the built-in calendaring app included with the iPhone, and you're pretty limited as to what you can do to your appointments.
- Use Spanning Sync, BusySync, or the equivalent (discussed in the next section, "Synchronizing Google Calendar with a Desktop (or Mobile) Calendar Program") to sync Google Calendar with iCal, and then sync iCal with your iPhone either manually via iTunes or automatically using MobileMe. The process is illustrated in Figure 13.1.

> **NOTE**
>
> If you're up to date with your tech news, you might think that you could use CalDAV to sync Google Calendar with iCal (free!), and then sync iCal with your iPhone either manually via iTunes or automatically using MobileMe, but alas, at this time you cannot. Six months from now, who knows? You can find more details later in this chapter in "Using CalDAV to Synchronize Apple iCal with Google Calendar."

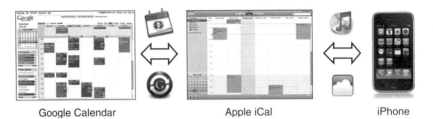

Google Calendar   Apple iCal   iPhone

FIGURE 13.1 From Google Calendar to iCal via Spanning Sync or BusySync, and from iCal to iPhone via iTunes or MobileMe. Whew!

The second solution is probably easier overall, but it comes with some factors you need to be aware of:

- Spanning Sync and BusySync both cost money. Not a lot, and I think they're worth it, but they do require you to pay for them.

- If you manually sync your iPhone using iTunes, your calendar on your iPhone will update only when you sync. This could result in Google Calendar and iCal being in sync, with the iPhone wildly out of date, depending upon how often you sync your iPhone.

- If you automatically sync your iPhone using MobileMe, things will be in sync between Google Calendar, iCal, and your iPhone a lot more often, with a lot less effort. However, this brings me to my fourth point.

- MobileMe costs $100 a year, which is a lot of money to most people. Sure, you get a lot of cool features with it, but it's still $100 (the family pack is a better deal, and it's a better deal on top of that if you buy it from Amazon). If you want your iPhone to be in sync with your Google Calendar with the least amount of out-of-sync time and the least amount of fuss, however, this is probably the way to go.

NOTE

The guys behind BusySync—a Spanning Sync competitor—have a good blog post explaining the interrelationships between "iCal, Google Calendar, BusySync and MobileMe" at http://blog.busymac.com/blog/mobileme/.

Windows Mobile

If you use a Windows Mobile device, you should look at the following solutions:

- **GmobileSync (http://rareedge.com/gmobilesync/; free)**—An open source app that syncs Outlook Mobile with Google Calendar.
- **Google Calendar Sync (http://www.google.com/support/calendar/bin/ answer.py?answer=98563; free)**—Synchronizes Google Calendar with Outlook, which then syncs with Outlook Mobile.
- **GooSync (http://www.goosync.com; free or $35)**—You must install a SyncML client on your phone.
- **OggSync (http://oggsync.com; free or $30/year)**—Automation requires the paid version.
- **SyncMyCal (http://www.syncmycal.com/pda_home.htm; $25)**—Free version is very limited.

SYNCHRONIZING GOOGLE CALENDAR WITH A DESKTOP (OR MOBILE) CALENDAR PROGRAM

It's nice that you can read your Google Calendar in desktop and mobile programs, but what you really want to do is synchronize your calendars, so a change in one is a change in the other. For instance, if you like Outlook and Google Calendar, it would be preferable—maybe even mandatory—for you to create, edit, or delete an appointment at either location and have it reflected in the other.

A Quick Look at Several Calendar Synchronization Programs

In Chapter 5, "Migrating Calendars to Google Apps," I looked at several programs you can use to sync your local desktop calendars with Google Calendar, including the following:

- **BusySync (www.busymac.com; $25)**—For Mac OS X users who want to synchronize Apple iCal with Google Calendar.
- **GCALDaemon (http://gcaldaemon.sourceforge.net; free)**—For Windows, Mac OS X, and Linux users who want to synchronize Sunbird/Lightning, iCal, KOrganizer/Kontact, and Evolution with Google Calendar. The

best tutorial for Windows is at http://lifehacker.com/software/google-calendar/geek-to-live-sync-google-calendar-and-gmail-contacts-to-your-desktop-251279.php; for KMail, see http://www.linux.com/feature/122054.

- **iCal4OL (http://ical.gutentag.ch; $23)**—For Windows users who want to synchronize Outlook with Google Calendar.

- **OggSync (http://oggsync.com; $30/year)**—For Windows users who want to synchronize Outlook and Exchange with Google Calendar.

- **ScheduleWorld (www.scheduleworld.com; free)**—For Windows, Mac OS X, and Linux users who want to synchronize Sunbird/Lightning, iCal, Outlook, Evolution, and some mobile devices with Google Calendar.

- **SpanningSync (http://spanningsync.com; $25/year or $65)**—For Mac OS X users who want to synchronize iCal with Google Calendar. Highly recommended.

If you'd like more info about any of those, go back to Chapter 5, "Migrating Calendars to Google Apps."

In addition to those programs that were previously covered, I'd like to introduce a few new ones that you may want to investigate:

- **CalGoo (http://www.calgoo.com; free)**—For Windows and Mac OS X users who want to synchronize Outlook or Apple iCal with Google Calendar.

- **CompanionLink (http://www.companionlink.com/products/companionlinkforgoogle.html; $30)**—For Windows users who want to synchronize desktop calendars (ACT!, GoldMine, Lotus Notes, Novell GroupWise, Outlook, Palm Desktop) or mobile devices (BlackBerry, iPhone, Palm, or Windows Mobile) with Google Calendar. Certainly the most complete solution. A tutorial for Outlook is at www.jakeludington.com/downloads/20061006_companionlink_for_google_calendar.html.

- **Google Calendar Sync (http://www.google.com/support/calendar/bin/answer.py?answer=98563; free)**—For Windows users who want to synchronize Outlook with Google Calendar. Sync 2-ways or 1-way. Highly recommended (even by Microsoft). Note, however, that it doesn't work with Outlook if your data is stored on an Exchange server, only if your data is stored in a local PST file.

- **GoogleSync (http://googlesync.sourceforge.net; free)**—For Mac OS X users who want to sync iCal with Google Calendar. Open source and uses built-in Apple technologies.

- **KiGoo (http://www.getkigoo.com; free)**—For Windows users who want to synchronize Outlook and Exchange with Google Calendar.

- **Provider (https://addons.mozilla.org/en-US/thunderbird/addon/ 4631; free)**—For Windows, Mac OS X, and Linux users who want to synchronize Sunbird/Lightning with Google Calendar using this Thunderbird extension.

- **SyncMyCal (http://www.syncmycal.com; $25)**—For Windows users who want to synchronize Outlook with Google Calendar.

Check out the ones that interest you. With all the choices we have available, it's a great time to want to sync your desktop calendar with Google Calendar.

Using CalDAV to Synchronize Apple iCal with Google Calendar

I'm focusing this entire section on using Apple iCal and Google Calendar, not because of the widespread use of iCal—which is certainly true on Apple's machines—but instead because Google's recent support of CalDAV points the way toward a possible future of calendar synchronization. Thanks to Google Calendar's new support for the CalDAV protocol, it's now possible to sync iCal and Google Calendar without any third-party software at all. As Google extends support to other desktop calendar programs, it won't be long until you can sync your favorite desktop calendar with Google Calendar.

> **NOTE**
>
> To learn more about CalDAV, start with Wikipedia's article on the subject at http://en.wikipedia.org/wiki/CalDAV. For the actual detailed protocol, see www.ietf.org/rfc/rfc4791.txt. Finally, for information about how Google Calendar works with CalDAV, check out the CalDAV Developer's Guide at http://code.google.com/apis/calendar/developers_guide_caldav. html.

However, there are many caveats to using CalDAV with iCal:

- CalDAV support is present only in the version of iCal found in Leopard. If you're using an older version of Mac OS X, you'll need to follow the instructions for iCal found previously in this chapter in the section titled "Accessing Google Calendar in a Desktop Calendar Program."

- You have to create a separate CalDAV account in iCal for each calendar, even if all the calendars you're connecting to are under the same account at Google Calendar (more about this later in this section).

- You can't sync an existing calendar at Google with an existing calendar in iCal; instead, you'll first need to transfer all the appointments from iCal to Google and then sync with the Google calendar or copy events around from within iCal. Either way, it's not as easy as Spanning Sync or BusySync, which allow you to choose arbitrary calendars in iCal and Google Calendar that you want to sync.

- This could be a biggie for a lot of folks: Calendars synced via CalDAV cannot sync with MobileMe, which means they can't sync with an iPhone. And nope, you can't sync it to your iPhone manually using iTunes either. You just cannot sync a CalDAV calendar with the iPhone in any way at this time (with the key phrase in that sentence being "at this time").

> **TIP**
>
> If you have any problems syncing iCal and Google Calendar using CalDAV, or if you just want to know about any problems that may still be in place, check out Google's list of Known Issues, at www.google.com/support/calendar/bin/answer.py?answer=99360.

If you're still interested, open iCal, and go to Edit, Preferences, Accounts, and press +. Enter the following information (I'll be using my heavymetalmassage.com account as an example, but you should enter your own info):

- Description: **Heavy Metal Massage**. This will become the title of your CalDAV calendar list.
- Username: **scott@heavymetalmassage.com**
- Password: **123456**
- Account URL: **https://www.google.com/calendar/dav/scott@heavymetal-massage.com/user**. Notice that you enter your Google Apps email address into the URL.
- Do not check Use Kerberos v5 For Authentication.

Click Add. iCal will begin grabbing your data from Google Calendar (it could take a few minutes, depending upon how much data you have in your calendar, but later syncs are instantaneous). Meanwhile, you'll be plopped back on the Accounts tab of iCal's preferences, on the Account Information screen.

Most of the information on the Account Information screen is already filled in based on the answers you gave when you created the account, but you can change

Refresh Calendars to Every 15 Minutes. You have five choices, so select the one that's right for you. Note that you can also force a refresh by pressing Command+R on your keyboard.

Close the Preferences window. You're ready to add, edit, and delete appointments in a calendar shared between Google Calendar and iCal.

If you want to add additional (or *secondary*) calendars, you'll need to perform a different set of steps.

Sign in to your Google Calendar and then go to Settings, Calendars, and click the name of the secondary calendar you want to add. On the Calendar Details tab, scroll down to the Calendar Address section, where you'll see an enormously long email address given as that calendar's Calendar ID, something like this:

```
heavymetalmassage.com_09sbrfw7iuytf6yrfhgnv4h7oc@group.calendar.google.c
om
```

Copy the Calendar ID address and then open iCal. Repeat exactly the steps you just performed to add the initial Google calendar to iCal, with one exception. For Account URL, use the Calendar ID you just copied instead of your Google Apps email address:

```
https://www.google.com/calendar/dav/heavymetalmassage.com_09sbrfw7iuytf6
yrfhgnv4h7oc@group.calendar.google.com/user
```

Click Add and again change the Refresh Calendars setting if you want.

Close the Preferences window. You're ready to add, edit, and delete appointments in a secondary calendar shared between Google Calendar and iCal.

This is great, but there's one annoyance. It's not a biggie, but for a perfectionist like me, it rankles. After adding two calendars via CalDAV to iCal, the list of calendars in the left column of iCal looked like Figure 13.2.

FIGURE 13.2   You have separate accounts for each individual calendar, even if they're part of the same Google Calendar!

See what happens? I have two calendars—Scott Granneman and Home—both at Google Calendar in the same Heavy Metal Massage account. But when I connect to those via CalDAV in iCal, I have to create a separate account for each one instead of having both under Heavy Metal Massage. Like I said, annoying, but not a deal breaker. But I hope it gets fixed soon.

For this annoyance, and all the others I mentioned at the beginning of this section, I don't think that the new CalDAV support in Google Calendar spells doom for Spanning Sync, BusySync, and the other Mac OS X-based calendar synchronization tools (which I mentioned in "Synchronizing Google Calendar with a Desktop [or Mobile] Calendar Program" earlier). If you can live with the restrictions that come with CalDAV, it's a great solution. But many people are going to file it under "Interesting, but I'll check it out later to see if they've fixed a few things."

RECEIVING NOTIFICATIONS ABOUT EVENTS

Information about what's going on with your calendar is vitally important to many people. Even though Google Calendar is a web-based program, there are still lots of ways you can be notified about appointments.

Most desktop calendar programs can let you know in some way that you have an upcoming event, usually with a sound or pop-up notification. If you stick to the web-based version of Google Calendar, you can always set it to notify you in three ways that an appointment is coming up:

- SMS text messaging
- Web browser pop-up
- Email

If you want something extra, you have a few options.

If you use Firefox, you can install the Google Calendar Notifier extension (https://addons.mozilla.org/en-US/firefox/addon/2528). It works, but it's also no longer maintained. However, it's open source, so someone else could take up the mantle.

If you use a Mac, you can install the Google Notifier (http://toolbar.google.com/gmail-helper/notifier_mac.html), a free tool from Google. This software also works with Gmail, as I explained in Chapter 9's "Receiving Notifications About New Emails."

SECURING YOUR CALENDAR

The best way to secure your calendar and its data is to access it only via HTTPS, so all traffic between your web browser and Google is encrypted. Although your login uses HTTPS, everything after that does not, which is unfortunate. You can fix that, however, in one of three ways:

- **Install the userscript found at http://diveintomark.org/projects/ greasemonkey/gmailsecure.user.js**—This works in Firefox with Grease-monkey, with Stylish, or with Opera and IE with some tweaking. Note that you'll have to change the @include line to be http://www.google.com/ calendar/.

- **Install Better GCal (https://addons.mozilla.org/en-US/firefox/addon/ 5299)**—Select Always Use Secure Connection (HTTPS) on the General tab of this Firefox extension.

- **Install CustomizeGoogle (https://addons.mozilla.org/en-US/firefox/ addon/743)**—Select Secure (Switch to HTTPS) on the Calendar tab of this Firefox extension. Highly recommended because many of the other features this extension offers are invaluable.

Someday Google will probably add an Always Use HTTPS feature like it recently did for Gmail. Until that day, however, you'll have to rely on one of the previous solutions.

> **TIP**
>
> If you really want to get under the hood and geek out, check out Nathan Harrington's excellent article "Integrate encryption into Google Calendar with Firefox extensions" available at www.ibm.com/developerworks/linux/ library/wa-googlecal/index.html. Here's his description of the paper: "Building on the incredible flexibility of Firefox extensions and the Gnu Privacy Guard, this article shows you how to store only encrypted event descriptions in Google's Calendar application, while displaying a plain text version to anyone with the appropriate decryption keys." Very cool.

CHANGING GOOGLE CALENDAR'S APPEARANCE

With userscripts and some other software, you can make changes to Google Calendar that are purely cosmetic. In the same way that make-up on a woman or a nice haircut on a man can make a big difference, however, some of those purely cosmetic changes in Google Calendar can make using it a lot more enjoyable.

Giving Google Calendar a New Skin

Don't like the way Google Calendar appears? Industrious coders have come up with new "skins" that can change the way Google Calendar looks in ways that range from small to radical. Far to the right on the Whoa! scale, Google Calendar Redesigned completely changes how Google Calendar's UI looks, as Figure 13.3 shows:

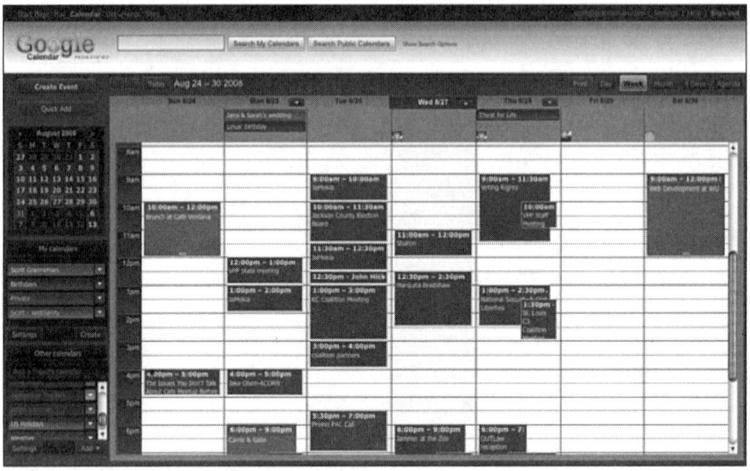

FIGURE 13.3   Now that's a new interface!

I really like it, except for the tiny fonts, which are hard for me to see.

Here are some interesting skins for Google Calendar you may want to try and how you can get them. After you install the skin, refresh Google Calendar in your web browser to see the results. If things blow up, don't panic—just reverse what you did and refresh Google Calendar in your browser again, and you'll be back to normal.

- Google Calendar Redesigned
    - Install Better GCal (https://addons.mozilla.org/en-US/firefox/addon/ 5299). Select Redesigned on the Skins tab of this Firefox extension.
    - Install the Google Redesigned extension for Firefox (http://www. globexdesigns.com/gr/). This is the best route to go if you like this look for Google Calendar (and Gmail).

- Google Calendar Restyle
  - Install the userstyle found at http://userstyles.org/styles/6525. Works in Firefox with Greasemonkey, with Stylish, or with Opera and IE with some tweaking.
- Google Air Skin
  - Install the userscript found at http://userscripts.org/scripts/show/9691. Works in Firefox with Greasemonkey, with Stylish, or with Opera and IE with some tweaking.

Collapsing the Header and Sidebar

Google has done a fine job organizing the user interface of Google Calendar, but sometimes you want the maximum browser real estate possible devoted to just the calendar itself. In cases like that, you can install a userscript that can temporarily hide the sidebar, the header, or both. Figure 13.4 shows what the default looks like and then what Google Calendar looks like sans header and sidebar.

Header andSidebar present   Header and Sidebar collapsed

FIGURE 13.4   With a header and sidebar and without.

If this looks interesting to you, look at one of the following solutions:

- Install the userscript found at http://userscripts.org/scripts/show/8507. Works in Firefox with Greasemonkey, with Stylish, or with Opera and IE with some tweaking.
- Install Better GCal (https://addons.mozilla.org/en-US/firefox/addon/5299). Select Collapse Header and Sidebar on the General tab of this Firefox extension.

You can set the default state of the header and the sidebar: open or closed. In addition, you can set a keyboard shortcut that hides and reveals the header and sidebar. By default, z toggles the sidebar, and Z toggles the header. If you don't like that, no problem—change it!

Wrapping Text in Events

A lot of people find the month view in Google Calendar useful, but there's one annoyance with it: By default, the text describing your appointment is cut off instead of wrapped, so "Bruce Springsteen @ Scottrade Center" becomes "Bruce Springst," which isn't all that helpful. Fortunately, if you install one of the following solutions, you can fix that little problem:

- Install the userscript found at http://userscripts.org/scripts/show/5850. Works in Firefox with Greasemonkey, with Stylish, or with Opera and IE with some tweaking.

- Install Better GCal (https://addons.mozilla.org/en-US/firefox/addon/5299). Select Text Wrap Events on the General tab of this Firefox extension.

After the solution is installed, month view gets a lot more useful, as the close-up in Figure 13.5 makes clear.

Without text wrap   With text wrap

FIGURE 13.5   In month view, text wrap helps when you're trying to decipher your appointments.

ADDING NEW FEATURES

As awesome as Google Calendar is, it doesn't do everything. However, clever users and developers have taken it upon themselves to add new features in a variety of ways. In this section I call out a few interesting ways to add some cool features to Google Calendar.

Adding To-Do's to Google Calendar

For some reason, Google still hasn't added a good to-do manager into any of its online properties, a feature for which many people have been begging for years. While we're waiting for Google to produce such a service, you can use what is easily the best online to-do service out there: Remember The Milk (www.rememberthemilk.com), which is free, easy to use, and powerful. Even better, you can integrate RTM into Google Calendar with ease.

If this sounds interesting to you, point your browser to http://www.rememberthemilk.com/services/googlecalendar/. Scroll down to the section on the page labeled "Adding to Google Calendar for Google Apps users"; do *not* go to the one labeled "Adding to Google Calendar," because that one won't work.

Enter your domain name (heavymetalmassage.com, in my case) and click the button labeled Google Calendar. Your calendar will load, and you'll be prompted to add a calendar named Remember The Milk. Click Yes, and a moment later you will see a new calendar on the left side in the Other Calendars section: Remember The Milk. In addition, you'll see small blue checkmarks on each day. When you click one, you'll see the tasks for that day, as shown in Figure 13.6.

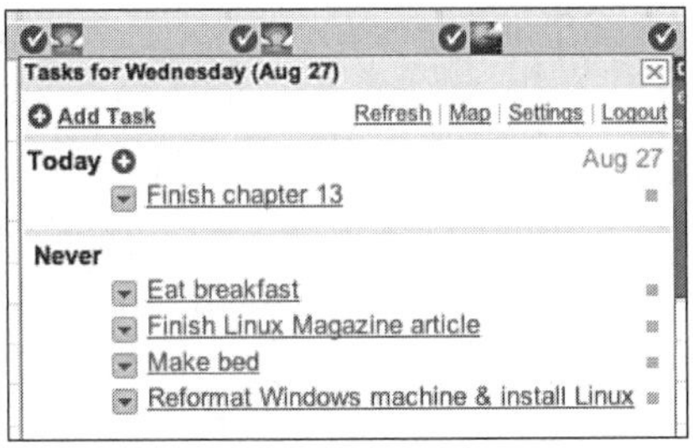

FIGURE 13.6   Remember The
Milk + Google Calendar = yummy!

Within Google Calendar, you can now do the following with Remember The Milk:

- View, add, and edit tasks
- Mark tasks as completed or postponed
- See tasks based on location

That's a nice way to get to-do's in your calendar—now let's hope that Google develops its own task manager or, better yet, just buys Remember The Milk.

Integrating Google Calendar with Gmail

Some people would like to be able to see their email and their calendar at the same time. If that sounds cool to you, install the userscript found at http://userscripts.org/scripts/show/24877, which works in Firefox with Greasemonkey, with Stylish, or with Opera and IE with some tweaking.

After installing the userscript, your Google Calendar upcoming events appear on the right side of Gmail. Keep an eye on the Better GCal extension for Firefox (https://addons.mozilla.org/en-US/firefox/addon/5299) because this script may be added to it soon.

SOLVING COMMON PROBLEMS

As with all things in life, you're going to find little gotchas. Here are a few of those and their solutions.

Can I Access and Use Google Calendar Offline in a Web Browser?

Google Calendar is awesome software, but it has one downside: You have to be online to use it. Granted, if you synchronize it with a desktop calendar (covered previously in "Synchronizing Google Calendar with a Desktop [or Mobile] Calendar Program"), you're covered if you're offline, but it would still be nice to be able to use the web interface even if you're not connected to the Net.

Google Gears is a web browser plug-in developed by Google that allows users to take web apps offline, change the data, and then, when they reconnect to the Internet, synchronize offline changes back to the online app. It's slick and works well, but right now the only product in Google Apps that supports it is Google Docs (the fantastic Google Reader also supports it, but that's not part of Google Apps for some weird reason). Rumors keep floating into the press that Google will be adding Gears support to Google Calendar "real soon now," but it's yet to show up. One day it will, and then you'll be able to take Google Calendar offline. Until then, use your desktop client—and keep checking the tech blogs and websites for news that Gears has finally been added to Google Calendar.

> **NOTE**
>
> For more on Gears, go to http://gears.google.com, where you can install it if you're using Firefox or Internet Explorer (Safari support is almost here). If you're not using Google Reader, you should be—go add the service at http://reader.google.com.

How Do I Copy an Appointment from one Google Calendar to Another?

If you have more than one calendar in your Google Calendar—in my case, Scott Granneman, Work, and Personal—you might find that you created an event in one calendar that better belongs in another. You could delete it and then re-create it in the correct calendar, but that's too much work.

Instead, click the event so you can see its details. At the top of the details page you'll see a drop-down menu labeled More Actions. Select it, and then you'll see that you can copy the event to any of your other calendars. So if I had three calendars—Scott Granneman, Work, and Personal—and I was viewing an event on the Scott Granneman calendar, the More Actions menu would say Copy to Work and Copy to Personal. Make your choice. A few seconds later Google makes the move, and at that point you can click Save.

Back on your main calendar screen, you'll see that that there are two copies of the event, but they're in different calendars. Click the time listed for the wrong one (not the words describing the event, although you can do that, too—you'll just be adding more clicks to the process), and a small pop-up will appear. If you click Delete on that pop-up and then confirm your choice by clicking Delete in the confirmation dialog, the old event will disappear from the old calendar, leaving it in its proper place on the new calendar.

My Calendar Entries Disappeared! Where Did They Go?

Well, you could have been hacked, but that's probably not what happened. Before you go into freak-out mode and start changing your password, keep reading first to see if this describes your problem.

This super-annoying issue goes back to the mess I discussed in the introduction to this book, in which you can create a Google account using an email address that is also used with a Google Apps account, and the two are actually two completely separate accounts! In other words, let's imagine that before I ever created a Google Apps account for heavymetalmassage.com, I went ahead and created a regular ol' Google account using scott@heavymetalmassage.com as the login. I then created a Google Calendar in which the sign in is scott@heavymetalmassage.com and filled it with data.

Fast forward a couple of months when I decide to create a Google Apps account for heavymetalmassage.com. Of course, I create a user of scott@heavymetalmassage.com, and when I do so, I also create a Google Calendar for that user.

And now things get really confusing. If I'm not really careful about where I sign in, I could be looking at an old calendar without realizing it. Or invitations could still show up at my old, non-Google Apps calendar, invitations that I'll never see because I only check my new Google Apps calendar. And none of the invitations on my old calendar are migrated over, which means that I have to do that manually (fortunately, that's not too difficult, as I covered in "Exporting Calendars from Google Calendar" in Chapter 5).

You have two choices at this point:

- Stop using the old non-Google Apps calendar. This is my recommended path. Empty it out and then don't use it.

- Change the email address associated with the old non-Google Apps account. Go to https://google.com/accounts/, sign in with your email address that's causing the confusion, and click Change Email. Enter a new email address—one that's not currently used for any other Google account, whether Google Apps-related or not—and your password, and click Save Email Address.

Actually, why not do both? Change the email address but then stop using the old calendar as well. That should prevent any confusion going forward.

Let's hope Google figures out a way around this confusion. The problems with different accounts are not getting any easier, and it really is a pain for a lot of people.

CONCLUSION

This chapter covered a lot of material, which is no surprise. Google Calendar has a great web-based interface, but many people are still wedded to their desktop calendar programs. Obviously, I left some out, but I can't include everything, or this book would weigh twice as much. If you want to learn more about Google Calendar so that you can solve your specific issue, check out the resources I mention in the Acknowledgements. New features and ideas relating to Google Calendar appear every day, and many of them are true light-bulb-over-the-head moments.

Part IV

Google Docs

CHAPTER 14

Things to Know About Using Google Docs

Google Docs is really great software, but people often think of it in the wrong way. Yes, it's a free online office suite (unless you're using Google Apps Premier Edition, but even then, the programs are free for everyone else) with a word processor, a spreadsheet, and a presentation program (named, respectively, Documents, Spreadsheets, and Presentations—who has the job at Google of naming programs? Fire 'em!). And because it's online, it has features that no other desktop-based office suite, such as Microsoft Office, OpenOffice.org, or Apple's iWork, possesses. We examine many of those features throughout this chapter.

But some people line up Google Docs' feature set against that of Microsoft Office and then think, "Aha! Google Docs only has x number of features, and Microsoft Office has x^8 features, so Google Docs must be terrible!" Nothing could be further from the truth.

Most people—the vast majority of humans who use Microsoft Office—never use more than a few features the program offers in the first place. When it comes to those essential features that 95% of people actually use, Google Docs has it covered. And it's adding new features all the time. On top of that, it has features that Office doesn't have, such as Gadgets and Forms.

Finally, remember that Google Docs is but a baby compared to the doddering old man that is Microsoft Office. Give Google Docs time, and it will mature in ways that will surprise everyone, like the kid with a stutter who develops into a silver-tongued orator, or the ugly child who becomes a beauty queen. It will be very interesting watching Google Docs mature, but now is the time to gain experience using it. You'll be glad you did.

> **NOTE**
>
> Throughout this chapter, I use "document" to refer to work created or edited in Documents, "spreadsheet" to refer to work created or edited in Spreadsheets, and "presentation" to refer to work created or edited in Presentations. If I'm talking generically about all three programs, I use "file" to refer to work created or edited in any of them.

GOOGLE DOCS

I'm going to look at each program in Google Docs separately in this chapter, but in this first section we look at big things you should know about Google Docs overall. These are things that apply to all three programs, and they help to make it clear why Google Docs is already great and why it holds so much promise of further innovation.

Getting Schooled with Google Docs

As a former high school teacher and current Adjunct Professor at Washington University in St. Louis, I wish my high school students had been able to use Google Docs—and I'm thrilled that my current college students can. It makes all the sense in the world.

Schools can save money and avoid having to install the expensive Microsoft Office (if they absolutely need a desktop office suite, I always pull for OpenOffice.org), and students can work without having to transfer files back and forth between school and home. In the case of my students at Wash U., the computers in the lab in which I teach are set up to revert to their original installation state when they reboot. Before Google Docs, I can't tell you how many times students would be taking notes in Word when they would accidently hit the power button with their knee, or pull a power cable, or Windows would crash, or the power would go out. Poof! No more notes. Gone. Now, with Google Docs, a loss of power doesn't spell disaster.

If you're involved in education, I strongly urge you to teach your students and fellow teachers about Google Docs. They'll thank you for it.

Remember that users need email addresses to create a Google Apps account so that they can log in and use Google Docs. In the case of schools, this can sometimes be tricky, especially when you factor in the bureaucracy under which many schools seem to labor. In addition, Google's Terms of Service state that students must be at least 13 years old to use Google Docs, so keep that in mind as well.

Ideally, your school will sign up for Google Apps Education Edition and set up accounts for all students, teachers, and staff. If your Tech Coordinator can't or won't do that, you still have options. If your school provides students with email addresses, they'll all have the same domain name, which means they can use the Team Edition of Google Apps (which I covered in Chapters 1 and 2). This is simple, fast, and will get your students on Google Docs—and able to collaborate with each other—in minutes.

> **TIP**
>
> If your school doesn't want to support Google Apps and for some reason blocks the Team Edition (which admins can do, as I discussed in Chapter 2's "Team Edition"), your students can use their personal email addresses to create non-Google Apps Google accounts.

After everyone is able to use Google Apps, the possibilities for education, no matter the age of the students, are endless. Here are a few ideas to mull over:

- Teachers can keep track of attendance and grades with a spreadsheet. If they're team teaching, this comes in handy (and I say that from experience—I team teach a course at Washington University in St. Louis titled "Technology and the Law," and we use a spreadsheet for just this purpose).

- Tests and quizzes can be created as online forms, with answers automatically stored—with timestamps!—in a spreadsheet.

- Teachers can add comments, notes, and corrections to students' documents, with no paper and nothing to carry back and forth.

- Teachers can create a template for the evaluation forms they have to fill in for their students.

- An entire class or team can use a common spreadsheet to track data from experiments.

- Lesson plans and notes can be shared with other teachers and administrators.

- Students can work together on class presentations.

- Students can anonymously publish their writings on the Net for others to view.

- Younger children can use some of the presentation templates (discussed in the next section) to easily organize photos from a field trip or vacation into a coherent narrative.

- Students can learn the basics of word processing, spreadsheets, and presentations without spending a dime.

> **NOTE**
>
> For more ideas, as well as some inspirational stories, read the blog post "Educators in Portugal, Mexico, and Germany Speak Out" at http://googledocs.blogspot.com/2008/07/educators-in-portugal-mxico-and-germany.html.

Saving Time with Templates

It can be a pain to create new documents from scratch every time you need to do something important. One of the most popular amenities of Microsoft Office is its myriad of templates. Likewise, Google Docs now offers more than 300 templates for documents, spreadsheets, and presentations; they are designed to perform a variety of functions.

To view the templates, go to New, From Template (you can also go to http://docs.google.com/templates). A new tab or window will open in your browser, and you can then search for templates, or you can sort the templates in four ways:

- **Application**—All Types, Documents, Spreadsheets, or Presentations
- **Popularity**—Most Users or Highest Rating
- **Category**—All categories, Albums & Flipbooks, Business, Calculators, Calendars & Schedules, Cards & Certificates, Labels & Business Cards, Letters & Faxes, Miscellaneous, Personal Finance, Presentation Designs, Resumes & Cover Letters, Statistics, or Students & Teachers
- **Templates I've Used**

By default, All Types of applications and All Categories are chosen. The listings all follow the same, uh, template, with Figure 14.1 showing you what they all look like.

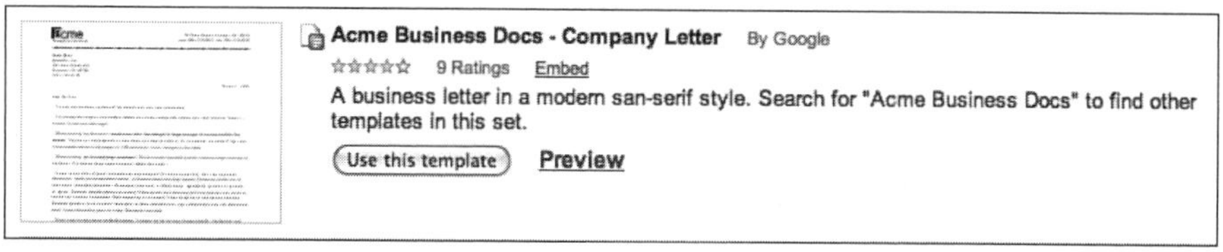

FIGURE 14.1   All the template listings look like this.

Clicking either the screenshot of the template or Preview opens up another tab or window so you can see what it will look like in more detail. If it's a presentation, you can use forward and back arrows in the bottom left of the window to see all the master slides, which is a great touch. If you like what you see, click Use This Template and start filling in your words and numbers.

I'd like to call out a few templates that you might find interesting, but you should take some time and scan through the entire list. You may find lots that you can use.

- **Comprehensive Travel Itinerary https://docs.google.com/ View?docid=dd8nn97m_88dnh2mmc**—Print out two copies: one to take with you and one to leave back with the people watching your house while you're gone. Really useful.

- **Gas Mileage Log (https://spreadsheets.google.com/pub?key= pyU3xkckhpI2nn_rmp5jDSQ)**—In times of high gas prices, this could be a great way to save some money, or at least keep track of how you're spending it.

- **Wedding Album, Guest List, Planner, Budget Manager, Checklist, Payment List (http://docs.google.com/templates?q=wedding& sort=hottest&view=default&pli=1)**—Planning a wedding? Everything you need is right here.

- **Sales Invoice (https://spreadsheets.google.com/pub?key= pyU3xkckhpI2OBBzCJUl7aQ)**—A very nice invoice, with automatic calculations of the amount your customers owe you.

- **Video Christmas Card (https://docs.google.com/Present?docid= dd8nn97m_61d35bnjhh)**—A very cool idea—embed a holiday video from you and your family and then publish it on the Web.

- **Budget Planners (https://docs.google.com/templates?q= budget&sort=hottest&view=default)**—Lots of different planners to help you create and stick to a budget, whether you're in college, a homeowner, or a businessperson.

- **Presentations (https://docs.google.com/templates?type= presentations&sort=hottest&view=default)**—Currently, there are 64 templates actually intended for presentations (13 of the templates in Presentations are for cards, certificates, and invitations). Although many are ugly as sin (something Microsoft is guilty of as well in PowerPoint, but mercifully avoided by Apple in Keynote), there are some good ones, including Autumn Leaf, Hokkaido Shell, Latitude, Photo Album, Scrapbook Album, and Venture Capitalist Pitch.

Here's one template that falls under "nice idea, but no thanks": Avery Address Labels. You're expected to manually enter all the addresses, which is nuts. The whole point of labels I create on my computer is that I can automatically fill them in with data from a spreadsheet or database so I don't have to manually type it in!

> **NOTE**
>
> The Official Google Docs Blog entry that announced templates has a bunch of links to various templates in it, as well as some videos talking about templates that you might find interesting. You can see the blog post at http://googledocs.blogspot.com/2008/07/templates-bring-docs-to-life. html.

Going Offline with Google Gears

It's great that you can use Google Docs when you're online—that's what allows you to use it without worrying about installing the software on your PC or finding out that you left a copy of the file you need to work on at the office—but there are times when you need to work on a document or spreadsheet when you're not connected to the Net. To solve this problem (and a few others), Google developed Gears, an open source extension for your web browser that allows you to run web-based apps offline, and when you take them back online, sync the changes you made offline back to the equivalent online files.

To install Gears, go to http://gears.google.com and download the software. Install it, restart your browser, and you're ready to go. To use Gears, go to Google Docs and press the new Offline link in the upper right of the page, right by the Settings link. When you're asked if it's alright to use Gears with this website, give your OK.

When you take your files offline, they're stored on your computer. Where they're stored, however, depends on your operating system and web browser. Table 14.1 shows those locations.

TABLE 14.1 The locations for files temporarily stored locally via Google Gears

OPERATING SYSTEM	WEB BROWSER	LOCATION FOR GEARS FILES
Windows Vista	Internet Explorer	C:\Users\USERNAME\AppData\LocalLow\Google\Google Gears for Internet Explorer
Windows Vista	Firefox	C:\Users\USERNAME\AppData\Local\Mozilla\Firefox\Profiles\PROFILE.default\Google Gears for Firefox
Windows XP	Internet Explorer	C:\Documents and Settings\USERNAME\Local Settings\Application Data\Google\Google Gears for Internet Explorer
Windows XP	Firefox	C:\Documents and Settings\USERNAME\Local Settings\Application Data\Mozilla\Firefox\Profiles\PROFILE.default\Google Gears for Firefox
Mac OS X	Firefox	/Users/USERNAME/Library/Caches/Firefox/Profiles/PROFILE.default/Google Gears for Firefox
Mac OS X	Safari	/Users/USERNAME/Library/Application Support/Google/Google Gears for Safari
Linux	Firefox	/home/USERNAME/.mozilla/firefox/PROFILE.default/Google Gears for Firefox

The first time you use Gears, it may take a while to sync files, but after that, it will go much more quickly. If you have problems syncing, try refreshing your web browser (for a complete refresh, hold down Shift while you click the Refresh or Reload button). If that doesn't help, uninstall and reinstall Gears.

When you're working offline, you can tell in one of the following ways:

- The word Offline next to your email address at the top of the window turns into a green check mark on the Docs list page and a gray arrow on the open Document's page if you've changed the file; if you haven't yet changed the file, you'll instead see a gray circle with a slash through it.

- A big yellow box will appear at the top of documents informing you that you are Editing in Offline Mode.

If the green check mark or gray arrow turns into a red exclamation point, you have a problem, and you're not really editing offline. It may look like you are, but Google doesn't think so. In that case, select all your work in your Document and save it to another file on your machine. Don't close your browser or the Document on which you were working; instead, wait until you're online again and make sure your changes are saved. If they're not, you have them saved in the file you created on your computer.

If you and a person with whom you've shared a file have both taken that file offline, you'll know when you log back in to Google Docs and see Edited Offline next to the file in question. If your edits and the other person's edits don't conflict, no problem. However, if conflicts exist, you'll be notified. You can choose to go ahead and overwrite the document with your changes or back off. Or you could go ahead and commit your changes and then use Show Differences to compare the different edits that were made.

As cool as it is, there are caveats to using Gears:

- Each of your computers and browsers syncs separately. If you're using more than one computer, you'll need to sync each one separately. The last one to sync back "wins," so keep that in mind as well. If you're using more than one browser on your computer, you'll need to sync each one separately. And the last one to sync back "wins" as well. My advice? Don't use more than one browser on a computer to sync your files and try not to use more than one computer at a time, or you run the risk of getting very confused and overwriting your own work (not a huge deal because you can always revert to earlier versions at Google Docs, but still annoying and potentially perplexing).

- Don't use it on a computer you share with someone else, especially if it's a public computer at a café, for instance. If you do, you make it possible for others to potentially read your files on the local PC.

- Although you can view documents, spreadsheets, and presentations offline, you can edit only documents. With spreadsheets and presentations, you can look but you can't touch.

- You can't create new documents offline. You can, however, create a few blank documents before you go offline that you can edit later (remember, you can't edit spreadsheets and presentations offline, so it doesn't matter whether you create blank files).

- If you use Windows and you're getting connection errors, check out Google's help page with suggestions to fix those problems at www.google.com/support/gears/bin/answer.py?hl=en&answer=70998.

Even with those caveats, however, I'd still recommend that you check out Google Gears—it's fascinating software, and it has come a long way in a short time. Eventually, all Google Apps will support it, so it's a good idea to start learning about it now.

NOTE

To learn more about Google Gears, go to Google's web page for the software at http://gears.google.com. A video about how to work with Google Docs offline using Google Gears is available at http://www.youtube.com/watch?v=7cyHYEfpRVA.

Sharing, Collaborating, and Publishing

All three programs in Google Docs allow you to make your files available to other people and even to specify certain people as collaborators so they can work with you on selected files.

The broadest thing you can do with a file is make it available for anyone in the world to view. To do this, click the Publish tab in Spreadsheets and Presentations, click the Share button in Documents, and select Publish as Web Page (I expect that it will soon be a button in all three programs). In all three programs, the document isn't actually out there for everyone to see until you click a Publish button to verify your choice. However, each program presents small differences between some additional features associated with publishing.

With Documents, you have the following options:

- **A check box allows you to Automatically Republish When Changes Are Made**—This is a great idea if you want readers to always see the most up-to-date version of your document.

- **A check box allows you to specify that Viewers Must Sign In With a heavymetalmassage.com Account to View the Published Document**—If you want to limit who can view even a published document, check this. And of course, it uses your domain name, not mine.

- **A button allows you to Post to Blog**—Google Docs as blog publisher! Who knew?

With Spreadsheets, you get no additional options. Publish or not, and that's it.

With Presentations, you get one option: A checkbox allows you to specify that Viewers Must Sign In With a heavymetalmassage.com Account to View the Published Document. If you want to limit who can view even a published presentation, check this. And of course, it uses your domain name, not mine.

Most of the time, when folks publish a file, they do it intending for it to be like a web page online, available to anyone who wants to view it, and that's how I treat it for the rest of this section.

The next level up from publishing is sharing. To get started, click the Share tab in Spreadsheets and Presentations, click the Share button in Documents, and select Share With Others (as with publishing, I expect that Share will soon be a button in all three programs).

The Share This Document screen allows you to set who can manage, edit, and view your file. If it looks similar to the Google Sites sharing screen (which we talk about in Chapter 16's "Sharing," it should because it's very close to the same concept.

Under Invite People, you have two options (I'm reversing the order, from least permissions to most):

- **As Viewers**—People can view the file but can't edit (in other words, they can look but can't touch); users can export a copy of the file to their computers.

- **As Collaborators**—People can edit and view the file, can export a copy of the file to their computers, and can invite and delete other Viewers and Collaborators if the Owner also checks the box next to Collaborators May Invite Others. Keep in mind that Collaborators can go to the Revisions tab and see all older versions of your file, which you might not want. To prevent this, before you share a file, rename the original with all the revisions to **Backup of Embarrassing Revelations** and then create a new file named **Embarrassing Revelations** into which you copy the text of the original. The new file will lack all revisions, so you're safe.

In addition to those two options, there's a hidden role as well—Owner—which isn't listed because there's only one owner: you. However, Owners can edit, view, and delete the file, export a copy of the file to their computers, and can invite and delete other Viewers and Collaborators. Because only one owner can exist at a time, it's also possible for you to transfer ownership of a file: on the Docs List page, check the box next to the file you want to reassign and choose More Actions, Change

Owner. Enter the email address or use the Contact Picker, change the Message if you feel like it, and click Change Owner. It's yours no longer.

> **NOTE**
>
> Spreadsheets have a third option in addition to Viewers and Collaborators—To Fill Out a Form—which is another way of inviting people to enter data in a form you create, as I discuss in "Filling in Forms" later in this chapter.

Needless to say, think carefully about whom you add and what role you assign them. Make sure you know and trust your fellow Collaborators!

> **NOTE**
>
> With Documents and Spreadsheets, the people you specify as Viewers or Collaborators must have Google or Google Apps accounts.

Make a choice, enter the email addresses for the people you want to include in that role (separated by commas), and click the Invite button to send invitations to them.

You have Advanced Permissions (although Spreadsheets calls them Advanced Options) that you can set for Viewers and Collaborators as well. The same three options show up for all three programs, with an additional one for Spreadsheets. These are shown as check boxes next to the following settings:

- **Collaborators May Invite Others**—If you want to give collaborators the right to invite others as either Viewers or Collaborators, check this box. Again, if you do this, be sure you trust your collaborators.

- **Invitations May Be Used by Anyone**—If you're sending the invitation to a mailing list, check this because it allows everyone in a group to access your file with just one invitation.

- **Anyone at heavymetalmassage.com May ___ This Site**—If you check this box, you have a choice: Edit or View. You can very quickly enable everyone at your domain to edit your new file, or you can allow everyone to view and then add specific individuals in your domain as Collaborators. If your file is intended for only a subset of people in your organization, don't check this box.

Spreadsheets also have an additional option: a check box next to Notify Me at scott@heavymetalmassage.com, followed by a drop-down menu with the following options that will notify you of the following:

- Every Time the Spreadsheet Changes
- Every Day, with a Summary of Changes
- According to Advanced Rules

If you want to keep close track of a spreadsheet you've shared, check that box and then choose the option that meets your needs. I also expect this feature to migrate to Documents and Presentations someday.

On the right side of this page is a list of your site's Viewers and Collaborators. To revoke someone's privileges on your site, click the Remove link next to the person's email address.

WARNING

After you have published or shared a file, to make sure that it is truly unavailable, you must Delete the file and then empty the Google Docs Trash.

The really neat thing about collaboration is that more than one person can work on a file at the same time, with changes showing up on everyone's copy of the file. Of course, more than one person can't work on the same line in a document or cell in a spreadsheet, or anarchy would ensue.

On top of that, some other restrictions exist on collaboration:

- You can share a document or presentation with a maximum of 200 people (and that's 200 total, whether they're Viewers, Collaborators, or a mix of the two), but only 10 of them can edit or view that document at the same time.
- You can share a spreadsheet with an unlimited number of people, but only 50 can edit that spreadsheet at the same time.

I often have students at Washington University in St. Louis work in tandem on papers and other work, and Google Docs' collaboration capabilities are truly stunning. The first time people start editing a document together, but working from different computers in a lab, a collective gasp goes out. Even now, I still find it impressive—and amazingly useful.

DOCUMENTS

Documents originally began as a product named Writely that Google purchased and completely remade in its own image. I was an early user of Writely, and Google has certainly improved it in a hundred different ways. It's now a darn good online word processor. Oh, there are others that have more features, but on the whole, Documents has what most people need in a simple word processor. On top of that, I know that Google is working hard to improve Documents all the time, so much so that I can't wait to see what new features Google is going to roll out next. It won't be long before Documents rivals some desktop word processors, a nice development for all of us.

> ## ⚠ WARNING
>
> Keep in mind the limits of Documents you create in Google Docs: Each document can be at most 500KB, with an additional 2MB for each embedded image. You can have at most a mix of 5,000 documents and presentations and 5,000 images.
>
> As for PDFs, those you upload from your computer can be no bigger than 10MB, and those you import from the Web top out at 2MB. You can have a maximum of 100 PDFs at Google Docs.

Changing Styles

This is kind of a non-obvious feature because many users won't really know what to make of it. If you know Cascading Style Sheets (CSS), you can change how your documents look by changing the CSS associated with each one. And even if you personally don't know CSS, find your friendly neighborhood web developer who does, and ask her to help you.

If you're going to edit your document's CSS, you should be aware of the following limitations:

- Attempts to change the background of the document's body will be commented out or ignored.

- External images cannot be inserted with an external, fully qualified domain name; instead, import the images you want to use to another document and then go to Edit, Edit HTML to find the image's unique ID and reference that in your CSS.

- Images inserted via CSS don't appear when you go to File, Print or to File, Download File As, PDF.

- If you use CSS to set a style for the body, first go to Edit, Document Styles and select Turn Off All Styles, or use the `!important` declaration.

- You can't edit CSS if your document is currently offline thanks to Google Gears.

- You can't reference external styles using the link element (`<link href="http://www.example.com/styles/main.css" type="text/css" rel="stylesheet" />`), so you're stuck with having to repeat any styles you want to use in every document in which you want to use them. Blech.

To change your document's CSS, go to Edit, Edit CSS. When you do, a CSS Edit box opens up into which you can enter your CSS. When you've finished, click OK.

> **NOTE**
>
> For more on this feature, read http://groups.google.com/group/Google-Docs/web/styles-in-google-docs. You can find a very nice CSS-styled resume that a Googler created to show off some advanced CSS at http://docs.google.com/DocAction?docid=df9n32wb_21crpb47cr. If you'd like to set up legal-style numbered headers (1, 1.1, 1.2, 1.2.1, and so on), read http://docs.google.com/View?docID=ajg93xcp56zc_11fz3zxqfc, but be forewarned: The bane of every CSS developer's existence—Internet Explorer—doesn't yet support the CSS used in that document.

Following are some CSS samples you might want to use to achieve various effects.

Setting Fonts

You can set a few fonts by going to Edit, Document Styles, but if you want more control, try the following:

```
body {
  font-family: Calibri, Verdana, "DejaVu Sans", "Lucida Sans",
Helvetica, sans-serif;
  font-fize: 16px;
}
```

Adding an Image

Adding images is a bit tricky because you're not allowed by Google to do this:

```
div.quote {
  background-image: url("http://www.d20srd.org/images/bkg_base.jpg");
}
```

You cannot refer to images in this way; instead, you must perform a different set of steps.

1. Create a document called Image Storehouse or something like that. In that document, go to Insert, Picture. Select bkg_base.jpg either from your computer or by pointing to its URL if it's already on the Web. After the image has been placed into the document, go to Edit, Edit HTML and find the img element that references bkg_base.jpg in the HTML. It will look something like this:

   ```
   <img src="File?id=dgcc9j32_33cn8tt7gp_b" style="width: 683px;
   height: 724px;" id="wlzi">
   ```

2. Copy the value of the src attribute of img; to whit, File?id=dgcc9j32_33cn8tt7gp_b. Now in your CSS to reference the image, use this code:

   ```
   div.quote {
     background-image: url("File?id=dgcc9j32_33cn8tt7gp_b");
   }
   ```

3. You can now refer to File?id=dgcc9j32_33cn8tt7gp_b in any of your documents.

This isn't the easiest process, but you wouldn't be messing around with the CSS of your document if you didn't have some technical knowledge to begin with, so it's not too onerous.

Watermarking Your Documents

Do you want to add a watermark across your document's pages, such as Confidential, Top Secret, or Draft? Use this CSS:

```
body {
  background-image: url("File?id=efbb9j32_46cn6uv9gp_a");
  background-repeat: no-repeat;
  background-position: 50% 20px;
}
```

The secret to this is the image you choose to use. Make sure it nestles unobtrusively into the background so that readers can still easily see the text.

Putting a Border Around Every Image

If you know you'd like a one-pixel black border around every image you place in a document, make it easy on yourself and set that up in your CSS.

```
img {
  border: 1px solid #000;
}
```

Printing Page Numbers

Before Google rolls out a new feature for Docs, it usually inserts code for testers. Super-intrepid bloggers comb through the HTML, CSS, and JavaScript that make up Google Docs looking for hints of those new features, and when they find something, they let us all know. Eventually, most of those hidden features become unhidden features, but in the meantime, you can try them out and get a feel for them now, in all their rough, unfinished states.

For instance, it's easy to add page numbers that show up when you print a document created with Google Docs: go to File, Print Settings and check the box next to Include Page Numbers. Specify the location of the numbers and click OK. When you print, numbers will appear where you specified: 1, 2, 3, and so on.

The problem is that there's no way to tell Google that you want it to print 1/3, 2/3, 3/3, for instance, or 1 of 3, 2 of 3, 3 of 3. Rather, there's no way, unless you edit the HTML.

First of all, make sure you turn off Include Page Numbers if you've already set it. Next, go to Insert, Header or Insert, Footer, depending on where you want your page numbers to appear. After you've enabled the Header or Footer, click inside it and click the Center or Right button to position your page numbers (if you want them on the left, you don't need to click any of the buttons). Now type something easy to find at the spot where you want the page numbers to go, like ARGLEBARGLE.

Go to Edit, Edit HTML and find ARGLEBARGLE in the HTML. In my case, it looked like this:

```
<p id="dwce" style="text-align: right;">ARGLEBARGLE</p>
```

Replace ARGLEBARGLE with the following HTML code:

- To insert the page number: `<span class="google_pagenumber">1</span>`
- To insert the page count (the total number of pages): `<span class="google_pagecount">1</span>`

In my case, my code looked like this:

```
<p id="dwce" style="text-align: right;"><span class="google_pagenumber"
id="w9ns0">1</span>/<span class="google_pagecount"
id="w9ns1">1</span></p>
```

Click Save and then click Back to Editing the Document. Don't worry if you see 1/1 in your Header or Footer because that's what Google sees at this point. But print your document, and you'll see 1/3, 2/3, 3/3. If you'd rather use the 1 of 3 structure, your code would look like this:

```
<p id="dwce" style="text-align: right;"><span class="google_pagenumber"
id="w9ns0">1</span> of <span class="google_pagecount"
id="w9ns1">1</span></p>
```

I expect that eventually this will be doable through a point-and-click process (my goodness, I certainly hope so!), but for now, this is what you have to do.

Keyboard Shortcuts

Google Docs is eminently usable with a mouse, but if you learn the key commands that Google thoughtfully provides, you can use Google Docs far faster and more efficiently.

I'm not going to go through all the keyboard shortcuts that Google Docs possesses because you can find the complete list at the Google Docs Help Center at http://docs.google.com/support/bin/answer.py?answer=66280.

Table 14.2 lists some of the shortcuts for Documents that I use all the time. However, do check out the link I just gave you because you are sure to find others that are just as useful.

TABLE 14.2 Some of my favorite Google Docs keyboard shortcuts for Documents (Note: Mac users, it's Command instead of Ctrl)

Keyboard Shortcut	Meaning
The Usual Suspects	
Ctrl+a	Select all
Ctrl+x	Cut
Ctrl+c	Copy
Ctrl+v	Paste
Ctrl+s	Save
Ctrl+z	Undo
Ctrl+p	Print
Formatting	
Ctrl+b	Bold
Ctrl+i	Italicize
Ctrl+1	Heading (H1)
Ctrl+2	Sub-Hheading (H2)
Ctrl+space	Remove formatting
Content	
Ctrl+k	Insert link
Ctrl+m	Insert comment

Remember, these are just a few of the many keyboard shortcuts that you can use. Check out the links I provided at the beginning of this section for more. And one final thought: It's not vital that you learn all the shortcuts. Instead, learn the ones that will be of most use to you.

Spreadsheets

Of all the programs in Google Docs, Spreadsheets is the most complex and powerful, and it also receives more work and attention from Google. It's amazing what

Google developers have managed to do with Google Spreadsheets—the features and power of the program are first rate for an online app and maybe even for a desktop app as well. If all you do with a spreadsheet is enter some names and addresses for your holiday card list, you can definitely do that in Google Spreadsheets, but you won't be taking full advantage of all that it has to offer. If you use Excel for complex formulas and calculations, definitely give Google Spreadsheets a try. You may be pleasantly surprised.

 WARNING

Keep in mind the limits of spreadsheets at Google Docs: a maximum of 256 columns and no limit on rows, but a maximum of 200,000 cells or 100 sheets, whichever comes first. A spreadsheet can have no more than 50,000 (50 freakin' thousand!) cells with formulas in them, with no more than 10,000 GoogleFinance formulas, 10,000 GoogleLookup formulas, and 500 Import formulas in those 50,000 total. You can have at most 1,000 spreadsheets, and you can have 11 open at one time.

Leveraging Formulas and Functions

Formulas are at the heart of the power of spreadsheets. Sure, a lot of people use a spreadsheet like a simple database and simply enter rows and columns of text, like holiday card addresses or wedding guests. But spreadsheets really show off their true capabilities when you use formulas to calculate, manipulate, and process data. Even something as simple as telling a spreadsheet to divide the contents of cell A1 by the contents of cell B1 and place the results in cell C1 can be amazingly helpful and produce invaluable information that helps people make better decisions.

A *function* is basically a shortcut for a formula. For example, this is a formula for adding up numbers in cells A1, B1, and C1:

```
=A1+B1+C1
```

But what if you wanted to add the contents of 25 cells, A1 through Y1? Writing out a formula to do all that is possible, but it's also terribly tedious. Instead, you could use the SUM function, which is a prebuilt chunk of code that performs a specific action—in this case addition—to a specified set of data, like this:

```
=SUM(A1:Y1)
```

A function is really a formula; it's just a prebuilt formula that you can use as a shortcut. In recognition of that reality, and in order to avoid mind-numbing repetition, use the words "formula" and "function" interchangeably throughout this section.

You have two ways to add a function to your spreadsheet:

- Double-click an empty cell, select the Formula tab, and then click a link on the right side of the Formula bar. By default, Sum, Count, Average, Min, Max, and Product appear, along with More. If you click More, a pop-up appears (shown in Figure 14.2) that makes it easy for you to pick any of the hundreds of functions Google has created.

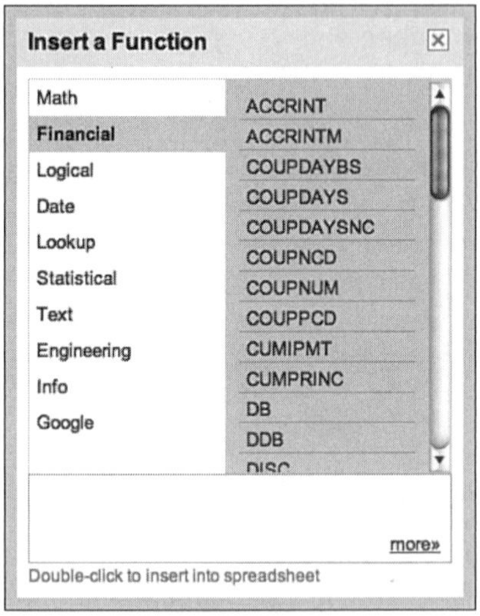

Insert a Function

Math	ACCRINT
Financial	ACCRINTM
Logical	COUPDAYBS
Date	COUPDAYS
Lookup	COUPDAYSNC
	COUPNCD
Statistical	COUPNUM
Text	COUPPCD
Engineering	CUMIPMT
Info	CUMPRINC
	DB
Google	DDB
	DISC

more»

Double-click to insert into spreadsheet

FIGURE 14.2 Google sorts its hundreds of functions by area, helping you zoom in on the one you want.

- Type **an** = and then start typing the first few letters of the function's name. Google will autocomplete the name of the function, helping to make sure you don't misspell anything, as you can see in Figure 14.3. Even better, it will also show you what parameters it needs to do its job.

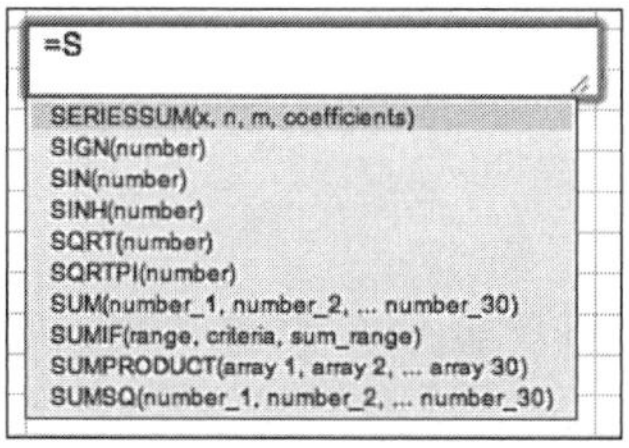

```
=S
  SERIESSUM(x, n, m, coefficients)
  SIGN(number)
  SIN(number)
  SINH(number)
  SQRT(number)
  SQRTPI(number)
  SUM(number_1, number_2, ... number_30)
  SUMIF(range, criteria, sum_range)
  SUMPRODUCT(array 1, array 2, ... array 30)
  SUMSQ(number_1, number_2, ... number_30)
```

FIGURE 14.3   Auto-complete makes it easy to enter functions you use all the time.

All formulas start with either an equal sign (=) or a plus sign (+). However, within a function you can use math operators as needed, listed in Table 14.3.

TABLE 14.3   Math operators usable in Spreadsheet formulas

OPERATOR	MEANING	EXAMPLE
+	Addition	=1+1
-	Subtraction	=2-1
*	Multiplication	=1*2
/	Division	=2/1
^	Power	=2^2

You can also compare values in your formulas, with the result being a Boolean value of either TRUE or FALSE. Table 14.4 lists the ways to compare values.

TABLE 14.4   Ways to compare values in Boolean expressions in Spreadsheet formulas

OPERATOR	MEANING	EXAMPLE
=	Equality	1=1
<>	Inequality	1<>2
<	Less Than	1<2
<=	Less Than or Equal To	1<=2
>	Greater Than	2>1
>=	Greater Than or Equal To	2>=1

You can use () to group calculations and also to avoid mixing math expressions and Boolean expressions. For example:

```
=((2^2)+(4-1)) >= 5
```

You can also use the ampersand (&) to concatenate text strings (although you may instead find the Combines Text Strings Formula, discussed in a later section, to be more appropriate). Suppose you have a first name, like Carson, in cell A1 and a last name, like Napier, in cell B1, and you want a complete name in cell C1, with a space between the first and last name. This example, which you would put in C1, shows how to do it with the &:

```
=A1&" "&B1
```

If you want to introduce text, place it between quotation marks, as in the previous example, in which " " inserts a space between names.

I'm not going to go through all the formulas you can use in Spreadsheets because you can find the complete list at the Google Docs Help Center, at http://docs.google.com/support/spreadsheets/bin/answer.py?answer=82712 (and also because this book would be about twice as long as it already is). But I would like to call out a few that are interesting and give you an idea of the breadth, power, and usefulness of the functions in Spreadsheets.

> **TIP**
>
> If you enter a formula incorrectly, Google Spreadsheets will look at you quizzically and, instead of data or your incorrect formula, it will show you ?#Error Parse Error? in the cell. That's its way of telling you to fix your function.

The Google Finance Information Formula

If you want to track stocks, you'll love this. Select the Formulas tab, double-click in a blank cell, and click More. Select Google and then double-click GoogleFinance to insert it. Close the Insert a Function window and take a look at what you just inserted:

```
=GoogleFinance(symbol, attribute)
```

The parameters are as follows:

- Symbol is required, and it must be the stock symbol of the company or fund you want to research.

- Attribute isn't required, but if you leave it out, Google returns the price of the company or fund by default. You can enter Price (the default), High, Low, Open, Volume, and many others. In addition, you can also refer to other cells with B12, A10, and so on.

Your parameters must be surrounded by quotation marks to work. For example, here's what I'd enter to find out Apple's current price:

```
=GoogleFinance("AAPL")
```

I didn't need to enter an attribute because I wanted the price, which is the default. But if I instead wanted the daily volume, I'd use this formula:

```
=GoogleFinance("AAPL", "volume")
```

> **NOTE**
>
> For more on the Google Finance formula, see http://docs.google.com/support/spreadsheets/bin/answer.py?answer=54198. There's even a video there to help you out. In particular, you may be interested to know that you can enter additional parameters to get historical quote information. More information is available at the link.

The Combines Text Strings Formula

Recently I was looking to buy a house, so I created a Google Docs spreadsheet that I could share with my realtor. I created 24 columns for all the stuff I wanted to track, and in particular I wanted to be able to sort on address data, including the street name, or all of the street numbers on a given street (I was very much targeting certain areas of St. Louis). As a result, the first four columns of my spreadsheet were labeled like this:

- **Street #**—Just the number of the building: 12, 1201, 12001.
- **NSEW**—The four cardinal directions, obviously not used at all addresses.
- **Street**—Amherst, Waterman, Big Bend. No directions, though—that's the job of the previous column.
- **Address**—The complete address: 1229 W. 9th St., 6047 Waterman, 466 S. Odell.

I didn't actually enter the data into the Address column. Instead, I used the CONCATENATE formula to do the work of joining the other three columns for me.

To do this, select the Formulas tab, double-click in a blank cell, and click More. Select Text and then double-click CONCATENATE to insert it. Close the Insert a Function window and take a look at what you just inserted:

```
=CONCATENATE(text_1, text_2, ... text_30)
```

The parameters are as follows:

- A reference to another cell: A2, B2, and C2, in my case, which corresponded to the data in Street #, NSEW, and Street (the headers were in A1, B1, and C1).
- If you want to enter a text string, enclose it in quotation marks.

In my case, I entered this into D4:

```
=CONCATENATE(A2, " ", B2, " ", C2)
```

I then selected cell D2 and, while holding the Shift key down, grabbed the bottom-left corner of the cell and dragged downward about 50 rows, thus duplicating the formula in each cell while incrementing the cell references for each row. D3, in other words, referenced A3, B3, and C3, whereas D4 referenced A4, B4, and C4, and so on.

You can see some partial results in Table 14.5:

TABLE 14.5 An example of my house search Spreadsheet, showing the results of the CONCATENATE function

STREET #	NSEW	STREET	ADDRESS
1229	W.	9th St.	1229 W. 9th St.
3546		Arsenal	3546 Arsenal
7227		Dartmouth	7227 Dartmouth

Google puts everything together as per my formula: 1229 plus a space (that's what " " is) plus W. plus a space plus 9th St. concatenated produces 1229 W. 9th St.

Notice, though, that there was no data for a direction (no N, S, E, or W) associated with Arsenal or Dartmouth, so the concatenation ignored those cells. Google didn't insert a space to represent those cells; it just skipped them instead, which is exactly what I wanted.

The Import Data From External Source Formula

This one is very cool. My best friend, Jans Carton, is a huge Dungeons & Dragons fan (I know, I know…), and he has created one of the very best D&D sites on the Web at www.d20srd.org. Basically, he took the 3rd Edition rules, marked them up by hand in vibrant, semantically correct HTML, cross-linked the living heck out of the whole thing (over 75,000 internal links!), and presented it in a smart package that thousands of people use every month.

Throughout the site he has placed tables of data governing the various particulars of the D&D rules. For instance, on www.d20srd.org/srd/combat/combatStatistics.htm he has the table shown in Figure 14.4.

Table: Size Modifiers	
Size	Size Modifier
Colossal	-8
Gargantuan	-4
Huge	-2
Large	-1
Medium	+0
Small	+1
Tiny	+2
Diminutive	+4
Fine	+8

FIGURE 14.4   Evidently, when it comes to modifiers in D&D, size does matter!

That's a beautiful table, and it's great that it's available to D&D players on the Web, but what if you want to use that data to perform some calculations? You could re-keystroke that table's data in your spreadsheet, and that wouldn't be a horrible fate, but this is the age of computers. Retyping that data would be drudgery, whereas we have an army of computers that will mindlessly obey our every whim! Google Spreadsheets and the Import Data From External Source function to the rescue!

To use this formula, select the Formulas tab, double-click in a blank cell, and click More. Select Google and then double-click ImportHtml to insert it. Close the Insert a Function window and take a look at what you just inserted:

```
=ImportHtml(url, query, index)
```

The parameters are as follows:

- URL should be the complete address to a web page.

- Query can be either List or Table, depending on the kind of data you want to import into your spreadsheet. If you enter List, the formula pays attention to <ul> (unordered or bulleted list), <ol> (ordered or numbered list), and <dl> (definition list) elements on a web page. If you enter Table, it looks for <table> and that's it.

- Index is a number identifying the specific list or table whose data you want. The number starts with 1 and increases sequentially, but lists and tables are numbered differently in two separate indexes. In other words, if a page consisted, in order, of List A, Table Y, List B, and Table Z, then List A would be 1 and List B would be 2, whereas Table Y would be 1 for tables and Table Z would be 2 for tables.

To insert the data from Jans's table into a spreadsheet, you'd use the following:

```
=ImportHtml("http://www.d20srd.org/srd/combat/combatStatistics.htm",
"table", 1)
```

This formula tells Google you want the first table from the given URL (note that the URL and Query must be in quotation marks, but the Index is not). I pasted this into cell B40 in a spreadsheet, and after a few seconds, the results popped in, automatically taking up two columns and ten rows (if there had been data in any of those cells, Google would have asked me if I wanted to overwrite it). You can see what happened in Figure 14.5 (some of the text is left-aligned, and some is right-aligned because of the cell's formatting; obviously I would immediately remedy that).

Size	Size Modifier
Colossal	-8
Gargantuan	-4
Huge	-2
Large	-1
Medium	+0
Small	+1
Tiny	+2
Diminutive	+4
Fine	+8

FIGURE 14.5 From Jans's website to a Google spreadsheet.

Now that this data is in a spreadsheet, it can be referenced and used by other cells and even other spreadsheets, making it far more useful. Well, not to me because I don't play D&D, but to those that do, I'm sure you're already thinking of what you can do with this.

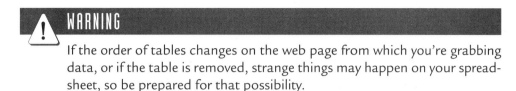

> **WARNING**
>
> If the order of tables changes on the web page from which you're grabbing data, or if the table is removed, strange things may happen on your spreadsheet, so be prepared for that possibility.

Filling in Forms

If you go to the New menu in Google Docs, you may notice that Form is a choice along with Document, Spreadsheet, and Presentation. In actuality, a Form is just a special kind of spreadsheet, and Google added Form to the New menu to make it a lot easier to find that capability. What does it do? It's actually a *great* feature: You can create a form that makes it easy for you to publish, and gather responses automatically, and then view the resulting data in a Google spreadsheet.

> **NOTE**
>
> Google has a nicely comprehensive help page on forms at http://documents.google.com/support/spreadsheets/bin/answer.py?hl=en&answer=87809.

When you select New, Form, a new tab or window opens up into which you can begin building the questions you want to ask, as you can see in Figure 14.6.

Fill in a title and enter some information about your form into the appropriate fields. Now the hard work begins: creating the questions.

> **WARNING**
>
> At this time, the form interface is apparently lacking an autosave function, so don't forget to click Save constantly. I'm sure this will be remedied shortly.

Google starts by providing the fields for your initial question, but you don't have to use what Google provides. On the top right of the first question's box, you can see three buttons, shown in close-up in Figure 14.7.

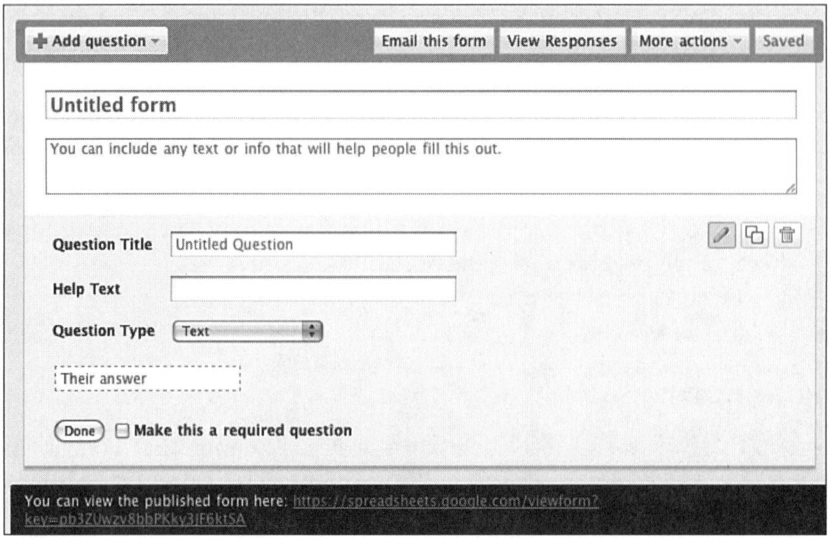

FIGURE 14.6   The initial interface for creating a form.

FIGURE 14.7   Edit,
Duplicate, and Delete each
question in your form.

The buttons, in order, are Edit, Duplicate, and Delete. Clicking Edit toggles between view mode (what the people filling out the form will see) and edit mode (what you, as the form's creator, see). Duplicate copies the contents of this question's box into a new question box on top of the current one (it's easy to move your questions, so that's no big deal—you just click in any blank area in the question box and drag after your cursor turns into a four-headed arrow). Delete does just that, removing that question's box for good.

TIP

You can delete any question's box, but you must always have at least one question box in your form. Google won't let you delete the last one.

You can create six kinds of questions:

- **Text**—Produces a small text box into which users type their answers. Good for questions that require short answers: Credit Card Number, Bank Account Number, or ATM PIN.

- **Paragraph Text**—Produces a bigger text box into which users type their answers. Good for questions that require a longer, more detailed answer: Describe your favorite haircut, Where were you the night of October 12? Provide a complete history of all life on Earth.

- **Multiple Choice**—Also known as radio buttons. Produces a series of choices, but users can choose only one. Good for multiple choice answers in which only one is allowed: Who's your favorite Beatle? Which of the following foods do you like the least? Grade you expect in this course.

- **Check boxes**—Produces a series of choices, and users can choose as many as are applicable. Good for multiple choice answers in which several options can be chosen at the same time: What do you want on your soyburger?, Select the albums on which the E Street Band plays with Bruce, or I'm interested in learning the following ballroom dances.

- **Choose From a List**—Also known as a drop-down menu. Pretty much the same thing as the Multiple Choice option, except with a drop-down instead of radio buttons. If it were me, I would have bagged Multiple Choice and kept Choose From a List.

- **Scale (1-n)**—AKA Hot or Not. Choose a scale between two numbers (1 through 5 is the default, but you can go all the way up to 10), provide a label for 1 and another for the other end (let's say 5), and users click a radio button to indicate where they lie along that scale. Good for questions in which you want to offer users a range of possibilities along a scale: Rank the band Rush on a scale ranging from awesome to godlike; Rate the clowns at last night's rodeo, and How did you like the heavy metal I played while you received a massage?

To add a new question, click the Add Question button on the top left of the form's window and select one of the six options. The new question box appears on the bottom of your current questions, but again, you can move it by clicking and dragging. You can change the kind of question you're asking anytime by selecting a new one from the Question Type drop-down. You can also make a question mandatory by checking the box next to Make This a Required Question.

After you've completed the form, you can do the following:

- **View the Published Form**—At the very bottom of the form is a link to the web page containing your form, which you can view to see how it looks or to fill in with test data.

- **Email This Form**—Click the Email This Form button, enter email addresses or use the Contact Picker, and choose whether to include the form in the email. I don't recommend including the form in the email because the differences between email programs make this a dicey proposition at best (in fact, Outlook 2007 won't display your form at all, so there are millions of users right there). Don't do it. Instead, let the email contain a link to the form so people can safely—and consistently—fill it out on the Web.

- **View Responses**—Click this button to load a page that shows you a summary of results, along with a link to See Complete Responses. You can read a bit more about this feature just a few paragraphs after this list.

- **Embed the Form in Your Website**—Go to More Actions, Embed to receive a line of code from Google that you insert into the HTML on your website to embed your form. This helps preserve your branding, even though it's still obvious that the form came from Google, thanks to the "Powered by Google Docs" at the bottom of the form.

- **Edit Confirmation**—Go to More Actions, Edit Confirmation to change the message people see after they've submitted your form.

If you want to delete a form, you have to go back to the main Google Docs screen, find your form, check the box next to it, and click Delete.

The responses are particularly interesting. The initial page Google displays with the responses you've received to your form contains attractive graphs and summaries. Figure 14.8 displays a sample.

If you click See Complete Responses, a spreadsheet opens up with the actual data your form has gathered, including a Timestamp column in A that contains the date and time of each response. Because that data is in a spreadsheet, you can start to do all sorts of fun things with it, such as creating your own formulas to measure results and generating your own graphs based on what you want to visualize.

One word of advice, however: if you want to insert a new row for totals or anything else, do it at the top of the results, not the bottom. New data is added after the bottom row of results, but the top is left alone. New columns to the right of those generated by Google are always fine. And you can certainly create another sheet and reference the data in the first, if you'd like.

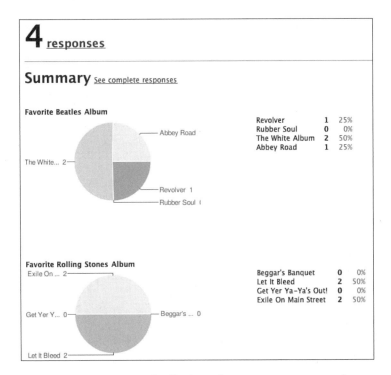

FIGURE 14.8   Google displays the responses to your form in an attractive, useful way.

⚠ WARNING

Keep in mind that the limits of any Google spreadsheet apply to the spreadsheet generated by your form: a maximum of 256 columns and no limit on rows, but a maximum of 200,000 cells across all sheets.

Clarifying with Charts

Like other spreadsheet programs, Google Spreadsheets makes it easy to visualize your data with a chart. To create a chart from your data, it's best that you select your data first—you don't have to, but it does make things easier for you—and then go to Edit, Insert, Chart (you can also click the little chart-looking button on the right side of the Edit bar and then choose Chart). When you do, the Create Chart screen appears, shown in Figure 14.9.

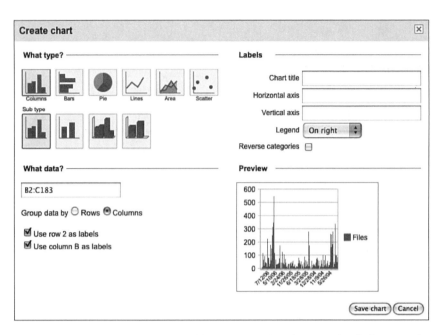

FIGURE 14.9 Google Spreadsheets provides the standard chart tools you need.

You can create six kinds of charts, and each one has between two and five subtypes:

- Columns
- Bars
- Pie
- Lines
- Area
- Scatter

In Figure 14.9 you can see that the range has already been filled in next to What Data?, but you're free to change those cell references or even add a range if you created a chart without first specifying your data.

On the bottom right of the Create Chart screen, Google shows you a preview of your chart as you make your choices. This is a handy way to buzz through the various chart types to find the exact one you need.

When you're happy with your chart, click Save Chart, and you're back in your spreadsheet, but with your chart now floating above your data. To move your chart, click it and drag it where you'd like it to go. When you click it, a small menu—labeled Chart—appears in the top left. From this menu, you can do the following:

- **Edit Chart**—This takes you back to the Create Chart screen, except that it's now labeled Edit Chart. Everything else is the same.

- **Delete Chart**—Watch as I put the chart under this handkerchief... annnd—abracadabra! It's gone!

- **Save Image**—This turns your chart into a PNG file, which you can then download onto your computer. After you have that PNG, you can import it into a document or presentation which, unfortunately, is the only way right now to get your chart into a file like that.

- **Publish Chart**—Provides you with an HTML image link (something like `<img src="http://spreadsheets.google.com/pub?key=pa7ZUwzv5rwP3_ 21kj2CjVg&oid=2&output=image" />`) you can paste into a website so that anyone else can see your chart.

- **Move to Own Sheet**—This creates a new sheet that contains nothing but your chart, making it much easier to see and work with.

Google doesn't offer the 50 gazillion charts that Excel does, but it doesn't have to—the charts that 90% of users actually need are already available. New ones will be added over time, but for now, you can do a lot with the charts that Google Spreadsheets has in its arsenal.

Embedding Gadgets

In addition to charts, Google takes its concept of gadgets (widgets that perform some function with data, also used in Sites and Start Page) to spreadsheets as well. To use a gadget with your data, it's best that you select your data first—you don't have to, but it does make things easier for you—and then go to Edit, Insert, Gadget (you can also click the little chart-looking button on the right side of the Edit bar and then choose Gadget). When you do, the Add a Gadget screen appears, shown in Figure 14.10.

You can create seven kinds of gadgets, with subtypes under each one:

- Charts
- Tables
- Maps
- Web
- Diagrams
- Finance
- Custom

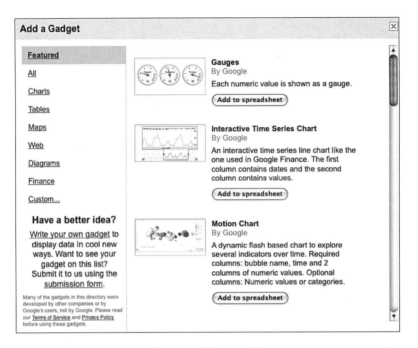

FIGURE 14.10   Google Spreadsheets allow you to insert several sophisticated gadgets.

This allows you to import gadgets that you have created. If you want to do this, read http://code.google.com/apis/gadgets/ and http://code.google.com/apis/visualization/; you can ask questions at http://groups.google.com/group/Google-Gadgets-API.

You can also view every gadget on one screen by clicking All or view gadgets for which Google wants to increase awareness by clicking Featured.

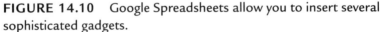

NOTE

See a complete list of all the gadgets you can use at the Google Docs Help Center at http://documents.google.com/support/bin/answer.py?answer=99488&topic=15165.

I'm not going to go through every gadget that Google has to offer, but just to give you a taste of what they can do in your spreadsheets, I'll call out three in which you might be interested.

- **Organizational Chart**—Create a classic Org Chart from a Google spreadsheet, as shown in Figure 14.11.

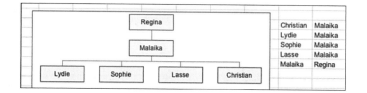

FIGURE 14.11   Underlings go in the first column, with the manager in the second.

- **Map**—An interactive map on which you can click, pan, and zoom, as shown in Figure 14.12. See an example at http://spreadsheets.google.com/pub?key=pnLDJiBKx5IjckJz69Yv0cA.

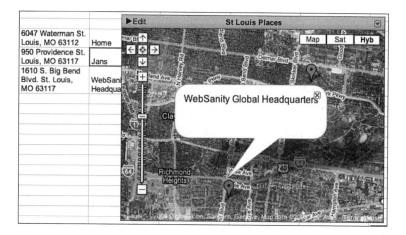

FIGURE 14.12   Addresses go in the first column, with optional descriptions in the second.

- **Interactive Time Series**—A series of points graphed over time, in which you can zoom in on certain time periods for greater detail, as shown in Figure 14.13.

Gadgets are really nifty additions to Google Spreadsheets, so be sure to play with them, and if you're feeling ambitious, create your own.

1	10/6/06	11
2	9/9/06	69
3	9/7/06	24
4	9/6/06	113
5	8/11/06	63
6	8/10/06	17
7	8/9/06	91
8	8/8/06	72
9	8/7/06	46
10	8/3/06	41
11	8/2/06	36
12	8/1/06	10
13	7/22/06	72
14	7/20/06	25
15	7/13/06	221
16	7/12/06	78
17	7/11/06	76
18	6/27/06	14
19	6/25/06	108
20	6/22/06	32
21	6/21/06	175

FIGURE 14.13 Dates go in the first column, with numeric values in the second.

Keyboard Shortcuts

Google Docs is eminently usable with a mouse, but if you learn the key commands that Google thoughtfully provides, you can use Google Docs far faster and more efficiently. I'm not going to go through all the keyboard shortcuts that Google Docs possesses, as you can find the complete list at the Google Docs Help Center, at http://docs.google.com/support/bin/answer.py?answer=66280.

Table 14.6 lists some of the shortcuts for Spreadsheets that I use all the time. However, check out the link I just gave you, because you are sure to find others that are just as useful.

TABLE 14.6 Some of my favorite Google Docs keyboard shortcuts for Spreadsheets (Note: Mac users, it's Command instead of Ctrl)

KEYBOARD SHORTCUT	MEANING
The Usual Suspects	
Ctrl+x	Cut
Ctrl+c	Copy
Ctrl+v	Paste
Ctrl+s	Save
Ctrl+z	Undo
Ctrl+p	Print

TABLE 14.6 Continued

KEYBOARD SHORTCUT	MEANING
Formatting	
Ctrl+b	Bold
Ctrl+i	Italicize
Rows, Columns, and Cells	
F2	Edit active cell
Ctrl+spacebar	Select entire column
Shift+spacebar	Select entire row
Moving	
Enter	Move to next cell in column
Tab	Move to next cell in row
Ctrl+PgDn	Move to next worksheet

Remember, these are just a few of the many keyboard shortcuts that you can use. Check out the links I provided at the beginning of this section for more. And one final thought: It's not vital that you learn all the shortcuts. Instead, learn the ones that will be of most use to you.

PRESENTATIONS

Presentations is the newest of the three Google Apps amigos, and as such, it has the least complexity of the three programs. However, there are still a few items I want to call out. At the same time, I don't want to go over the obvious. For instance, embedding a video is right in front of you—just click the Insert Video button (there are also buttons for Insert Image, Insert Text, and Insert Shape). Jumping back to prior versions of your presentation is also conspicuous; it's a big tab labeled Revisions—one of the only two tabs currently in the program! So instead, I'm going to look at a few of the not-so-obvious features in Presentations that you might just find indispensable.

> ⚠️ **WARNING**
>
> Keep in mind the size limits of presentations at Google Docs: a maximum size of 10MB, with uploaded files no bigger than 2MB, and emailed files no bigger than 500KB. You can have at most a mix of 5,000 documents and presentations and 5,000 images.

Delivering Presentations

Of course, the whole point to creating a presentation is…presenting it! And when you're presenting, it's often very helpful to have notes for yourself to which you can refer so you don't have to type *everything* out on the slide.

To enter a speaker's note, click the icon for that function in the bottom right of the Presentations window. You can see the icon, which can be easy to miss, in Figure 14.14.

FIGURE 14.14 The View Speaker Notes icon is at the bottom right of the Presentations window.

After you click it, a frame opens on the right of the window in which you can type pretty much anything. When you finish, close it by clicking the X in the upper-right corner, or just leave it open so it's always available to you.

When you're ready to give your presentation, start it up in one of the following ways:

- Click the Start Presentation button in the upper-right corner.
- Press Ctrl-F5

After you start the presentation, it will load in another tab or window in your web browser, depending on your browser's settings. You can invite others to see it online by copying and sharing the URL Google gives the presentation in the upper-right corner of the window. While others are viewing it, you can chat with them using the chat interface on the right side of the screen.

To view your notes yourself, click the View Speaker Notes link on the right side of the window. Again, Google opens them in another tab or window in your web browser, depending on your browser's settings, but you really want them to open in another window. If you open them in another tab, you'll be switching back and forth between your presentation and your notes about the presentation, which will quickly grow tedious and distracting.

To open the link in another window instead of another tab, do the following, depending upon your browser:

- **Firefox**—Right-click the link and select Open Link in New Window.
- **Internet Explorer**—Right-click the link and select Open in New Window.
- **Safari**—Right-click the Speaker Notes tab and select Move Tab to New Window.

As you advance through your slide show, the notes in the other window (or tab, if you went that route) will advance in step with the presentation slide. Now that's slick—and useful!

Rearranging Slides

Moving slides around is a key function in preparing a presentation: Should this slide go before that one? Or after this one? How about these five? Should they go at the beginning or the end? And so on.

Unfortunately, Presentations doesn't have a separate slide sorter view yet, like PowerPoint and Keynote. Instead, you have to move slides around in the area to the left of the screen, where the slides are listed. The longer your presentation, the more this will grate on you. Let's hope Google fixes this soon.

Start by choosing the slides you want to move. To select contiguous slides (slides that are next to each other), click the first slide and then, while pressing Shift, click the last slide in the series that you want to select. To select noncontiguous slides, click the first slide and then, while pressing Ctrl on a Windows or Linux box and Command on a Mac, click the other slides you want to include.

Now you'll have to move the slides using one of the following techniques:

- Drag the slides to the new position in which you want them. If you hold down Ctrl as you drag, you'll be duplicating the slides instead of moving them.
- Right-click the selected slides and choose Move Slide Up or Move Slide Down. To make copies of the slides, choose Duplicate Slide.

Resizing Objects

After you insert an object—be it image, text, shape, or video—you can easily move it anywhere on your slide. Select the object, and your cursor turns into a four-headed arrow. At that point, just drag the object wherever you'd like it to go.

You can also resize objects, but this can be a bit tricky. When you click an object, a resize handle appears at each corner, as you can see in Figure 14.15.

FIGURE 14.15 See the four resize handles at each corner of this picture of my cute lil' puppy, Libby.

If you click one of those resize handles and drag, you will resize the picture. However, the resulting dimensions will not remain locked in the proportions they were in when you started, so you will quickly end up with an object that doesn't look quite right. An example of this is in Figure 14.16. Poor Libby!

FIGURE 14.16 I changed the width, but the height stayed the same.

When you resize, you almost always want to keep the object's proportions locked. To do so, hold down Shift as you click and drag the resize handle. This will constrict your changes so they stay in proportion.

If you want to move or resize multiple objects at the same time, hold down the Shift key as you select each object, or click and drag over all the objects, joining them together as one unit.

Keyboard Shortcuts

Google Docs is eminently usable with a mouse, but if you learn the key commands that Google thoughtfully provides, you can use Google Docs far faster and more efficiently.

I'm not going to go through all the keyboard shortcuts that Google Docs possesses because you can find the complete list at the Google Docs Help Center, at http://docs.google.com/support/bin/answer.py?answer=66280.

Table 14.7 lists some of the shortcuts for Presentations that I use all the time. However, check out the link I just gave you because you are sure to find others that are just as useful.

TABLE 14.7   Some of my favorite Google Docs keyboard shortcuts for Presentations (Note: Mac users, it's Command instead of Ctrl)

KEYBOARD SHORTCUT	MEANING
The Usual Suspects	
Ctrl+x	Cut
Ctrl+c	Copy
Ctrl+v	Paste
Ctrl+s	Save
Formatting	
Ctrl+b	Bold
Ctrl+i	Italicize
Slides and Screens	
Ctrl+m	Insert new slide
PgDn	Move down one screen
PgUp	Move up one screen

Remember, these are just a few of the many keyboard shortcuts that you can use. Check out the links I provided at the beginning of this section for more. And one final thought: it's not vital that you learn all the shortcuts. Instead, learn the ones that will be of most use to you.

SOLVING COMMON PROBLEMS

As with all things in life, you're going to find little gotchas. Here are a few of those and their solutions.

When I Right-Click in Firefox, the Google Docs Menu Is Covered Up by the Web Browser's Menu!

This can be very frustrating: If you use Firefox, when you right-click while editing files or in the Docs list, two overlapping menus can appear: Google Docs' and Firefox's. There are a couple of things you can do to fix this:

- Hold down Shift when you right-click to use Firefox's menu instead of Google Docs'.
- In Firefox, go to Tools, Options, Content if you use Windows; Firefox, Preferences, Content if you use Mac OS X; or Edit, Preferences, Content if you use Linux. Make sure Enable JavaScript is checked and then click Advanced next to Enable JavaScript. In the new window, check the box next to Disable or Replace Context Menus and click OK. After this change, right-clicking will show only the Google Docs' menu, not Firefox's.

CONCLUSION

This has been a long, detailed chapter, but Google Docs is a rich, complex, powerful set of programs, and it is getting richer, more complex, and more powerful all the time. Really, an entire book could be written on the subject of Google Docs, but in this chapter I've tried to hit the high points to give you an idea about how to utilize Google Docs more effectively if you're already using it and to get you to try it if you haven't already.

FURTHER READING

There's always more to learn, so here are some resources that you might find handy if you want to learn more about the Google Apps Start Page:

- Tour: http://www.google.com/google-d-s/tour1.html
- Overviews and high points: http://www.google.com/a/help/intl/en/users/dands.html

- Google Apps for Admins Help Topics

    - Google Docs: http://www.google.com/support/a/bin/topic.py?topic=10719

    - Documents: http://documents.google.com/support/bin/topic.py?topic=15114 (or try http://documents.google.com/support/?fulldump=1 for all help topics concatenated)

    - Spreadsheets: http://documents.google.com/support/spreadsheets/ (or try http://documents.google.com/support/spreadsheets/?fulldump=1 for all help topics concatenated)

    - Presentations: http://documents.google.com/support/presentations/ (or try http://documents.google.com/support/presentations/?fulldump=1 for all help topics concatenated)

- Google Apps for Users Help Topics: http://documents.google.com/support/?ctx=ausers&hl=en

- Interactive Video Guides: http://services.google.com/apps/resources/overviews/welcome/topicDocs/index.html

- YouTube

    - Google Docs YouTube Channel: http://www.youtube.com/view_play_list?p=372A76C86AF35D52

    - Google Docs Community Channel: http://www.youtube.com/GoogleDocsCommunity. Videos from users who like Google Docs and want to share their knowledge.

    - Lee LeFever's "Google Docs in Plain English": http://www.youtube.com/watch?v=XyjY8ZLzZrw.
      A fun, quick intro to the topic.

    - "Teachers and Principals Talk about Google Docs": http://www.youtube.com/watch?v=TYPjJK6LZdM

- For developers

    - Screencasts on the Spreadsheets Data API: http://services.google.com/apps/resources/admin_breeze/SpreadsheetsAPI/index.html

    - Google Apps APIs discussion group: http://groups.google.com/group/google-apps-apis)

    - Google Docs Data APIs discussion group: http://groups.google.com/group/Google-Docs-Data-APIs

- PDFs for training support staff: http://services.google.com/apps/
  training/user_support/DocsSpreadsheets/DocsSpreadsheetsUserSupport.pdf
- Discussion group: http://groups.google.com/group/GoogleDocs. The official
  Google Docs Help Group.
- Blog: http://googledocs.blogspot.com. The Official Google Docs Blog
- FAQs
  - Google Docs FAQ: http://docs.google.com/View?docid=dgzdcn6d_
    195txp2zgn. Really ugly, but it contains some useful information.
  - Google Spreadsheets FAQ: http://gssfaq.googlepages.com. Hasn't been
    updated in a few years.
- Known issues: http://documents.google.com/support/bin/request.py?
  contact_type=known_issues_2. Discover the problems Google knows about
  and what it's doing about them.
- Support options: http://documents.google.com/support/bin/request.py?
  contact_type=contact_policy&ctx=docs&hl=en

Integrating Google Docs with Other Software and Services

Google Docs is nice and is constantly getting better. You're pretty much forced to use Google Docs in a web browser (with a few exceptions, discussed in this chapter), but that still hasn't stopped smart folks from integrating Google Docs with other software, even if it's on their computers.

In this chapter, I present tips, tricks, and software you can use to enhance Google Docs to more closely fit your needs.

WORKING WITH GOOGLE DOCS USING OPENOFFICE.ORG OR STAR OFFICE

Microsoft is working to integrate online support into Office so that you can access and edit Word, Excel, and PowerPoint files stored in Microsoft's cloud computing experiment, Office Live Workspace. But it's no big shocker that Microsoft isn't doing anything to support Google Docs in Office, due to the intense rivalry between the two companies.

The free and open source office suite OpenOffice.org (OOo) has stepped into the breach in a handy way. Well, let me be more precise: OOo developers have stepped up and written several extensions for OOo that allow it to work with Google Docs in some smart ways. It wouldn't surprise me, however, to see OOo eventually support Google Docs out of the box someday.

To install either of these extensions, go to Tools, Extension Manager and press the Add button. Select the downloaded extension file (it will end in .oxt), and OpenOffice.org will install it. Restart OOo, and you're ready to use the new functionality.

OoGdocsIntegrator

The free OpenOffice.org2GoogleDocs extension allows you to import and export files to and from Google Docs. You can download it from http://extensions.services.openoffice.org/project/OoGdocsIntegrator and read more about it at its official home, http://code.google.com/p/oo-googledocs-integrator/.

One big caveat is that you need version 6 of the Java Runtime Environment (JRE) for this extension to work. Once you install the extension, a new menu appears named OOIntegrator and offers the following choices:

- **Zoho**—You can ignore this unless you use Zoho, a competitor to Google Apps.
- **Google**—This is the one you want, obviously.
- **History**—Past searches and other items you may want to revisit.
- **Settings**—Go here first and enter your Google Apps username and password.
- **About**—Find out more about OoGdocsIntegrator.

Once installed, you can now upload and download files—even multiple files!—to and from your computer and Google Docs.

WARNING

Mac OS X users in particular will have to be on Leopard (Tiger and anything earlier is unsupported unless you try out http://landonf.bikemonkey.org/static/soylatte/) and will need to download the latest Java from http://developer.apple.com/java/. Even with that, however, this extension still won't work because it crashes OpenOffice.org 3 beta on Mac OS X Leopard when you select Google from the OOIntegrator menu. By the time you read this, it may have been fixed, but at least you've been warned.

OpenOffice.org2GoogleDocs

The free OpenOffice.org2GoogleDocs extension allows you to import and export files to and from Google Docs. You can download it from http://extensions.services.openoffice.org/project/ooo2gd and read more about it at its official home, http://code.google.com/p/ooo2gd/.

The formats it supports are listed in Table 15.1.

TABLE 15.1 Formats supported by OpenOffice.org2GoogleDocs.

	DOCUMENTS	SPREADSHEETS	PRESENTATIONS
Export to Google Docs	DOC, ODT, RTF, SXW	CSV, ODS, XLS	PPS, PPT
Import from Google Docs	ODT		PPT

One big caveat—you need version 6 of the Java Runtime Environment (JRE) for this extension to work. After you install the extension, a new toolbar appears, as you can see in Figure 15.1.

FIGURE 15.1 The OpenOffice.org2GoogleDocs toolbar in OpenOffice.org.

This extension also supports Zoho, but you can ignore those buttons (the ones with the little Z on them). Instead, the first button in Figure 15.1 allows you to upload files from your machine to Google Docs, while the second button downloads files from Google Docs to your computer. When you press either of them, you're prompted to log in with your Google Docs username and password.

If you want to import files, press the enormous Get List button, shown in Figure 15.2, and shortly thereafter you'll see a list of your files at Google Docs.

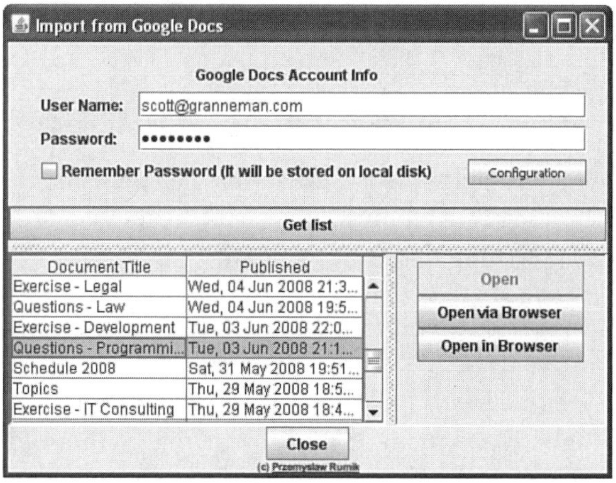

FIGURE 15.2 Log in and you'll see the files stored at Google Docs.

This is a nice extension that brings some much-needed functionality to both Google Docs and OpenOffice.org.

> ⚠️ **WARNING**
>
> Mac OS X users in particular will have to be on Leopard (Tiger and anything earlier is unsupported unless you try out http://landonf.bikemonkey.org/static/soylatte/), and you will need to download the latest Java from http://developer.apple.com/java/. However, even with that, this extension won't work apparently because the Apple JRE update is 64-bit only, while much of the extension is 32-bit, which means they don't play together nicely.

ACCESSING GOOGLE DOCS ON A MOBILE DEVICE

We live our lives on the go now, and as smart phones get more powerful and more capable, we'll increasingly be using them to access our work. Right now, Google Docs is available to mobile users, but it's not fully there yet, as you'll see.

Generic Instructions

If you want to view Google Docs on your mobile device, point its web browser to http://docs.google.com/a/YOURDOMAIN/m. Log in, and there you are: your files, but read-only, and probably in little-bitty type. But at least you can see them as you go about your day, untethered to your computer. As for editing, who knows when that will be available? It'll have to happen someday, but I wouldn't hold my breath.

BlackBerry

You can view documents and spreadsheets (but not presentations) by using your BlackBerry's web browser to go to http://docs.google.com/a/YOURDOMAIN/m. No editing at the time I'm writing this book, though.

iPhone

If you use an iPhone, you're in luck…kinda. You can view (as in no editing, just viewing) your Google Docs using Safari by going to http://docs.google.com/a/YOURDOMAIN/m. You can't edit them, though, and the text can be kind of teensy-weensy on the iPhone's screen.

Instead, you should think about downloading the free MiGhtyDocs from the Apps Store at http://phobos.apple.com/WebObjects/MZStore.woa/wa/viewSoftware?id=287327494&mt=8 (the link opens iTunes, so it might be a lot quicker to just open iTunes and search for the app). After you install it, you can access your Google Docs with the following restrictions:

- You cannot view presentations or spreadsheets, just documents.
- You can't edit documents; you can only view them.

However, on the plus side, you don't have to be online to view your documents, as MiGhtyDocs caches them so you can view them offline. Someday we may see something more full-featured, but for now, we'll have to be grateful for what we have.

GETTING DOCUMENTS INTO GOOGLE DOCS

You can import a wide variety of file types into Google Docs, but you can't import everything under the sun. In addition to file types, you have another limitation in terms of size.

- **Documents**
    - Formats: DOC, HTML, ODT, RTF, SXW, TXT
    - Size: 500KB
- **Spreadsheets**
    - Formats: CSV, ODS, TSB, TSV, TXT, XLS
    - Size: 1MB
- **Presentations**
    - Formats: PPS, PPT
    - Size: 10MB if uploaded from your computer directly; 500KB if emailed; 2MB if imported by supplying a URL
- **PDFs**
    - Formats: PDF (duh!)
    - Size: 10MB if uploaded from your computer directly; 2 MB if imported by supplying a URL

Generally, importing a file manually is the same, no matter the file type. On the Docs List page of Google Docs, click Upload, choose the file you want to upload, give it a name (or leave this blank if you want to use the file's current name), and press Upload File. Alternatively, you can specify a URL of a file that already exists on the Web, or you can even email the file to a special email address that Google Docs specifies at the bottom of the page. When your file finishes uploading, Google Docs will open the file in a new tab so you can start working on it.

Needless to say, this process rapidly becomes soul-destroying in its dreary monotony if you have more than just a few files to upload. Throughout the rest of this section, I show you some solutions that allow you to upload files in bulk (as well as some that won't). Ahhh...thank goodness for automation!

Using Firefox

As popular as Firefox has gotten in the last few years, and as clever as developers are at coming up with cool extensions for the open source web browser, it's no surprise that there are several ways you can use it to open files in Google Docs.

Opening Links with the Send to Google Docs Firefox Extension

Install the Send to Google Docs extension for Firefox (https://addons.mozilla.org/en-US/firefox/addon/8552), and you turn all of Firefox into a feeder for Google Docs. When you find a link to a Word doc, a PDF, a file in Open Document Format, or anything else that Google Docs supports, just right-click the link and select Send to Google Docs. A moment later, Google Docs will open, and the file will be ready for editing. Quick and easy is always nice!

Uploading and Managing Files with the gDocsBar Firefox Extension

This is a really cool, useful extension, one that people who use Firefox and Google Docs will love. Install the gDocsBar extension (https://addons.mozilla.org/en-US/firefox/addon/6363), restart Firefox, and you just gained a powerful tool. To see the gDocsBar, do one of the following:

- Go to View, Sidebar, Google Docs Bar
- Press Cmd-Shift-y if you use a Mac and Ctrl-Shift-y if you use Windows or Linux.

After you do, and after you log in, you'll see something like Figure 15.3.

You can see the files you have in Google Docs using several different criteria:

- **View all files**—Filter, All Types
- **View files by type**—Filter, Documents (or Spreadsheets or Presentations)
- **Sort files by title, data, or author**—View all files or view files by type and then click Title, Date, or Author

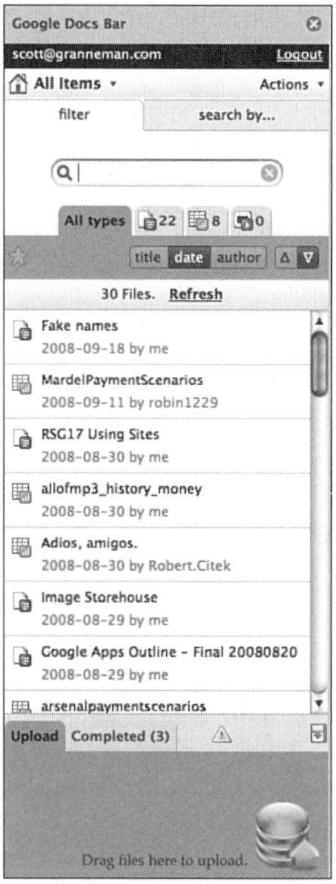

FIGURE 15.3   The Google Docs Bar in all its useful glory.

- **List files in ascending or descending order**—View all files or view files by type; click Title, Date, or Author and then click the up or down arrow
- **View starred files**—View all files or view files by type and then click the pale gold star
- **Search for files**—Filter, search box
- **View files in a specific folder**—Drop-down menu at the top left; default to All Items
- **Search by name, author, or content**—Search By tab

When you see a list of the files you want, you can open a file by simply clicking it. To create a new file, go to Actions and select the file type you want to create.

If you want to upload files from your computer to Google Docs, drag them into the blue area at the bottom of the tab. A few moments later, your files will be copied to Google Docs. If you don't see the blue upload area, press the small icon on the bottom right of the tab, which shows up when that area of the sidebar is collapsed.

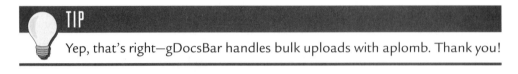

TIP

Yep, that's right—gDocsBar handles bulk uploads with aplomb. Thank you!

There's a lot more you can do with gDocsBar, but I'll let you explore to discover all its capabilities. One hint: right-click and you'll find some nice actions. The one downside is that gDocsBar doesn't yet support PDF uploads. For many people, this won't be a problem. And even without PDF uploads, gDocsBar is still great.

TIP

Another great Firefox extension that lets you upload more than one file at a time to Google Docs is Firefox Universal Uploader, available at https://addons.mozilla.org/en-US/firefox/addon/4724. It has a dual-pane interface like a lot of FTP programs, and it works well. Give it a try.

Utilizing the Google Toolbar for Firefox

If you're using the Google Toolbar with Internet Explorer, then skip this section—or read it and feel jealous. This feature works only with the Google Toolbar for Firefox (available at http://toolbar.google.com), and it's a nice one.

First make sure the feature is enabled. On the Toolbar, go to Settings, Options and check the box next to Google Docs. Press OK to save your settings.

Now you can open files at Google Docs in several different ways:

- Drag the files from your computer into Firefox.
- Click a link on a web page that points to a file type supported by Google Docs (this is very similar to the Send to Google Docs Firefox Extension, discussed a bit earlier).
- Double-click a file on your computer. If it's a file type supported by Google Docs, it will open online in that program.

That last option can really drive some folks nuts, so you might not want to enable this feature (of course, opening Word first and then selecting the file you want to open from inside Word still works, as does right-clicking a Word file and telling Windows you want to open it with Word).

Using Windows

If you use Windows and want to move some of your files from your local machine up to Google Docs, install the free Documents List Uploader, available at http://code.google.com/p/google-gdata/downloads/list (you need to have .NET 2.0 first; if you need it, you can get it from Windows Update). Once you've provided it with your Google Apps username and password and the program is running, you can move files (yes, it supports bulk uploads) using one of the following methods:

- Right-click the files and select Send to Google Docs.
- Drag the files onto the DocList Uploader window.

It's fast, it works well, and if you right-click a file listed in the Documents List Uploader, you can open it in your browser or delete it. All in all, this program is a must for Windows users.

> **NOTE**
>
> For more information about the Documents List Uploader, see http://googledataapis.blogspot.com/2008/01/easily-upload-your-documents-to-google.html.

Using Mac OS X

If you use Mac OS X and want to move some of your files from your Mac up to Google Docs, install the free GDocsUploader, available at http://code.google.com/p/gdocsuploader/. When you start the program, you're prompted for your Google Docs username and password. If you open the program, you're prompted to select a file to upload (only one a time, unfortunately).

Alternately, drag the program (when it's not running) to your Dock so it sits there all the time. After that, simply drag your files onto GDocsUploader on your Dock. A few moments later, they appear at your Google Docs account. Voila!

ENCRYPTING YOUR CONNECTION

The best way to secure your files at Google Docs is to access them only via HTTPS so that all traffic between your web browser and Google is encrypted. Google Docs uses an HTTPS connection as long as you change the initial http to https. In my case, I bookmarked the https connection, and that's what I always use.

If, however, you want to ensure that you're always accessing Docs via a secure Internet connection, you can use one of the following:

- **CustomizeGoogle extension for Firefox (https://addons.mozilla.org/en-US/firefox/addon/743)**—Select Secure (Switch to HTTPS) on the Docs tab of this Firefox extension. An excellent extension with many essential settings.
- **Google Secure Pro Greasemonkey script (http://userscripts.org/scripts/show/5951)**—Works in Firefox with Greasemonkey or with Opera and IE with some tweaking.

SEARCHING YOUR DOCS FROM YOUR MAC OS X DESKTOP

Mac OS X users already have Spotlight, the best desktop search tool on any platform. With the free and open source Precipitate, Mac users can now integrate Google Docs with Spotlight (or Google Desktop for Mac if that's installed).

Download Precipitate from http://code.google.com/p/precipitate/ and install it (it's actually a Preference Pane, not an actual app). After it's installed, go to System Preferences to view it. You'll see what's shown in Figure 15.4.

FIGURE 15.4 The Precipitate Preference pane.

Enter your Google Apps Username and Password, check the box next to Google Docs, and press Refresh Now. Give Precipitate some time to index your files; in fact, it may take up to an hour between the time that you add or change a file at Google Docs and when Precipitate indexes it.

Now when you perform a search using Spotlight, results from the contents of your Google Docs are also included. If you select a result from one of your Google Docs, the file opens in your default web browser, which is great.

There's only one downside—at this time, Precipitate doesn't automatically update itself, so you'll need to manually check every once in a while. But that's a small price to pay for such a cool add-on.

DEFAULTING TO GOOGLE DOCS

If you want to make Google Docs the default office program on your computer, you'll need to install the Google Toolbar for Firefox. I discussed what to do earlier in this chapter in the "Utilizing the Google Toolbar for Firefox" section. To my knowledge, this is the only way to set Google Docs as your computer's default for the various file types that Google Docs understands.

SOLVING COMMON PROBLEMS

As with all things in life, you're going to find little gotchas. Here are a few of those and their solutions.

My docs disappeared! Where did they go?

This is the same problem as the one discussed in Chapter 13's "My calendar entries disappeared! Where did they go?" Read this section and then read Google's solution specific to Docs at https://docs.google.com/support/bin/answer.py?answer=66656. Basically, if your email address is exactly the same at both your original Google account and your Google Apps account, you can import your docs from the non-Google Apps account into the Google Apps account. This is a good thing.

Finally, keep in mind going forward that you access Docs at different URLs, depending on if you're accessing it as part of Google Apps or not:

- Google Apps Docs: http://docs.google.com/a/YOURDOMAIN
- Google Docs: http://docs.google.com

How can I use all of Google Docs' features in Safari?

If you find that some features don't work in Safari on Mac OS X, there's a sneaky workaround that may enable you to get more use out of Safari. If you see a Develop menu in Safari, skip ahead a paragraph; otherwise, close Safari, open Terminal, and enter the following command, followed by Enter:

```
defaults write com.apple.Safari IncludeDebugMenu 1
```

Open Safari, and you should now see a Develop menu. Go to Develop, User Agent, and select Firefox 2.0.0.12 – Mac. Now when you go to Google Docs, Google thinks you're actually using Firefox instead of Safari, and it gives you all of Google Docs' features.

CONCLUSION

There's a lot you can do to integrate Google Docs into your full computing experience, but we still don't see the flexibility with Google Docs that we do with Gmail or Google Calendar, for instance. This may be due to the inherent nature of Google Docs, or it may be that developers simply haven't focused on Google Docs enough yet. Given more time, we'll see, but I'm betting on the developers.

Part V

Google Sites

Setting Up Google Sites

When you first go to your main Google Sites page at https://sites.google.com/a/yourdomain.com, you're not going to see any settings at all. You won't see any settings until you actually create a site. Then you can go into Settings and make some configuration choices.

To create a site, click the Create New Site button and enter the following information (I'll be using my heavymetalmassage.com account as an example, but you should enter your own info):

- **Site Name: Heavy Metal Massage Office Info**—You can enter whatever you want here; just make it meaningful to you.

- **Your Site Will Be Located At**—In this case, it's heavy-metal-massage-office-info. This is automatically filled in by Google, based on what you entered in Site Name. You can change it (I'd leave it alone), but you can't use spaces.

- **Site Categories**—For example, office. Completely optional, these are essentially labels (like in Gmail and Google Docs) that allow you to quickly find all sites sharing the same label. If you only have a few sites, don't bother.

- **Site Description**—Information about running and maintaining our office. Also completely optional, the purpose of this entry is to give users an idea of what each site on your list of Google Sites is about. If you only have a few sites, and their names are obvious, don't bother.

- **Collaborate With**—Everybody at heavymetalmassage.com, for instance. This determines who can access and edit the site. We discuss this important setting in more detail in the "Sharing" section later.

- **Site Theme**—Charcoal, for example. This determines what the site looks like. We discuss this in more detail in "Themes" later.

After making your settings, choose Create Site. A moment later, Google will finish creating your site. After you access it, go to Site Settings in the upper right of your browser window.

Sharing

The Sharing screen allows you to set who can manage, edit, and view your site. If it looks similar to the Google Docs sharing screen, it should—it's very close to the same concept.

Under Invite People, you have three options (I'm reversing the order, from least permissions to most):

- **As Viewers**—People can view the site, and that's it; in other words, they can look but can't touch.
- **As Collaborators**—People can create, edit, move, and delete pages; add attachments or comments to pages; add or remove pages to sidebar navigation; and subscribe to site and page changes.
- **As Owners**—People can do everything collaborators can: They can change the site's name, theme, and layout; invite other viewers, collaborators, or owners; and delete the site.

Needless to say, think carefully about who you add and what roles you assign. Make sure you know and trust your fellow owners!

> **NOTE**
>
> The people you specify as Viewers, Collaborators, or Owners will need Google or Google Apps accounts.

Make a choice, enter the email addresses for the people you want to include in that role (separated by commas), and click Invite These People to send invitations to them.

If you check the box next to Anyone at heavymetalmassage.com May ___ This Site, you must choose Edit or View. You can very quickly enable everyone at your domain to edit your new Google Site, or you can simply allow everyone to view and then add specific individuals in your domain as Collaborators and Owners. If your site is intended for only a subset of people in your organization, don't check this box.

If you check the box next to Anyone in the World May View This Site (Make it Public), you are allowing everyone who can access your site via the Web to view but not edit the site, with no login required. If you have a site that is appropriately public, this is a great way to unveil it to the globe.

On the right side of this page is a list of your site's Viewers, Collaborators, and Owners. To revoke someone's privileges on your site, click the Remove link next to his email address.

APPEARANCE

There are three tabs under appearance: Themes, Site Elements, and Colors and Fonts. Together, they govern how your site looks to your viewers and editors. Let's walk through each one.

Themes

Google provides several themes on this page. You can check out each one before you apply it by clicking the Preview link under each theme. After you've settled on one you like, select the option button under the theme and click Save Changes. Keep in mind that if you made changes on the Colors and Fonts tab, discussed shortly, those changes will be nuked from orbit when you apply a new theme.

When Google rolled out Sites, there were vague promises that users would eventually be able to create their own themes. Unfortunately, as of this writing, that hasn't come to pass. This is really too bad because out of all of the themes Google offers, none are what you could call businesslike. They tend to be cartoony, or cute, but there's nary a plain or serious one in the bunch. Sure, you can always create your own on the Colors and Fonts page, but that's a lot of work for many users. Instead, Google should either hire people to create more themes or allow third parties to submit themes that can be approved by Google and made available to all Google Sites owners.

Site Elements

This page allows you to select what components go on your site and where they should go.

Start by pressing the Change Site Layout button, which opens the screen shown in Figure 16.1.

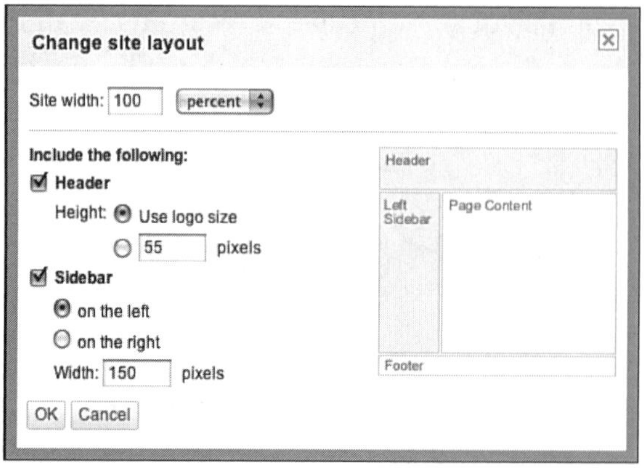

FIGURE 16.1 Change sizes and positions of key site elements.

You can make the following changes:

- **Site Width**—Width can be in either a percentage of your viewer's browser window or hard-coded as a set number of pixels. For most sites, a width of 100 percent (which is the default) should be just fine.

- **Header**—I'd leave this box checked so that a header is included. It's a good spot for your organization's logo, the name of the site, and other key information.

- **(Header) Height**—You can set the height of your header to either your logo or a set number of pixels you specify. For most sites, the logo's height should work well.

- **Sidebar**—Leave this box checked because a sidebar is very useful for navigation and other extremely useful widgets.

- **Left/Right**—You can place the sidebar on the left or right side of your site. Because western cultures are used to reading from left to right and because most other sites your users will have seen place navigation on the left, you probably should leave the sidebar on the left.

- **(Sidebar) Width**—You can set the width of your sidebar in pixels. The default of 150 should be fine, but feel free to adjust it slightly if need be.

Click OK when you're finished in the Change Site Layout screen.

Back on the main Site Elements screen, you can change two things: your Header and your Sidebar.

With the Header, you can change your logo, which, if you previously set the Header height to your logo, will change the height of your header.

TIP

Google recommends that your logo be 145 pixels wide and 52 pixels tall.

With the Sidebar, you can add, edit, and delete widgets that appear to your users. By default, two are included, Navigation and Recent Site Activity, but you can remove them (I don't recommend that, however). Some of the other widgets you can add include the following:

- **Text**—Any text or HTML you'd like.
- **My Recent Activity**—Things the signed-in user has done.
- **Countdown**—Count the days down to a date you enter.

There aren't very many right now, but Google will undoubtedly add more in the coming months.

Colors and Fonts

If you're feeling artistically inclined, or if you just don't like the way a theme you've chosen looks, then head to this tab, where you can change the fonts and colors for many aspects of your site, including the following:

- Site background color
- Site background image
- Site link color
- Header title color
- Header background color
- Header background image
- Page font

And quite a bit more, actually. If you're interested, check it out. Just remember that changing a theme blows away anything you've done on this tab, so be prepared for that.

OTHER STUFF

This page is kind of a catch-all for other features of your site not covered by Sharing or Appearance. Several of the fields here allow you to alter choices you made when you were creating the site, including

- **Site Name**—You can change the name here, but it won't change the URL that was generated when you created your site.
- **Site Category**
- **Site Description**

Let's look at a few of the more interesting, useful fields on this page in a bit more detail.

Statistics

If you'd like to view statistics, graphs, and reports on visitors to your site, check the box next to Enable Google Analytics for This Site and then paste your Google Analytics Account ID into the field. You need to first have a free Google Analytics account before you can do this, which you can sign up for at www.google.com/analytics/.

> **TIP**
>
> You can find the information you need to set all this up at http://sites.google.com/support/bin/topic.py?topic=14656 at Google's Help Center.

Web Address Mapping

By default, your Google Site is going to be at a URL that looks something like https://sites.google.com:443/a/heavymetalmassage.com/heavy-metal-massage-office-info/ (the actual URL depends on your domain and your site name). If you'd rather be able to use a different domain name—in my case, http://office.heavymetalmassage.com—you can do that here.

Click Map This Site, and you'll be taken to your domain's control panel, to a page titled Add a New Web Address Mapping. Enter the following information:

- **Site Location**—For instance, heavy-metal-massage-office-info. This should be prefilled in for you, based on the site from which you just came. If you

made a different page your site's home page, the URL will include that page
in it.

■ **Web Address**—For example, office. Enter the subdomain you want here.
Keep in mind that you're going to need to change your DNS, so make sure it's
something that DNS supports. In other words, no spaces or weird characters.

Now go to your DNS provider and add a CNAME with your subdomain pointing
to ghs.google.com. In my case, I go to Go Daddy and sign in to the Total DNS Control Panel. Then I click Add New CNAME Record and enter the following information:

■ Enter an Alias Name: `office`

■ Points to Host Name: `ghs.google.com`

■ TTL: `1 Hour`

I click OK, wait a bit, and then I can go to http://office.heavymetalmassage.com
to get to my site.

There's one caveat here, though: For this to work, your site needs to be public.
As in exposed to the world, as I covered earlier in this chapter in "Sharing." However, this isn't going to be attractive to everyone.

You can choose not to share your site with everyone on the Web, and things will
still mostly work in a way that will probably be fine with most people. You still need
to map the web address at Google and set up a CNAME at your DNS provider.
When you go to http://office.heavymetalmassage.com, however, you end up at
http://sites.google.com/a/heavymetalmassage.com/heavy-metal-massage-office-
info/Home, and you have to log in to your Google account to see anything.

In other words, you can use the "easy" URL to help people get to the site, but
after they're there, the easy URL disappears, and the longer, more complicated
sites.google.com URL takes over. For most organizations, though, this won't be a big
deal. The easy URL is for those in the know to remember how to get to the site; at
the same time, the site is protected from just any ol' Netizen seeing it.

TIP

Don't forget that your users can get to the page listing all your Google Sites
by going to the URL you set up for Google Sites in Chapter 2's "Creating
Custom URLs." For instance, in my case, I tell users to log in to
http://wiki.heavymetalmassage.com to see the list of all sites used by folks
involved with Heavy Metal Massage.

Google Webmaster Tools Verification

Google Webmaster is a fantastic collection of resources for people who run any kind of website. If you create a Google Site and make it public, you can use a few Google Webmaster Tools with it. First, though, you must verify your site with Google Webmaster.

To do so, sign into Google Webmaster Tools at https://www.google.com/webmasters/tools/siteoverview with your Google Account. Next to your Google Site, click Verify. For Choose Verification Method, select Add a Meta Tag. Google will provide you with a unique meta tag, which you need to copy.

Back on the settings page, in the field next to Enter Your Google Webmaster Tools Meta Tag Verification Below, paste in the entire meta tag you just copied at Google Webmaster Tools (it will look something like `<meta name="verify-v1" content="IHk8prUJGoHm3wa9moW5saIp6akmqDdLc2qMXsfaocb6g=" />`).

After you've verified your Google Site with Webmaster Tools, Google Sites will then generate an XML-based sitemap file for you automatically. You can find that file at an address like this:

```
http://sites.google.com/a/yourdomain/yoursite/system/feeds/sitemap
```

In my site's case, it would be found at

```
http://sites.google.com/a/heavymetalmassage.com/heavy-metal-massage-
office-info/system/feeds/sitemap
```

You can then submit the sitemap to Google at Webmaster Tools. Why do that? Google explains the very good reasons for doing so at www.google.com/support/webmasters/bin/answer.py?answer=40318.

Delete This Site

If you no longer want your site, click Delete This Site, click the Delete button when you're asked to confirm your decision, and say bye-bye to your site. Like the dodo, it's gone.

SOLVING COMMON PROBLEMS

As with all things in life, you're going to find little gotchas. Here's one of those and its solution.

Why Can't I Share My Site with People Outside My Domain?

If you try to share your site and find that you cannot, your Google Apps administrator has limited your sharing rights. To change this, your admin will need to go to your domain's Google Apps control panel, Service Settings, Sites and change Users Cannot Share Sites Outside This Domain to one of the other settings.

CONCLUSION

Sites is one of the newest additions to Google Apps, so it's not surprising that there aren't a lot of settings for it yet. Give it time, and as Google expands its features, it will offer more ways to customize how sites look, act, and perform.

FURTHER READING

- Why businesses use Google Sites to share knowledge: www.google.com/a/help/intl/en/users/sites.html
- Google Apps for Admins Help Topics: www.google.com/support/a/bin/topic.py?topic=14229
- Google Apps for Users Help Topics: http://sites.google.com/support/
- Interactive Video Guides
    - Google Sites Welcome: http://services.google.com/apps/resources/overviews/welcome/topicWelcome/page10.html
    - Google Sites: http://services.google.com/apps/resources/overviews/welcome/topicSites/index.html
- Google Sites Video Tour: www.youtube.com/watch?v=X_KnC2EIS5w
- Discussion Groups
    - Google Sites Help Group: http://groups.google.com/group/sites-help
    - APIs: http://groups.google.com/group/google-apps-apis
- Google Sites Blog: http://googlesitesblog.blogspot.com
- Google Sites FAQ: www.google.com/support/sites/bin/topic.py?topic=15024
- Google Apps Frequently Reported Issues: www.google.com/support/a/bin/request.py?contact_type=known_issues
- Support Options: www.google.com/support/sites/bin/request.py?contact_type=contact_policy&hl=en

Things to Know About Using Google Sites

Google Sites is really a wiki, even though Google does everything it can to hide that fact from its users. You may not have ever edited a wiki, but most web users have at least read a wiki: Wikipedia, the largest wiki in the world (http://en. wikipedia.org for those of you who haven't been there). A wiki is essentially a website that can easily be edited by nontechnical people, and that's pretty much what Google Sites is. In the spirit of reducing tech-speak for a general audience, however, Google hides the fact that Sites is a wiki—but it is.

At this time, Google Sites has a long way to go. Google acquired Sites by purchasing a company named JotSpot in late 2006; almost a year later, Google unveiled Sites, a rebranded, reworked JotSpot. In many ways, however, Google Sites is far less capable and robust than JotSpot was when Google bought it, and Google has quite a way to go to restore that functionality.

However, this is often the case with Google's products: A service is released that is pretty bare bones, and over time, Google improves it with more features and a slicker interface. That's why even though I'm critical of Google Sites now, I believe that eventually it will be a useful tool in your online Google Apps toolkit—one day. For now, use it; you'll be able to do basic things with it, but don't expect a lot out of it.

THINKING ABOUT HOW GOOGLE SITES FITS INTO GOOGLE APPS

If you've investigated Google Apps before, you may wonder why this book isn't looking in any detail at Google Web Pages. The reason is that Google is phasing out

Web Pages in favor of Sites, as the notice at the top of http://pages.google.com/-/about.html makes clear. For this reason, it behooves you to start moving anything you have at Web Pages over to Sites.

If you're going to continue using Web Pages for the time being (if you like living on the edge, in other words), some good advice for maximizing the service can be found at http://jvanbaelen.googlepages.com/gpcinfo.html.

You may find the two services very similar, and on the surface, they both seem the same because they both allow you to make websites. The names of the services, however, indicate their different focuses: Web Pages is very much focused on individual pages, whereas Sites is about creating and maintaining entire websites. Yes, you can use Web Pages to make a site, but that's not its strength. Sites, though, is about using a website to collaborate and work on a unified series of content.

In fact, I was very underwhelmed when Web Pages came out, and Google never really expanded the service much beyond the rudimentary. Ironically, though, Web Pages offers features that Sites currently lacks, such as the capability to use JavaScript and IFrames in your HTML. At this time, Sites is pretty bare bones in many ways as well, although it seems that Google is adding new features at a much more robust rate than it ever did with Web Pages.

If you find that Google Sites doesn't meet your needs, you can experiment with many wiki-based alternatives out there. Here are a few interesting options:

- **Deki Wiki** (http://opengarden.org; free or starting at $2,495/year—yes, over $2,000!)—An excellent, innovative wiki that installs in a virtual image.

- **MediaWiki** (http://www.mediawiki.org; free)—If you're feeling techie, download and install this free, open source wiki that is the same software that powers Wikipedia. It's powerful but not as user-friendly as many other options.

- **PBwiki** (http://pbwiki.com; free or starting at $100/year)—Very easy to use, very powerful, and very popular.

- **Socialtext** (http://socialtext.com; free or starting at $10/user/month)—Business-focused wiki with both products and services available.

- **Wetpaint** (http://www.wetpaint.com; free)—Targeted at nontechnical users; recently added social networking features.

- **Wikia** (http://www.wikia.com; free)—Free for those providing content under an open license. From the people who gave us Wikipedia.

- **Wikispaces** (http://www.wikispaces.com; free or starting at $60/month)—A wiki built on open source tools and intended for a general audience.

- **Zoho Wiki** (http://wiki.zoho.com; free or commercial when out of beta)—Part of the amazing series of online Zoho apps. Google's closest competitor in terms of features and functionality, surpassing it in some areas.

CREATING SEVERAL KINDS OF PAGES

Unlike many wikis, Google Sites allows you to create five kinds of pages. When you click Create New Page, you'll see Figure 17.1.

FIGURE 17.1   You can choose from five kinds of page types.

The five you can choose from are the following:

- **Web Page**—A standard blank page in which you put any content. A nice general canvas, but not good for extremely specific tasks.

- **Dashboard**—Two columns, two rows, four placeholders for various Google gadgets (the same Google gadgets available in other Google Apps). Weirdly, when you click the Gadgets button, you see the same thing as the Insert menu, but anything you insert other than a gadget doesn't seem to quite work correctly. Seems pretty half-baked to me.

- **Announcements**—Chronological information like news, updates, and yes, announcements. However, adding new posts is awkward and not very intuitive, and you have very little control over how the posts are formatted or how they behave. Also half-baked.

- **File Cabinet**—A collection of documents and folders with version history so you can revert to earlier revisions as needed. Files can be added from your hard drive or the Web. However, if you click documents that Google Docs supports, the files are downloaded to your computer instead of opening in Google Docs! Integration, Google, integration!

- **List**—Easily the best of the four specialized page types, this allows you to create a table of sortable data. You can use the built-in templates—Action Items, Issue List, or Unit Status—or create your own. Very nicely done. Now we need more page types with this level of usefulness, usability, and polish to really make Google Sites a contender.

Google Sites allows you to arrange each page in a hierarchy that you control, which is useful, and each page also has a version history that allows you to revert to earlier revisions as needed. These are nice features, but they're standard with most services that are like Google Sites. I expect better from Google, and I'm sure we'll get it, given time.

INSERTING OTHER CONTENT INTO YOUR PAGES

You can attach files to any page at a Google Site—just click Attachments at the bottom of a page, click Choose File, and upload a file from your computer. You can keep uploading changed versions of that file, and Google Sites will hold on to the revisions and allow you to view any of them. Keep in mind, however, that all your sites together share a 10GB pool of storage space, although Education and Premier accounts also receive an additional 500MB for each user at the domain.

 TIP

After you've attached a file, if you're in edit mode, you can drag the link to the attachment into the editing field to quickly create a link to that file.

One of the strongest features of Google Sites is that it's easy to insert lots of rich content over and above text and pictures. If you're editing a page and select the Insert menu, you'll see the choices shown in Figure 17.2.

I'm not going to go through all of your options because many are self-explanatory, but I do want to call out a few that are particularly interesting.

- **Table of Contents**—If you're going about using Headers (inserted using the Format menu), Google Sites will automatically build a TOC for you based on your headers.
- **Google Calendar**—Paste in the URL for the HTML version of your Google Calendar (discussed in Chapter 11's "My Calendars" section), set some formatting and display options, and you have an embedded, updated calendar in your Site.
- **Picasa Web Slideshow**—Picasa is Google's online photo sharing website, and you can embed slideshows from that service in your Site.

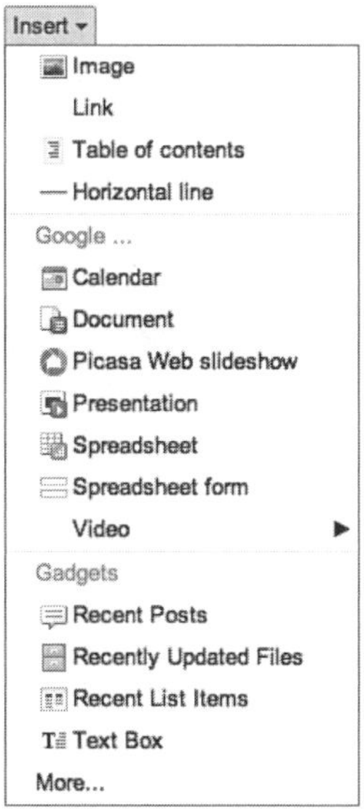

FIGURE 17.2   You can insert a variety of content into your Sites page.

- **Document, Presentation, Spreadsheet**—Embed files created by Google Docs in your Site. Nicely, it shows a list of your documents so you can pick the one you want, although you can also paste in a URL if you'd like. However, there are silly limitations: You can't edit the inserted document, and none of its content is searchable. A near miss.

- **Spreadsheet Form**—Enter the URL for a spreadsheet form you created, and it appears on your page. Users can fill in the form and submit their entries.

- **Google and YouTube Video**—Embedding videos can be really handy, especially for training sites.

- **Google Gadgets**—The same Google Gadgets available with other Google Apps services. Some are extremely useful, many are of marginal use at best, and some have absolutely no place in a business setting.

Google has five sample Sites available for you to view; you should take a look at them because they contain some good examples of embedded content, as well as design and overall usability. You can find them at www.google.com/sites/overview.html.

UTILIZING THE MORE ACTIONS MENU

When you're not editing a page, you see three buttons at the top of it: Create New Page, Edit Page, and More Actions. Don't ignore the More Actions button, which, when clicked, displays a menu like that in Figure 17.3.

FIGURE 17.3 The More Actions menu contains some key functions.

I'm not going to go through all your options because many are self-explanatory, but I do want to call out a few that are particularly interesting.

- **Subscribe to Page Changes**—Choose this, and you'll receive an email every time the page changes. In the email, new content is highlighted in yellow, and deletions are formatted with a red strikethrough. After you subscribe, this command changes to Unsubscribe to Page Changes.

- **Page Settings**—This offers several functions, so I'll discuss it after this list.

- **Move**—Have you placed a page in your site hierarchy and want to reposition it? Use this.

- **Delete**—Remove a page, but not really. You can still bring it back from the dead by going to the page and clicking the Recover Page button.

- **Subscribe to Site Changes**—Like Subscribe to Page Changes, but for the entire site. Warning: this may result in a flood of email!

- **Site Sharing**—A shortcut to the Sharing page at Site Settings, discussed in Chapter 16's "Sharing" section.

Page Settings is a bit more complicated than the other choices, so I want to discuss it separately. When you choose it, a small window opens that presents you with five check boxes and a text box:

- **Show This in Navigation in the Sidebar**—A good idea, unless your Sidebar is growing cluttered with too many items.

- **Show Page Title**—Another good idea, to make things more usable for readers.

- **Show Links to Sub-Pages**—Very useful, as it displays links at the bottom of a page to pages under the current one.

- **Allow Comments**—If you don't want visitors to be able to leave comments on a specific page, uncheck this. Most useful on public Sites.

- **Page URL**—Enter new text into this text box if you want to change the URL for the page. Some characters, such as spaces, aren't allowed. In a thoughtful touch, any pages linking to the changed URL have that URL updated, so you never have to worry about broken internal links.

Some key functions are present only under More Actions, so get used to heading there when you need to change your page or your Site.

WORRYING ABOUT SECURITY

Google Sites has some nice features built in to it that protect your content. While you're editing a page, Google automatically saves your edits continuously, minimizing the risk that you'll lose important content if you're suddenly disconnected. That's great.

Also on the good side of the security ledger, Google Sites invisibly rewrites any links outside of a Site (those pointing to any domain besides sites.google.com, in other words) so that `rel=nofollow` is appended in the HTML. Why do that?

Spammers will often try to place links pointing to web pages promoting whatever garbage the spammers want to push to drive up those web pages' Google rankings. In other words, if a spammer can manage to put links on blogs, websites, bulletin boards, and everywhere else, all pointing to http://www.buymycrap.com/ear-enlargement.htm, all those links will hopefully drive up that site in Google rankings when someone searches for "ear enlargement."

As Google's indexing software crawls the Net, if it sees `rel=nofollow`, it ignores that link and doesn't count it toward a site's ranking in Google's search index.

Because Sites is a free service, there's nothing in place to stop spammers from creating hundreds of fake Sites, all pointing to http://www.buymycrap.com/ear-enlargement.htm. By using `rel=nofollow` automatically, with no way to disable it, Google minimizes the attractiveness of Google Sites to spammers. And I'm for anything that hurts spammers.

> **NOTE**
>
> You should know, however, that Google keeps track of the links people click on to go outside of your Site. It's all part of Google's search engine database, so it knows what links people find most useful and can therefore raise those in its search results.

CONCLUSION

Google Sites is still the newest addition to Google Apps, and it has a long way to go. But it does have some very useful features, and those point the way forward to a service that has as much functionality, usability, and innovation as Gmail or Google Calendar. For now, feel free to use Google Sites, but don't expect a lot from it; at the same time, keep an eye on it for further growth and improvement.

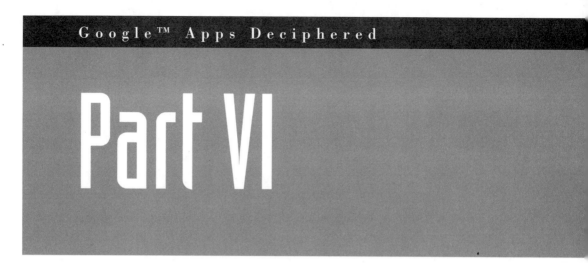

Part VI

The Other Services

Things to Know About Using Google Talk

It's great that Google Apps includes a chat program (actually, *four* chat programs, as you're about to see) because IM is a fantastic business productivity tool. On top of being able to know whether someone is available to talk, the ability to make phone calls, transfer files, and much more make IM one of the essentials for a modern computer. It's just too bad, as you'll see, that Google kind of muddies the waters by including several versions of its software, each with different features—and worst of all, none of them really match up to the best IM or VoIP programs out there. It's not that Google's IM programs are bad; it's just that they're not as innovative, interesting, or useful as other alternatives.

> **NOTE**
>
> So what do I recommend? At WebSanity, we use Skype (www.skype.com) for voice, IM, and file transfer—it's free, runs on every major operating system, and all traffic is automatically encrypted. Otherwise, Pidgin (www.pidgin.im) is a great choice—it's free, open source, runs on every major operating system, and has tons of plug-ins and add-ons.

THE FOUR VERSIONS OF GOOGLE TALK AND THEIR FEATURES

When it comes to chat, someone at Google apparently thinks that the company's motto needs to be, "You can't have too many options!" How else to explain that there are no fewer than four chat programs available for users? Three of them share the name Google Talk in some form or other, and the fourth is simply Gmail Chat—even though it (mostly) uses the same IM network as the others. Oh boy.

Okay, if you're ready, here are the four chat programs:

- **Google Talk**—The standalone program you run on your Windows PC, like AIM, Yahoo Messenger, and Windows Live (formerly MSN) Messenger.
- **Google Talk Labs Edition**—A standalone program you run on your Windows PC that is based on Adobe's Flash.
- **Google Talk Gadget**—A Flash-based gadget you run on your Start Page.
- **Gmail Chat**—Chat built into Gmail (and the new versions of iGoogle, which may or may not ever see the light of day in the Start Page; for more info, see Chapter 19's "Trying Out the New Start Page").

Some features are shared among all four programs, but each has unique capabilities as well. Table 18.1 is my attempt to delineate exactly which program does what, to help you make a better decision about which one to use.

> **NOTE**
>
> To keep things simple, I refer to each program by its full name whenever I discuss it. In other words, I never refer to the Google Talk Gadget as just Google Talk, but always with its full name.

TABLE 18.1   Google's four chat programs and their features.

Feature	Google Talk	Google Talk Labs Edition	Google Talk Gadget	Gmail Chat
Requirements				
Operating System Support	Windows	Windows (requires Adobe Flash)	Windows, Mac OS X, Linux (requires Adobe Flash Player in web browser)	Windows, Mac OS X, Linux (web-based)
Basic Communications				
Chat (IM)	✓	✓	✓	✓
PC-to-PC Voice Calls	✓		✓ (only if Google Talk is running in the background)	

Feature	Google Talk	Google Talk Labs Edition	Google Talk Gadget	Gmail Chat
PC-to-Landline or Cell Voice Calls				
Video Calls				
Chat Details				
AIM Integration				✓
Go Invisible		✓	✓	✓
Sending Offline Messages	✓			✓
Receiving Offline Messages	✓		✓	✓
Chat History	✓	✓	✓	✓
Off The Record Chats	✓	✓	✓	✓
Multi-User (Group) Chats		✓	✓	✓
Emoticons		✓	✓	✓
Call Details				
Send Voicemail	✓			
Receive Voicemail	✓			✓
Email				
Gmail Notification	✓	✓		✓
Send Email	✓ (requires Gmail)	✓ (requires Gmail)		✓
Other Features				
File Transfer	✓			
Video and Image Embedding		✓	✓	
Music Status Messages	✓			
Themes	✓			

Next, I walk through a few of the features mentioned in the table so they're a little clearer, and I can better discuss how the four programs implement them.

Voice Calls

- Supported by: Google Talk, Google Talk Gadget (if Google Talk is running on the PC)

Let's dispense with the obvious first: No version of Google Talk is able to perform PC to landline, PC to cell, or video calls. At this time, it's just not possible, no matter which chat program you try. Further, you can't have group calls either, so it's just you and another person. Maybe sometime in the future this will change.

Two versions of the software can make PC-to-PC calls. However, in both cases, it's Google Talk that's doing all the work! You can use the Google Talk Gadget to initiate calls, but it's Google Talk that actually handles them, and it has to be running.

NOTE

Google has a nice list of recommended headsets at www.google.com/talk/accessories.html. If you can, get a USB headset—it will work easier and sound a lot better.

AIM Integration

- Supported by: Gmail Chat

If you use AOL Instant Messenger or connect over the AOL Messenger Network (Apple iChat will do that, for instance), you'll like Gmail Chat. In addition to talking to others using Gmail or people federated to Google's chat network, you can also chat with those who use AIM's network.

If you use Yahoo Messenger, you may see integration with that network coming soon as well, according to a press release dated June 12, 2008 (www.google.com/intl/en/press/pressrel/20080612_yahoo.html). But don't hold your breath—it took years between the time Google and AOL announced Google Talk and AIM integration and when it finally appeared.

Go Invisible

- Supported by: Google Talk Labs Edition, Google Talk Gadget, Gmail Chat

If you don't want people to know you're online, but you want to still stay online so you can send and receive IMs, you want invisible mode. In fact, invisible mode even works with AIM if you use Gmail Chat.

Unfortunately, if you use Google Talk, there is no invisible mode. Google's advice? Block users and then unblock them when you want them to be able to see you again! Needless to say, that's nuts and not a very good solution to the problem.

A better solution for Google Talk users is gAlwaysIdle, which is free and available at www.galwaysidle.com. That program at least allows you to set your status as idle, even if you're not, which will hopefully discourage people from contacting you. Again, not the best solution, but better than unnecessary blocking!

Sending and Receiving Offline Messages

- Sending supported by: Google Talk, Gmail Chat
- Receiving supported by: Google Talk, Google Talk Gadget, Gmail Chat

If a buddy isn't online, but you want to send him a message, you can with two of Google's chat programs. In terms of receiving a message sent to you while you are offline, however, three of Google's chat programs will show you such a thing. When it comes to offline messages, Google Talk Labs Edition is nowhere to be found.

Interestingly, if someone has sent you an IM while you were offline and you sign in to Gmail before you sign in to Google Talk or the Google Talk Gadget, the message will show up as an unread email in your Inbox. Otherwise, it will appear in the chat program.

Finally, if either you or your chat partner went off the record (discussed later in "Off the Record"), you won't be able to send messages offline until you change that status.

Chat History

- Supported by: Google Talk, Google Talk Labs Edition, Google Talk Gadget, Gmail Chat

Google automatically saves your chats in Gmail's Chats label/folder. This allows you to save and search them at any time, just as you would with email. If you don't like that, read the very next section.

Off the Record

- Supported by: Google Talk, Google Talk Labs Edition, Google Talk Gadget, Gmail Chat

As I pointed out in the previous section, Google normally saves your chats at Gmail (in the Chats label/folder, naturally) so you can search them at any time. If you take a chat off the record instead, it will not be saved in your chat history or in the chat history of the person to whom you're IMing—as long as that person is using a Google product to chat. If she's not, she could easily save your conversation, so make sure you know what software your chat partner is using.

Keep another thing in mind: If you take a chat with someone off the record, your chats will continue to be off the record until you reverse it. So don't forget!

Multiuser (Group) Chats

- Supported by: Google Talk Labs Edition, Google Talk Gadget, Gmail Chat

Chatting one to one online is nice, but sometimes you need to have a group conversation. Unfortunately, if you use Google Talk, you're out of luck. If you're using any of the other three Google chat programs, however, you can include as many people as you want in your chat room. If you started the conversation and then leave, no worries—the group chat will merrily continue along until the last person has turned out the lights and shut the door.

Emoticons

- Supported by: Google Talk Labs Edition, Google Talk Gadget, Gmail Chat

We all love emoticons—they're fun, and they help communicate in a textual environment. For some bizarre reason, Google Talk doesn't support them! Be that as it may, Table 18.2 shows some of the emoticons that you can use with the other Google chat products.

TABLE 18.2 Oooooh! Emoticons!

:-o	B-)	:-|	;-)
:D	:'(	=)	:-)
:(	=D	:-D	:-/
x-(	;)	;^)	:P

I'm not going to show you what they look like once you've typed them, however—I'll leave that fun to you.

Sending and Receiving Voicemail

- Sending supported by: Google Talk
- Receiving supported by: Google Talk, Gmail

If you try to call someone when both parties are using Google Talk, and the other person doesn't answer, you can leave a voicemail for them. Or if you want, you can go directly to voicemail by choosing Send Voicemail in Google Talk.

Either way, you can leave a message up to ten minutes long (which should be plenty for anyone, even my Uncle Gussie, who does like to stretch a story out a bit longer than is sometimes necessary). The message ends up as an email in your recipient's Gmail account, with an MP3 attachment containing what you said. In my case, the email will be titled "Voicemail From Gussie Granneman (598 Seconds)." If I were reading Gmail in my web browser, I could just click the Play button that appears and then listen to the message, or I could download the MP3 and listen to it anywhere I can play MP3s.

If you're using Google Talk, you'll see a small telephone icon at the bottom of the program's window. The number next to that icon will tell you the number of voicemail messages waiting for you. Click that icon, and Gmail opens so you can access your message.

And no, at this time Google Talk doesn't support creating a custom welcome message for your voicemail. You'll just have to find another outlet for your humor.

File Transfer

■ Supported by: Google Talk

If you're using Google Talk, and your chat partner is using Google Talk—and only Google Talk, because none of the other programs will work!—you can send files back and forth to each other. There's no limit on file size or file type (unlike Gmail, which prevents lots of different kinds of files from being emailed, as I covered in Chapter 8's "Checking for Viruses"), so you can send pretty much anything back and forth. Of course, you can continue chatting while your files are winging their way back and forth across the Internet.

> **TIP**
>
> If you can't find your files, look in My Documents and you'll see a folder named Google Talk. They're in there.

Video and Image Embedding

- Supported by: Google Talk Labs Edition, Google Talk Gadget

When you're chatting, often someone will send you a link to a cool video or a funny slideshow. Normally, you'd have to click the link, which would open the video or slides in your browser, forcing you to leave the chat temporarily. However, if you're using Google Talk Labs Edition or the Google Talk Gadget, you can view the movie or pix in the chat window.

When your chat partner sends you the URL, you'll see a tiny thumbnail preview, with the name of the video and its length. If you click Play, the video begins, as you can see in Figure 18.1:

FIGURE 18.1 The chat program shows you the video so you don't have to leave the chat.

Otherwise, you can click Go to Page and see the video in its natural habitat on YouTube (or any of the other video services). This is a clever little feature that I wish more chat programs offered.

Music Status Messages

- Supported by: Google Talk

This is kind of a weird but fun one. It's supported only by Google Talk, so it's Windows only. Basically, if you enable this feature (Settings, Audio), Google Talk shows the artist and song you're listening to in your IM status. When you stop playing music, your status reverts to the defaults.

The following music players are supported:

- iTunes
- Windows Media Player
- Winamp
- Yahoo Music Engine

On top of that, if you opt in to Music Trends, every song you listen to will be added to a gigantic tally of the music Google Talk users are listening to around the world. Google then displays charts showing the top 20 favorite songs by country and genre. If you then click the name of the artist, song, or album, you're taken to Google Music Search, an under-the-radar collection of search pages all about music.

In addition to adding your listening choices to the global pool, you can also view your private listening history, which is a nice way to suddenly realize you're listening to *way* too much Celine Dion.

Themes

- Supported by: Google Talk

Don't like the way Google Talk looks? Change its theme! Go to Settings, Appearance, Chat Theme and pick a different one that suits you. Keep in mind, though, that you're the only one who will see it—the people with whom you're chatting will have no idea.

ACCESSING GOOGLE TALK IN A DESKTOP PROGRAM

You don't have to use Google's clients to chat on the Google Talk network. In this section we look at other alternative clients on a variety of operating systems.

But keep in mind two warnings:

- If you receive a message advising you that The gmail.com Certificate Failed the Authenticity Test, you can ignore it. Go ahead and sign in—you're safe.

- I'll be using my heavymetalmassage.com account for examples throughout this section, but you should enter your own info.

Using an SSB (Site-Specific Browser)

Many people think that the Google Talk Gadget is superior to Google Talk in many ways, as long as you don't care about file transfers or voice calls. If you think that way, the problem is that you have to keep your browser open all the time to use the Google Talk Gadget. Even if you convert the tab with the Google Talk Gadget into another window, you can't use Alt+Tab (or on the Mac, Command+Tab) to switch back and forth between your chat and your web browser. One window has the Google Talk Gadget, and one has your web stuff that you're using, and because they're both the same program, it can be problematic.

> **NOTE**
>
> On Macs, you can switch between windows within the same Application by using Command+~ (that's the tilde, to the left of the 1).

Of course, you could load the Google Talk Gadget in one web browser—IE, for example—and then use Firefox for your main web browsing. But most people have a favorite web browser that they want to use all the time.

Into this breach steps a new idea: SSBs, or Site-Specific Browsers. SSBs are web browsers, but they're stripped down and simplified, and instead of loading just any old website in one, the idea is that each SSB is focused on a single site or web app. For instance, I have Google Reader in one SSB and the website of Twitter in another. To my Mac, those are separate programs named Google Reader and Twitter. I can switch to them as I can with any other program, and if one goes haywire, it doesn't affect the other—or any of my web browsers. Because they are simpler and lack my 50 billion extensions, they take up a smaller memory footprint on my computer. Finally, each one feels like a separate program instead of just a website or a tab in a web browser.

NOTE

To find out more about SSBs, read Wikipedia's article on the subject at http://en.wikipedia.org/wiki/Site_Specific_Browser.

Several SSB frameworks exist out there now, but these are the ones I would look at if I were thinking about using an SSB on my computer:

- **Prism**—http://wiki.mozilla.org/Prism. Based on Firefox. Very good with one of the largest SSB user bases.
- **Fluid**—http://fluidapp.com. Based on Safari and Mac OS X-only. Very nice with a responsive developer and helpful users.
- **Bubbles**—http://bubbleshq.com. One of the first SSBs, but Windows-only. Provides some nice extensions that make it work well with certain popular websites.
- **Google Chrome**—http://www.google.com/chrome. Google's new web browser (discussed in Appendix C) makes it easy to turn any website into an SSB.

They all work basically the same: You start the SSB program, fill in a few essential details (URL, most importantly), click OK, and a moment later you have an instance of the specific website running in its own window, seemingly in its own program. With Fluid, for example, I'd fill in the following fields:

- **URL**—http://talkgadget.google.com/talkgadget/client.
- **Name**—Google Talk Gadget. Obviously, use a name that's meaningful to you and describes your "program."
- **Location**—Applications. This is where you want the "program" you're creating to reside. On Macs, /Applications; on Windows, Program Files; on Linux, /usr/bin.
- **Icon**—Use Website Favicon. Where do you want the "program" icon to come from? Normally, the website's favicon (the little icon you see in the Address bar to the left of the URL) would work but not with the Google Talk Gadget. Instead, I recommend going to the Fluid Icons group at Flickr (www.flickr.com/groups/fluid_icons/) and searching for Google to find some beautiful icons. Best of all, those will work with other SSBs besides Fluid.

I then click Create, and soon enough I have the Google Talk Gadget running in its own window, as shown in Figure 18.2.

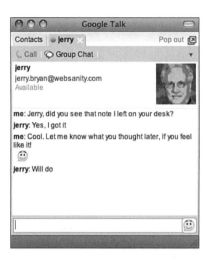

FIGURE 18.2 It's web-based
Google chat, but it looks and
acts like a desktop chat program.

The process would be much the same with Prism or Bubbles. Google Chrome has been out for about two days as I'm writing this, so I'll let you figure out how to create an SSB with it, but I will point you to a very short video at www.youtube.com/watch?v=R0Mgf66GOr4 that explains the process.

TIP

You can create an SSB for any of the Google Apps we've looked at in this book. If you use Gmail all the time, turn it into an SSB. The same goes for Google Calendar, Google Docs, Google Sites, or any of the others. After you do, be sure to check out the extensions and add-ons each SSB provides, as many of them are Google-specific: Prism (https://wiki.mozilla.org/Prism#Bundles), Fluid (http://code.google.com/p/fluiduserscripts/), and Bubbles (http://bubbleshq.com/scripts). Try it—you might find that you really like it.

Adium

In Adium, go to Preferences, Accounts and click the + icon in the bottom left. Select Jabber and then enter the following information on the Account tab:

- Jabber ID: `scott@heavymetalmassage.com`
- Password: `123456`. If you don't enter your password here, you'll be prompted to do so every time Adium starts. It's your call.

On the Options tab, enter the following information:

- Connect Server: `talk.google.com`
- Resource: `Adium`
- Port: `5222`
- Check the box next to Require SSL/TLS.

Click OK to close Accounts and then close Preferences.

You're ready to IM folks via the Google Talk network in Adium.

Firefox

If you're a big Firefox user and a big Google Talk user, it would be nice if you could put those two things together. Actually, you can, and you have a choice as to how you do it:

- Install the gTalk Sidebar extension for Firefox from https://addons.mozilla. org/en-US/firefox/addon/4708. Whenever you want to IM, open the sidebar and go to it.
- Go to http://hostedtalkgadget.google.com/a/heavymetalmassage.com/ talkgadget/m in Firefox and bookmark it (it's the iPhone version of the Google Talk Gadget). Then go to Bookmarks, Organize Bookmarks, and find the bookmark you just created. Select it and then click More to expand it so you can see more bookmark data. Check the box next to Load This Bookmark in the Sidebar and close the window. Now when you go to the site in your bookmarks, it will load in Firefox's sidebar.

Try both and see which one you like the best.

iChat

In iChat, go to Preferences, Accounts and click the + in the bottom left. On the Account Setup screen, enter the following information:

- Account Type: `Jabber Account`
- Account Name: `scott@heavymetalmassage.com`
- Password: `123456`

Click the triangle next to Server Options to expand it and then enter the following information:

- Server: `talk.google.com`
- Port: `5223`
- Check the box next to Use SSL.
- Do not check the box next to Use Kerberos v5 for Authentication.

You're ready to IM folks via the Google Talk network in iChat.

> **NOTE**
> You'll need to be running Tiger or Leopard on your Mac to connect iChat to Google Talk.

Kopete

In Kopete, go to Settings, Configure, Accounts and click New. On the first screen of Add Account Wizard, choose Jabber and click Next.

On the Basic Setup tab, enter the following information:

- Jabber ID: `scott@heavymetalmassage.com`
- Check the box next to Remember Password.
- Password: `123456`
- Don't check the box next to Exclude From Connect All.
- Don't check the box next to Exclude From Global Identity.

On the Connection tab, enter the following information:

- Check the box next to Use Protocol Encryption (SSL).
- Check the box next to Allow Plain-Text Password Authentication.
- Check the box next to Override Default Server Information.
- Server: `talk.google.com`
- Port: `5223`

Click Next. On the Congratulations screen, click Finish.

You're ready to IM folks via the Google Talk network in Kopete.

Meebo

Meebo is a very useful website that allows you to login to your IM accounts on the following networks: Google Talk, AIM, Yahoo, and MSN. After you are logged in, you can chat with all your buddies on those networks.

Before you log in to Google Talk using your Google Apps domain, however, you'll have to make sure you've set up your domain's SRV records.

After you do so, go to http://www.meebo.com and log in to the Google Talk box.

Pidgin

In Pidgin, go to Accounts, Add/Edit (or Manage if you haven't added any accounts yet). On the Basic tab, enter the following information:

- Protocol: `XMPP`
- Username: `scott.` Your Pidgin username is the part of your Google Apps email address before the @.
- Domain: `heavymetalmassage.com`. Your Pidgin domain is the part of your Google Apps email address after the @.
- Resource: (Leave it alone.)
- Password: `123456`
- Check the box next to Remember Password. Don't do this if you're paranoid.
- Local Alias: (Leave blank.)
- Check the box next to New Mail Notifications. Check this if you want to know if new Gmail has arrived.
- Check the box next to Use This Buddy Icon for this Account. After doing so, change the icon; if you don't care, don't check the box.

On the Advanced tab, enter the following information:

- Check the box next to Require SSL/TLS.
- Do not check Force Old (Port 5223) SSL.
- Do not check Allow Plaintext Auth Over Unencrypted Streams.
- Connect Port: **5222**
- Connect Server: **talk.google.com**
- File Transfer Proxies: **proxy.jabber.org:7777**
- Proxy Type: Use GNOME Proxy Settings.

Click Save to close the Add Account window and then close the Accounts window.

You're ready to IM folks via the Google Talk network in Pidgin.

Psi

In Psi, go to Account Setup and click Add. On the Add Account screen, enter the following information:

- Name: **Heavy Metal Massage**
- Do not check Register New Account.

Click Add, and the Account Properties window opens. On the Account tab, enter the following information:

- Jabber ID: **scott@heavymetalmassage.com**
- Password: **123456**
- Check the box next to Automatically Connect on Startup. If you don't check this box, you'll have to manually connect every time you start Psi.
- Check the box next to Automatically Connect After Sleep. It's for your convenience, but you don't have to check it.
- Check the box next to Automatically Reconnect if Disconnected. This is really helpful and reduces a major annoyance.
- Check the box next to Log Message History. If you don't want to save your chats, uncheck this box.

On the Connection tab, enter the following information:

- Connection Proxy: **None.** If you do need to set up a proxy, click Edit and do so.

- Check the box next to Compress Traffic (If Possible).
- Check the box next to Send Keep-Alive Packets.
- Check the box next to Manually Specify Server Host/Port.
- Host: `talk.google.com`
- Port: `5223`
- Encrypt Connection: `Legacy SSL`
- Do not check the box next to Ignore SSL Warnings.
- Do not check the box next to Probe Legacy SSL Port.
- Allow Plaintext Authentication: Over Encrypted Connection.

Click Save to close Account Properties and then click Close to remove the Jabber Accounts window.

You're ready to IM folks via the Google Talk network in Psi.

Trillian Pro

In Trillian Pro (not Trillian, but Trillian Pro—the free version won't work), go to Trillian, Connections, Manage My Connections, Plugins, and make sure that Jabber is checked.

Now go to Identities and Connections. Click Add a New Connection, Jabber and enter the following information:

- Jabber ID: `scott@heavymetalmassage.com`
- Password: `123456`
- Check the box next to Automatically Connect to This Account on Startup.

Click Connect and enter the following information:

- Server Host: `talk.google.com`
- Server Port: `5222`
- Do not check Use Legacy SSL for Connection.
- Check the box next to Attempt to Reconnect When Connection Is Lost.

Click Save Settings and then click Close to get out of Trillian Preferences.

You're ready to IM folks via the Google Talk network in Trillian Pro.

ACCESSING GOOGLE TALK ON A MOBILE DEVICE

In addition to logging in to Google Talk on your desktop, you can also check Google Talk from a mobile device.

BlackBerry

If you use a BlackBerry, open your device's web browser and go to www. blackberry.com/googletalk. Install the program, launch it, log in, and you can chat via Google Talk on your BlackBerry.

iPhone

Right now there isn't a native version of Google Talk for the iPhone, so you have to open up Safari and point it to http://talkgadget.google.com/a/heavymetalmassage. com/talkgadget/m. Unfortunately because it's a browser-based app, you'll be signed out the second you go to a different screen in Safari or leave that program for another. Basically, then, you can use it to change your status or have a short chat with someone, but that's about it.

Nonetheless, if you like Google Talk in Safari and intend to use it, add it as a bookmark or add it to your home screen.

SECURING YOUR CHATS

Keeping what you're chatting about private is just as important as protecting your email conversations. However, understand that there are two kinds of encryption:

- **Client-to-Server Encryption**—In this case, communication between your IM program (the client) and the IM server are encrypted. However, the IM server needs to pass your message along over the Internet, and at that point encryption goes out the window. This kind of encryption is good only if you're worried about people on your network (at a coffee shop, for instance, or at work) listening in with packet sniffers and finding out what you're talking about and with whom.

- **End-to-End Encryption**—This kind of encryption makes sure that everything—from your IM client to your IM server across the Internet to the other person's IM server to their IM client—is encrypted. If anyone at any point along that route grabs some packets and looks at them, they see only gibberish, which means they got bupkus.

You can do both with Google's chat clients, as you'll see.

Client-to-Server Encryption

You can use several solutions when it comes to encrypting the traffic between the various Google chat programs and Google's chat servers (remember, after that, it will be viewable by anyone who grabs the packets, unless you use end-to-end encryption, discussed in the next section):

- According to a Google employee posting at http://bit.ly/Mw5Rw, all connections between Google Talk and Google's servers are automatically encrypted.

- If you're using Gmail Chat and you're connecting to Gmail via an SSL connection so that you see https instead of just http in your browser's address bar, you're safe—your chats and your email traffic are encrypted from your browser to Google's servers.

- If you're using the Google Talk Gadget or the Google Talk Labs Edition, there's nothing you can do—it's just not secure.

This is all nice, but really what you want is end-to-end encryption. That way, no matter where your packets are grabbed, it's all just gibberish to the bad guys.

End-to-End Encryption

You can use several solutions when it comes to encrypting all the traffic between your Google chat program and the chat programs used by the people with whom you chat:

- Use Psi as your Google chat client (discussed earlier in "Psi"). After you download the client at http://psi-im.org you'll need to install and set up GnuPG from http://gnupg.org, and finally configure Psi to work with GnuPG. You can find the instructions you need for that at http://psi-im.org/wiki/Encryption. Keep in mind, the other person will need to use Psi or another chat client that supports GnuPG for the encryption to work successfully.

- If you use Windows, check out the free SimpLite at www.secway.fr/us/products/all.php. After it is installed and configured (see www.secway.fr/us/manuals/simplite_jabber/manual.php), you can chat with anyone else using Google Talk, AIM, MSN, or Yahoo! over a completely encrypted connection.

- Use Pidgin and install the Pidgin Encryption plug-in from http://pidgin-encrypt.sourceforge.net. Instructions for configuring it are found in Lifehacker's tutorial "Geek to Live: Encrypt your instant messages with Gaim," at http://lifehacker.com/software/instant-messaging/geek-to-live—encrypt-your-instant-messages-with-gaim-228878.php (keep in mind that Pidgin at that time was called Gaim; other than that, everything is the same). The other person needs to be using Pidgin as well, but that shouldn't be a problem because it runs on Windows, Mac OS X, and Linux.

- Use the OTR (Off-the-Record) Messaging plug-in from www.cypherpunks.ca/ otr/ (Off-the-Record has nothing to do with Google's similarly named feature, discussed earlier in "Off the Record.") You need the plug-in only if you use Pidgin on Windows or Linux; if you use Adium on Mac OS X, Off-the-Record is already built in (see http://chris.milbert.com/AIM_Encryption/#MacOTR), but you'll need to enable it in Preferences.

The only problem with end-to-end encryption is that it's not enough for you to encrypt your end. You absolutely must make sure that the person with whom you're IMing is doing the same thing you are. Otherwise, you're fooling yourself.

SOLVING COMMON PROBLEMS

As with all things in life, you're going to find little gotchas. Here are a few of those and their solutions.

I Have More Than One Google Apps Account and Would Like to Chat Using Two or More at the Same Time.

You have two ways to accomplish this:

- Install both Google Talk and Google Talk Labs Edition on your PC. You can run them at the same time (even though Google warns against this), each using a different account. Voila!

- Find the shortcut to Google Talk in your Start menu, right-click it, and choose Properties (if you use a shortcut on the desktop, do the same thing there as well). In the Target field, it should already say something like "C:\Program Files\Google\Google Talk\googletalk.exe" /startmenu. To the end of that, add **/nomutex** so that that it looks like **"C:\Program Files\Google\Google Talk\googletalk.exe" /startmenu /nomutex** and then click OK. You can now launch Google Talk multiple times, each with a different Google Apps account. Just remember—if you have shortcuts to Google Talk in the Start menu and on the Desktop, you have to change both if you want to be able to click either to start the program.

Why Can't I Connect to Google Talk?

First, make sure your firewall allows you to connect on the ports that Google Talk needs:

- TCP connections to talk.google.com on port 443, 5222, or 5223, depending upon how your client was configured.
- For voice calls or file transfers, you also need to enable UDP connections to anywhere on any port or (thank goodness there's an or!) open up port 443 for both incoming and outgoing connections.

On its website (www.google.com/support/talk/bin/answer.py?hl=en&answer= 24962), Google provides instructions for many widely used desktop firewalls, including the following:

- McAfee Personal Firewall. In particular, if Google Talk is crashing, you should read http://knowledge.mcafee.com/solution/mcafee/tutorials/vse/vse_third-party_application_crash_when_scriptscan_is_running.htm.
- Norton Personal Firewall
- Trend Micro PC-cillin
- Windows Firewall
- ZoneAlarm

How Do I Block Google Talk on My Network?

Easy—block DNS lookups to the following domains by having them return 127.0.0.1:

- talkgadget.google.com
- talk.google.com
- talkx.l.google.com

Google Talk: How Can I Record Voice Conversations?

If you want to record your voice chats, you have several options:

- **Audacity (http://audacity.sourceforge.net; free)**—A free and open source audio recorder and editor that's so good I wrote a book on it (http://safari.oreilly.com/9780132366571).

- **SoliCall SoftPhone Add-on (http://www.solicall.com; free)**—A small program that not only records but also helps reduce background noise.
- **Total Recorder (http://www.highcriteria.com; $18 and up)**—Easy to use, powerful, and inexpensive. An old favorite.

The important thing, however, is to try these out *before* you need to record that all-important call! Do not wait until the last minute and try to use one of these programs without testing first because setting things up to record a voice chat can be a bit tricky. Test before you trust.

Google Talk Gadget: One of My Chat Tabs Disappeared!

The Google Talk Gadget (and Google Talk Labs Edition) allows you to organize your chats into tabs. However, you can have only four tabs open at the same time. If you IM someone else, or if someone else IMs you, the new tab will knock another tab out of the stack. Which one gets bumped? The one that has been unused the longest.

Google Talk Gadget: Why Can't I Copy and Paste?

This is a common complaint. Because the Google Talk Gadget is built on Adobe's Flash, copying and pasting with the keyboard often gets funky and doesn't work right. Frankly, the easiest thing to do is to right-click with your mouse and copy and paste that way.

Otherwise, Table 18.3 goes over how to copy and paste with your keyboard.

TABLE 18.3 Copying and Pasting via the Keyboard in the Google Talk Gadget Is a Pain

OPERATING SYSTEM	COPY	PASTE
Windows	Press Ctrl, Press c, Release c, Release Ctrl	Press Ctrl, Press v, Release v, Release Ctrl
Linux	Press Ctrl, Press c, Release c, Release Ctrl	Press Ctrl, Press v, Release v, Release Ctrl
Mac OS X	Press Cmd, Press c, Release c, Release Cmd	Press Cmd, Press v, Release v, Release Cmd

Yup—I know what you're thinking, and I agree.

Conclusion

As you can see, thanks to Google's wise decision to base Google Talk on an open standard like Jabber, you can do quite a bit in terms of accessing and using the Google Talk network, even in terms of accessing other IM networks. That's great, and Google is to be commended for that. I do hope Google works harder on its IM clients, however—it's okay now, but there's still a lot to do to catch up to the innovations other IM clients bring to the table. Knowing Google, though, there's a good chance we'll see interesting updates to the various Google chat clients someday.

Further Reading

There's always more to learn, so here are some resources that you might find handy if you want to learn more about Google Talk and its various incarnations:

- Overview: www.google.com/a/help/intl/en/users/talk.html
- Google Apps for Users Help Topics
  - Google Talk Client and Google Talk Gadget: www.google.com/support/talk/
  - Gmail Chat: http://mail.google.com/support/bin/topic.py?topic=12870
  - Headsets and Accessories: www.google.com/talk/accessories.html
- Palin Ningthoujam's "10 Tools to Get the Most Out of GTalk": http://mashable.com/2008/08/21/gtalk-tools/
- Interactive Video Guides: http://services.google.com/apps/resources/overviews/welcome/topicTalk/index.html
- Google Talk Gadget video at YouTube: www.youtube.com/watch?v=oPTP3rXKHvc
- For developers:
  - Google Talk for Developers Help Pages: http://code.google.com/apis/talk/talk_developers_home.html
  - Google Apps APIs discussion group: http://groups.google.com/group/google-apps-apis
- Discussion groups:
  - Google Talk Discussion: http://groups.google.com/group/Google-Talk-Discussion
  - Google Talk Help Discuss: http://groups.google.com/group/Google-Talk-Help-Discuss

- Google Talk Discussion and Troubleshooting: http://groups. google.com/group/google_im
- Google Talk Labs Edition: http://groups.google.com/group/google-talk-labs-edition-discussion-group
- Google Talkabout (official blog): http://googletalk.blogspot.com
- Google Talk Labs Edition FAQ: www.google.com/talk/labsedition/faq.html
- PDFs for training support staff: http://services.google.com/apps/training/user_support/Chat/ChatUserSupportModule2Issues.pdf
- What's New on Google Talk?: www.google.com/talk/about_whatsnew.html
- Known Issues:
  - Google Talk: www.google.com/support/talk/bin/static.py?page=known_issues.cs
  - Google Talk Labs Edition: www.google.com/talk/labsedition/knownissues.html
- Support Options: www.google.com/support/talk/bin/request.py?contact_type=contact_policy

Things to Know About Using Start Page

The Google Apps Start Page is a customizable web page that lets you add independent boxes of content and programs, called Google Gadgets, to create something dynamic and useful.

Well, that's the marketing, anyway. But as you're going to see, Start Page has a long way to go before it matures into something truly practical.

DECORATING WITH THEMES

If you use Start Page with a regular ol' Google account (in that case, by the way, it's not called Start Page—it's called iGoogle), instead of a Google Apps account, you get your choice of a wide array of themes you can pick for your page, including the following:

- **Google's Themes Directory (http://www.google.com/ig/directory? type=themes)**—There are a lot here, but many of them are absolutely hideous.

- **Artist Themes for iGoogle (http://www.google.com/help/ig/art/ gallery.html)**—Themes from more than 70 artists, many of them very cool. (I really like the Dale Chihuly theme at http://www.google.com/help/ig/ art/artists/chihuly.html.)

- **inThemes (http://inthemes.com)**—An unofficial collection of themes, each one reviewed so it isn't offensive to the eye.

Google also provides information for those interested in creating their own themes, with the Developer's Guide at http://code.google.com/apis/themes/docs/dev_guide.html an essential resource. The official Google Themes API discussion group at http://groups.google.com/group/google-themes-api would also be handy.

Alack and alas, Google Apps users get absolutely *none* of this. We're stuck with whatever our Google Apps admins can conjure in the settings for Start Page back in the Google Apps Control Panel I looked at in Chapter 6 (see the "Start Page" section). And if you don't remember, those settings are pretty bare bones: colors, layout, header, and footer. *Borrring.*

Sure, I understand that some companies might not want their employees changing the look and feel of their Start Pages willy-nilly because they're worried about branding, but c'mon. How about giving admins a setting they can enable that allows users to pick themes if the organization allows? Colors are one thing, but it wouldn't hurt to have a gorgeous glass sculpture by Chihuly in front of me on my Start Page to inspire me. Or at least make me happy with so much beauty.

So it turns out that this section in the book doesn't cover a feature that's available, but one that really should be available to all Google Apps users.

GOING GA-GA FOR GADGETS

Really, the Google Start Page is all about one thing: Google Gadgets. Without the gadgets, the Start Page is just another search page; with the gadgets, it can be a powerful productivity tool.

To add new gadgets, click Add Stuff in the upper right of your Start Page. You'll be taken to Add Stuff to Your Homepage at http://partnerpage.google.com/YOUR-DOMAIN/default/directory?dpos=top&gasp_action=directory (yes, iGoogle users would go to a completely different page—such is what happens when you do not unify services). There you can search or sort by categories, including Popular, News, Tools, Communication, Fun and Games, Finance, Sports, Lifestyle, and Technology. To see more information about the gadget, click the screenshot or illustration. When you find a gadget that you'd like to use, click Add It Now. When you've finished looking at gadgets, click Back to Homepage in the upper-left corner.

To remove a gadget from your Start Page, click the X in the gadget's upper-right corner. Like Tiramisu on my plate, it's gone in a flash.

With those basics out of the way, let's look at what gadgets can do for you. But really, the best way to learn is to start playing with any that look interesting.

> **NOTE**
>
> If you have technical folks available, you can create your own gadgets. Start at the iGoogle Developer Home, at http://code.google.com/apis/igoogle/.

COLLABORATING WITH GADGETS

Here's another feature that iGoogle users have, but which Google Apps users don't. In iGoogle, you can share any gadget with any of your contacts. That means you and other people can collaborate on the content and data in a gadget, just like you can with Google Docs. Well, not *can*, but *could*—if the Google Start Page gave Google Apps users that feature.

For instance, if I add the Sticky Note gadget to my iGoogle page, I can then click the triangle that's in the upper right corner of every gadget (the one next to the delete X and the minimize) and select Share This Gadget. When I do, I see a pop-up window like the one in Figure 19.1.

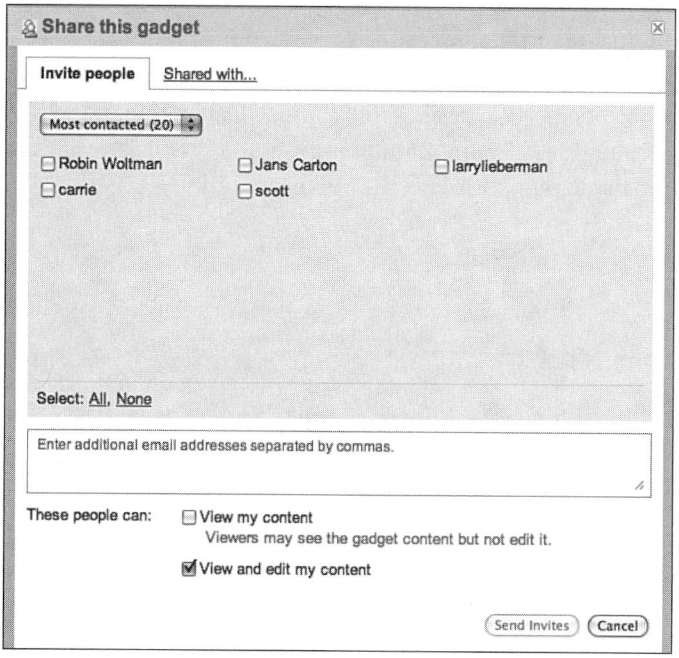

FIGURE 19.1   I can share a gadget's data? Cool! Oh, yeah, not in Google Apps. Fail.

I can choose contacts with whom to share, enter other email addresses, control what they can do (view only, or view and edit), see who I've shared with, and remove people from sharing. That's really cool, except that I can't do any of it in Google Apps.

Google, I'm paying you for the Premier Edition of Google Apps! Let's get moving on the features!

SOLVING PROBLEMS WITH GADGETS

There are lots of Google Gadgets, and they do everything from serious to silly, from useful to useless. In this section I want to look at a few gadgets that solve interesting problems that users might face.

Keeping Track of Customers

Customer Resource Management (CRM) software is becoming more vital to companies every day. After all, companies are nothing without their customers, and without good ways to track contacts with current and potential customers, failure is guaranteed.

A company named Etelos has jumped into the Start Page market with Etelos CRM for Google Apps, a CRM program that integrates into your Google Start Page. There are four editions—Personal, Professional, Enterprise, and Developer—with different features and price points, ranging from free to $44.95 per month. You can see one of the many screens Etelos CRM gives you in Figure 19.2.

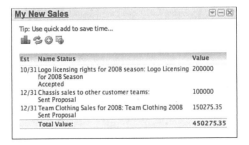

FIGURE 19.2 Track your sales prospects and much more with Etelos CRM.

Rather than go through its feature list, I'll instead point you to the Etelos web pages on the program, available at www.etelos.com/store/store.espx?store=2467& storetab=on. There's a full list of features and lots of screenshots and video examples. You can also request a free trial to give the program a whirl before you buy.

Managing Projects

Etelos, introduced in the previous section, also makes Etelos Projects for Google Apps, a project management gadget for your Start Page. There are five editions—Single Project, Personal Projects, Professional Projects, Enterprise Projects, and Unlimited Projects—again with different features and price points, ranging from free to $99.95 per month, and all with unlimited users. One thing they all have is collaboration with other users, which is vital to project management. You can see an Etelos Projects screen in Figure 19.3.

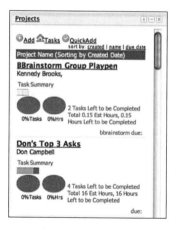

FIGURE 19.3   Manage your projects, tasks, and time with Etelos Projects.

Because it's tied into Google Apps, Etelos Projects works with Google Spreadsheets and Google Calendar, which is fantastic. Rather than go through all the other features, I'll instead point you to the Etelos web pages on the program, available at www.etelos.com/store/store.espx?store=2463&storetab=on. There's a full list of features and lots of screenshots and video examples. You can also request a free trial to give the program a whirl before you buy.

Accessing Backed Up Files

I've been using Dropbox for several months, both with my company and in writing this book, and I'm really loving it. What exactly is it? The video at www.getdrop-box.com/screencast will definitely help to make things clearer, but in short, it's backup and autosyncing of data done *really* well. I put files and folders in my Dropbox folder, and a few moments later they appear in the Dropbox cloud. If I install Dropbox on another computer, the folders and files I'm syncing with Dropbox appear on that computer soon after, seamlessly. As I change the files, they are instantly updated at Dropbox and on any other of my computers running Dropbox, too.

Best of all, I can sync with someone else's computer. So I could create a folder in my Dropbox folder on my Mac and then share it with my buddy Robert. When he accepts, it shows up on his Linux box, with all the folders and files I shared in it. If either of us changes any files or folders, those changes are autosynced with each other and at Dropbox. Slick!

Michael Freeman has created a really cool Dropbox gadget for your Start Page that shows you all the files and folders you're currently syncing. At this point, however, if you go to Add Stuff, the gadget doesn't appear (that may very well have been remedied by the time you're reading this book, though). To add it, go to Add Stuff and then click Add by URL at the top of the page. Enter the following URL and click Add: http://dl.getdropbox.com/u/232/gadgets/dropbox_redir_mf-v2.xml.

When you do, you may see a warning asking you if you want to proceed. Click OK, go back to your Start Page, and you should see the new Dropbox gadget.

There's one problem, however: The content within the gadget is wider than the space Google gives the gadget to fit within (this wouldn't be a problem with canvas view, which I discuss later in "Trying Out the New Start Page"). To fix this, you'll need to install a Greasemonkey script, also by Michael, available at http://userscripts.org/scripts/source/29469.user.js.

NOTE

If you don't remember what Greasemonkey is, check out "A Note on Adding Scripts to Your Web Browser" at the beginning of Chapter 9 for a refresher. Greasemonkey scripts are written for Firefox, but most of them will work in Safari and Internet Explorer with some tweaking.

After you install the Greasemonkey script, the Dropbox gadget will fit into your Start Page just like all the other gadgets, as you can see in Figure 19.4.

FIGURE 19.4   The Dropbox gadget allows you to access the files and folders you're syncing with Dropbox.

To find out more about Michael's Dropbox gadget, read his blog post at http://spanishgringo.blogspot.com/2008/07/my-dropbox-gadget.html. Good job, Michael!

Keeping Track of Tasks

I last discussed RememberTheMilk, the excellent online task management service, in Chapter 13 in reference to integrating the service into Google Calendar ("Adding To-Do's to Google Calendar"). However, the people behind RememberTheMilk also have a gadget that you can add to your Start Page that will help you keep track of all the things you have to do.

To get it, click Add Stuff and then search for RememberTheMilk, and you'll find the gadget. After you add it, you'll see a box that looks something like Figure 19.5 on your Start Page:

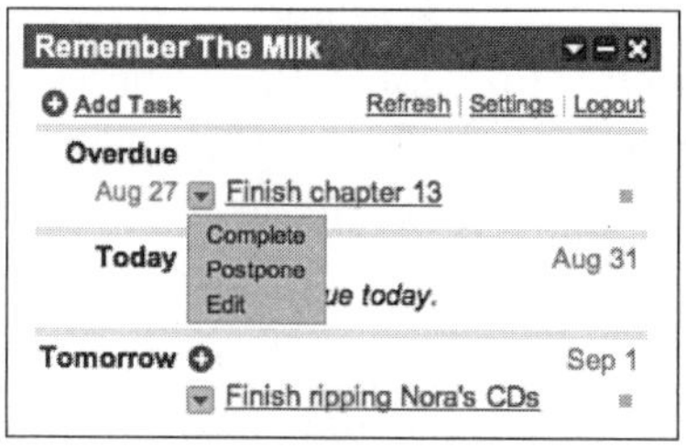

FIGURE 19.5   Manage your tasks with the RememberTheMilk Google Gadget.

You can do all the following with this gadget:

- Review tasks that are coming up as well as those that have fallen behind
- Add new tasks
- Edit existing tasks
- Mark tasks as complete
- View tasks without a due date
- View tasks that fall in a specific list

To find out more, head over to RememberTheMilk's page on their gadget at http://www.rememberthemilk.com/services/igoogle/.

LIMITING THE GADGETS USERS CAN ADD

My complaint in Chapter 6 still holds water: There are far too many gadgets that have absolutely no place in a business setting. I mean, really, Hooters Model of the Day? Okay, maybe if you worked at Hooters. But for anyone else, adding that Gadget to his Start Page could very well lead to a sexual harassment lawsuit. It's ridiculous that Google doesn't give admins a way to block that stuff.

If you're using the Educational Edition of Google Apps, you're in luck (the rest of you are still left holding the fuzzy end of the lollipop). According to a post at http://groups.google.com/group/apps-edu-circle/browse_thread/thread/198209ee00d0d086, Google has now implemented a new feature that allows Google Apps admins who work in educational settings to limit end users' choices for gadgets to only official Google Gadgets. Bingo! No more Maxim Hot Babe of the Day.

If you want other gadgets to be available, you have to add each one by URL. This could of course turn into a full-time job, so I don't know how schools are going to handle that burden. Unfortunately, I have the feeling that many admins are simply going to enable the official gadgets and be done with it, which is really too bad. But what else can they do?

There's one more caveat: If a kid has already added the Better Sex Tip of the Day or Grand Theft Auto IV Official Widget to his Start Page, it won't be automatically removed. Instead, you'll have to log in to the little goober's account and remove it yourself. Sigh.

If this ability to limit gadgets sounds like something you need, go to www.google.com/support/a/bin/answer.py?answer=45473, read the instructions, and then click the link to the request form at the bottom. Fill it in, and the inappropriate gadgets should be gone within five days or so. You can tell by logging in to your Google Apps Control Panel and visiting the Start Page editor.

Now, this is fine and dandy for Educational Edition customers, but what about the millions of businesses out there? How long until this absolutely vital feature is available for them as well? We need some communication on the subject, Google!

ACCESSING YOUR START PAGE FROM A MOBILE DEVICE

Here's another place where Google Apps users lag behind the Start Page. iGoogle users can access and view a version of iGoogle that's specially formatted for their mobile devices, but we Start Page users have to load up the Start Page in the web browser that comes with our iPhone or BlackBerry and hope for the best. The results aren't that great, as you can see in Figure 19.6, which shows my granneman.com Start Page on my iPhone.

FIGURE 19.6   My Start Page on my iPhone, in portrait mode.

Sure, I can double-tap to see content in larger than microscopic fonts, but at this point, the iPhone has been out over a year, and there's still no Start Page optimized for it.

If you look carefully, you'll see the blank areas in Figure 19.6. Those are where certain modules didn't load, like those requiring Flash, which the iPhone doesn't support.

I can also rotate the phone so the page appears in landscape mode, as in Figure 19.7, but that doesn't help much, either.

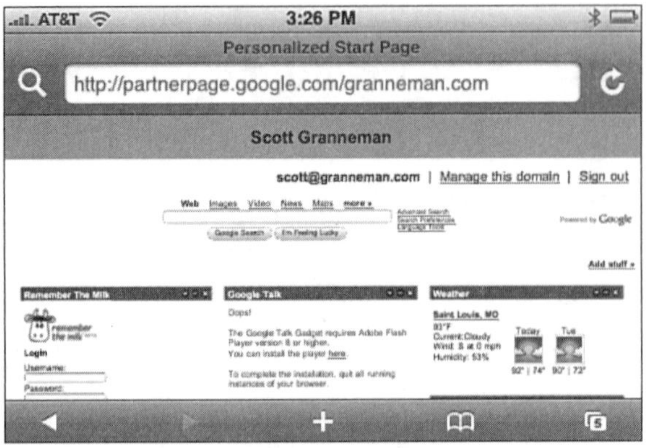

FIGURE 19.7 My Start Page on my iPhone, in landscape mode—not much better, eh?

All in all, the Start Page on mobile devices is, at this time, a disappointment. I'm certain it will be improved some day, but it's too bad that the Start Page is still so user-unfriendly.

TRYING OUT THE NEW START PAGE

This is my last section complaining about the Google Apps Start Page, I promise.

If you were using iGoogle instead of the Start Page, you could right now check out what promises to be a very nice improvement in layout and behavior. If you have a Google account (not a Google Apps account, but a plain ol' Google account) and have signed up for an iGoogle page, you can perform a simple step that will allow you to see the new interface.

Go to your normal iGoogle page, located at http://www.google.com/ig. In the Address bar at the top of your web browser, enter in the following and press Enter:

```
javascript:_dlsetp('v2=1');
```

You'll now be looking at the new iGoogle interface. If you decide that you don't like it and want to go back to the old style, enter this into your web browser's Address bar and press Enter:

```
javascript:_dlsetp('v2=0');
```

If that doesn't work, go to www.google.com/ig/sandbox. You may have to aver that you're a developer, but Google doesn't perform any checks. But if you blow something up, you're on your own! (I doubt that'll happen, though.)

What are some of the new features you get in the new iGoogle?

- Tabs run down the left side of the page instead of the top, and the tabs are expandable so you can see the individual gadgets on each tab.
- A Gmail-like Chat box is present by default on the left side of the screen, with group chat and AIM integration targeted for final release.

The most interesting new change, though, is that Gadgets can now use *canvas view*, in which they take up the entire width and height of the Start Page area. The new canvas view makes Gmail, Google Reader, Google Calendar, weather, and other supported gadgets much easier to access and use. Figure 19.8 shows the official Google Weather gadget at its normal size:

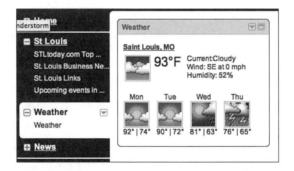

FIGURE 19.8 The Weather gadget at normal size.

Now let's maximize it using canvas view, as seen in Figure 19.9:

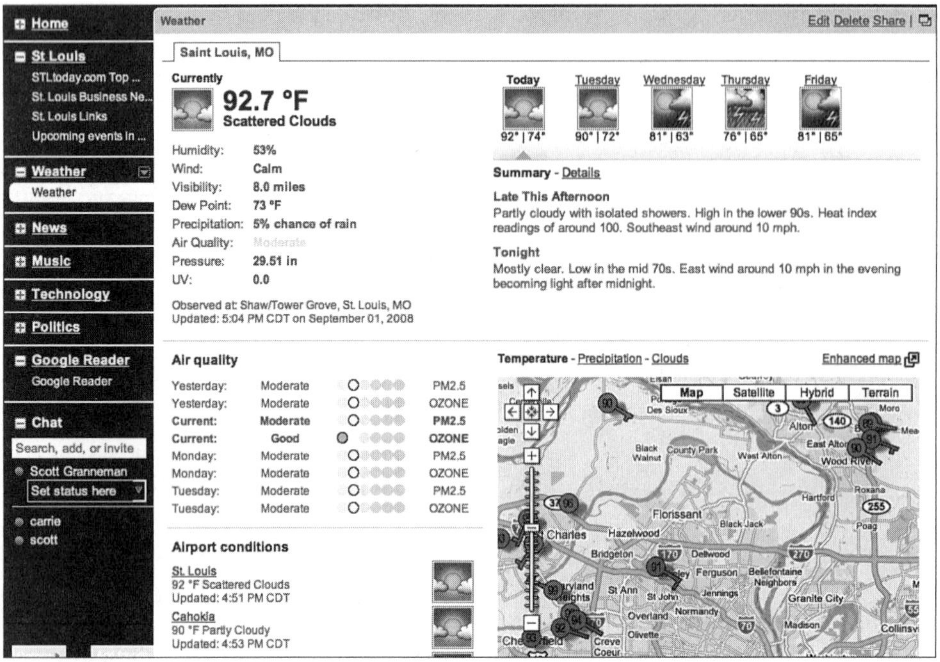

FIGURE 19.9 The Weather gadget is now a lot more useful!

Quite a difference! Now I get complete current conditions, including air quality, airport conditions, temperatures throughout the area, a five-day forecast, and more. Canvas view is a great addition to iGoogle.

To view a gadget in canvas view, do one of the following:

- Expand the tab by clicking the + in front of the tab's name and then click the name of the gadget listed below.
- There are two buttons at the top right of every gadget: Menu and Maximize (a third, a four-sided arrow, appears only when you hover over a gadget's title bar). Click Maximize to put the gadget into canvas view.

If you want to collapse the gadget back to its normal size, click the Restore icon that appears in the upper right of an expanded gadget.

Personally, I can't wait until all the new features in the new iGoogle make their way to the Google Apps Start Page. Until they do, Start Page is going to be but a pale shadow of iGoogle.

Solving Common Problems

As with all things in life, you're going to find little gotchas. Here are a few of those and their solutions.

Why Can't I Add Certain RSS Feeds to My Start Page?

If you try to add a password-protected RSS feed to your Start Page, it will fail. This is the case with Google Reader as well, and it's something that people have been hollering about for years. Google needs to fix this one. There's no reason not to do it.

How Do I Reorder My Tabs?

Tabs? Have you been looking at iGoogle instead of the Google Apps Start Page? iGoogle has tabs, true, but Start Page does not. No tabs for you!

With the current interface of iGoogle, reordering tabs is a complex, very clever hack that Google Blogoscoped describes at http://blogoscoped.com/archive/2008-04-10-n68.html. In the new iGoogle, which I described earlier in "Trying Out the New Start Page," you can easily reorder tabs within the iGoogle interface. That's good.

Except that Start Page doesn't even have tabs at this point. Sigh. Here's hoping.

Conclusion

I've complained a lot in this chapter about Start Page's deficiencies, with good cause. Start Page is a great idea, but its actual execution is slapdash at best. It pales in comparison to the current iGoogle and is humiliated—with its ice cream cone thrown in the ditch and a wedgie on top of that—by the new iGoogle that's coming 'round the bend. Right now, Start Page is usable, but that's being charitable, considering the level of polish and innovation that Gmail, Google Calendar, and Google Docs bring to the package. If Google wants Start Page to be taken seriously as a business tool used by people all over the world, it needs to get to work—stat.

FURTHER READING

There's always more to learn, so here are some resources that you might find handy if you want to learn more about the Google Apps Start Page:

- Overview, with factoids: http://www.google.com/a/help/intl/en/users/start_page.html
- Google Apps for Admins Help Topics: http://www.google.com/support/a/bin/topic.py?topic=14229
- Google Apps for Users Help Topics: http://www.google.com/support/bin/topic.py?topic=1592&ctx=ausers&hl=en
- Interactive Video Guides: http://services.google.com/apps/resources/overviews/welcome/topicStart/index.html
- For developers:
  - Screencasts on the Google Gadgets API: http://services.google.com/apps/resources/admin_breeze/APIGoogleGadgets/index.html
  - Google Apps APIs discussion group: http://groups.google.com/group/google-apps-apis
  - iGoogle Developer Forum discussion group: http://groups.google.com/group/Google-Gadgets-API
  - iGoogle Developer Blog: http://igoogledeveloper.blogspot.com
  - Official Google Gadgets API Blog: http://googlegadgetsapi.blogspot.com
- PDFs for training support staff: http://services.google.com/apps/training/user_support/Start_Page/StartPageUserSupportModule2Issues.pdf
- Google-Labs-iGoogle Discussion Group: http://groups.google.com/group/google-labs-igoogle
- Known Issues: http://groups.google.com/group/Google-Gadgets-API/web/known-issues

Things to Know About Using Message Security and Recovery

Message Security and Recovery (formerly Policy Management and Message Recovery, but still really Postini, the company and service that Google purchased in 2007) offers a variety of important email services to Google Apps Premier Edition customers. Basically, you route your email through Postini, and Google takes care of security, recovery, and adherence to policy. Admins have an enormous level of tight control over exactly what Postini does for your organization, making it an absolutely essential service to many.

Message Security and Recovery is actually a large and complex topic, deserving of a book in its own right. In this chapter, I go over some of the features of Postini and walk you through some basic usage of the service. The last section in the chapter, "Further Reading," contains a wealth of information you can use to learn as much as you want about Message Security and Recovery.

> **TIP**
>
> Keep in mind that while Premier Edition customers get Postini as part of their package, the service offers other features besides those available in Google Apps. To find out more, visit Postini's home page at www.postini.com.

FEATURES OF MESSAGE SECURITY AND DISCOVERY

At the end of this chapter, in "Further Reading," I point you to several places you can go to learn more about all the cool and useful things that Postini can do for you.

In this section, however, I look at the big features available to Google Apps Premier Edition users and admins.

Policy Management

Every organization has policies about the kinds of email messages allowed in and out of its workers' email boxes. Policy Management is just that: It allows admins to craft Postini so that it matches the organization's policies when it comes to email.

Emails are inspected carefully by Google, and then a range of activities are applied to them, including block, allow, redirect, quarantine, log, or even encrypt. Rules can cover a variety of policies, including the following:

- Messages with certain words can be flagged for review.
- Messages from a certain domain are blacklisted so users never see them.
- Messages with a certain kind of attachment are quarantined for review by admins.
- Social Security numbers or credit card numbers are blocked.

In addition to these rules, Postini generates detailed reports that admins can use to verify how well the policies are working. All-in-all, it's invaluable to modern businesses and organizations.

Message Recovery

It's happened to everyone—an important message is deleted, and there's no way to get it back. With Postini, this hopefully becomes a thing of the past. By default, Postini saves the last three months of all of your users' email messages. Admins can recover deleted messages from the previous 90 days at any time by searching for and restoring the messages. If admins desire, they can set up Personal Archives for users that allow them to perform the same function.

If 90 days isn't enough, you can always buy longer periods of time, ranging from one to ten years. Prices start at $1500 (which isn't that much, in the scheme of things) and go up from there.

Message Discovery

Searching for the occasional random message is nice, but what if (I really hope not, but still...) your organization is involved in a lawsuit? Or what if you have to conform to certain regulations and need to prove it to the lawyers? Or what if a certain kind of message is constantly needed? Then you'll want Message Discovery.

This feature is search on steroids. Your searches can be way more complicated, and you can save them for constant reuse. In addition, you can export your search results (perfect for the lawyers!) and even hold messages so that they're not automatically discarded according to policy. All-in-all, it's a powerful and amazingly useful feature for the litigious times in which we live.

Using Message Security and Discovery

As I said in the introduction to this chapter, Postini is actually a large and many-headed beast, so there's no way I can go over all of it and keep this book to a reasonable length. Instead, in this section, I hit some high points to give you a slight taste of how you would use the service.

Administration Console

When you log in to your Administration Console using the URL that was emailed to you when you signed up for the service, you're in the heart of Postini. From the Console, you can perform the following tasks:

- Search for Users, Organizations, or Domains
- Quickly go to a specific user's Settings or Quarantine that user (you'll need the user's email address)
- Add, Delete, or Move Users
- Perform tests on your SMTP, MX Records, and Firewall
- View a graph showing you email activity for your domain over the last 60 minutes
- View a table showing email activities for your domain over the last 60 seconds, including valid messages, spam, virus-laden messages, errors, average message size, total bytes, and the number of blocked messages

To get back to the Admin Console at any time, click Home in the upper right corner of the Postini page.

User Overview

Once you select a user on the Administration Console, you go to the User Overview screen, shown in Figure 20.1.

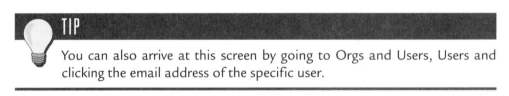

FIGURE 20.1   You can control all aspects of a user's account.

Let's walk through some of the various services and settings you can control for a user's account.

> **TIP**
>
> You can also arrive at this screen by going to Orgs and Users, Users and clicking the email address of the specific user.

Spam Filtering

You can turn spam filtering off or on, but I really wouldn't recommend turning it off for obvious reasons. Once it's on, you have four types of spam you can filter along a sliding scale, from Lenient to Aggressive:

- Sexually Explicit
- Get Rich Quick
- Special Offers
- Racially Insensitive

Virus Blocking

You can turn virus blocking on or off, but I can see absolutely no reason to disable this service. In addition, you can set how often users are notified that an email was blocked due to a virus problem. Unless you change it, this is set to your Organization Default, which you configure at Orgs and Users, Orgs, Notifications. However, you can alter the notification to

- Once Per Day
- Immediately
- Disable Notifications

Sender Lists

This section gives you more granular control over senders and whether or not email messages can get through your filters. You can specifically change the following by adding specific email addresses or domains:

- **Approved Senders**—Always allow messages from these addresses, regardless if they look like spam or not. Email addresses on this list take precedence over domains on the Blocked Senders list; in other words, if you add foobar.com to the Blocked Senders list and bob@foobar.com to the Approved Senders list, mail from bob@foobar.com will still get through to your users, but mail from alice@foobar.com will still be blocked.
- **Blocked Senders**—Welcome to the blacklist!
- **Approved Recipients**—Always allow messages sent to these addresses from your organization.

User Access

This screen allows the admin to determine what users themselves can change when it comes to settings. Many of the permissions allow an individual user to read and/or modify the settings. The defaults are intelligent, but each organization is going to want to review these settings and alter them to fit existing policies.

Reports

Postini provides a large number of reports on a wide variety of email-related topics, sorted into Inbound and Outbound. While all of them deserve your attention, here are a few of the more interesting:

- **Traffic by Domain (Inbound and Outbound)**—Which domains are sending the most traffic? To whom?

- **Traffic by Recipient (Inbound)**—Which users are getting the most mail?

- **Spam by Domain (Inbound)**—Which domains are sending your organization the most spam?

- **Virus by Domain (Inbound and Outbound)**—Which domains are sending viruses to you? Who appears to have a virus inside your organization?

- **Content Manager by Account (Inbound and Outbound)**—Which accounts had the most bounced messages? The most quarantined messages? How many messages have been processed per account? How many bytes?

CONCLUSION

Most organizations will never need Message Security and Discovery, which is one of the reasons Google makes it available only to Premier Edition customers. However, for those who do need it, Postini is absolutely vital to have and makes Google Apps all the more attractive and even necessary. Many organizations require some sort of policy management and message recovery, and Postini is among the best in its field. To learn all you need to know, go through the wealth of materials provided for you in the "Further Reading" section that follows. You'll find that Postini is a powerful service that will help you greatly.

FURTHER READING

There's always more to learn, so here are some resources that you might find handy if you want to learn more about Message Security and Discovery:

- Overviews and High Points
    - Welcome to Google Apps Security Services: www.google.com/a/help/intl/en/security/index.html
    - Choose the package that fits your needs: www.google.com/a/help/intl/en/security/compare.html
    - Postini Features in Google Apps Premier Edition: https://www.google.com:443/support/a/bin/answer.py?answer=77041&topic=12977
    - Message Center Quick Start, available in Word: (www.postini.com/webdocs/mc/quick_start/mc_qs_ee_en.doc) or PDF (www.postini.com/webdocs/mc/quick_start/mc_qs_ee_en.pdf)

- Personal Archive Quick Start, available in Word: (www.postini.com/webdocs/archiving/personal_arch/pa_qs_en.doc) or PDF (www.postini.com/webdocs/archiving/personal_arch/pa_qs_en.pdf)

- Google Apps for Admins Help Topics
  - Google Message Security & Compliance Help Center: www.google.com/support/appsecurity/
  - Message Security and Discovery (Postini): www.google.com/support/a/bin/topic.py?topic=14840
  - Activation Step-by-Step Guide for Policy Management and Message Recovery by Postini: www.postini.com/webdocs/activate_pg/wwhelp/wwhimpl/js/html/wwhelp.htm
  - Activation Overview: www.postini.com/webdocs/activate_overview_pg/
  - Activation Help: http://groups.google.com/group/PostiniSupportFor-GoogleApps/web/activation-help
  - Message Security & Compliance Documentation (available in HTML or PDF): www.google.com/support/appsecurity/bin/bin/answer.py?answer=87514
  - Google Message Security & Compliance Help Center: www.google.com/support/appsecurity/bin/topic.py?topic=13834
- Interactive Video Guides
  - Getting Started Tour: www.postini.com/webdocs/training/pgmr_train_overview/
  - Your First Week: Next Steps for Administrators: www.postini.com/webdocs/training/pgmr_train_next_steps/
  - Video tutorials for admins: www.google.com/support/appsecurity/bin/answer.py?answer=87508 (Includes Message Security and Compliance Activation Overview, Understanding and Working with MX Records, Successfully Deploying Message Security and Compliance, Administration Console Basics, Customizing the User Experience, Message Discovery: Configuring Journaling to Archive All Messages, Add Users, Aliases, and Mailing Lists, Add Domains and Domain Aliases, Add Administrators, and Search Your Message Archive)
  - Email Security Tour video: www.google.com/support/appsecurity/bin/answer.py?answer=87508
- Product Overview and Tour Videos
  - Google Apps Security Services Quick Tour: www.youtube.com/watch?v=DlnmZ2AtD-A

- Postini Policy Management and Message Recovery Demonstration: www.youtube.com/watch?v=vOyW_6Dsbn8
- Google Message Security, powered by Postini: www.youtube.com/watch?v=6Gk67oytpyo
- Screencasts
  - Message Security and Compliance Activation Overview: www.postini.com/webdocs/training/en/seccomp_actover/engage.html
  - Understanding and Working with MX Records: www.postini.com/webdocs/training/en/email_activate/email_mxrecords.html
- Admin Guides
  - Administrator's Guide: www.postini.com/webdocs/pgmr_admin/wwhelp/wwhimpl/js/html/wwhelp.htm
  - Documentation and Training page: http://groups.google.com/group/PostiniSupportForGoogleApps/web/documentation-and-training-for-policy-management-and-message-recovery-by-postini
- Discussion Groups
  - Postini Support for Policy Management and Message Recovery for Google App: http://groups.google.com/group/PostiniSupportForGoogleApps/
  - Google Message Security Discussion: http://groups.google.com/group/gms-discuss
- FAQs
  - FAQ for Message Recovery: http://groups.google.com/group/PostiniSupportForGoogleApps/web/FAQs+for+Message+Recovery+by+Postini
  - FAQ for Policy Management: http://groups.google.com/group/PostiniSupportForGoogleApps/web/FAQs+for+Policy+Management+by+Postini?version=8
  - Message Center FAQ: www.postini.com/webdocs/mc_resources/faq_inter/faq_inter_en/engage.html
  - Message Security Overview FAQ: www.google.com/support/appsecurity/bin/answer.py?answer=92706&ctx=sibling
- Instructor-Led Webinars: www.google.com/support/appsecurity/bin/answer.py?answer=97518
- Google Apps Frequently Reported Issues: www.google.com/support/a/bin/request.py?contact_type=known_issues

Things to Know About Using Google Video

Just as I was finishing up this book, Google announced the newest member of Google Apps: Google Video. Although it caused a bit of a scramble on my part to add this chapter to the book, it also shows just why Google Apps is so interesting as a product.

The fact that Google would add a very nice feature like this one—and that users don't have to do anything to use the feature because it just appears—is a big part of the strength behind cloud computing as it's embodied by Google Apps. If Google Apps were a desktop program that had to be installed on a computer, it might be months or even years before customers were using Google Video; because Google Apps is a set of web apps that run in the cloud, it was easy for Google to roll out a major new feature like this to its users.

So what is Google Video? Basically, it's a white label version of YouTube that Google Apps customers can use to host videos that they want their users to see inside an organization. Video has been getting cheaper to create and edit for years. With a Flip Ultra video camera (only $125 at Amazon) and Windows Movie Maker or iMovie on a Mac, a nontechnical user can now easily shoot and edit a nice-looking and informative video (I should know—I require students in one class to create videos, and they do a bang-up job). The problem is, if that video is meant for internal use only, where can the worker put it?

Google's YouTube seems like an obvious answer, except that then it's available to the world, so there goes security, privacy, and control. Instead, what Google has done is take the best parts of YouTube—its ease of use, its support for a wide range of video formats, and its incredible bandwidth—and integrated it into Google Apps. Now any organization can use Google's infrastructure to make videos easily available to everyone in that organization.

> **NOTE**
>
> Keep in mind, Google Video is about hosting videos, not creating them. You still need to take care of that on your own.

Here are the salient facts about the new Google Video:

- It's free as part of Google Apps Premier Edition subscriptions.
- Each user gets 3GB of storage for videos.
- Videos can be viewed an unlimited number of times—there's no restriction on that.
- There are a few restrictions and recommendations on the videos themselves, as listed in "Upload" later.
- Google Video is coming for Education Edition users later in 2008, with a free trial until March 9, 2009. After that, it will cost $10 per user, per year. The idea is that faculty and staff will upload videos for students to see and use.

How can your organization use Google Video? Here are a few ideas, some cribbed from Google:

- Product training and how-to's (in which case, a screencast—explained at http://en.wikipedia.org/wiki/Screencast—may be needed)
- Reports
- Introducing employees and staff
- HR introductions to various policies and procedures
- Corporate announcements
- Interviews and focus group results

The nice thing is that Google Video democratizes video in an organization, making it easy for any employee with a Google Apps account to add videos to the mix.

CHANGING CONTROL PANEL SETTINGS

If you signed up for a Premier Edition account after Google Video came out, you'll see Google Video enabled by default.

If you already had a Premier Edition account and your Google Apps admin had gone to Domain Settings and checked Automatically Add New Google Services, then Google Video will appear without your admin having to do anything.

If you don't see Google Video yet, you can add it—just log into your Control Panel, click Add More Services, and click Add It Now under Google Video.

> ## NOTE
>
> If you don't see Google Video as an option on Add More Services, you must first switch to the Next Generation English version of the Control Panel on the Domain Settings, General page. After you add Google Video, you can switch back to the non-English, old school version of the Control Panel and still keep it.

To change Google Video's settings, go to Service Settings, Video. On that page you can do the following:

- **Web Address**—Change the URL your users go to for Google Video. By default, your videos are found at http://video.google.com/a/ heavymetalmassage.com (of course, with your domain, not mine), but you can change it to something else, like http://video.heavymetalmassage.com. After you make the change here, you'll need to log in to your DNS provider and add a CNAME record pointing to video (or whatever else you choose) to ghs.google.com. For examples showing you how to change DNS, see Chapter 2's "Configuring DNS."

- **Recommended Tags**—Enter some tags here that you'd like your users to see by default as suggestions when they upload videos.

- **Statistics**—Here you can see how you're doing when it comes to your allowed disk quota. In addition, you can download a CSV file (which will open in Google Docs) showing you who your top video uploaders are, so you can thank or warn them as needed.

- **Disable Video**—Don't want Google Video any longer? You can disable it here.

Click Save Changes when you're finished. You just configured Google Video.

USING GOOGLE VIDEO

When your users go to http://video.heavymetalmassage.com (using your URL, of course), you're going to see three tabs: Home, My Videos, and Upload. At the top of each of those tabs you'll see a search box that allows you to search through the videos to which you have access.

Let's walk through those tabs.

Home

This initially shows you the most recently uploaded and most viewed videos. In both categories, you see the following for each video:

- Thumbnail
- Title
- Length
- Date recorded
- Person who uploaded it
- Number of views
- Number of people who have viewed it

If you'd like to see all the videos that were recently uploaded or all the most viewed videos, click See All in the appropriate category. On the resulting pages, you can sort by a variety of factors, including Rating, Total Views, and Upload Date.

My Videos

This one's easy—it's just the videos you've uploaded. That's it. You can sort them by a variety of factors, including Rating, Total Views, and Upload Date.

Upload

This screen is the real meat and potatoes because this is where you get your videos into Google in the first place. Most of the fields here are pretty self-explanatory, but you need to know the following guidelines about the kinds of videos you can upload:

- To start with, don't break copyright laws; make sure you have the right to the videos you upload.
- Your videos can be in the following formats, in alphabetical order: ASF, AVI, FLV (but not SWF), MOD, MOV, MPEG, MPG, MP4, RA, RAM, and WMV.

- Acceptable codecs are H.263, H.264, Motion JPEG, and MPEG 1/2/4 (MPEG 4 or MPEG 2 with MP3 audio is recommended).

- Your bitrate should be above 260Kbps.

- Your frame rate should be above 12fps (30fps is recommended)

- At least 640×480 resolution.

- An aspect ratio of 4:3.

- De-interlace your video.

- No more than 300MB in file size.

After you upload your video, which can take quite some time depending upon its file size and the speed of your Internet connection, Google will process your video for display. This usually takes about 1–3 times the duration of your video, so a 5 minute video will take anywhere from 5 to 15 minutes. After it's processed, it appears on the Home and My Videos tabs, and you can begin viewing and sharing it.

For each video, you have two check boxes:

- **Show Download Link to Viewers**—If you want viewers to be able to download your videos—and I normally think that its a good idea (and realize that it's very easy to get around this restriction anyway, so it's practically meaningless to uncheck this box)—check the box.

- **Anyone at heavymetalmassage.com Can View**—This makes it easy on you. Anyone in your Google Apps domain can see the video, so you don't have to send out invites to everyone.

As you can with Google Docs, you—the video's owner—can invite other people as viewers or collaborators. The permissions, in order from least to most, break down as follows:

- Viewers can watch videos but can't change anything about them, and they can download videos on a case-by-case basis if those with greater permissions allow them.

- Collaborators can watch videos, modify data about the videos, see or change the sharing list, hide or reveal links so viewers can download videos, and delete tags viewers submit.

- Owners can do everything Collaborators can, but they can also delete videos.

If you embed the video or use it as a gadget elsewhere in Google Apps (more about that in the next section, "Viewing Videos"), the settings you make in regard to sharing apply there as well. Users must be signed in to Google Apps to see the video or do anything else to it for that matter.

If you allow only Alice to see the video, but you've embedded it in a spreadsheet that you also allow Bob to see, Alice will be able to see the video in the spreadsheet, whereas Bob will see the spreadsheet but not the video. And if you embed it in one of your Google Sites and share that site, the video's sharing settings take priority. So again, Alice and Bob may both be able to see your Google Site, but only Alice will see the video in the Site.

VIEWING VIDEOS

To view a video, click its title or thumbnail. If the resulting page, shown in Figure 21.1, looks a bit like YouTube (albeit a bit cleaner and nicer), that shouldn't be a surprise.

FIGURE 21.1   Viewing a video of a little boy wearing a great big football helmet.

There are a few features you should notice, however:

- **Scenes**—Under the video is a + that opens up scenes, a series of thumbnails showing your major points in the video. Click a thumbnail, and you jump to that portion of the video. You can't choose the scenes or delete the ones that appear; that's solely up to Google. This, by the way, is a feature not currently offered in YouTube.

- **Comments**—Users can leave comments about the video. The commenter's name automatically appears, which is great—no more anonymous comments, the kind that have made YouTube comments synonymous with "stupid."

- **Ratings**—Users can rate the video from one to five stars.

- **Tags**—Users can tag the video. As they type, Google will attempt to auto-complete the tags based on those entered by the domain's Google Apps admin (see "Changing Control Panel Settings" earlier in this chapter) or on those previously entered by the specific user. Like comments, tags are not anonymous. To see who entered a tag, hover over the tag, and a tooltip appears with the person's name. Owners and Collaborators can delete inappropriate tags. If users click a tag, they go to a page listing all videos matching that tag.

- **Embed This Video**—Clicking the Show link provides users with two links: one to embed the video in a web page—Google Sites, for instance—and one to add the video as a gadget on the Start Page or in Google Docs' Spreadsheets. Remember that the video's permissions are still in place even if it appears in other Google Apps programs, such as Google Sites and Google Docs.

- **Downloads**—If you enable downloads (and if you're an Owner or Collaborator, you can disable downloads at any time by clicking Hide Download Links From Viewers), users have two choices: Standard and High. Both are in the MP4 format, which is great, with Standard being roughly half the size of videos downloaded as High.

- **Edit**—This allows those with permission to change the video's Title and Description or delete it.

- **Share**—Basically a streamlined view of the same permissions covered previously in "Upload."

ACCESSING GOOGLE VIDEO ON THE IPHONE

If you use an iPhone and you're logged in to your domain's Google Video site, or you're accessing one of your other Google Apps resources on which a video has been embedded (Sites or Docs, for instance), you can still view the video. Download the video in Standard quality; as you do so, the iPhone automatically opens the video and begins playing it.

SOLVING COMMON PROBLEMS

As with all things in life, you're going to find little gotchas. Here are a few of those and their solutions.

Why Can't I Upload Any Videos?

If you receive an error message about a content match, Google has identified your video as violating the copyright of some company or organization. As a result, Google won't host your video. More information about this policy is at http://video.google.com/support/bin/answer.py?hl=en&answer=82734.

If there's been a mistake, and you think your video should be allowed, you can file a dispute by going to http://video.google.com/support/bin/answer.py?answer=82442 and following the steps outlined there.

CONCLUSION

Google Video can be an extremely useful new service to organizations using Google Apps. As video grows more important as a means of communication, and as it becomes easier for nontechnical people to create videos, Google Video will prove an easy, powerful way to collaborate and educate. If you don't currently use the Premier or Education Editions of Google Apps, don't worry—I'm certain that Google Video will some day be available to all editions of Google Apps. It's simply too important an app and too central to what Google is trying to do with Google Apps.

FURTHER READING

There's always more to learn, so here are some resources that you might find handy if you want to learn more about Google Video and its various incarnations:

- Overview with factoids: http://www.google.com/a/help/intl/en/users/ video.html

- Google Apps for Admins Help Topics: http://www.google.com/support/ a/bin/topic.py?topic=15588

- Google Apps for Users Help Topics:

    - Google Video Help Center: http://video.google.com/support/. Not specific to the Google Video in Google Apps, but helpful nonetheless.

    - YouTube Help Center: http://www.google.com/support/youtube/. Not specific to the Google Video in Google Apps, but helpful nonetheless.

- Videos at YouTube:

    - Google Video for business: How we use it at Google. http://www. youtube.com/watch?v=iWzwLGJ0BIo

    - How customers are using Google Video for business: http://www. youtube.com/watch?v=_c7z-kdi4kU

- Google Video FAQs: http://www.google.com/support/a/bin/answer.py? answer=106608

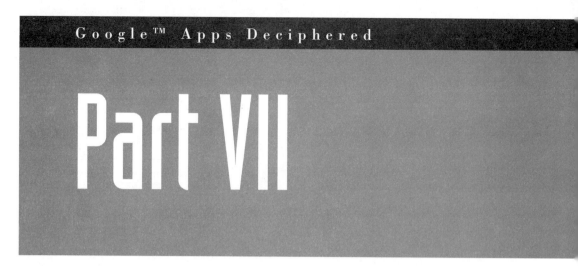

Part VII

Appendices

Backing Up Google Apps

I trust a lot of my digital life to Google, but I don't trust blindly. I fully understand that everything mechanical can fail, which includes hard drives, networks, and entire systems. Even though Google is a gigantic company full of brilliant people, mistakes and failures can still happen. It's best to be prepared. I'm not saying don't use Google Apps—after all I'm writing a book on the subject, and I rely on Google Apps every single day—but I am saying that you should definitely have a backup strategy in place.

In this appendix, I give you a few tips for backing up your vitally important data stored in Google Apps. There's one important thing you need to remember about your backups, however: As a locksmith once said to me when he gave me a key that he had just copied, test before you trust. Test your backups to make sure they work before you rely on them. There's nothing worse than that sickening feeling in the pit of your stomach when you realize that the backup you desperately need just doesn't work.

BACKING UP GMAIL

Backing up Gmail is actually quite easy. You have several methods you can choose from:

- Enable POP access on your Gmail account, create another Gmail account, and then pull email from the original Gmail account using POP. This is free, easy, and happens automatically in the background, so you don't need to worry about it. The disadvantage, however, is that the backup will not reflect the original Gmail account as you delete messages. Your backup will contain every bit of mail you have ever received (except for Spam and Trash, which most likely isn't going to be a problem), which may be far more than you want. If you want to continue using Gmail on the Web, don't forget to check Keep Mail's Copy in the Inbox or Archive Mail's Copy in Gmail's POP settings.

■ Enable IMAP access on your Gmail account, create another Gmail account, and then pull email from the original Gmail account using IMAP. This is free, easy, and also happens automatically. The advantage of this method over POP is that the new account will perfectly reflect your original account. The disadvantage is that if you delete a message in the original account, it will also be deleted in the backup account.

■ You can also set up a desktop email client to grab your email using POP (again, messages in Spam and Trash will not be downloaded). The disadvantage of this method is that the client will only back up your mail when it is running. You either need to leave the client running all the time or remember to open the program on a semi-regular schedule. If you don't mind the possibility of perhaps missing an email or two, this may be just fine. The advantage of this method is that your backed-up email is completely under your control.

■ Tell Gmail you want to forward all new email to another email address. This method allows you to back up your email to a Gmail account, a Yahoo Mail account, or even a private Google Group (instructions for that can be found at www.googletutor.com/2007/03/29/using-google-groups-to-backup-gmail/).

■ Finally, there are many third-party programs designed to back up Gmail. I discussed some of them in Chapter 9, "Backing Up Your Email." If you'd like to learn about more, do a Google search for "back up gmail," and you'll find lots of options that you can pursue.

TIP

If you use Linux, you really must take a look at Matt Cutts' article, "How to back up your Gmail on Linux in four easy steps," available at www.mattcutts.com/blog/backup-gmail-in-linux-with-getmail/. Another good one is George Donnelly's "How To Backup Your Gmail or Google Apps Account Daily," at http://georgedonnelly.com/unix/how-to-quickly-set-up-a-daily-backup-of-your-gmail-account. Both focus on the free and open-source program getmail.

BACKING UP GOOGLE CONTACTS

Backing up your Google Contacts isn't hard. In chapters 4 and 10 of this book, I discussed several programs that synchronize your Google Contacts with your desktop address book. If you run one of those programs, then your Google Contacts will be backed up. Of course, you'll need to back up your Contacts once they're on your local computer, but that's true of everything you back up.

BACKING UP GOOGLE CALENDAR

Backing up your Google Calendar is actually very easy. In Chapters 5 and 13 of this book, I pointed you toward a number of programs that synchronize your Google Calendar with your desktop calendar. Run one of those, and your Google Calendar is constantly backed up. If you use Apple's iCal, you can also back up your Google Calendar automatically—and for free—thanks to the new CalDAV support that Google recently introduced (see Chapter 13 for all the details).

Finally, if you don't want to synchronize your Google Calendar, you can always grab your Google Calendar data in a desktop program instead. I covered how to do that at length, in most of the major desktop calendar programs, in Chapter 13. The nice thing about accessing but not synchronizing is that you make it impossible for an error in your desktop calendar to propagate to your Google Calendar, given that accessing Google Calendar in a desktop program means that it's read-only.

BACKING UP GOOGLE DOCS

Google allows you to download Google Docs…one file at a time. Eeek! That isn't going to fly. Fortunately, other folks have stepped up to the plate and developed solutions that allow you to download your files in bulk, automatically. That's much better. Here are a few programs that will do what you want:

- **Gdatacopier**
  http://code.google.com/p/gdatacopier/
  A command line tool that relies on Python and the Google Data APIs Python Client Library (gdata-python-client), which means it will run on Windows, Mac OS X, and Linux, and can be scripted to run automatically with cron. Be sure to read the documentation on the wiki, which has plenty of examples.

■ **Syncplicity**
www.syncplicity.com
Currently Windows-only, but with a Mac app promised and maybe a Linux client after that, this is a clever program that syncs files in your Windows Documents folder with other computers, with Syncplicity's servers, and with Google Docs. Free for 2GB and two computers or $10 per month for more data and machines. Watch the video overview at www.syncplicity.com/Video/Overview.aspx.

■ **Google Docs Download**
http://1st-soft.net/gdd/
A Greasemonkey script (for more on Greasemonkey, see Chapter 9's "A Note on Adding Scripts to Your Web Browser") that makes it easy to manually download some or all of your Google Docs in the formats you choose. Combine this with the awesome Firefox extension DownThemAll (http://www.downthemall.net), and you have a bulk download solution, albeit one that can't be automated with cron.

■ **OpenOffice.org2GoogleDocs**
http://extensions.services.openoffice.org/project/ooo2gd
An extension that allows you to open one document at a time in OpenOffice.org on your computer. Because OpenOffice.org runs on Windows, Mac OS X, and Linux, theoretically this should work on any platform; however, I had major problems on Mac OS X and Linux. It worked fine on Windows, though.

BACKING UP GOOGLE SITES

Google Sites doesn't yet have a built-in capability to back up a site, but supposedly this is coming. Unfortunately, it's supposed to have been coming since early spring 2008. In other words, I wouldn't hold my breath.

There are various programs available—for Windows, Linux, and Mac OS X—that allow you to download websites. The problem, however, is that most Google Sites are protected via HTTPS and password protection. If your program doesn't support HTTPS and passwords, your only choice is to temporarily make your Google Site public, download it with the program, and then quickly hide your Site again. Of course, during the time your Site is public, someone could stumble across it, or a search engine could index it, leading to potentially disastrous results. It's far safer to use a program that supports HTTPS and password protection.

Fortunately, there's a free, open source, and powerful program that runs on every major operating system and is specifically built to download websites efficiently and quickly: Wget. Where you download Wget depends upon your OS:

- **Linux**—Wget should already be included with your distro. If it's not, use your distro's package manager to find, download, and install it. Typically, the program will be found at /usr/bin/wget.

- **Mac OS X**—Even though OS X is in reality a UNIX, for some reason Apple doesn't bother to include Wget, which is certainly annoying. The easiest way to install Wget on your Mac is to go to this URL and download the appropriate package: http://rudix.org/packages.html. While you're there, notice that there are other really cool UNIX software packages you can grab. After you install it, you'll find the program at /usr/local/bin/wget.

- **Windows**—If you've installed Cygwin (www.cygwin.com), then you can run Wget from inside it. However, this is too UNIX-y for most Windows users. If you'd rather use a GUI, then you'll probably want to install WinWGet, which you can download from www.cybershade.us/winwget/. What's nice about this program is that the GUI shows you the command line options in it, so you'll be able to follow along in the example I provide here, which focuses solely on the command line.

Once you've installed Wget, create the directory into which you're going to download your site, open your terminal, cd into that directory, and enter the following command (use your own domain name and site name instead of heavymetalmassage.com/office/):

```
wget -r -v -p -w 7 —random-wait —cut-dirs=5 -nH -E -k -np —no-check-
certificate -D sites.google.com -X /support,/system/app/pages -R
compare*,revisions*,createPage* -np —http-user="scott@granneman.com"
https://sites.google.com:443/a/heavymetalmassage.com/office/
```

Let's walk through the options in that command one by one so you understand what it is you're telling Wget to do.

- -r
  Start at the base URL—
  https://sites.google.com:443/a/granneman.com/house/—and
  recursively grab every web page under it.

- -v
  Be verbose and tell you what the program is doing.

- -p
  Download page requisites, the files necessary to display a web page correctly, such as images, CSS, and scripts.

- -w 7
  Wait that number of seconds between requests. Otherwise, Wget will hammer Google's servers, and Google might block you.

- --random-wait
  Wait random times between requests, with the amount of time a random number between 0 and 2, times the number of seconds specified with -w.

- -nH
  Prevents Wget from placing all of the downloaded files in a directory named sites.google.com. If you would instead like that, remove this option.

- --cut-dirs=5
  If you don't use this option, Wget will create a subdirectory corresponding to every subdirectory you're requesting in the URL. In other words, all of your content will be inside a subdirectory named a/yourDomainName/ yourSiteName. If you'd like all your content to be placed into those subdirectories, remove this option.

- -E
  Append .html to the end of every downloaded web page, if it's not already there. This makes it easy for you to browse the site locally or place it on a web server.

- -k
  Convert the links in all downloaded files so that you can view the website locally.

- -np
  The np option is short for "no parent," and it tells Wget to go recursively down through the Site's directory structure and never to follow a link above it. This prevents Wget from grabbing content that's not actually in your Google site.

- --no-check-certificate
  Don't check if the SSL certificate at https://sites.google.com is good or not. If you leave this off, your command will fail with "ERROR: Certificate verification error for sites.google.com: unable to get local issuer certificate."

- -D sites.google.com
  This limits the download to the sites.google.com domain. If you don't specify this, Wget will try to download from several different Google domains.

- `-X /support,/system/app/pages`
  Excludes two subdirectories common to all Google Sites. `/support` contains help files, which you undoubtedly do not want, and `/system/app/pages` contains all the different revisions made to your site. If you do want all the revisions, remove `/system/app/pages` from the option above (there should not be a space before `/system/app/pages`).

- `-I /system/app/pages/sitemap`
  Tells Wget to grab the site map from inside the `/pages` subdirectory you excluded in the previous option.

- `—user="scott@heavymetalmassage.com"`
  Your Google Apps username, which, as always, is your email address.

- `https://sites.google.com:443/a/heavymetalmassage.com/office/`
  The URL of the Google site you'd like to download.

You might notice that a password isn't specified. You could use `—http-password=123456`, but that would be a bad idea given that your password would now show up in your command line's history (if you're using the Windows GUI, this isn't a concern). Instead, create a file in your home directory named `.wgetrc` (note the dot in front of the name, as that's required) and in it place the following line:

```
http_passwd = 123456
```

Press Enter to run the command and then wait. The larger your site, the longer you're going to have to wait. Don't be surprised if it takes a long time to download your entire site. If you're really concerned about backing up your site on a regular basis, create a cron job that automatically runs the command at a specified time every night.

> **TIP**
>
> For more about Wget and cron, see my book *Linux Phrasebook*, which covers Wget in Chapter 15's "Download Files Non-interactively" and cron in the same chapter's "Securely Transfer and Back Up Files."

Also be aware that the site you're downloading is going to consist of static web pages. The pages aren't going to be dynamically generated, they aren't going to contain any cool widgets you may have installed, and they certainly aren't going to be wiki pages any longer. Until Google makes it easy for people to download their Sites, this is the best you can hope for. But at least you'll have all of your content—well, at least the content that isn't dynamic—so you'll be able to view it or even post it on a web server like Apache or IIS as a stopgap measure.

BACKING UP GOOGLE TALK

First, if you set Google Talk to save your chats (for info on that, see Chapter 18's "Chat History"), then all of your conversations are backed up at Gmail.

Google Talk stores the following files on your PC:

- Avatars
- Chatlogs
- Themes
- Vcards

Google Talk stores these files in different places, depending on which version of Windows you're using (remember, it only runs on Windows):

- **Windows XP**—C:\Documents and Settings\USERNAME\Local Settings\ Application Data\Google\Google Talk
- **Windows Vista**—C:\Users\USERNAME\AppData\Local\Google\Google Talk

Back those folders up, and you've backed up important data that Google Talk uses.

As far as backing up your buddy list, remember that your buddy list is really your Google Contacts list. As long as you're backing up Google Contacts according to the method I outlined previously in this appendix, your buddy list should be safe and sound.

BACKING UP START PAGE

In keeping with Google's apparent disinterest in improving or modernizing the Start Page (see almost all of Chapter 19, "Things to Know About Using Start Page"), there is apparently no built-in way to back it up. In reality, however, this isn't that big of a deal because the entire Start Page is essentially dynamic. Considering there really isn't any way to use elements of the Start Page apart from the Start Page, there isn't much point in backing it up. And anyway, the Start Page as it currently stands is so anemic, so problematic, that I for one wouldn't miss it too much if it disappeared one day and I found that I hadn't backed it up.

BACKING UP GOOGLE VIDEO

There isn't really any way to back up Google Video at this time. My advice is to keep a copy of any video you upload on your computer or backed up somewhere. Besides, your local copy is undoubtedly of better quality than what you could download from Google itself.

CONCLUSION

Unfortunately, many people use Google Apps without taking extra precautions to ensure that their data is protected. Google does a good job of protecting your data overall, but it can make mistakes, and it has. Remember, there are two kinds of people in the world: those who have suffered a catastrophic data loss and those who will. Some day something bad could happen to your stuff, and when that day arrives, you'll be glad that you had a backup strategy in place.

Dealing with Multiple Accounts

The key to using Google Apps is the Google Apps account. A Google Apps account, however, can quickly turn problematic if you're not careful, due to the existence of multiple accounts.

When it comes to multiple accounts, you're looking at two different problems:

- It's possible to have a Google Apps account *and* a regular ol' non-Google Apps Google account, both with the same email address. Warning: cloudy skies and rough waters ahead.

- Many people have more than one Google Apps account. This can cause problems when you're trying to access more than one at the same time in a web browser, but there are ways to mitigate any issues.

THE PROBLEM WITHOUT A GOOD SOLUTION

Earlier in this book, in Chapters 13 ("My Calendar Entries Disappeared! Where Did They Go?") and Chapter 15 ("My Docs Disappeared! Where Did They Go?"), I discussed the confusion that can result if you have both a Google account and a Google Apps account with the same username. Yes, this can happen.

To understand how and why, remember that Google offers an enormous number of services, most of them not part of Google Apps (Google Reader, for instance, as well as Blogger, Knol, Picasa Web Albums, YouTube, and so on), but all of them accessible via a Google—not a Google Apps, but a Google—account. Further, most of the services provided as part of Google Apps are also available to people who don't use Google Apps and simply have a Google account. Gmail works this way, as does Docs, Calendar, Sites, Talk, and Start Page (though it's known as iGoogle, and it's about 100 times better—see all of Chapter 19).

When you create a Google account, you supply an email address that will serve as your username. In my case, I've been using scott@websanity.com since we founded WebSanity several years ago, so I used that to create a Google account in order to use Google Docs, Gmail, and Google Calendar. Then we decided to switch over to Google Apps for websanity.com, so I now had a Google Apps account for scott@websanity.com *in addition to* the scott@websanity.com Google account.

That means two Google Docs have the same login—scott@websanity.com—but each is completely different. Even the URLs are different. The one associated with my Google account is at https://docs.google.com, while the one connected to my Google Apps account is at https://docs.google.com/a/granneman.com/. This is, to say the least, a bit confusing.

This mess can also happen in reverse. I've been using scott@granneman.com for over a decade, but I never used it with a Google account. I did, however, set up Google Apps for granneman.com a few years ago, and as part of that, I created a Google Apps account for scott@granneman.com. Later, I wanted to log in to Google Reader using scott@granneman.com, so I had to create a separate Google account using the same email address that I used with my Google Apps account.

That's OK except that I wanted to email some of the posts I read in Google Reader. To do so, I press Email under the post, type in the email address, and press Send. After doing this 25 times, it gets old. I want autocompletion of email addresses as I'm typing, just like in Gmail. Google Reader offers this feature, but it uses your Google Contacts as the address book. However, I don't have Google Contacts for the scott@granneman.com Google account because I don't have Gmail set up for the scott@granneman.com Google account—because the only scott@granneman.com I want to have Gmail for is already set up in Google Apps. Aaagh!

Now, I can set up Gmail with my scott@granneman.com Google account, but I can't actually use scott@granneman.com as the actual Gmail address because that's taken by my Google Apps account. So Google is able to know that much, but that's about it. I have to create a new Gmail address that I will use when I log in to my scott@granneman.com Google account, so I decide on rscottgranneman@gmail.com. Now I can add addresses to the Google Contacts associated with my Google account (still separate from my Google Apps account, keep in mind).

However, a big problem crops up—I can send Google Reader posts via email to my friends, which is great, but the return address is now rscottgranneman@gmail.com and no longer scott@granneman.com, even though I'm still logging in to Google Reader with scott@granneman.com! There was no way to change it so that scott@granneman.com was still used as the From address. So after a few days of that annoyance, I decided to forgo editing Google Contacts, which meant canceling Gmail for the scott@granneman.com Google account, which meant getting rid of rscottgranneman@gmail.com. I did so, and for the next week, whenever I logged in to Google Reader as scott@granneman.com, the page would reload a second later to helpfully inform me that I was now logged in—as rscottgranneman! Finally, a week later, rscottgranneman mysteriously disappeared.

But here's the weird part—like Jason or Freddy Krueger, my Contacts from the brief time I was rscottgranneman@gmail.com live on...unkillable. When I start to type an address into a post I'm emailing from Google Reader, if it's for the ten or so people I added into Google Contacts while it was around, the address autocompletes. Anyone else, nada. But of course there's no way for me to add more addresses or change the ones that are already there because there's no way to get back to Google Contacts for my scott@granneman.com Google account.

> **TIP**
>
> I just found out as this book was going to press that you can in fact get to your non-Google Apps Contacts without first logging in to Gmail. The address you need is https://mail.google.com/mail/contacts/ui/ContactManager. Again, this is *not* for Google Apps, but for non-Google Apps accounts.

This is a huge mess. A colossal ball of confusion. And unfortunately, there's really nothing at this time we can do about it—except avoid, if at all possible, using the same email address with Google accounts and Google Apps accounts. The real solution to this debacle will have to come from Google when it releases a way to unify accounts. Until then, be careful.

THE SOLVABLE PROBLEM

The real problem that I'm addressing in this appendix, however, is that of multiple Google Apps accounts. In my case, for instance, I have four different personal or work-related Google Apps accounts. However, on top of those, I also have to periodically log in to clients' Google Apps accounts to try and help them with their various issues. This can lead to mounting frustration as I find out that I've been logged out of my work account because I logged in to fix a client's account.

You might think that simply opening up a new Firefox tab for each account would resolve the problem, but that doesn't work. It may for a short time, but then something somewhere crosses its wires, and involuntary logouts raise their ugly heads.

Fortunately, though, you have a wide variety of choices when it comes to solving this issue.

SOLUTIONS

When it comes to the problem of multiple accounts, you have several possible solutions.

Working in Separate Web Browsers

You can use separate web browsers, with your first Google account in Internet Explorer and your second in Firefox. Or if you're on a Mac, your first Google account in Safari and your second in Firefox. Linux users could do this with Firefox and Konqueror. Opera also makes a good second browser, and it runs on all the major operating systems.

Nowadays, it's easy to run lots of web browsers on your computer. My own computer, for instance, has the following web browsers on it: Safari, Firefox, Opera, Camino, Flock, WebKit (the nightly build of Safari), and even Amaya, a browser put out by the World Wide Web Consortium. Soon I'll be able to add Google Chrome to that list as well. If I were running Windows, I could add Internet Explorer to that list. I can run any combination of these at the same time, with a different Google account in each.

Creating Multiple Instances of Internet Explorer

If you repeatedly start up IE by clicking its icon and not by pressing Ctrl-n to create a new window, you can open as many different IE windows as you'd like, each with a different Google Apps account in it. This can be a quick and dirty way to use multiple accounts if you're still using Internet Explorer.

Getting Specific with an SSB (Site-Specific Browser)

Back in Chapter 18, I introduced you to Site-Specific Browsers (SSBs). This is one solution to the problem of multiple Google Apps accounts, and it may be my favorite.

Unfortunately, it won't work with Fluid, the Mac OS X-based SSB, thanks to its reliance on Safari and the way that browser stores cookies. That's too bad, but you still have your pick from three other SSBs, and they all work well:

- **Prism, the Firefox-based SSB http://labs.mozilla.com/projects/ prism/)**

  This is great because Prism is a cross-platform solution, so you can run it on Windows, Mac OS X, and Linux.

- **Bubbles, the Windows-only, IE-based SSB (http://bubbleshq.com)**

  It's not cross-platform, but if you're stuck on Windows and don't like Firefox, it'll work just fine.

- **Google Chrome (www.google.com/chrome)**

  Open Gmail, or Google Calendar, or whatever you want to use as an SSB and then click the little page icon to the right of the Omnibox and select Create Application Shortcuts. Save the icon on your Desktop. Repeat with the other Google Apps accounts. Now you can click any or all of those icons and have multiple Google Chrome applications, each tuned to a separate Google Apps account.

Hiding with Google Chrome's Incognito Mode

Google Chrome (covered in Appendix C) supports Incognito Mode, in which nothing you do in the browser is saved (that's why many people are calling it "Porn Mode" instead). What's fortunate for our needs, however, is that it's possible to access one Google Apps account in Google Chrome as you normally would with that browser and then open another instance of Chrome in Incognito Mode to view another, separate Google Apps account.

To do this, log on to your normal Google Apps account in Chrome and then press Ctrl-Shift-n to open a new window in Incognito Mode. Log in to your other Google Apps account in that window, and you are now accessing two different Google Apps accounts at the same time.

Understand, though, that when you close the Incognito window, Chrome forgets everything you did in that browser, including usernames and passwords. You'll have to log in again and repeat the entire process the next time you want to view that Google Apps account.

Running the IE Tab Extension for Firefox

Let's say you have two Google Apps accounts, one for Heavy Metal Massage and one for Granneman.com. If you're running Firefox on Windows, you can install the IE Tab extension for Firefox (https://addons.mozilla.org/en-US/firefox/addon/1419), which allows you to run Internet Explorer inside one of your Firefox tabs. That means that inside Firefox, you could have one tab viewing Heavy Metal Massage while another tab (that's actually Internet Explorer *inside* Firefox) views Granneman.com.

> **NOTE**
>
> This extension will work on Windows only. It won't work on Macs or Linux because those operating systems don't have Internet Explorer built in.

If you go into IE Tab's preferences, you can set it so that any time you go to any web page at Granneman.com, it automatically loads with Internet Explorer inside your Firefox tab. I understand this probably sounds a little weird, so here are some instructions to help make it clearer.

After you install the IE Tab extension, go to View, Toolbars, Customize. Find the button for IE Tab and drag it somewhere onto your toolbar. Press Done to close the Customize window. Now go to the Heavy Metal Massage Google account in a Firefox tab. When it loads, press the IE Tab button. You'll notice that the screen reloads, but if you look carefully you'll notice several other changes as well. In the bottom right of the Firefox window, you should see a little tiny blue IE icon appear that lets you know that the page is now loaded using Internet Explorer inside your Firefox tab. Also the IE Tab icon that you just pressed will change. Instead of a blue E, it will now display the Firefox icon, meaning that if you now press that button, the page will reload again and go back to displaying its contents using Firefox.

While the tab is still using Internet Explorer, open up a new tab and go to your other Google account, Granneman.com in my case. Notice that the account will load just fine. Go back to Heavy Metal Massage, which is being displayed with Internet Explorer inside Firefox. Notice that you can use that account as you please. You can go back and forth between the tabs without any problem, with one account running in one tab and the other account running in the other tab. However if you click the IE Tab button while you're in the tab using Internet Explorer, the tab will change back to Firefox, and you'll be back to the original problem: You will only be able to view the same account in all your tabs.

Now let's automate the process so that when you go to Heavy Metal Massage, Firefox will automatically load the site using Internet Explorer. That way you won't have to think about it. In Firefox, go to Tools, IE Tab Options. In the Options window, select the Sites Filter tab and add the address for your Google Apps in the text box next to URL. You'll need to enter the address for each of your Google Apps one at a time and press the Add button for each one in order for this to work (the * at the end of each one is a wildcard, and it is required). In my case, I would use the following:

- **Google Apps**—http://www.google.com/a/heavymetalmassage.com/*
- **Control Panel**—https://www.google.com/a/cpanel/heavymetalmassage.com/*
- **Gmail**—https://mail.google.com/a/heavymetalmassage .com/* (If you haven't turned on automatic SSL access, explained in Chapter 7's "Browser Connection," you should probably also add http://mail.google.com/a/heavymetalmassage.com/.*)
- **Calendar**—https://www.google.com/calendar/hosted/heavymetalmassage .com/*
- **Docs**—https://docs.google.com/a/heavymetalmassage .com/*
- **Start Page**—http://partnerpage.google.com/heavymetalmassage .com/*
- **Video**—http://video.google.com/a/heavymetalmassage .com/*
- **Sites**—https://sites.google.com/a/heavymetalmassage .com/*

Once you've finished, press OK to close the IE Tab Options window. Now try going to any of your Google Apps in a tab that is not using IE. As soon as you try to go to the selected Google App, IE Tab should take over and display the page with Internet Explorer inside Firefox.

Creating Separate Firefox Profiles

Closely related to running separate web browsers, you can actually run more than one copy of Firefox at the same time, but—and here's the kicker—each copy must use a different profile. So what's that mean?

Firefox stores your bookmarks, settings, extensions, and more—basically, all the information that you use with your browser—in a *profile*. In reality, a profile is simply a folder containing all of the files needed by Firefox. You can set up multiple profiles with different settings in each and then start up Firefox using a specified profile. Normally, you can run only one instance of Firefox with one profile at a time. However, there is a little known trick that will allow you to start multiple instances of Firefox, each using its own distinct profile.

To begin, you need to set up multiple profiles. In my case, let's say I want to set up three different profiles, one each for three different Google Apps accounts: Heavy Metal Massage, Granneman.com, and WebSanity. Here's how I would create a new Firefox profile on each OS I use (yes, you'll need to use the command line, and note that you cannot use spaces in your profile name):

- Windows: Go to Start, Run, and type the following, pressing Enter after each line:
  - `"C:\Program Files\Mozilla Firefox\firefox.exe" -CreateProfile HeavyMetalMassage`
  - `"C:\Program Files\Mozilla Firefox\firefox.exe" -CreateProfile Granneman`
  - `"C:\Program Files\Mozilla Firefox\firefox.exe" -CreateProfile WebSanity`
- Mac OS X: Open Terminal and type the following, pressing Enter after each line:
  - `/Applications/Firefox.app/Contents/MacOS/firefox -CreateProfile HeavyMetalMassage`
  - `/Applications/Firefox.app/Contents/MacOS/firefox -CreateProfile Granneman`
  - `/Applications/Firefox.app/Contents/MacOS/firefox -CreateProfile WebSanity`
- Linux: Open your favorite terminal app and type the following, pressing Enter after each line:
  - `/usr/bin/firefox -CreateProfile HeavyMetalMassage`
  - `/usr/bin/firefox -CreateProfile Granneman`
  - `/usr/bin/firefox -CreateProfile WebSanity`

To view your list of profiles, open the Firefox Profile Manager using the following command for your OS:

- Windows: `"C:\Program Files\Mozilla Firefox\firefox.exe" -ProfileManager`
- Mac OS X: `/Applications/Firefox.app/Contents/MacOS/firefox -ProfileManager`
- Linux: `/usr/bin/firefox -ProfileManager`

When the Profile Manager opens, you'll see something like what is shown in Figure B.1.

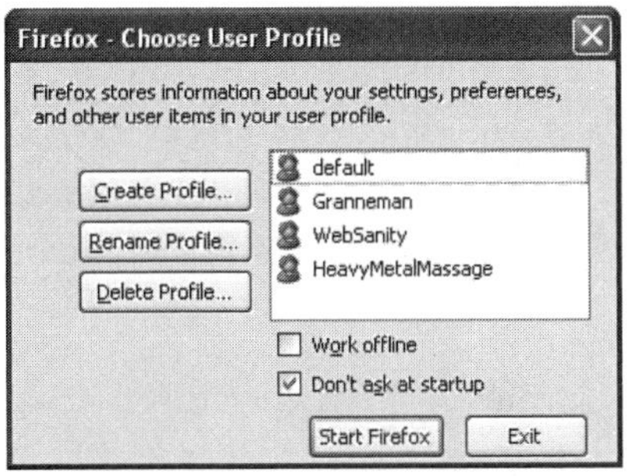

FIGURE B.1   The Firefox Profile Manager with three new profiles for Google Apps accounts.

You can review your profiles, delete them if you no longer need them, and even create a new profile if necessary. To start Firefox with a new profile, bring up the Profile Manager, uncheck Don't Ask at Startup, and select the profile you want to use. The problem with this method is that you can start only one instance of Firefox; you cannot run multiple copies of Firefox at the same time using the Profile Manager. However, by unchecking Don't Ask at Startup, Firefox will not show you the Profile Manager every time you start the program, enabling you to easily choose a profile.

If you want to run multiple copies of Firefox, each using a specific profile, start by closing all open instances of Firefox and then using the following command (in this case, I'm telling it to start with Heavy Metal Massage):

- Windows: "C:\Program Files\Mozilla Firefox\firefox.exe" -no-remote -P HeavyMetalMassage

- Mac OS X: /Applications/Firefox.app/Contents/MacOS/firefox -no-remote -P HeavyMetalMassage

- Linux: /usr/bin/firefox -no-remote -P HeavyMetalMassage

Then after Firefox is running, start another instance of Firefox that uses a different profile entirely:

- Windows: "C:\Program Files\Mozilla Firefox\firefox.exe" -no-remote -P WebSanity

- Mac OS X: `/Applications/Firefox.app/Contents/MacOS/firefox -no-remote -P WebSanity`

- Linux: `/usr/bin/firefox -no-remote -P WebSanity`

Repeat as needed with your other profiles. You can run as many different versions of Firefox, each utilizing a different profile, as you'd like.

Of course, you probably don't want to use the command line to start Firefox all the time. Instead, you'll probably want icons that you can click. Here's how to create those icons:

- Windows: Right-click your Desktop and select New, Shortcut. Next to Type the Location of the Item, enter "`C:\Program Files\Mozilla Firefox\firefox.exe" -no-remote -P HeavyMetalMassage` and press Next. On the next screen, use a name like Firefox (Heavy Metal Massage) for your shortcut and press Finish. Repeat for your other profiles.

- Mac OS X: Go to Applications, AppleScript, Script Editor. In the top box, enter in `do shell script "exec /Applications/Firefox.app/Contents/MacOS/firefox -no-remote -P HeavyMetalMassage`" and then click File, Save. For Save As, enter Firefox (Heavy Metal Massage); for File Format, choose Application. Select where you'd like the file to go (either the Desktop or Applications is good) and press Save. Now you can double-click Firefox (Heavy Metal Massage).app to open Firefox with the HeavyMetalMassage profile. Repeat for your other profiles.

- Linux (GNOME): Right-click the Desktop and select Create Launcher. Enter the following information, press OK, and then repeat the entire process for your other profiles:

  - Type: Application
  - Name: Firefox (Heavy Metal Massage)
  - Command: `/usr/bin/firefox -no-remote -P HeavyMetalMassage`
  - Comment: Launch Firefox using the HeavyMetalMassage profile

- Linux (KDE): Right-click the Desktop and select Create New, Link to Application. On the General tab, enter **Firefox (Heavy Metal Massage)**. On the Application tab, enter the following information, press OK, and then repeat the entire process for your other profiles:

  - Description: Launch Firefox using the HeavyMetalMassage profile
  - Comment: Launch Firefox using the HeavyMetalMassage profile
  - Command: `/usr/bin/firefox -no-remote -P HeavyMetalMassage`
  - Work Path: (leave blank)

Remember that if you click your regular Firefox icon—the one that isn't pointing at a profile you created—then Firefox will open using your default profile.

> **TIP**
>
> You can create multiple profiles with Google Chrome too. For more information, see Amit Agarwal's "Create Separate Profiles in Google Chrome for Family Members and Stay Extra Safe" article at http://www.labnol.org/software/create-family-profiles-in-google-chrome/4394/.

Swapping Cookies with the CookieSwap Extension for Firefox

This is an interesting and smart extension that still has a little ways to go, but that shouldn't prevent you from using it now as long as you accept its shortcomings. Basically, CookieSwap keeps track of three different sets of cookies so that you can log in to up to three different Google Apps accounts (actually, you don't have to use it with Google Apps—any three different websites that use cookies will do).

> **TIP**
>
> CookiePie is another similar extension that some people like better, so you might want to check it out. You can find it at http://www.nektra.com/oss/firefox/extensions/cookiepie/. Another thing you might want to do is search Mozilla Add-ons for "cookie," which will provide you with a list of results at https://addons.mozilla.org/en-US/firefox/search?q=cookie&cat=all&show=100. Many of those results will be useless, but you may find some gold in there.

To add CookieSwap, go to https://addons.mozilla.org/en-US/firefox/addon/3255 and install it. Restart Firefox, and you'll see Profile 1 in the Firefox status bar at the very bottom of your browser. Type in the URL to your first Google Account or select it from your bookmarks and log in.

Now right-click the CookieSwap menu and select Profile 2. Type in the URL to your second Google Apps account or choose it from your bookmarks and log in. Repeat with Profile 3 for your third Google Apps account if you have one.

When you want to go to Profile 1's Google Apps account, right-click the CookieSwap menu, select Profile 1, and go to the Google Apps account that corresponds to that profile. You can do the same for the other Google Apps accounts in other tabs.

Needless to say, this extension has some rough edges:

- You have to remember to change the profile before you go to the website. It would be much nicer if the profile automatically switched when it detected that you visited the Google Apps account.

- You're stuck with Profile 1, Profile 2, and Profile 3 for names, which aren't exactly helpful. Sure, one of your options when you right-click CookieSwap is Manage Profiles, but that just brings up an alert box that tells you that the feature isn't actually in place yet! You can rename profiles—and the alert box tells you how—but it's a manual process that may scare off some users.

- You're limited to three profiles. Some people have more Google Apps accounts than that.

Still, this extension is promising. I just hope the developer improves it a bit so that it becomes more useful.

> **NOTE**
>
> You can read more about the CookieSwap extension at http://cookieSwap.mozdev.org. In particular, the help page at http://cookieswap.mozdev.org/help.html is very, uh, helpful.

A Few Gmail-Only Solutions

If all you care about are your multiple Google Apps Gmail accounts, then one of the following could work for you. These won't help if you want to view two different Google Docs or Google Calendar accounts at the same time, however, so be aware of that limitation.

- **Mailplane**

  http://mailplaneapp.com

  A Mac OS X app that lets you consolidate your Gmail accounts into one place. A very cool program with some interesting features. Definitely worth checking out.

- **Gmail Manager**

  https://addons.mozilla.org/en-US/firefox/addon/1320

  A Firefox extension that allows you to manage as many Gmail accounts as you'd like. Very good, and very easy to set up.

There are many others. You can tell because they will reference Gmail instead of Google Apps as a whole.

CONCLUSION

The problems outlined in this appendix can crop up naturally, simply by using Google's services, if you aren't careful. Though Google has not yet solved the complicated relationship between a Google account and a Google Apps account, we can be comforted knowing that those with more than one Google Apps account can find solutions to their issues.

Google Chrome: A Browser Built for Cloud Computing

After I'd finished writing this book, but before we had finished the editing process, Google released Chrome, its own web browser. This was huge news, so much so that even my nontechnical friends were texting me to ask about it. In actuality, I think it's a much bigger deal than most people realize, and it's certainly much bigger than a web browser.

However, Chrome is still a beta, and as such it displays a number of flaws (hopefully most of these bugs will be long squashed by the time you're reading this):

- No extensions, toolbars, or skins
- No way to zoom text and images, just text
- No way to remember zoom levels on a per site basis
- No way to display the Address bar, bookmarks, or settings when you create an application shortcut (discussed in "Application Shortcuts")
- No support for subscribing to RSS feeds in the browser (Personally, I don't care because I use Google Reader, but some might want such a thing.)
- No way to add a word to the spelling dictionary
- No way to sort by Name or Keyword by clicking the column title in the Edit Search Engines window

Nothing's perfect, but Google Chrome sure is interesting. Let's look at how, but before we do, let's ask why.

WHY?

So why in the world is Google building its own browser? I mean, we already have three browsers duking it out—Internet Explorer, Firefox, and Safari—with a whole host of other excellent browsers available to Web users: Konqueror, Flock, and Opera, to name but a few. So why did Google jump into the fray?

The answer may be staring us right in the face. Let's juxtapose two statements, both from Google, about its new browser.

During a Q & A after introducing Chrome, Google cofounder Sergei Brin had this to say: "I think operating systems are kind of an old way to think of the world. They have become kind of bulky, they have to do lots and lots of different [legacy] things. We want a lightweight, fast engine for running applications."

Chromium is the name of Chrome's open source project. On the User Experience page for Chromium, Google states: "In the long term, we think of Chromium as a tabbed window manager or shell for the Web rather than a browser application. We avoid putting things into our UI in the same way you would hope that Apple and Microsoft would avoid putting things into the standard window frames of applications on their operating systems."

> **NOTE**
>
> You can find Sergei Brin quoted at http://googlewatch.eweek.com/content/google_chrome/google_clearly_sees_chrome_as_the_clouds_future.html, and the User Experience page for Chromium at http://dev.chromium.org/user-experience.

Taken together, it seems clear that Google sees Chrome as not just similar to the operating systems we use today, but also as something that transcends them. Google's entire business (with a few very minor exceptions) is built around the Web. It needs web browsers that run their web-based programs as fast, as efficiently, and as powerfully as possible, but it can't count on the big three browser makers to produce the browsers of tomorrow.

- Microsoft hates Google and would love nothing more than hurting the company it sees as its biggest rival. Further, Microsoft is still very much tied to the desktop paradigm and will move into cloud computing in a big way only if it is forced to do so by declining profits and migrating users, and even then it will only do so kicking and screaming. Finally, Web users have learned from painful experience that Microsoft's commitment to improving Internet

Explorer is spotty at best, and that's being extremely generous. Internet Explorer 8 is shaping up as a nice upgrade, but even so, there's still plenty of funny business happening when it comes to support for standards.

■ Apple's main focus is on its hardware and its best of breed operating system. It started developing Safari because Microsoft had abandoned IE on the Mac, and users expect operating systems to include web browsers. Now that the iPhone is becoming an important financial center to Apple, mobile Safari is a key selling point. But Apple's ultimate commitment isn't to bettering the Web or advancing the future of cloud computing. (The screw-ups with MobileMe during the summer of 2008 demonstrate that.) It's to making the hardware it sells more attractive and useful.

■ Firefox has done yeoman's work fighting the IE monopoly, and it has made huge strides. If anyone else is going to do interesting things with the web browser, it's going to be the Mozilla Foundation and not Microsoft and Apple. It's true that Google supplies the lion's share of the Mozilla Foundation's funding because it pays for pushing Firefox users to root around the Web with Google's search engine. However, Google ultimately has next to no control over Firefox and where it chooses to go with its web browser. Firefox is open source, which is its strength, but its open source nature also means that Google can't control Firefox.

Because Google can't count on Microsoft, Apple, or the Mozilla Foundation to do what it needs, it's doing the work itself. It's going to make a browser that transcends browsers and turns them into machines for running the cloud computing apps that attract users and power Google's twin aims: organizing the world's information and making a profit from doing so by selling ads everywhere. Browsers up until Chrome were built first and foremost to display web pages; browsers after Chrome will be built to run web-based applications.

Even if Chrome doesn't end up taking an enormous share in the browser market, it will still succeed in two other ways. First, its innovations will pressure Microsoft, Apple, and Mozilla to better their own browsers in ways that will improve the Web for everyone. JavaScript will get faster, security will get tighter, and UIs will become easier to use. As that happens—as the Web increasingly becomes the place people go to do their work and have their fun—Google wins.

Second, by open sourcing Chrome and its components, Google makes its innovations attractive to other browser makers. Google chose the BSD license for Chromium (see http://code.google.com/chromium/terms.html), one of the most liberal open source licenses out there. Where the GPL requires that code changes made publicly available must be given back to the original project, the BSD license does no such thing. The GPL says, in essence, "You may take, but you must share," whereas the BSD license says, "You may take and do what you wish." Both have their place, and both are important, but in this case, Google is maximizing the attractiveness of its code to other companies and organizations interested in improving their web browsers. And again, when that happens, Google wins.

In the last quarter century, Microsoft understood that the PC was to be the central computing platform, and it sought to dominate that platform long before any other company realized the strategic position into which Microsoft was placing itself. In the coming quarter century, Google better than anyone else understands that the Web will be the platform, and it is trying to position Chrome as the foundation of the transition to cloud computing that is inexorably coming.

FEATURES

Of course, what you really want to know about are the features. Complete information on all the cool features in Google Chrome can be found in "Further Reading" at the end of this appendix. For now, though, let's quickly hit on some of the most interesting ideas that Google has baked into Chrome. Keep in mind, not every feature listed is brand new. Some came from Opera, some from Safari, and some from Firefox. However, remember what Picasso said: "Good artists copy. Great artists steal!"

Omnibox

The address bar is now more than a place in which to type URLs; it's a combined address bar and search box, hence the name Omnibox. Search history is shown as you type, as well as sites based on your bookmarks and even suggested sites based on popularity rankings by Google.

In addition, the Omnibox learns from the searches you perform on specific sites. For instance, let's say I go to the Saint Louis Zoo's website to find out information about the Lowland Gorilla. I click the Search link in the upper right of every page, and on the resulting Search page I type in `lowland gorilla`. The results page shows up, and there's my info on that animal. Nothing out of the ordinary.

But the next time I start to type in `stlzoo.org` in my Omnibox, on the right side I see Chrome telling me that if I click Tab, I will be able to search the Saint Louis Zoo website directly from the Omnibox. You can see this message in Figure C.1.

FIGURE C.1   The Omnibox allows me to search specific sites directly.

If I click Tab, the Omnibox changes to display "Search stlzoo.org" in it, and when I type my search terms and then press Enter, that's what will happen: My search will be performed using the search engine provided by the Saint Louis Zoo.

But what if I don't want to have to type **stlzoo.org** to start a search of the Saint Louis Zoo website? Is there a faster way to do it? Sure! Right-click in the Omnibox and select Edit Search Engines. When you do, the Search Engines window opens, with two columns: Name and Keyword, as shown in Figure C.2.

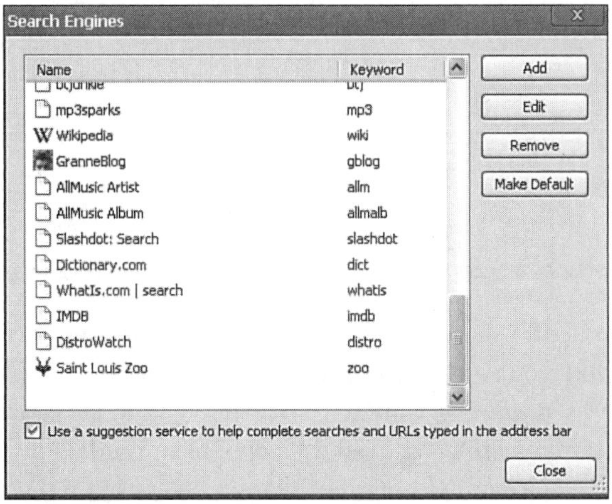

FIGURE C.2   You can set each search engine's keyword to make it easier to search in the Omni-box.

Notice in Figure C.2 that Google has automatically entered stlzoo.org as a search engine, with its keyword—the thing you type in the Omnibox to invoke it— also as stlzoo.org. Double-click that line, and you can edit the following information about that particular search engine:

- Name: **Saint Louis Zoo**. I changed it from stlzoo.org to something more meaningful to me.

- Keyword: **zoo**. I changed it from stlzoo.org to something shorter and easier to remember.

- URL:
  http://www.stlzoo.org/find/results.htm?cx=013289413871174106925%3A_k8gc5uf2o&cof=FORID%3A11&q=%s&sa=Search
  Leave this alone unless you really know what you're doing; it's the search URL that Google detected. Your actual search query is inserted where you see %s.

After I've made my choices, I click OK to close the Edit Search Engine window and then click Close to shut the Search Engines window. Now if I type **zoo** into the Omnibox, Chrome tells me that if I click Tab, I can search the Saint Louis Zoo site, which is both shorter to type and much easier to remember.

You can also add search engines to the list manually if you'd like. Suppose that www.heavymetalmassage.com didn't offer a search engine on its site (as if!) and you wanted the ability to search the site using the Omnibox. Right-click in the Omnibox and choose Edit Search Engines. Click the Add button and enter the following information:

- Name: **Heavy Metal Massage**

- Keyword: **massage**

- URL:
  `http://www.google.com/search?q=site:www.heavymetalmassage.com+%s`

Click OK, Close, and then try your new search in the Omnibox. It works because it utilizes the fact that you can search Google and tell it that you only want results from a specific website by prefacing your search terms with `site:www.domainofsite.com`. However, this trick relies on Google, so if Google hasn't indexed the site yet or hasn't indexed much of it, you're out of luck, but that's not very often the case.

TIP

One thing I noticed that is hopefully just a bug in this new browser: If you search a site that uses Google as its search engine, Chrome doesn't detect that you originally performed a search on that site and so doesn't automatically add that site's search engine to its list. For an example of this, go to http://boingboing.net and use the site's search engine. You'll wind up at a www.google.com URL. Now check your search engine list in Chrome, and boingboing.net won't appear. You can add it manually, of course, but that's more work!

You can even perform simple calculations and convert from one thing to another in the Omnibox. Try the following queries in the Omnibox and notice what it shows you before you ever press Enter.

- `number of miles in a lightyear`
- `6047 / 36`
- `87 * 6`
- `number of acres in a square mile`
- `(3 + 2) * 6`
- `14 euros in us dollars`

This doesn't work yet in the Omnibox, but it does at Google, so I expect it will shortly.

V8

JavaScript is at the heart of most sophisticated web apps these days, like Gmail, Google Calendar, and Google Docs—actually, pretty much every program that's part of Google Apps. When there's a problem with your browser's JavaScript because of a bug, or slowness, or anything else, the programs you're trying to run in your browser suffer.

Recognizing all this, Google decided that when it came time to create Chrome, it would create its own highly tuned JavaScript Virtual Machine. It's fast—really fast—but it also has advanced features such as precise garbage collection, incremental garbage collection, and on-the-fly code compiling. In short, in many ways it's a huge leap forward, and the fact that Google is open sourcing it means that any other browser makers can use it as well, another benefit for all web users.

> **NOTE**
>
> For more on V8, read *eWeek*'s informative article "Google Chrome JavaScript Is Powered with a V8 Engine," at www.eweek.com/c/a/Search-Engines/Google-Chromes-JavaScript-is-Powered-with-a-V8-Engine/.

Dynamic Tabs

Google Chrome is very much centered around its tabs, as you'll see in several sections in this appendix, such as "New Tab Page," "Crash Control," and "Safe Browsing." Correspondingly, Google spent a lot of time making tabs easy to use in

Chrome. You can change the order of tabs with drag and drop (in fact, it's the smoothest dragging I've ever seen on any browser), but you can also turn a tab into a window by dragging it out of the browser, as shown in Figure C.3.

FIGURE C.3   Drag a tab out of a window, and you create a new window.

To reverse the process, drag it back to its original window—or to another window you've created in the meantime.

Application Shortcuts

Back in Chapter 18, in a section titled "Using an SSB (Site-Specific Browser)," I talked about SSBs, stripped down web browsers that handle a specific website as though it were a desktop application. Google Chrome has this concept already built in. If you want to view Gmail in Chrome as though it were a desktop app dedicated to that purpose—if you want to view Gmail in an SSB, in other words—visit the site in Chrome. To the right of the Omnibox is a little page icon that lets you work with the current webpage. Click the page icon and select Create Application Shortcuts. When you do, you'll see the window shown in Figure C.4.

FIGURE C.4 It's labeled Google Gears, but this window allows you turn any website into an SSB.

Choose where you want the shortcut to this site to go—the Desktop, the Start menu, or the Quick Launch bar (different choices will appear on Mac and Linux machines) and click OK.

When you do, the site immediately moves into an SSB. If the site was in a tab, it's now in its own window. The tabs disappear, as well as the Omnibox, the bookmarks bar, and any other icons that let you control the page or Chrome's settings. If you click the shortcut that now appears in the places you specified previously, the site opens in the SSB.

To delete the website-as-application, delete the shortcuts you told Chrome to create.

By the way, you might have noticed that after you selected Create Application Shortcuts, the window was labeled Google Gears. That's a bit confusing, and I hope that Google will make things a bit clearer for users, but that should also emphasize to you that Google Gears is baked into Chrome and is automatically helping it work with websites that you've decided to turn into applications viewed via SSBs.

NOTE

For a refresher on Google Gears and what it does (and why it's so cool), go back to Chapter 13's "Can I Access and Use Google Calendar Offline in a Web Browser?" and Chapter 14's "Going Offline with Google Gears."

New Tab Page

When you open a new tab, Chrome displays a super-useful screen you can see in Figure C.5.

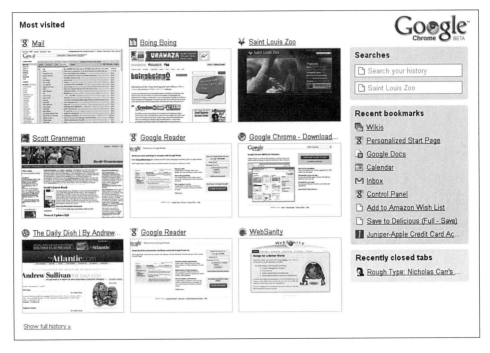

FIGURE C.5   The new tab page in Chrome.

The features on this tab include the following:

- Your nine most visited websites, arranged in a 3×3 grid and with a screenshot of each. Click the screenshot or the title of the website displayed above each screenshot to go to the site.

- A link to Show Full History if you want to see all the pages you've visited.

- A Searches box that displays your most recently used search boxes, so you can quickly use those search engines again.

- A list of your most recent bookmarks.

- A list of recently closed pages.

This is all great to have so close at hand, and I think most users will love it.

Crash Control

It's happened to me hundreds of times: I have several (OK, a lot) of tabs open in Firefox, when something goes haywire on one of them. The result? The entire browser crashes, or it all comes to a screeching halt and I have to kill the browser and restart it.

This should be a thing of the past with Chrome. Each tab is running independently of all others, so if one crashes, the others are unaffected. You'll know the tab has crashed when you see the message shown in Figure C.6.

Aw, Snap!

Something went wrong while displaying this webpage. To continue, press Reload or go to another page.

FIGURE C.6   Weirdly, this crashed tab makes me laugh.

If you want to find out how much of your system resources each tab is using, that's easy because Chrome includes a Task Manager similar to the Windows Task Manager. To see the Chrome Task Manager, click the little page icon to the right of the Omnibox and go to Developer, Task Manager, or press Shift+Esc. The Task Manager, shown in Figure C.7, will open.

Task Manager - Google Chrome			
Page	Memory	CPU	Network
Browser	31,568K	3	N/A
Tab: Google Reader (3)	21,832K	9	7.9 kB/s
Tab: Google Chrome	6,460K	0	0
Tab: Mail - Inbox - scott@granneman.com	17,508K	1	0
Tab: Scott Granneman	6,200K	0	0
Tab: Boing Boing	16,720K	0	0
Plug-in: Google Gears 0.4.17.0	1,220K	0	N/A
Plug-in: Shockwave Flash	36,444K	17	0

Stats for nerds   End process

FIGURE C.7   It's sheer brilliance for a browser to have its own Task Manager.

Each tab and browser plug-in is listed, along with its usage of Memory, CPU, and Network bandwidth. If a particular process is running out of control or is just taking up too much memory, processing, or bandwidth, you can kill it by selecting it and clicking End Process.

Even better is the link in the bottom left labeled Stats for Nerds. Click it and a new web page opens that will have the hearts of nerds everywhere aflutter.

Incognito Mode

Want to browse without leaving behind any search history? Go to the page icon to the right of the Omnibox and select New Incognito Window. Now you can browse without Chrome saving any history, and when you close the window, any cookies are deleted as well. No trace left behind whatsoever. This is great for public kiosks and when you're searching sites that you might not want anyone else to know about. I'll leave it up to you as to what kinds of sites those could be.

Safe Browsing

Phishing is a real problem on the Net, but Chrome has antiphishing protection built in, thanks to a constantly updated list of phishing sites that Chrome acquires from Google. If you do go to a phishing site, you'll see the warning shown in Figure C.8.

FIGURE C.8   Chrome tells you that you'd better not visit that site!

The same is true for sites that host malware and try to infect browsers and computers that visit them.

In addition, Chrome sandboxes each tab so that what happens in that tab stays in that tab and will not affect other tabs, the browser as a whole, or your computer.

Finally, all pop-up windows are blocked, which is standard on most browsers nowadays. Google does things a little differently, though—it informs you about the pop-up by displaying the title bar of the blocked window at the bottom of your tab.

To see it, click the title bar of the blocked window; to dismiss it, click the X. Either way, the pop-up is contained in the tab that spawned it.

User Interface Niceties

Besides the big stuff I've covered previously, Chrome also has its share of nice little touches that make using it a pleasure. Here's a small list, but you'll find more as you use the browser:

- If you accidentally close a tab, press Ctrl+Shift+t or open a new tab and find the one you just closed in the Recently Closed Tabs section.

- You can resize any large text box by dragging the lower-right corner to make it bigger.

- Copy a new tab into a new window by right-clicking the tab and choosing Duplicate.

- If you right-click the Back button or left-click and hold down the mouse for a few seconds, Chrome shows you the list of previous pages you visited. The same is true for the Forward button.

- If you right-click a link in a tab and select Open Link in New Tab or middle-click a link, the new tab opens directly to the right of the current tab.

There are many more. Use the browser, and I guarantee you'll find some small thing that makes you smile at the attention Google Chrome's developers paid to their browser.

Looking at the About: Pages

For years, browsers have included hidden access to special pages with advanced (or, in some cases, fun) information on them. In Firefox, for instance, try typing the following into the Address bar and pressing Enter:

- `about:config`—Shows all of Firefox's settings, both those exposed in Options/Preferences and those hidden but still usable.

- `about:crash`—Crashes the active tab and displays the sad tab image, which you can see in "Crash Control" in this appendix.

- `about:plugins`—Shows information about your browser's plug-ins.

- `about:Mozilla`—I'm not going to tell you—just do it.

Google Chrome also has about: pages. Following is an alphabetical list of many of them, along with what they do.

- **about:cache**—A list of hyperlinks to all the web pages cached by Chrome. Click the link to see the headers returned by the web server for the specific file, as well as a packet dump for the file.

- **about:dns**—By default, Chrome prefetches DNS records for pages you might visit in order to speed things up. This page shows you the results of that prefetching.

- **about:hang**—Hangs the processes occurring in this tab. It doesn't crash, so you can still see what's in the tab, but no further input or output will occur. Note that the other tabs will continue running without a problem.

- **about:histograms**—If you're not a developer, don't bother; if you are, you'll love it.

- **about:internets**—A fun little Easter egg that hearkens back to two famous Internet memes: George W. Bush's repeated references to the "Internets" (see http://en.wikipedia.org/wiki/Internets) and Sen. Ted Stevens' famously clue-less description of the Internet as "a series of tubes" (see http://en.wikipedia.org/wiki/Series_of_tubes). Just try it—and notice what it says on the tab!

- **about:memory**—Complete information about the real and virtual memory used by the browser's tabs and processes, as shown in Figure C.9. Even includes information about other running web browsers! See "Crash Control" earlier in this appendix for more.

About memory *Measuring memory usage in a multi-process browser*

Summary

Browser	Memory			Virtual memory	
	Private	Shared	Total	Private	Mapped
Chrome 0.2.149.29	104,988k	4,466k	109,454k	113,500k	19,900k
Firefox 3.0.1	26,524k	4,872k	31,396k	19,276k	2,728k

Processes

PID	Name	Memory			Virtual memory	
		Private	Shared	Total	Private	Mapped
4068	Browser	30760k	6928k	37688k	28680k	6412k
996	Tab 4 Google Chrome	3164k	2536k	5700k	7864k	2580k
948	Tab 2 Google Reader	24744k	4324k	29068k	27560k	2580k

FIGURE C.9 About:memory tells you about Chrome and other running browsers.

- **about:network**—If you've ever used the Live HTTP Headers extension for Firefox, you'll want to use this page, which is the same thing with a different interface. If you have no idea what I just wrote, you won't need this page.

- **about:plugins**—Lists information about the plug-ins that Chrome is using.

- **about:stats**—Nerd-vana. A list of internal Counters and Timers for developers only. Gotta love the subtitle on the page: "Shhh! This page is secret!"

- **about:version**—Shows the current version number of the browser, as well as the browser's user-agent.

So-called normal users will never even know about these pages or even find them useful, but developers, web builders, and nerds will find them tremendously useful and fun. Thanks, Google!

SOLVING COMMON PROBLEMS

As with all things in life, you're going to find little gotchas. Here are a few of those and their solutions.

How Do I Block Ads?

At this time, there isn't an ad-blocker extension for Chrome. Heck, at the time I'm writing this, Chrome has been out for about a week, and it doesn't have any extensions at all, much less one for blocking ads. However, Google has said that Chrome will support add-ons, and I expect that one of the first that will appear will be an ad blocker.

In the meantime, you can always use a free ad-blocking proxy like Proxomitron. Download Proxomitron from www.proxomitron.info and then install and configure it. When you've finished, it will sit running in your Windows system tray taking up a mere 3MB or so of RAM.

In Google Chrome, click the little wrench icon to the right of the Omnibox and go to Options, Under the Hood, Change Proxy Settings. (This is the same as the Internet Options control panel.) Click the LAN Settings button and check the box next to Use a Proxy Server for Your LAN. Enter the following information:

- Address: **localhost**
- Port: **8080**
- Check the box next to Bypass Proxy Server for Local Addresses.

Click OK to close Local Area Network (LAN) Settings and then click OK to close Internet Properties. Google Chrome is now using the Proxomitron web-filtering proxy. It's not as easy or as powerful as Adblock Plus for Firefox, for instance, but it'll work until such a thing appears for Google Chrome. In fact, by the time you're reading this, it may already have appeared, and you can safely ignore my advice here.

> **TIP**
>
> If you don't like Proxomitron, you can always use a similar program: Privoxy. See the instructions at http://lifehacker.com/5046529/how-to-block-ads-in-google-chrome. Download Squad published a nice article, "4 Free Proxies To Block Ads in Google Chrome (or any browser)," at www.downloadsquad.com/2008/09/08/4-free-proxies-to-block-ads-in-google-chrome-or-any-browser/, that is also very useful.

Can I Change How Chrome Looks?

The Automatic Theme Switcher for Chrome lets you do just that. You can download it from http://chromespot.com/index.php/topic,289.0.html. You can find themes at www.altafsayani.com/2008/09/03/download-google-chrome-themes/ and at http://chromespot.com/forumdisplay.php?f=19. By the time you're reading this, however, there may be an official theme repository, along the lines of Firefox's Themes directory. At this time, an official collection of themes is at www.chromeplugins.org/.

Where Are the Chrome Plugins?

Google Chrome Plugins and Themes, at www.chromeplugins.org, is an unofficial repository that has the start of a decent collection, but I'm sure that Google will eventually unveil an official site.

One that particularly interests me is Greasemetal, a hack that brings Greasemonkey-like functionality to Chrome. You can read more about it at http://greasemetal.31tools.com/.

How Do I Back Up Chrome?

If you use Windows, you can download the free Google Chrome Backup from www.parhelia-tools.com/products/gcb/googlechrome.aspx. You'll need .NET 2.0 for it to work, but you can get that from Windows Update.

How Do I Update Chrome?

Click the little wrench icon to the right of the Omnibox and then choose About Google Chrome to see the window displayed in Figure C.10.

FIGURE C.10   The About window tells you if there's a new version of Google Chrome.

If you can update the program, at the bottom of the window you'll see the message, A New Version of Google Chrome Is Available alongside an Update Now button. Click the button, and Chrome automatically downloads and installs the latest version of the software.

This is nice, but I'm assuming that this entire process will become far more noticeable in later builds. Like Firefox, Chrome needs to notify the user when a new version is available and not keep that information hidden away in an obscure location. But Google knows that, and I'm sure things will be different soon.

> **TIP**
>
> If you're feeling like living on the bleeding edge, you can install the Google Chrome Channel Chooser (http://dev.chromium.org/getting-involved/dev-channel/), which brings you the latest developer releases as they happen. Be prepared for instability!

Does Google Chrome's EULA Say That It Owns Everything I Do with Chrome?

Within a day of Chrome's appearance, people in the blogosphere were freaking out over some of the terms Google placed in Chrome's EULA, specifically those found in Section 11, which stated that Google had "a perpetual, irrevocable, worldwide, royalty-free, and non-exclusive license to reproduce, adapt, modify, translate, publish, publicly perform, publicly display and distribute any Content which you submit, post or display on or through, the Services." Whoa!

Granted, those are pretty scary—and crazy—terms of use for a web browser. But basically Google had made a mistake. Within a day, Rebecca Ward, the Senior Product Counsel for Google Chrome, was quoted on www.mattcutts.com/blog/google-chrome-license-agreement/ with this to say about the issue:

> In order to keep things simple for our users, we try to use the same set of legal terms (our Universal Terms of Service) for many of our products. Sometimes, as in the case of Google Chrome, this means that the legal terms for a specific product may include terms that don't apply well to the use of that product. We are working quickly to remove language from Section 11 of the current Google Chrome terms of service. This change will apply retroactively to all users who have downloaded Google Chrome.

The next day, Section 11 of the EULA was changed to say this:

> You retain copyright and any other rights you already hold in Content which you submit, post or display on or through, the Services.

End of problem.

CONCLUSION

At the time I'm writing this, Google Chrome has been out for only a few days, but it's already made a huge splash, and some websites are seeing a substantial number of

Chrome users in their logs. I predict a great future for the web browser. It has Google behind it, but more importantly, it's built on solid, innovative technology that makes browsing faster, safer, and easier. If you use Google Apps, you owe it to yourself to check those programs out in Google Chrome. You just may have found the perfect browser for cloud computing.

FURTHER READING

There's always more to learn, so here are some resources that you might find handy if you want to learn more about Google Chrome:

- The famous 38-page comic book by Scott McCloud, "Google Chrome: Behind the Open Source Browser Project": http://www.google.com/googlebooks/chrome/index.html
- Overviews
  - A fresh take on the browser: http://www.google.com/chrome/intl/en/why.html?hl=en
  - Getting Started Guide: http://www.google.com/support/chrome/bin/topic.py?topic=14658
- Google Apps for Users Help Topics: http://www.google.com/support/chrome/
- YouTube videos
  - Google Chrome announcement: http://www.youtube.com/watch?v=LRmrMiOWdfc
  - Features: http://www.google.com/chrome/intl/en/features.html
  - The story behind Google Chrome: http://www.youtube.com/watch?v=JGmO7Oximw8 10
  - Features of Google Chrome: http://www.youtube.com/watch?v=Xlh8gSF_hhE
- For developers
  - Information for web developers: http://www.google.com/chrome/intl/en/webmasters.html
  - FAQ for web developers: http://www.google.com/chrome/intl/en/webmasters-faq.html
  - Chromium (the open source project): http://code.google.com/chromium/

- Chromium Developer Documentation: http://dev.chromium.org/Home
- Chromium-Announce discussion group: http://groups.google.com/group/chromium-announce
- Chromium-discuss discussion group: http://groups.google.com/group/chromium-discuss
- The Chromium Blog: http://blog.chromium.org
- Google Chrome Help Discussion Group: http://groups.google.com/group/google-chrome-help
- Known Issues
  - http://www.google.com/support/chrome/bin/request.py?contact_type=known_issues_2
  - http://www.google.com/support/chrome/bin/topic.py?topic=14686
- Support options: http://www.google.com/support/chrome/bin/request.py?contact_type=contact_policy

Index

G

Q-R

Also Available in the Negus Live Linux Series

Live Linux® CDs
Building and Customizing Bootables
Christopher Negus | 0132432749 | ©2007

Create Custom Versions of Linux That Run "Live," Without Installation!

"Live" Linux® CDs let users run Linux on any PC, without affecting the operating system and data already present there. Live Linux distributions, such as Knoppix, are now among the most popular versions of Linux. What's more, because Linux is open source, you can customize your own Live Linux distribution for virtually any purpose. *Live Linux® CDs* is the first start-to-finish guide to creating, building, and remastering your own Live Linux distributions.

Bestselling *Linux Bible* author, Christopher Negus, walks you step-by-step through building complete Linux systems that run from CDs, DVDs, flash drives, and other bootable media. First learn exactly how Live Linux works and then walk through creating Live Linux distributions based on five different systems: KNOPPIX (Debian), Fedora/Kadischi, Gentoo, Slax (Slackware), and Damn Small Linux. Working from complete examples on the accompanying DVD, customize all these specialized bootable Linuxes.

Ajax Construction Kit
Building Plug-and-Play Ajax Applications
Michael Morrison | 0132350084 | ©2008

Supercharge Your Sites with Ajax Right Now...No Scripting Expertise Needed!

You've heard how great Ajax is—how it can help make your Web sites more usable, more interactive, more responsive, more successful. *Ajax Construction Kit* lets you put Ajax to work right now, even if you've never written a script! Just learn a few essentials, check out a few examples, and then run the live CD and discover all the plug-and-play code you need to hit the ground running.

Ajax Construction Kit's built-in applications work right out of the box. The CD contains all software needed to run Ajax examples in Windows, Mac OS X, or directly from the Linux live CD. And with easy guidance from Michael Morrison, you'll gradually deepen your understanding—learn how to customize, extend, and reuse these applications—and even build skills for creating new ones. Walk away an expert.

The Official Damn Small® Linux® Book
The Tiny Adaptable Linux That Runs on Anything
Robert Shingledecker, John Andrews, Christopher Negus | 0132338696 | ©2008

Make the Most of Today's Smallest, Fastest Linux Distribution—Damn Small Linux!

Damn Small Linux (DSL) is a super-efficient platform for everything from custom desktops to professional servers. Now, DSL's creator and lead developer have written the first definitive, practical guide to this remarkable system. *The Official Damn Small® Linux® Book* brings together everything you need to put DSL to work in just minutes. Simply learn a few essentials, boot the live CD, and master the rest...one step at a time, hands-on.

If you're new to Linux, you can quickly discover how to use DSL to take your data on the road, safely running your programs and personal environment on nearly any computer. Easily adapt DSL to run on anything from an alternative device (Internet appliance, hand-held, diskless PC, or mini-ITX system) to an older PC that might otherwise be headed for a landfill.

Practical PHP and MySQL®
Building Eight Dynamic Web Applications
Jono Bacon | 0132239973 | ©2007

Build Dynamic Web Sites Fast, with PHP and MySQL...Learn from Eight Ready-to-Run Applications!

Suddenly, it's easy to build commercial-quality Web applications using free and open source software. With this book, you learn from eight ready-to-run, real-world applications—all backed by clear diagrams and screenshots, well-documented code, and simple, practical explanations.

Leading open source author Jono Bacon teaches the core skills you need to build virtually any application. You discover how to connect with databases, upload content, perform cascading deletes, edit records, validate registrations, specify user security, create reusable components, use PEAR extensions, and even build Ajax applications.

PRENTICE
HALL

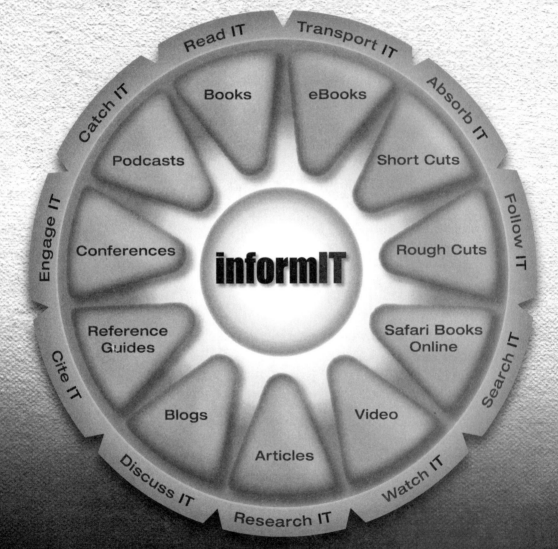

FREE Online Edition

Your purchase of **Google Apps Deciphered** includes access to a free online edition for 45 days through the Safari Books Online subscription service. Nearly every Prentice Hall book is available online through Safari Books Online, along with more than 5,000 other technical books and videos from publishers such as Addison-Wesley Professional, Cisco Press, Exam Cram, IBM Press, O'Reilly, Que, and Sams.

SAFARI BOOKS ONLINE allows you to search for a specific answer, cut and paste code, download chapters, and stay current with emerging technologies.

Activate your FREE Online Edition at
www.informit.com/safarifree

> **STEP 1:** Enter the coupon code: LANJIXA.

> **STEP 2:** New Safari users, complete the brief registration form.
> Safari subscribers, just log in.

If you have difficulty registering on Safari or accessing the online edition,
please e-mail customer-service@safaribooksonline.com